Cultural Psychology of Musical Experience

A volume in
Advances in Cultural Psychology
Jaan Valsiner, *Series Editor*

Cultural Psychology of Musical Experience

edited by

Sven Hroar Klempe
*Norwegian University
of Science and Technology*

INFORMATION AGE PUBLISHING, INC.
Charlotte, NC • www.infoagepub.com

Library of Congress Cataloging-in-Publication Data

A CIP record for this book is available from the Library of Congress
http://www.loc.gov

ISBN: 978-1-68123-484-7 (Paperback)
978-1-68123-485-4 (Hardcover)
978-1-68123-486-1 (ebook)

Printed in the United States of America

CONTENTS

PART I
CULTURAL PSYCHOLOGY OF MUSIC

PART II
MUSICAL SENSATIONS

PART III

MUSICAL EXPERIENCES

PART IV

MUSICAL TRANSFORMATIONS

PART V
MUSICAL FUNDAMENTALS

SERIES EDITOR'S PREFACE

The Voice of Music in Cultural Psychology

Writing this particular preface—my regular feature for books in this series—made me realize my own deep and profound incompetence in the subject matter of this book. Having been brought up in my native Estonia under the Soviet political power, I could be considered to have survived a "difficult childhood." After my relocation to "the West" some three decades ago, I have been hearing such easily deceptive attributions used widely. There exists a formidable hurdle in the understanding of the complexity of the human psyche when the social representation of "difficult childhood" is evoked.

In my case, nothing could be further from reality: my childhood was more than comfortable as it did not include any links with politics. Yet something was indeed missing in my childhood, and that was music. There was no music in my environment, I could never pick up the necessary semiotic code to navigate in the knowledge space of musical knowhow of instruments, notes, styles, and appreciation of concerts. Even my parents' efforts to make me "cultured" by way of hiring a piano teacher ended in a fiasco of the 11-year-old boy escaping from home after the third lesson. The effort was terminated, and I remained musically ignorant, only to develop intuitive appreciation of the mysterious flows of sounds later.

What did develop—over the last half century—is a curious mixture of appreciation of music in a deeply personal and completely uneducated way. Aside from deep feeling into classical music without any recognition of the

Cultural Psychology of Musical Experience, pages ix–xii
Copyright © 2016 by Information Age Publishing
All rights of reproduction in any form reserved.

authorship of the enjoyed pieces, my neighbors in the office were horrified by my playing endless versions of loud *forró* while I happened to be in my office, while my Brazilian visitors were mildly amused1. I could only excuse myself by referring to all of this mixed pattern as my *personal culture*—a convenient term I invented to cover all the complexity of sign-mediated processes in the *psyche* (Valsiner, 2000).

In contrast to my convenient personal excuses, the discipline of psychology can have no easy explanation for overlooking music as a centrally relevant psychological phenomenon that may be historically more ancient than any verbal human language. Historically minded psychologists may point their finger at the obvious fact that white rats or pigeons—the recognized animal models for much of psychology over the 20th century—do not sing or play in an orchestra. Higher primates—who have been taught to use various sign systems substituting human language in human-led laboratories—have not (yet?) been taught to sing or play even in a quartet (Krylov, 1809/2010). Reliance on animal models in the 20th century psychology—only to be surpassed by the deep trust in computers as the cognitive science unfolded—has been blind to music as an omnipresent reality in human lives. The realities of lullabies, choir singing, melodies emerging from violins, pianos, organs, guitars, and military marching bands have been left out of psychological science.

This was not always the case. The originators of contemporary psychology in the 19th century were completely immersed in music. Not only was music a central feature of their upbringing, they developed the skills and need to perform music themselves, and even composed it. Carl Stumpf, known best of all for his contributions to *Tonpsychologie*, was proficient in playing multiple instruments. Christian von Ehrenfels was composing under the guidance of Anton Bruckner. Alexius Meinong both composed music as well as performed it in a quartet that included his colleague Stefan Witasek. It is therefore not surprising that the magic of music—for instance, the question of how one can recognize a melody in its full from a scanty temporal presentation of its first notes—became the starting puzzle for the most comprehensive part of developing psychology at the end of the 19th century: the Gestalt movement. Information about the whole melody is not immediately available in the first notes heard, yet the music maker needs to anticipate the whole as the first notes become played, and the listener preknows what melody is to emerge from the notes just heard. Music breaks the border of the immediate past and the arriving future, extending beyond the here-and-now of the present. Yet both the music maker and music listener operate within the present. At first glance, this seems to be a basic paradox—knowing beyond the asymmetry of time. We could go to a fortune teller to hope to hear a story about our future, yet we preknow what kind of continuity of a melody should follow after the music begins.

A similar problem was faced around the same time (1890s and early 1900s) in developmental biology; the developing multicellular embryo could somehow anticipate its final expected form ahead of its own fruition. Hans Driesch's introduction of the notions of *equipotentiality* and *equifinality* were efforts to understand this miracle of anticipation of the final form. Talking in terms of music making, different instruments can be used to play the same melody (*equipotentiality*) and the recognized melody becomes considered at *that particular* known masterpiece that was once composed by that particular composer and performed by this particular group of musicians on that particular date (*equifinality*).

Yet equifinality is treacherous; if it were in place in its full form, there could be no innovation possible. All different performances of music would end in the same place—once recognized and canonized fixed set of melodies. Or, in human development every new generation could only—at most—reach the forms of their parents' generation. That is obviously absurd; every next generation in human history invents something new. In a similar vein, each performer of a classic melody introduces nuances to the canonized melody that make the new performances fresh and worth the trip to the concert location, rather than listening a "clean" version of the performance at home on some recording. At some moments, musicians make mistakes and may instantly create improvisations out of such mistakes (Klemp et al, 2008). Composers break the existing rules—knowingly—and are at first reprimanded, then tolerated, and—finally—appreciated by the new musical audiences with new perception patterns. Stravinsky, after all, was a troublemaker!

Music provides cultural psychology with two of the most important arenas for further investigation. First of all, it is a sign system that is free of iconic signs (in terms of C. S. Peirce). None of the sounds that musical instruments can make are iconic representations of the instruments themselves. Instead, music operates through the production of indexical signs— the sound of the violin is the temporary representation of the violin. Yet these indexical signs are assembled instantly into symbolic sign complexes—melodies. Hearing a particular play on a violin or a piano we as listeners are not interested in the affordances of the particular instruments, but immediately look for meaningful melodies, rather than treating the sounds as noise produced by the particular instrument.

Secondly, the rapid generalization of symbolic sign complexes in music happens first of all through the affective mechanisms and takes the pleromatic pathway (see Valsiner, 2014 for the contrast of *schematization* and *pleromatization*). It is only through the move from affective meaning complex of the melody *as heard* into the hyper-generalized feeling of the *Einfühlung* into the music as *felt through* that the music begins to be of importance in the personal culture. The primacy of intuitive understanding—through hyper-generalized field-like signs—dominates over the schematization efforts that may follow. Talking about music is a difficult task, in contrast to feeling into it.

The present volume is a notable landmark for cultural psychology. Its contributions open a number of new alleys for future research. Use of musical forms in the study of higher (and highest, i.e., generalized personal and existential) psychological functions is an opportunity research in cultural psychology should not overlook. The specific features of musical experiences described above can open new ways to create comprehensive theories of the human cognitive system that subordinate the rational to the affective metarational aspects of human lives spent in living, loving, and mourning. Finally, the volume should provide much material for thought in terms of practice. After all, singing, playing instruments, and dancing have been historically preceding the forms of human intervention that have confined human problems to a Freudian couch or to the regimes of behavior modification. It is not the behavior nor the unconscious that matters for human living, but the whole person who is each in one's own unique way interdependent with music.

—**Jaan Valsiner**

NOTE

1. As the given genre is that of North-Eastern Brazilian village dance music filled with erotic innuendos.

REFERENCES

Klemp, N., McDermott, R., Raley, J., Thibeault, M., Powell, K., & Levitin, D. (2008). Plans, takes, and mis-takes. *Outlines, 10*(1), 4–21.

Krylov, I. (1809/2010). The string quartet. In I. Krylov, *The frogs who begged for a tsar* (pp. 109–110). Moscow, Russia: Russian Information Service.

Valsiner, J. (2000). *Culture and human development.* London, England: Sage.

Valsiner, J. (2014). *Invitation to cultural psychology.* London, England: Sage.

INTRODUCTION

Sven Hroar Klempe

The close relationship between music and psychology is probably not so easy to trace. Nevertheless there are some connections, and some of them have played an important role in psychology as well. The most famous example of these is probably related to Christian von Ehrenfels's presentation of the argument for the Gestalt. In his first presentation of the term Gestalt in 1890 (von Ehrenfels, 1890/1988), he made a longer report on how a melody consists of more than just a sequence of individual pitches. The point he made in 1890 was repeated in a more condensed form in one of the very last publications of him:

> The starting point of the theory of Gestalt qualities was the attempt to answer a question: What is a melody? The most obvious answer: The sum of the individual tones which make up the melody. But opposed to this is the fact that the same melody may be made up of quite different groups of tones, as happens when the same melody is transposed into different keys. (von Ehrenfels, 1932/1988, p. 121)

What has to be highlighted here is that music represents a certain quality that exemplifies fundamental aspects of how the mind is working. Yet von Ehrenfels was not the only one to realize the importance of music as an entrance to discover psychological mechanisms or phenomena. Carl Stumpf had already showed the importance of the relation between phenomena

Cultural Psychology of Musical Experience, pages xiii–xix
Copyright © 2016 by Information Age Publishing
All rights of reproduction in any form reserved.

and mental activities, and by this demonstrated the "reality of relations" (Ash, 1998, p. 37), which prepared the ground for the term Gestalt and the forthcoming Gestalt psychology. Although Stumpf did not only refer to music, his main contribution to psychology is to be found in his two-volume theses on "tone psychology" (Stumpf, 1883,1890).

Yet the psychological interest in music did not completely start with Stumpf. If we go further back in the history, we find that also Wundt had a predilection for sounding stimuli in his experimental psychology, quite simply because he regarded the auditory organ as being "the best possible transfer of the physical stimulus to the sensory nerve rather than to any transformation of the stimulus" (Wundt, 1896/1897, p. 41). Yet these physiological considerations represented just one reason. Another as important reason was that experimental psychology was by then solely about sensation and was not focusing on higher cognitive functions like thinking or language. The aim was first of all to investigate the relationship between sensation and the notions they may generate. On this basis, Gustav Fechner referred to music as the "direct factor" in the sense that music "is independent from certain associated ideas" (Fechner, 1871/1978, p. 159). By using music as stimuli, they could focus on sensation as such without activating the intellect too much. This perspective on music indicates that it was regarded as something independent and quite different from language in the sense that music does not evoke clear or universally standardized ideas.

Although experimental psychology and the foundation of Wundt's laboratory in Leipzig in 1879 have been regarded as the starting point for psychology as a modern science, Wundt himself would probably not agree with that view. In his autobiography published in the very final year of his life he reviews experimental psychology as *hilfsmitteln* (Wundt, 1920, p. 201)—it was regarded as just a supporting discipline. To achieve a proper understanding of thinking and language the psychological approach had to focus on other aspects than sensation and physiology. Language and thinking are both characterized by apparently stability, but are in reality quite fluctuating entities. To follow him on this, one has to make a clear distinction between the capacity to talk and think, and the way we talk and think. Capacities are of course founded in certain physiological preconditions specific for human beings, whereas the ways we talk and think are not. The psychological interest lies in the way we talk and think, and this can be traced in the actual use of language in terms of telling stories and the way we use to act under certain circumstances. So in the aim of making "psychological analysis of the most general mental products, such as language, mythological ideas, and laws of custom, is to be regarded as an aid to the understanding of all the more complicated psychical processes" (Wundt, 1896/1897, p. 10). This statement forms the basis for Wundt's turn to the so-called "folkpsychology," which he also calls "social psychology." Yet it consists of elements we today rather would say belong to cultural psychology, specifically the way people behave, communicate, and interact with each other in a more or less larger population.

Wundt's motivation for concentrating on culture in other words was to leave the physiological aspects of psychological research by letting experimental psychology just define the first step in the achievement of building up psychology as a science. Thus the next step consisted of focusing on psychology as a mental science in terms of thinking and language. If so —and music was primarily related to experimental psychology—what actually did happen with music when this shift started? The answer depends very much on which trace one chooses to follow. In general one may say that music has never ever gained such an attention as it had around the turn of the previous century in psychology. Yet one interesting detail in line with this is that we may say that the same seems to be true when it comes to the cultural aspect of psychology. This ended up in social psychology, which after the Second World War turned into something quite different from Wundt's ideas of a folkpsychology. No matter how this is or is not defined, the aspect of music is not very visible in that tradition of research. Yet if we go back to around 1900 again, we may find another pathway that can tell us more about the outcome of the relationship between music and psychology.

We have to go back to Carl Stumpf again. Although he was comparable with Wundt by dealing with experimental psychology with a certain focus on music, some severe controversies between those two scholars also appeared. They were about how to define a music interval, the role of criteria for informants in the research, and how to approach musical judgments (Boring, 1929; Ash, 1998; Klempe, 2011). Yet underneath the surface of these controversies we see that Stumpf wanted to open up for ordinary people as informants, highlight a more complicated mathematical understanding of the intervals (based on the geometric instead of the arithmetic mean value), and stick to qualitative approaches investigations of musical judgments. At the same time Stumpf also changed his research activities by establishing a sound archive as a part of the psychological department in Berlin. There was even a huge activity on this, and in 1914 this archive is said to contain around 10,000 phonograph cylinders with recorded folk music from all over the world (Elschek, Michel, Porter, & Stockmann, 1997). At this time Erich Moritz von Hornbostel was the director of this archive. He had worked close to Stumpf as his assistant for a while before he became the director for the archive. Yet today he is primarily known as one of the most important pioneers in ethnomusicology. However Carl Stumpf also belongs to this group and by being so he contributed very much to questions around transcription of recorded music (Elschek et al., 1997).

Thus both Stumpf and von Hornbostel represented transition figures and founded a bridge between psychology and musicology. This was emphasized by the fact that von Hornbostel collaborated also with one of the most important musicologists in the early 20th century: Curt Sachs (1881–1959). He is first of all famous for a system for classifying musical instruments, which he developed in collaboration with von Hornbostel, and consequently is called the Sachs-Hornbostel system. On this basis Sachs had a great influence on musicology in general, not least when it comes to his understanding of the origin of music and how music is to be understood compared to language. From a Darwinian perspective, singing is regarded as a means for mating, some others would say it rises from facilitating teamwork, and the most widespread opinion, stemming from Rousseau and many others, says that it is descended from spoken language as a kind of intensified speech:

> But it matters that all of them...were failures because they started from two erroneous presuppositions. In the first place they took for granted that so complicated a thing as music had grown from one root, which of itself is more than improbable. Music bound to the motor of impulses of our bodies, to the vague images of our minds, and to our emotion in all its depth and width, eludes whatever attempt may be made to find any simple formula. The second mistake was to think of music and the language familiar to ourselves.... Critics have found fault with this theory...because it neglected what they considered the fundamental contrast: that music required well-defined intervals, while the pitches and steps of speech were irrational. (Sachs, 1943, p. 19)

Although Sachs's argument for making a clear distinction between music and language is not so convincing, because our understanding of an interval in music is not necessarily as fixed as this argument presupposes, this quotation rather tells us that just to make this distinction became very important. Sachs was not alone about arguing in this way. He is referring to an Italian article by Stumpf from 1885, which claimed the same. Hence music was not just from a musicological perspective, but also from a psychological perspective, regarded as an independent system of communication, first of all characterized by a complexity due to the composite lived human lives.

The lines and connections that have been drawn here demonstrate that four different fields were more or less united and regarded as having very much in common: psychology, anthropology, musicology, and ethnomusicology. During the whole 20th century those sciences have been more or less defined as separate and different, partly because they have developed different methodologies and research traditions, and partly because they even may contradict each other. However this has changed during the last 20 years. We see that psychology has accepted more anthropological approaches, and ethnomusicology has more or less been included in normal musicology in terms of what have got the name "new musicology" (Scott, 2005). On this basis it is time to continue the project that started up at the end of the 19th century, but more or less stranded because the scientific basis became divided into separate and unconnected disciplines.

These historical lines form in many ways the background for this book. Yet it does not directly follow up the research questions formulated by Stumpf, von Hornbostel, and Sachs. This book rather aims at arranging a meeting point or an arena in which different aspects of psychology and musicology touch and encounter each other due to how the two fields might be defined today. In line with this, it consists of a group of scholars who have their feet solidly grounded in psychology, social science, or musicology, but at the same time have a certain interest in uniting those three. Thus another aim of this book is to prepare the basis for a further growth of a cultural psychology that is able to include the experiences of music as a basis for understanding the ordinary human life.

On this background the book is divided into five different sections, in which the first aims to present some factors that have to be included in a cultural psychology of music. On this basis Christian Allesch poses some fundamental questions around our understanding of both psychology and musicology. He emphasizes that the two have a common ground in modern aesthetics. Yet this is just a starting point for finding a deeper connection between the mysterious origins of music, its structure, and the way humans include music in their ways of striving for meaning in their lives. Tania Zittoun is continuing by focusing on sound as a part of our everyday environment, and forms a certain semiosphere, which includes noise, sound, and music. By means of reported experiences of sound and music experiences she demonstrates how these experiences invades our daily lives and make the big changes for an individual. Jacob Belzen follows up the big changes in a person's life by focusing on the ambiguous relationship between music and religion. On the one hand they may have a common origin and are in practice united, but on the other hand they represent two different stands and have been even as much in conflict during the history. Based on these contributions, the cultural psychology of musical experiences cannot easily be defined, but they demonstrate anyway the importance of music as a factor in the semiospheric process of meaning making for an individual.

The second part is pursuing the real experiences of sound as sensational events. In this respect Karen Rodriguez is reporting how people by just sensing a noisy festival with opera performances and other sound events in a small Mexican city achieve a belonging to both each other and the city. This is followed up by Anne Danielsen's analysis of Public Enemy's *Fear of a Black Planet*, in which music and reality are mixed up, and the result is a type of musicalized reality. Sven Hroar Klempe is developing the aspect of musicalization further by demonstrating how the musical system can be separated from language by means of how they deal with ambiguities.

These aspects are elaborated from another perspective in Part III. Arild Bergh demonstrates how youngsters deliberately use music as a means for regulating their own emotions by the use of mobile phone technology. As Bergh is pointing at, this does not necessarily end up with just one type of music, and this aspect of dynamism and flexibility in borders between musical genres is what Petter Dyndahl is pursuing. Rolf Inge Godøy discusses how to define musical units in terms of timescales as tools for understanding differences in musical experiences in diverse cultures and genres.

The fourth part is focusing on different aspects of music used in healing. Andrea Korenjak is presenting a historical overview of how music was actually applied in medicine and psychiatry in early Western industrialization in Vienna. Lars Ole Bonde and Katarina Mårtenson Blom are investigating therapeutic imagery by means of Western classical music. Viggo Krüger and Brynjulf Stige are following up the Western perspective, but they present music therapy from the perspective of community psychology. Lise Jaastad on the other hand is presenting results from a fieldwork on the use of music in healing processes in Kenya. Thus music has been applied as a kind of alternative approach to the understanding of human life in different cultures and in different ways. This implies that there are different ways of understanding the musical system. This is pursued in Part V in which Olga V. Lehmann circles in silence as a phenomenon that articulates what is said between and underneath the tones, the phrases, and the chords. Martin Knakkergaard is examining the rhythm pattern in Michael Jackson's "Give In to Me" to show how close, but at the same time how different from regularity a preferred rhythm actually can be. Sven Hroar Klempe is terminating this part by demonstrating how easy it is to mix up an understanding of music as if it is language, and bring in some conclusions about how cultural psychology in the future can benefit from maintaining a clear distinction between language and music as two different perspectives on higher mental functions.

These contributions represent in many ways different perspectives and scientific strands. This is a necessary consequence of a project that aims at assembling disciplines that have been separated and developed individually for almost 100 years. On the other hand these contributions represent some aspects of the state of the art for those disciplines that have to be involved in a forthcoming cultural psychology of music. This is also the aim of this compilation of texts, specifically to form a basis and a starting point for a closer dialogue between musicologists, anthropologists, and psychologists to achieve a better understanding of the cultural psychology of musical experience.

REFERENCES

Ash, M. G. (1998). *Gestalt psychology in German culture 1890–1967: Holism and the quest for objectivity.* Cambridge, England: Cambridge University Press.

Boring, E. G. (1929). The psychology of controversy. *Psychological Review, 36,* 97–121.

Elschek, O., Michel, A., Porter J., & Stockmann, D. (1997). Musikalische transkription, dokumentation und edition. In D. Stockmann, (Ed.), *Neues handbuch der musikwissenschaft, band 12, volks–und popularmusik in Europa* (pp. 14–20). Darmstadt, Germany: Wissenschaftliche Buchgesellschaft.

Fechner, G. T. (1871/1978). *Vorschule der Aesthetik. 2 Bände in 1 Band. Beigebunden ist Zur experimentellen Aesthetik.* New York, NY: Georg Olms Verlag.

Klempe, S. H. (2011, Spring). The role of tone sensation and musical stimuli in early experimental psychology. *Journal of the History of the Behavioral Sciences, 47*(2), 187–199.

Sachs, C. (1943). *The rise of music in the ancient world, east and west.* New York, NY: W. W. Norton.

Scott, D. (2005). New musicology. In F. Gravesen & M. Knakkergaard (Eds.), *Gads musikleksikon, etbindsutgave,* (p. 1226). København, Denmark: Gads Forlag.

Stumpf, C. (1883). *Tonpsychologie: Erster band.* Leipzig, Germany: Verlag von S. Hirzel.

Stumpf, C. (1890). *Tonpsychologie: Zweiter band.* Leipzig, Germany: Verlag von S. Hirzel.

Von Ehrenfels, C. (1890/1988). On Gestalt qualities. In B. Smith (Ed.), *Foundations of Gestalt theory* (pp. 82–117). Wien, Austria: Philosophia Verlag.

Von Ehrenfels, C. (1932/1988). On Gestalt qualities. In B. Smith (Ed.), *Foundations of Gestalt theory* (pp. 121–123). Wien, Austria: Philosophia Verlag.

Wundt, W. M. (1896/1897). *Outlines of Psychology* (C. H. Judd, Trans.). Leipzig, Germany: W. Engelmann.

Wundt, W. M. (1920). *Erlebtes und erkanntes.* Stuttgart, Germany: Alfred Kröner Verlag.

PART I

CULTURAL PSYCHOLOGY OF MUSIC

CHAPTER 1

PSYCHOLOGICAL AESTHETICS, CULTURAL PSYCHOLOGY, AND MUSIC

Christian G. Allesch

Music, as a ubiquitous reality of our daily life, has been made a subject to scientific analysis by different disciplinary approaches. As a topic of musicology, it has been analyzed in its historical development, its formal structure, its social context, or in its cultural diversity (ethnomusicology). Within the context of systematic musicology, music traditionally has been analyzed also as a subject matter of musical aesthetics. Thus, the title of this chapter seems to refer to well-known and well-established fields of research.

However, my reference to a "psychological aesthetics" and to "cultural psychology" is to indicate that my approach to this interdisciplinary field does not go on quite in the same old way. I would like to demonstrate this at first by questioning the traditional conception of musical aesthetics.

THE TRADITIONAL CONCEPTION OF "MUSICAL AESTHETICS"

Musical aesthetics is usually defined as a philosophical discipline, which particularly reflects the "aesthetic" quality of musical perceptions and experience.

Cultural Psychology of Musical Experience, pages 3–20
Copyright © 2016 by Information Age Publishing
All rights of reproduction in any form reserved.

However, the term aesthetic was not unanimously used in the course of the history of this discipline. While Alexander Baumgarten, to whom the "foundation" of aesthetics as a subdiscipline of philosophy is usually attributed, referred to the Aristotelian concept of aesthesis, thus pointing to a rather general understanding of aesthetics as a science of sensory experience, later generations narrowed this concept to a "science of beauty and the fine arts." Like aesthetics in general, musical aesthetics followed a rather normative viewpoint in the 18th and 19th centuries. When Gustav Th. Fechner published his *Vorschule der Aesthetik* (1876/1978), in which he sought to establish an empirical "aesthetics from below" in opposition to the metaphysical concepts of German Idealism, his attempt was immediately interpreted as an infringement of the timeless rules of "ideal beauty." The historical development of musical aesthetics with some respect "mirrored" this division of viewpoints. While, for example, Arthur Schopenhauer argued that music is capable of representing the metaphysical organization of reality, favoring thus an idealistic concept of music, the representatives of romanticism focused on the capacity of music to express moods and emotions and other subjective states of mind. The thesis that the function of music is related to its representational capacity was vigorously contradicted by Eduard Hanslick (1854/1981) and other representatives of the "formalist" position, who emphasized that the formal structure of music was the only base of its aesthetic character.

From the point of view of psychological aesthetics, this aesthetic character of music cannot be explained by a mere "reacting" to or "recognizing" of an immanent aesthetic quality of a certain tonal structure. Although there is some evidence that also animals can be influenced by music, there is no reason for the assumption that there exists any comparable form of musical experience outside the human species. The reason for the development of musical sensibility as a crucial characteristic of mankind has to be traced back therefore to the evolution of human mind.

This leads us necessarily to cultural psychology because human evolution includes cultural evolution as a pivotal aspect. Anthropological evidence shows that there has never existed any human culture without music. In his *Geschichte als Weg zum Musikverständnis* (History as a Means of Understanding Music, 1977), Georg Knepler characterized music as "a form of expression of mankind, which is so elementary and universal that we cannot hope to understand its essence and functions unless we regard it fundamentally connected with human evolution" (Knepler, 1977, p. 52, author's translation). The evolution of music, Knepler argues, is therefore also the key to the evolution of man: "Dealing with the history of music means, consciously or not, dealing with the history of mankind" (Knepler, p. 49, author's translation).

In a similar way Wolfgang Suppan *(Der musizierende Mensch: Eine Anthropologie der Musik, 1984)* demonstrated that ritual activities in all contexts where they occur are associated with songs and other forms of musical expression. This also established a close connection between music and religion. In the early writings of cultural psychology, these topics formed a crucial part of the agenda. Wilhelm Wundt, for example, has dedicated three volumes of his *Voelkerpsychologie* to the topic of myth and religion. According to Wundt, art is "in any phase of its development ... in its forms the expression of the general activity of fancy, in its content an expression of the worldviews which are founded in particular in myth and religion" (Wundt, 1905, p. 94, author's translation).

THE ORIGINS OF MUSIC

It is in this context that we have to discuss the relation between aesthetics, culture and music. We know that many animals communicate by using voice and vocal signals. But this communication is limited to the functional context for which it was selected by evolution, and to a certain genetically fixed repertoire of tonal structures. Similar vocal signals were probably used in the early days of mankind; for example to coordinate activities in hunting or to warn each other to avoid perils in warlike activities. But this is not music and cannot explain the development of musical forms. Probably the development of musicality is part of a rather complicated evolutionary development of organic structures and mental abilities. On the organic part, some structural changes of larynx and glottis were necessary prerequisites for enhancing the extended flexibility of the human voice. But this enhancement of expressive qualities would not have produced an evolutionary advantage without certain coordinated changes in mental awareness and consciousness. There are some reasons to suppose that the ability to perceive musical structures in time and to be aware of aesthetic qualities in general is closely connected to the perception of time and to the awareness of personal identity in time. That means that sequences of tones can be perceived as musical structure (Gestalt) developing in time and that this development can be related to the continuance of a listening subject. We know from evidence of developmental research, that the ability to conceive musical periods is not existent from the beginning of life but develops in the course of the first years of age. But this implies that also this developmental function was constituted by an evolutionary process in prehistoric times.

With respect to the enlarged state of consciousness that is necessary for an aesthetic experience of music, some considerations may be helpful, which Wilhelm Revers had presented in his book on *Das Musikerlebnis* (The Experience of Music) in 1971. In this book Revers criticized the embarrassment of musical research of that time to conceptualize musical experience in terms of stimulus and response. Contradictory to that, he pled for an anthropological foundation of a theory of musical experience. This means not to start from the question which measurable "reactions" are elicited by a musical "stimulus," but to ask for the meaning of a sounding tone within the concrete life world of a listening individual. Of course this leads consequently to the anthropological question why this form of experience developed in the process of human evolution to a pivotal category of human experience. Revers answered this question by pointing to the fact that the audible world—even more than the visible world—opens the world as a space of resonance that enables us to get aware of our individual existence (Revers, 1971, p. 70, author's translation).

Ernst E. Boesch in his symbolic action theory (1991) distinguishes between "objective-instrumental" and "subjective-functional" qualities of action. This distinction is also relevant for an evolutionary interpretation of music. The term objective-instrumental thereby points to the fact that an action that is directed to reach an objective goal like to draw somebody's attention by a vocal call. Subjective-functional aspects of actions are characterized by their self-enhancing function, by resulting in a personal emotional benefit for the acting person. In this context Boesch argues that there are some similarities between listening to a piece of music and skiing: Following carefully the unevenness of the ground may have the objective-instrumental aim to come down safely, but may have also the subjective-functional reinforcement to experience one's own skillfulness and ability to master a difficult terrain. In the same way following a temporal contour in listening to music and thus experiencing one's own ability to master it may have an "I-strengthening" function (Boesch, 1975, p. 51f.; Allesch, 1993).

With respect to the evolution there are some reasons for supposing that tonal experience and performance are at least predominantly associated with objective-instrumental functions at the prehuman stage. Whether the singing of a bird has any "self-enhancing" function besides its evolved function as a tool of social communication, which is typical for the respective species, cannot be answered in an empirical way. But we may conclude from the fact that the variability of these "musical" productions is highly restricted, that these tonal structures are "signals" rather than "messages" or even modifications of a flexibly usable "language." At the human level, however, there is much evidence for subjective-functional qualities of musical activities (including the intentional listening to music, which by no means represents a "passive" reception). Furthermore, human activities are, in general, characterized by what Boesch calls the "polyvalence" of goals and processes: They do not represent themselves alone but may serve different goals at the same time: "Creating a *beautiful* vessel is more than simply producing a vessel; it enriches the functional quality object by one of private enjoyment, but likely one of social demonstration, of appeal or of individualization" (Boesch, 1991, p. 46).

It is the difficult task of evolutionary psychology to discover in which manner objective-instrumental and subjective-functional qualities of musical activities were interlinked in the evolution of human musicality and what forms the particular evolutionary "benefit" of producing differentiated sound patterns and of listening to such patters beyond their concrete denotative function. Hauser and McDermott (2003) presume that animal vocalizations were forged by natural selection in the hunter-gatherer societies to convey information about the emotional state of the caller—this refers to an objective-functional aspect of musical activity. Scherer and Zentner (2001) proposed a neurocognitive mechanism linking acoustic properties of sound directly to neural structures of the brainstem and primary cortex, which could explain the hedonic responses to sound features. This again points to an origin of such reactions in the early human evolution, but cannot explain why it came about.

Summing up the recent results of evolutionary musicology, Brattico, Brattico and Jacobsen (2009/2010, p. 20) state that "sound features ... may have added survival chances to the individuals that were able to better process or produce them, hence being associated in the phylogenesis with pleasurable sensations." This is a reasonable explanation for the evolution of the prerequisites of human musicality on an objective-instrumental level, and it may be as well a reasonable explanation of the evolution of complex tonal patterns of communication at the pre-human level. But it does not provide a thorough understanding of the aesthetic character of music. François-Bernard Mâche (2000) comes still closer to the problem when he argues that the aesthetic function of tonal structures, despite the fact that they originated in a natural context, have to be interpreted by their function as an intrinsic pleasure, as an unnecessary activity beyond mere survival.

It is exactly this point that leads us from explanations on the level of adaptive behavior to the complex processes of cultural evolution. We have to conceive the evolution of humanity— and of musicality as an essential aspect of humanity—as a process that fundamentally changed the relation of the individual and his world. It is only a particular aspect of this process that humans became able to process or produce tonal patterns in a more differentiated way. Furthermore, it seems plausible to assume that this ability to perceive sensory patterns in a more differentiated way is not restricted to the auditory part of perception, but just one aspect of a new symbolic form of perceiving reality. This limits the explanatory capacity of models which try to explain the emergence of an aesthetic experience of tonal structures exclusively by the association of isolated features of sounds to particular emotional connotations. In this sense, aesthetic experience as an evolved form of perceiving reality (including audible patterns and structures) may be interpreted as a by-product of a fundamental change of the structure of consciousness that characterizes the transition from prehuman stages to

Homo sapiens. With respect to tonal structures, an essential feature of this evolutionary process might be seen in a change of the temporal structure of consciousness. Although there is some evidence that animals are able to recognize changes in the temporal structure of tonal sequences, we cannot infer from this fact that animals, e.g., birds, have the same impression of a tonal *gestalt* as human beings. Already Augustine, in his treatise *De Musica* (VI, 2 [3]; Migne, 1844, vol. 32, col. 1164), made a distinction between *habere numeros* (to identify criteria like pitch or duration) and *sentire numerosum sonum* (the phenomenal equivalent in perception). Furthermore, Augustine distinguished between *memoria* and *recordatio* (and Aristotle in a similar way between *mnéme* and *anámnesis*), distinguishing in that way the process of a mechanical recall of tonal patterns from memory and the act of an intended remembering of a tonal context (like mother's voice or an important musical experience in the past).

THE EXISTENTIAL ASPECT OF MUSICAL EXPERIENCE

While there is no evidence that animals reflect on their past and their future, human beings are aware of the transitoriness of their personal existence. Recent theoretical constructions of social psychology like terror management theory (Greenberg, Solomon, & Pyszczynski, 1992) have recognized this fact as a crucial background for the explanation of individual behavior in a cultural context and of the evolution of cultures (Solomon, Greenberg & Pyszczynski, 2004). Empirical research on the base of this theory provided us with remarkable evidence that identifying with cultural symbols, which represent a continuity of one's own belief system beyond the limits of one's personal existence, may be a powerful means for coping with the threatening recognition of the limitedness of this personal existence. Cultures, from this point of view, do not merely provide an evolutionary benefit by mobilizing a collective protecting system for the survival of individuals and their communities, but represent a collective memory in which individual experiences are embedded and "objectified" and will survive the limits of personal existence.

This is at least one of the reasons we might presume for the rewarding function of rituals as they have developed in the emergence of human cultures. In this context, musical forms of rituals are particularly suited to fulfill this function because they do not require any particular knowledge or expressive talents but are based on abilities that are, at least to a large extent, available to all members of the respective communities. Brattico, Brattico, and Jacobsen (2009/2010) rightly point to the fact that "music enjoyment is typically a collective experience" and that "on the basis of anthropological observations and on studies of infant behavior, it is well demonstrated that music is able to strengthen social cohesion, coordination and cooperation within social groups" (Geissmann, 2000).

However, besides this rewarding function of collective musical activities, there may be supposed rewarding mechanisms also on the individual level: Wilhelm Revers (1971), for example, points to the fact that in performing musical activities human beings may experience that they are not only subject to the flow of time, but have the opportunity to actively structuring timely processes. Music, according to this concept, is in its very essence, "shaped time" (*gestaltete Zeit*). We find similar ideas in the aesthetic theory of Ernst E. Boesch, which refers to cultural psychology: In his book *Das Magische und das Schöne* (The Magical and the Beautiful, 1983), Boesch distinguishes two alternative ways or attitudes of facing reality. While the magic attitude expresses a distancing function, trying to avert the influences of the disturbing object or situation, the aesthetic attitude represents a tendency to incorporate the "strange" aspects of reality into the personal symbolic world by empathy; it stresses being in harmony with the world by the attempt "to expand the validity of the inner images" and "to transform counter-world into I-world" (Boesch, 1983, p. 316). According to Boesch, it is mainly this ability of "mastering" strange and threatening aspects of our life-world by the constructive power of empathy and imagination, which may explain the rewarding function of aesthetic experience.

This is one more argument for my supposition that it was not the enhancement of discriminatory abilities with respect to the perception and production of tonal stimulus material, which enabled an aesthetic or "hedonic" experience of sound, but the emergence of self-consciousness, which included a personal past and a personal future within the realm of perceived actual identity. In the context of a conscience that is able to conceive identity as consistency over time, the continuous sound of a horn or a human voice can not only represent a signal conveying a specific information, but a symbol of the time-encompassing identity of the producer as well as the listener. This might be at least one source of the aesthetic fascination of musical structures and, by the same token, distinguishes them from accidental noise.

In his essay "The Sound of the Violin," Ernst E. Boesch describes the psychological function of the action of making objects produce sound: He takes up reminiscences of his childhood, when he "used to tighten a blade of grass between the two thumbs and, by blowing into the thus formed interstice, produce a sharp, oboe-like sound" (Boesch, 1993, p. 74). Forming an instrument means, according to Boesch, "transforming nature into culture, forcing it to produce a sound which neither existed in "raw" nature, nor would have been possible to create without nature" (1993). Boesch continues,

> Yet the pleasure was immense and can be understood only by the extension of my childish action potential; it made me a creator, albeit in a tiny area. Mak-

ing objects sound, thus, is a bit like taming animals: it transforms a resistant non-I into a compliant extension of the I. (Boesch, 1993)

I think that this biographical observation refers to a mechanism which may be interpreted as an explanation for the evolutionary "benefit" of musical activity as well. In ontogeny as well as in phylogeny of human beings the experience of "mastering" resistant objects represents an important precondition for forming stable relations between the I and his environment and for strengthening self-efficacy. Boesch's narrative is, furthermore, a good example for the theoretical and practical relevance of his distinction between objective-instrumental and subjective-functional valences of actions: Producing a musical instrument does not necessarily fulfil a specific purpose with respect to individual survival (although instruments might be construed as a means of communication in hunting, for example). But in the reported example, the only purpose is a subjective one and it reflects—in evolutionary terms—a new state of consciousness which includes self-consciousness and the need for stabilizing one's own identity as essential aspects of individual existence. This can be an explanation, why forming an instrument and musical behavior may be perceived as actions with a high subjective-functional valence for an individual and, in consequence, have been integrated into cultural patterns of behavior.

However, we might put the question whether this valence may be inherent to any form of sound or is dependent on a certain (aesthetic?) quality of the sound. From observations of children playing, we may derive that in an early stage of development in fact the mere experience of producing sound (or noise) may fulfill an I-rewarding function. But we also know from empirical investigation of children's drawings that aesthetic needs are not satisfied by the kind of production that is characteristic for a certain stage but includes a tendency for differentiation and perfection (Schuster, 2010). The same is true for the musical productivity of children (Trehub, 2002, 2003). Also Boesch, in "The Sound of the Violin," distinguishes two aspects to be considered: the action of *making objects to produce sound*, and the *search for perfection of sound* (Boesch, 1993, p. 74).

Both activities arise from the same motivational source: to gain reinforcement from "mastering" an instrument or one's own voice. But this experience of mastering is—at least in most cases—inevitably connected with the desire for perfection: "to reach that elusive quality of tone which he feels to be moving, 'going to heart,' indefinable and yet inducing a reaction of content and fulfilment in the happy moments where he feels to have reached it" (Boesch 1993, p. 74). Referring to ethnological findings, Boesch argues that the ideational concept of the "perfect sound" can be found in myth stories and fairy tales of many cultures: The miraculous power of the perfect sound "tames wild animals, ghosts, heals the sick and appeals directly to the angels," it "provides the experience of an optimal action potential, able to realize perfection—although only for the fleeting moment of the sound's duration" (Boesch, p. 74ff.).

But what makes a perfect sound perfect or—put in a more generalized way—what is the "aesthetic" quality of an aesthetic experience? In his fascinating essay "Bedeutung ästhetischer Zeichen: Musik und Sprache" (1985), the musicologist Peter Faltin characterized the essence of aesthetic signs by the fact that they convey significance without denoting something. A perfect sound is not a "better description" of any reality it would pretend to describe; its perfection is based on the degree of mastery it reflects and on the ease and naturalness of its production. Again Boesch uses the paradigm of skiing in order to demonstrate this analogy: "The trace of the skilled skier becomes aesthetically pleasing by an effortless elegance of its curves, and similarly the beauty of sounds consists in a smooth flowing through the meanders of the melody" (Boesch, 1993, p. 79).

MUSICAL EXPERIENCE AND CULTURAL EVOLUTION

Arguments like these may explain why playing or listening to music may have an eminent subjective-functional valence for an individual. But, from the viewpoint of cultural psychology, this is just one side of the coin. As Brattico, Brattico, and Jacobsen (2009/2010, p. 22) rightly state, "Music enjoyment is typically a collective experience," and its evolution cannot be sufficiently explained by the individual benefit caused by its subjective functionality. I have argued that an important prerequisite for the I-rewarding function of musical experience has to be seen in a fundamental change of the capability of conscience that is supposed to have happened in the transitory stage from prehuman to human way of existence. With respect to the ability of perceiving aesthetic qualities of music, the intentional perception of time is probably the most important feature of this widening of conscience. But it seems reasonable to suppose that the same evolutionary change of the structure of mind entailed also other changes of human worldview, which concern the social and cultural aspects of living. Thus, the evolution of musical experience is likely to be inseparably embedded in the embracing process of cultural evolution. There is strong evidence that the most ancient musical forms emerged in the context of symbolic ceremonies and cultural rituals (Suppan, 1984). However, the emergence of symbolic action again presupposes the evolution of a mind that is capable of a symbolic understanding of the world and of his action and of that of others.

It is common conviction that "cognitive advancements such as music, language, culture, advanced tool use, symbolic art, social organization and hierarchical thought appeared as a result of an increasing number of sophisticated, innate, domain-specific faculties" (Livingstone & Thompson, 2009/2010, p. 94). But there have been discussions whether these faculties can be subsumed to a single faculty that was responsible for the emergence of all these cultural activities. According to Tomasello (1999, 2003), for example, the evolution of a theory of mind (ToM) was the essential progress that enabled *joint-attentional activities* and, in consequence, *dialogic interaction,* which might include musical forms. If we take Astington and Baird's (2005, p. 3) definition of ToM as the ability to understand "people as mental beings who have beliefs, desires, emotions, and intentions and whose actions and interactions can be interpreted and explained by taking account of these mental states," the concept of ToM is probably too general in order to explain the emergence of musical experience in its particular aspects. Some authors (Livingstone & Thompson, 2009/2010, p. 97) suggest a "two-stage model" of ToM (containing simulation theory as a basic empathy learning mechanism and theory as an explanation of the formation of complex mental models about the mind) in order to explain the emergence of cultural rituals. Nettl (2005, pp. 254–258) rightly points to the concept of identity as a significant aspect of musical experience. Livingstone and Thompson (2006, 2009/2010) emphasize *reflective thought* as a process responsible for "the continual refinement and progression of music and the arts" (2009/2010, p. 99). In contradiction to these theories and assumptions, which tend to focus on a single explanatory concept, Parncutt (2009/2010, p. 122) assumes that "music may have several origins in the sense that it emerged parallel to a number of changes in the human and prehuman condition over a long period."

It is in fact this aspect that may constitute the particular approach of cultural psychology to the phenomena of musical experience. Musical experience, within the general frame of a "psychology of music," was subject to rather different theoretical and methodological approaches in the historical development of this discipline. These particular approaches in general followed the paradigmatic trends of psychology as the "mother discipline" of music psychology (Allesch & Krakauer, 2005/2006). While in the age of behaviorism (and even in some experimental designs until now) musical experience was conceptualized as a "response" to musical "stimuli," after the "cognitive turn" it was preferably interpreted as the result of "top-down processes" and as the result of a complex process of mental analysis including pattern recognition, prototypicality judgments or expertise-based appraisal and resulting in aesthetic judgments and aesthetic emotions (for example, the model of aesthetic experience proposed by Leder, Belke, Oeberst, & Augustin, 2004). More recently, the psychology of music adopted the current trend to evolutionary interpretations of psychological phenomena and psychology's turn to new interdisciplinary connections with psychobiology and the neurosciences (for example, the model of music perception proposed by Koelsch & Siebel, 2005, which is very similar to the model of Leder et al. but refers more directly to the neural basis of music perception).

Until now, the cognitive psychology of music is one of the most successful research programs of psychology of the past 50 years. However, there are some shortcomings of this paradigm with respect to recognizing the cultural character of music and music experience. Jerome Bruner, one of the fathers of the "cognitive revolution," in his book *Acts of Meaning* (1990) criticized cognitive psychology in general for having abandoned its original intentions. These were, Bruner argued, to oppose behaviorism's stimulus-response doctrine and search for an explanation as to how the concepts of meaning and significance are represented in the human mind by which he meant "to discover and to describe formally the meanings that human beings created out of their encounters with the world" (Bruner, 1990, p. 2). The reason for this defection was, according to Bruner, that the protagonists of the cognitive turn succumbed to a fascination with information technology. The computer model became the leading metaphor for "information processing" despite all differences that might be assumed between a computer's hard and software and a human brain, which, unlike a computer, is construed to detect sense and meaning in the perceived world and to perceive it as a personal experience.

In order to correct this mistake, Bruner argues, psychology has to rediscover culture as the objective mediator of meaning in history. However, any psychology that "concerns itself centrally with meaning, . . . inevitably becomes *cultural* psychology" and "must venture beyond the conventional aims of positivist science with its ideals of *reductionism, causal explanation* and *prediction*" (Bruner, pp. xii–xiii). In its historical tradition, Wundt's *Voelkerpsychologie*, conceptualized as a "psychological history of the development of mankind" (Wundt, 1912), represented the most prominent example of a nonexperimental empirical approach to investigate the interrelations between the development of human culture and the development of human mind (Jüttemann, 2006). Recent approaches of cultural psychology focus on the dynamic interactions between man and his culture (Boesch, 1991; Boesch & Straub, 2007) distinguishing thereby cultural psychology as a general attempt to conceptualize the interrelation between man and culture from cross-cultural psychology as a means to test psychological hypotheses with respect to their cross-cultural universality. Richard Shweder (1990, p. 1) defined cultural psychology as "the study of the way cultural traditions and social practices regulate, express, transform and permute the human psyche" and characterized the particular point of view of cultural psychology by the fact that it interprets human beings as living in an intentional world composed of intentional objects forming the cultural background of our daily lives. This means that music as an objective part of our intentional world may be interpreted as a culturally formed structure that influences our personal experience but is formed by our intentions as well. From this point of view music (as an audible structure) and musical perception (as a corresponding function of the mind) do not figure as stimulus and response, but as meaningful structures characterized by intentionality. However, theoretical conceptions of cultural psychology that are dealing explicitly with music or musical experience are rather rare.

MUSIC FROM THE VIEWPOINT OF CULTURAL PSYCHOLOGY

Nevertheless, useful inference to a cultural-psychological conception of musical experience may be derived in particular from Ernst E. Boesch's symbolic action theory (1991)—I already referred to Boesch's concept of the "polyvalence" of action and objects and to his reflections on the self-rewarding function of the awareness of "mastering" a complex time-related structure as an essential aspect of the "hedonic" character of musical experience. In a recent publication Über *Musik* (About Music, 2005), Boesch presents some hypothetical assumptions about the origin of music: it might have been developed, on a first stage,

> as a reaction to noises and sounds, gradually followed by the handling of sounding objects, be it for the purpose of communication or just for play, but certainly at an early stage for magic defense and beseech. This magic use has been most lasting preserved within religious contexts – in the psalmody of monks, in hymns and songs of praise, with the particular monotonous solemnity which has been known still in Gregorian chants. This has been favored by the combination of music and speech which lent a particular power and insistence to the sound by beseeching words, and in this way the human voice became a privileged and certainly most important musical instrument. (Boesch 2005, p. 137)

According to Boesch, musical sound was used by man from the origins of music in three ways:

> for communication, for play (in order to experience pleasant, surprising or frightening sounds), and in the context of magical rites. All of these three forms of use had the common purpose to harmonize the relation of man to his world, be it in the intention to coordinate social action, be it by transforming neutral objects into instruments of enjoyment, or be it for magical use in order to overcome the resistance of the real world or to beseech the numinous world. (2005, p. 138)

A radical change of the cultural role of music was induced by its development from ritual practice to a form of art. According to Boesch (2005,

p. 139), the transformation of music to an art had, in principle, three consequences: first, its separation from magic (which survived in liturgy but lost its predominant role). Secondly, the growing complexity of musical forms and the development of polyphony made playing an instrument to a business of experts and caused the separation of performing artists and listening audience. Third, the growing complexity of musical forms divided even the audience into erudite experts and naive listeners. Thus, the immediate cultural function of music, namely to mediate between the inner world and the world outside, got lost by the development of modern culture.

We may derive from this arguments, that music as cultural phenomenon of the external world and musical experience as a particular form of personal awareness form an intricate interrelation. It was another cultural psychologist, Alfred Lang, who developed a "semiotic-ecological" model in order to conceptualize the relation between culture and psyche in semiotic terms. Lang interprets the process of forming meaningful in the external world (ExtrAsemiosis) and the formation of mental representations (IntrAsemiosis) as semiotic processes which include a referent (R), a presentant (P), and an interpretant (Int) as well as the processes of exchange between individual and culture, represented by acts of perception, experience (which Lang calls IntrOsemiosis) and acting (ExtrOsemiosis; Figure 1.1; Lang, 1992).

Within the context of this theoretical approach, experiencing music cannot be conceptualized as a mere reacting to certain acoustic stimuli, but is interpreted as a symbolic understanding based on a vocabulary developed by cultural tradition and mediated by those early experiences of elementary patterns of musical expression, which we can find in every culture. Furthermore, the individual experience of music must be conceived of in this theoretical context as an individual event in an individual's mind at a certain time and in a particular cultural context. Both the cultural context as well as the individual are subject to a process of development in time, however.

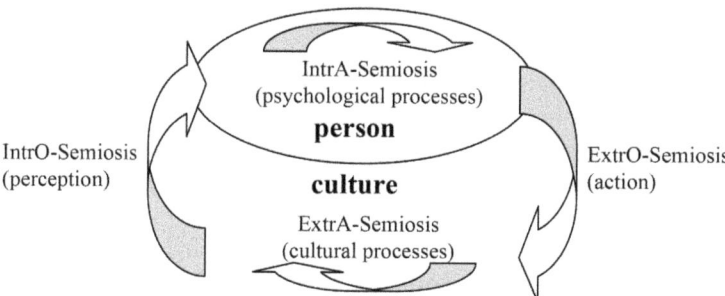

Figure 1.1 The "Semiotic Function Circle" (Lang, 1992).

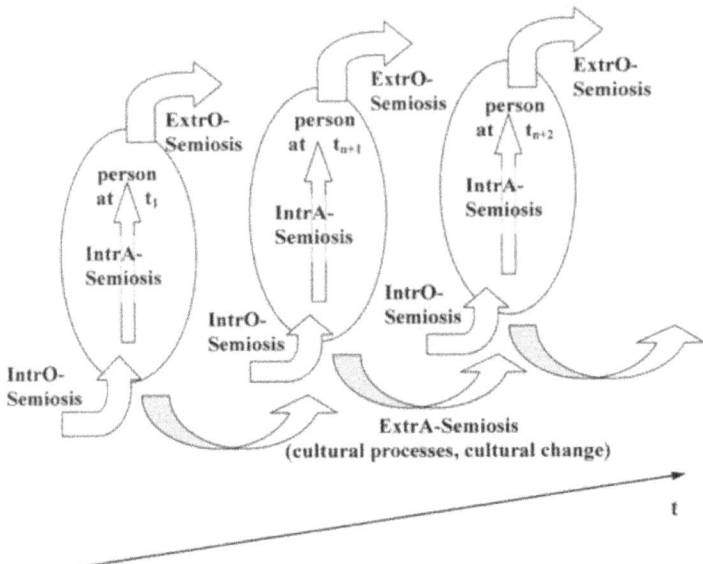

Figure 1.2 The Semiotic Function Circle: Exchanges between persons and the world in time (Lang, 1993).

Alfred Lang acknowledges this fact by introducing time as an additional dimension to his semiotic circle (Figure 1.2, Lang, 1993).

This means that any reliable assessment of the individual experience of music must consider the development of musical patterns within the respective culture as well as the individual's development with respect to dealing with cultural "codes" of musical expression. Maria Spychiger (2000, 2001) has implemented this model to music education: Neither musical activities nor the experience of music can be interpreted as isolated processes, but are embedded in a cultural process which can be conceptualized by using Lang's model (Figure 1.3).

In this model, IntrOsemiosis refers to the process of musical perception, the reception of the sound environment as well as the intentional listening to music. IntrAsemiosis characterizes the domain of musical experience (knowing music), creating musical ideas or subjective interpretation of musical structures. Musical activities like playing an instrument, composing or dancing represent the aspect of ExtrOsemiosis while the term ExtrAsemiosis refers to "musical culture with all the various things it includes—musical devices, musical events and works, and creatures living in it" (Spychiger, 2001, p. 61). This model "addresses the role of music as a connecting agent within cultural life and development" (Spychiger, 2001, p. 65) and is a good example for the possibility of reinterpreting musical experience and musical activities in theoretical context derived from cultural psychology.

Figure 1.3 The Semiotic Circle applied on musical activities (Spychiger, 2001).

To sum up, it is difficult to describe the actual or possible contribution to a psychological interpretation of musical experience since the concept of cultural psychology cannot be clearly delimited—neither in historical terms nor with respect to recent approaches: There are rather different forms of "culture-related psychologies" (Boesch & Straub, 2007) than a clearly structured scientific discipline. Anyway there are some plausible theoretical approaches to explain the difficult and complex network of relations between culture and individual and between music as a cultural fact and musical experience as its perceptual representation on the personal level. The examples I quoted reflect my personal preferences and do not pretend to represent an objective description of a widely accepted state of the art.

However, some plausible assumptions with respect to the essential questions, which a cultural-psychological approach to the phenomenon of musical experience should be able to answer: First, it has to find plausible interpretations of the concrete evolutionary mechanisms that governed the common evolution of human consciousness, of human culture and of aesthetic experience. Second, it has to develop plausible models in order to explain the interrelation between culture and individual. Third, it has, on the one hand, to be open for new methods to analyze the psychic representation of musical stimuli (including the fascinating facilities of neurocognitive science and neuroimaging), but on the other hand, it should never forget the reminder of Jerome Bruner that aesthetic and, in particular, musical experiences are not mere "reactions" to definable "stimuli," but "acts of meaning" that are determined by the existential situation of the experiencing individual as well as by the cultural context by which his way of experience has been coined.

REFERENCES

Allesch, C. G. (1993). The aesthetic as a psychological aspect of man-environment relations: Ernst E. Boesch as an aesthetician. *Schweizerische Zeitschrift für Psychologie, 52*, 122–129.

Allesch, C. G., & Krakauer, P. M. (2005/2006). Understanding our experience of music: What kind of psychology do we need? In R. Parncutt (Ed.), *Interdisciplinary musicology: Musicae scientiae* (Special issue; pp. 41–63). Liège, Belgium: Escom.

Astington, J. W., & Baird, J. A. (2005). Introduction: Why language matters. In J. W. Astington & J. A. Baird (Eds.), *Why language matters for theory of mind* (pp. 3–25). New York, NY: Oxford University Press.

Boesch, E. E. (1975). *Zwischen Angst und Triumph. Über das Ich und seine Bestätigung.* Bern, Switzerland: Huber.

Boesch, E. E. (1983). *Das Magische und das Schöne. Zur Symbolik von Objekten und Handlungen.* Stuttgart, Germany: Frommann-Holzboog.

Boesch, E. E. (1991). *Symbolic action theory and cultural psychology.* Berlin, Germany: Springer.

Boesch, E. E. (1993). The sound of the violin. *Schweizerische Zeitschrift für Psychologie, 52*, 70–81.

Boesch, E. E. (2005). Über Musik. In E. Boesch, *Von Kunst bis Terror: Über den Zwiespalt in der Kultur* (pp. 107–168). Göttingen, Germany: Vandenhoeck & Ruprecht.

Boesch, E. E., & Straub, J. (2007). Kulturpsychologie: Prinzipien, Orientierungen, Konzeptionen. In G. Trommsdorff & H.-J. Kornadt (Eds.), *Enzyklopädie der psychologie* (Vol. C/7/2): *Theorien und Methoden der kulturvergleichenden Psychologie* (pp. 25–95). Göttingen, Germany: Hogrefe.

Brattico, E., Brattico, P., & Jacobsen, T. (2009/2010). The origins of the aesthetic enjoyment of music: A review of the literature. In O. Vitouch & O. Ladinig (Eds.), *Musicae scientiae: Music and evolution* (Special issue; pp. 15–39). Liège, Belgium: Escom.

Bruner, J. S. (1990). *Acts of meaning.* Cambridge, MA: Harvard University Press.

Faltin, P. (1985). *Bedeutung ästhetischer zeichen: Musik und sprache.* Aachen, Germany: Rader.

Fechner, G. T. (1876/1978). *Vorschule der Aesthetik* (Reprint of the 3rd ed. 1925). Hildesheim, Germany: Olms.

Geissmann, T. (2000). Gibbon songs and human music from an evolutionary perspective. In N. Wallin, B. Merker, & S. Brown (Eds.), *The origins of music* (pp. 103–123). Cambridge, MA: MIT Press.

Greenberg, J., Solomon, S., & Pyszczynski, T. (1992): Why do people need self-esteem? Converging evidence that self-esteem serves an anxiety-buffering function. *Journal of Personality and Social Psychology, 63,* 913–922.

Hanslick, E. (1854/1981). *Vom Musikalisch-Schönen* (Reprint of the 1st ed., Leipzig 1854). Darmstadt, Germany: WBG.

Hauser, M. D., & McDermott, J. (2003). The evolution of the music faculty: A comparative perspective. *Nature Neuroscience, 6,* 663–668.

Jüttemann, G. (Ed.) (2006): *Wilhelm Wundts anderes Erbe. Ein Missverständnis löst sich auf.* Göttingen, Germany: Vandenhoeck & Ruprecht.

Knepler, G. (1977). *Geschichte als Weg zum Musikverständnis.* Leipzig, Germany: Reclam.

Koelsch, S., & Siebel, W. (2005). Towards a neural basis of music perception. *Trends in Cognitive Science, 9,* 578–584.

Lang, A. (1992). Kultur als externe Seele. In: C. G. Allesch, E. Billmann-Mahecha, & A. Lang (Eds.), *Psychologische Aspekte des kulturellen Wandels* (pp. 9–30). Wien, Austria: VWGÖ.

Lang, Alfred (1993). Zeichen nach innen, Zeichen nach aussen—eine semiotisch-ökologische Psychologie als Kulturwissenschaft. In P. Rusterholz & M. Svilar (Eds.), *Welt der Wirklichkeit: Welt der Zeichen* (pp. 55–84). Bern, Switzerland: Haupt.

Leder, H., Belke, B., Oeberst, A., & Augustin, D. (2004). A model of aesthetic appreciation and aesthetic judgment. *British Journal of Psychology, 95,* 489–508.

Livingstone, S. R., & Thompson, W. F. (2006). Multi-modal affective interaction: A comment on musical origins. *Music Perception, 24,* 89–94.

Livingston, S. R., & Thompson, W. F. (2009/2010). The emergence of music from the theory of mind. In O. Vitouch & O. Ladinig (Eds.), *Musicae scientiae. Music and evolution* (Special issue; pp. 83–115). Liège, Belgium: Escom.

Mâche, F.-B. (2000). The necessity of and problems with a universal musicology. In N. L. Wallin, B. Merker, & S. Brown (Eds.), *The origins of music* (pp. 473–479). Cambridge, MA: MIT Press.

Migne, J. P. (Ed.) (1844ff.). *Patrologiae cursus completus; pars Latina.* Paris: Siron.

Nettl, B. (2005). *The study of ethnomusicology: Thirty-one issues and concepts* (Revised ed.). Champaign, IL: University of Illinois Press.

Parncutt, R. (2009/2010). Prenatal and infant conditioning, the mother schema, and the origins of music and religion. In O. Vitouch & O. Ladinig (Eds.), *Musicae scientiae. Music and evolution* (Special issue; pp. 119–150). Liège, Belgium: Escom.

Revers, W. J. (1970). *Das Musikerlebnis.* Düsseldorf, Germany: Econ.

Scherer, K. R., & Zentner, K. R. (2001). Emotional effects of music: Production rules. In P. N. Juslin & J. A. Sloboda (Eds.), *Music and emotion: Theory and research* (pp. 361–392). Oxford, England: Oxford University Press.

Schuster, M. (2010). *Kinderzeichnungen: Wie sie entstehen, was sie bedeuten* (3rd ed.). Munich, Germany: Reinhardt.

Shweder, R. A. (1990). Cultural psychology: What is it? In J. Stigler, R. Shweder, & G. Herdt (Eds.), *Cultural psychology: Essays on comparative human development.* Cambridge, England: Cambridge University Press.

Solomon, S., Greenberg, J., & Pyszczynski, T. (2004): *The cultural animal: Twenty years of terror management theory and research.* In J. Greenberg, S. L. Koole, & T. Pyszczynski (Eds.), *Handbook of experimental existential psychology* (pp. 13–34). New York, NY: Guilford.

Spychiger, M. (2000). Hören und Zuhören im erweiterten Musikunterricht. In L. Huber & E. Odersky (Eds.), *Zuhören–Lernen–Verstehen* (pp. 149–165). Braunschweig, Germany: Westermann.

Spychiger, M. (2001). Understanding musical activity and musical learning as sign processes: Toward a semiotic approach to music education. *The Journal of Aesthetic Education, 35*(1), 53–67.

Suppan, W. (1984). *Der musizierende Mensch: Eine Anthropologie der Musik.* Mainz, Germany: Schott.

Tomasello, M. (1999). *The cultural origins of human cognition.* Cambridge, MA: Harvard University Press.

Tomasello, M. (2003). The key is social cognition. In D. Gentner & S. Goldin-Meadow (Eds.), *Language in mind: Advances in the study of language and thought* (pp. 47–58). London, England: MIT Press.

Trehub, S. E. (2002). The musical infant. In D. J. Lewkowicz & R. Lickliter (Eds.), *Conceptions of development: Lessons from the laboratory* (pp. 231–257). New York, NY: Psychology Press.

Trehub, S. E. (2003). Musical predispositions in infancy: An update. In R. Zatorre & I. Peretz (Eds.), *The cognitive neuroscience of music* (pp. 3–20). Oxford, England: Oxford University Press.

Wundt, W. (1905). *Völkerpsychologie: Eine Untersuchung von Sprache, Mythus und Sitte, (Vol. 2, Part 1: Mythus und Religion).* Leipzig, Germany: Engelmann.

Wundt, W. (1912). *Elemente der Völkerpsychologie: Grundlinien einer psychologischen Entwicklungsgeschichte der Menschheit.* Leipzig, Germany: Kröner.

CHAPTER 2

THE SOUND OF MUSIC

Tania Zittoun

What holds for play also holds for the St. Matthew passion.
—Donald W. Winnicott, 1968, p. 206

ouitchi-tchatchitchatchaouitchitchatchitchitchaNIAAAAAAH . . .
ouitchi-tchatchitcha.
—Simonds, 1988, p. 45

As people live and move through their physical, urban, material, geographical environment, they are constantly exposed to an endless variety of shapes, volumes, colors and sounds (Kharlamov, 2012; Maslov, 2012; Valsiner, 2007, 2008). These geographical environments thus guide our physical movements, and also, because we keep being exposed to shapes, colors and sounds at the periphery of our consciousness, they actually guide our thinking (Valsiner, 2011). First, in the here and now, street signs and colors suggest us to some places, inform us about the status of others, induce us to spend money, or to keep our way. Second, in a deeper sense, our long-term experience of the places in which we live is also the situated process by which we learn to move and to see; we therefore internalize and generalize these relationships to space, colors of the landscape, and textures of the buildings. Our spaces become the texture of our minds, in a very essential sense. Hence, the nostalgia of migrants for their homeland landscapes

Cultural Psychology of Musical Experience, pages 21–39
Copyright © 2016 by Information Age Publishing

or for the shape of the houses of their village speaks for such deep connections between our material environments and our identities and sense of what feels homely (Märtsin & Mahmoud, 2012). Third, we actually also participate to the transformation of the material space—we transform our gardens and houses, we paint walls and draw urbanistic plans.

Beyond the visual and the tactile, the space of music and sounds also calls for a special investigation. As spaces and colors, sounds are present in our physical environment. As much as physical spaces, they are perceived by humans through their senses and their physical, embodied experience; and as their experience of space, experiences of sounds needs to be treated, analyzed, these become signs for humans. Like physical spaces, sound is pervasive; first, it is always on the process of being experienced, catching our attention or disturbing us; second, it is also and always exposing us to endless social meanings; and third, we participate to sounds.

The notion of *semiosphere* has been proposed by Lotman to designate the world of culture in which we live, made out of semiotic units—the minimal conditions of carrying meaning through time and space among humans (if not other species)—and as "the result and the condition for the development of culture" (Lotman, 1990, p. 125). The notion was built in analogy to that of biosphere, used to designate "the totality and the organic whole of living matter and also the condition for the continuation of life" (Lotman, 1990, p. 125). If sounds are relevant to humans, whatever their cause is, it is because they become one of the modalities by which culture functions. Sounds constitute one of the modalities of the semiosphere in which we live; they constitute the soundscape of our lives (Müller, 2012; Schafer, 1993).

BOUNDARIES: NOISE, SOUNDS, MUSIC, MEANING

To contribute to a reflection of a possible cultural psychology of sounds and music, I will explore a few attempts made to reflect on people's experience of sound in specific spheres of experience. Using an old technique, I will approach sounds through contradistinctions: when the idea of sounds becomes blurred and meets a limit—noises, words, or music. This exploration is in no way exhaustive.

"Sound" designates "(what is heard because of) quick changes of pressure in air, water, etc." (Procter, 1995, p. 1378)—a sound is a vibration interpreted by an ear, and here, a human ear (with no major dysfunction). Something that is heard can also be interpreted in different ways.

The Cultural Construction of the Meaning of Sounds

In a foundational essay for cultural psychology, Boesch (2007) reflects on "the sound of the violin" and questions what makes its beauty. He examines the epigenesis of the violin through history and in different places in the world, as well as the developmental trajectory of the young violinist who needs to discipline his movement and hearing so as to produce a beautiful sound. The essay brings him to reflect on the mutual adjustment of person and instruments, through a life course and history, and mediated by dynamics of recognition. More relevant for the current discussion, Boesch particularly reflects on the tension that justifies the search for a "pure" sound —a utopia of something not yet heard, but powerful enough to mobilize the effort of civilization and musicians:

> Utopia is the imagination of a world entirely in harmony with our phantasms, of reality totally in tune with our inner experience. In other words, utopia abolishes the "I" "non-I" antagonism. The beautiful sound, an external phenomenon, yet produced by our mastery and corresponding to—or even surpassing—our ideal standards, thus becomes a proof of our potential to create a phenomenon which, by its appeal, symbolizes utopia. (Boesch, 2007, p. 186)

Eventually, Boesch suggests, the beautiful sound is a mythem, linked to a cultural ideal of purity, in opposition to noise—or "sound dirt" (p. 188). He goes as far as suggesting that rock music is looking for this "dirt"—through its noisy music, dirty clothes, and greasy hair.

But what is then noise? In such a view, noise is sound that has not been cultivated, either because it has not been produced by humans, or because humans have not yet developed a system to identify and name it. But noise is also very often simply the sound of others, as Gonseth, Knodel, Laville, & Mayor (2011) observe through the history of anthropological musicology.

If we now examine the perspective of individuals, the boundaries between sounds and noise appears slightly differently. In an intriguing case study of a Thui village in Northern Thailand, Chuengsatiansup (1999) describes the illness of women that is foremost manifested by a hyper-sensibility, or even a feeling, of being attacked by daily noises, "blasting motorcycles, drunkards, quarrelling neighbors, machines eating up the forest" (p. 297). These "noises" are perceived as highly unpleasant and participate to the ill state of these women, manifested by deep tiredness, numbness, insomnia, without having a physiological explanation. To account for this, the author proposes a complete analysis of the village's mode life, which has been questioned by regional and world legislative and economical changes, and was forced to undergo through deep transformation. Hence, for reason of animal protection, the traditional elephant trade became forbidden, which demanded to find new occupations for elephants and new trades for villagers; forest were being sold to large foreign groups that started to use extensively its woods, preventing traditional uses; the media brought new leisure to young men, such as motorbikes and alcohol. In that perspective, the "noises" that make women sick are actually the sounds of all the aspects that impose a rupture on the previous way of life of villagers and women: the sound of woodcutting is interpreted as the noise of machines destroying the physical environment, the sound of young mean having fun with their motorbike becomes the noise of young men risking death through dangerous mechanical objects. In that sense, a noise is a sound that is perceived as rupture—whether it designates a real source of danger, or because it questions who one is, the relationships between the person and her social and material environment, or one's vision of the future and the meaning of existence. Chuengsatiansup's (1999) coup de force consists in her analysis of the complete semiosphere: why specific sounds are interpreted as noises having the power to somatically aggress people can only be understood when these are put in relationship to other meanings, diffracted through other material means and modes. In that sense, even in this very basic sense, for what they designate and what they are not, sounds are part of a semiotic system.

Artists' Explorations: From Nonsound to Sound

What is a sound, and how sounds touch us or disturb us, has been systematically explored by musicians and composers. Since the beginning of modernity in the arts, mainly after industrialization and the First World War, the pursuit of beauty became secondary in painting and in music; artists engaged in making sense of, admired or denounced the new conditions of existence. In his 1913 futurist manifesto, Russolo enthusiastically asked his readers to learn to listen and discriminate the sounds of modernity, which could become a new material for creative invention. Over the last 100 years, and especially after WWII, musicians and composers have developed complex ways to create a wide diversity of sound experiences, using for this natural sounds, instruments, synthesizers, and new technologies. Since the 1950s, through stereophonic effects, multiple tracks, uses of samples and drones, and thanks to the quality of sound systems, headphones, and physical places, they manage to create sounds that have a deep spatial structure—it is now possible to literally hear sounds that move through space and have complex layered architectures—and a strong materiality: vibration, drums, palpitations, create deliberate physical experiences of pressure, tensions, etc. as in the sound showers of electronic music.[1] In such work, different sounds are transformed for new composition; whether they are natural or industrial, pleasant or not, noise-like or music, they thus become material for creation of new soundscapes. Musical research has thus questioned the limits between noise and sound, sound and music, sound and space; it definitely displays a deep understanding of what sound does to people, and how active listeners engage with sounds.

Some artists have thus explored the boundary between sound and its absence. In his musical piece "Composition 1960 # 5," the American composer La Monte Young demands the performer free butterflies in the performance area, with open windows and doors, the performance being finished when the butterflies are gone (Young, 1960). In such a case, the actual "vibration" caused by the wings of the butterflies is infinitesimal, yet why should it not be music?

Other artists have also developed reflections on our experience of conferring meaning to physical spaces and soundscapes, but this time exploring the boundaries between different semiotic modes. For example, in his partition *Circus On, Means for Translating Any Book Into a Performance Without Actors, a Performance Which is Both Literary and Musical or One or the Other*, John Cage (1979) asked performers to choose a literary text, and through some algorithm, to progressively replace words by their corresponding sound. In their "urban circus" performance directed by Volker Straebel,[2] artists thus played a scene of Döblin's *Berlin Alexanderplatz* (2003), going through a reading of the description of the place, with words being progressively replaced by the corresponding sounds produced by artists, working with objects, electro-acoustic instruments as well as historical archives. With time, a word-based description of an urban location became a soundscape meant to recreate the experience of Berlin in the 1930s. Such a piece can be seen as exploring the boundaries between two semiotic systems, that of verbal language, and that of a sound system, for it plays with the listener's experience of spaces. Can it be understood or interpreted in the same way if it is represented through sounds or through words?

Sounds Between Perception and Imagination

These contrasted examples highlight the importance of the active role of the listener in the construction of a soundscape: if words and sounds can be equivalent for the construction of an experience, if noise can be used for music, it is because "sounds" are simply perception, they are active constructions. To hear sounds, people draw on their experiences of past sounds, and use their imagination of things and spaces. Typically, one can make the hypothesis that the poetic power of La Monte Young's piece is partly due to the public's added meanings and imagination—drawing on personal experience and the cultural meanings of butterflies.

The role of people's imagination in hearing sounds is also demonstrated by our gullibility when it comes to identifying the physical causes of a sound. Sound effects engineers or designers precisely play with this fact when they prepare radio shows or soundtracks for theater or cinema: all kinds of tricks are used to create specific sounds,[3] which listeners happily attribute to their imaginary source. Hence, the flapping of a helicopter is better created with an undulating sheet of metal than by the recording of an actual helicopter, where the only clear noise becomes that of the motor. Consequently, people actually know many sounds through their fictional reconstitutions in the first place. Most of us can close our eyes and imagine the bomb whistling and blasting of WWI, or the deep pounding of galloping horses of hunting North American Indians, while never having approached such situations and having heard only their studio creations. Hence, we have an imaginary of sounds, which is fed by fictions: we read novels, see documentaries and movies, in which these sounds were precisely crafted. This imagination of sounds becomes our experience of such sounds, and there is little doubt that these fictional sounds shape our experience of daily sounds.

Altogether, such an exploration suggests that our ability to experience soundscapes is an active construction, for which we draw on our personal experiences of sounds and places, as well as on semiotic resources and cultural conventions available in our environment.

GENESIS OF SOUNDS

As any other sociocultural phenomena, sounds have also to be understood in time. In an ontogenetic perspective, audition can be considered as one of the first senses of the young infant already before birth. Sound plays a fundamental role in early interactions, as touch and smell— so that sound can be said to participate to the constitution of "sonor psychic envelop" (Anzieu, 1995)—one of the constituent of our thinking capacities. Boesch (2007) also describes the genesis of beautiful sound from such ontogenetic perspective; in his description, the child's exposure to sounds, perhaps through parents who play the violin, the exposure to teachers and audiences who react to their sounds as "good" or "bad," participate to the development of a sense of a "beautiful sound."

In terms of cultural history, how specific sounds became identified, admired, reproduced, or created, becomes one question—which Boesch addresses in his sociogenetic analysis of the sound of violin (2007), or that is at the heart of Müller's (2012) project of a history of sounds.

Sounds should be studied in their microgenesis. Studies like Chuengsatiansup's (1999) suggest the daily interactions and small scale processes by which sounds become noise. Cage's performance retraces the process of sense-making of sounds and places. As daily experience as well as literature reveals, in any new sphere of experience—an urban center or the jungle, a theater or a cafeteria—people have to differentiate harmless from dangerous sounds, or relevant from irrelevant ones. This is typically the case for young soldiers finding themselves on the front (Remarque, 1928/1989) or civilians learning to survive in a town under siege (Daiute, 2010): in both cases, recognizing the sound from different types of ammunition, shot in various conditions, becomes a condition for survival. It is also the case of refugees and migrants, who have to "learn" the soundscape from a new place to feel at home (Märtsin & Mahmoud, 2012).

At their various scales, such analyses suggest that the capacity to recognize sounds in a given place and time falls into the same dynamics as the socialization to, or enculturation, or progressive mastery of any other semiotic system. More generally, it is quite likely that mastering sounds as a semiotic system demands a progressive capacity to discriminate units in a sonor flow, to differentiate and name some of them, to take distance from their more physiognomic qualities, and to organize them (Werner & Kaplan, 1963).

When the groups in that environment have developed coding systems or other semiotic modes to codify these sounds, they might also have to use these secondary signs—music notation, names of ammunition type or of motors. And when these secondary systems are lacking, they can even be invented—such as the proposition to codify bird songs (Thompson, LeDoux, & Moody, 1994).

Like any semiotic mode, sounds are attached to other social modes of organization, specific group values and histories. People then learn what sounds are beautiful or ugly, authorized in public or to be kept private, such a body noises. People also learn to identify some sounds as representing wider values, such as the trumpets as dedication to a country, or the church bell as reassuring homely. Sounds thus organize our relationship to self, others, and the world in a deep way; all the complexity of power, ideologies, and myths can be found in our relationship to sounds. For such reasons, studying soundscapes should be, as any other semiotic system, part of the project of a cultural psychology.

EXPERIENCING SOUNDS AND MUSIC: PSYCHOLOGICAL AND ANTHROPOLOGICAL ACCOUNTS

Developing in a given soundscape, or having learned to master a new one after migration (from countryside to town, from one country to another), or a deep transformation of the environment (e.g., after a highway has been built, trees have been planted, etc.), or after having trained some specific skills and semiotic systems related to the production or the understanding of sounds (learning to read music, to edit sounds, to play an instrument), people have specific sound and musical experiences. Sounds, perhaps more than other semiotic modes, are deeply embodied and awake proprioceptive experiences; the vibrations of a car or a drum on the street communicate specific vibration to our bodies—internal organs as well as skin and ears:

our bodies amplify vibrations or various wavelengths, and perceive modification of the air pressure on surfaces. Because of the early genetic nature of our soundscapes, or this very organic nature of our perception, our experiences of soundscapes have physiognomic qualities—they are associated to states of the body and specific emotions. Perhaps more than with others semiotic modalities, this emotional and embodied anchorage remains in the background of our experiences of sounds (as shown by Werner & Kaplan, 1963). This anchorage might also explain the power of music—a universal, powerful phenomenon. Hence, experiences of sound and music demand to account for these embodied as well as interpretative aspects—sounds are both felt and meant. These aspects have been well observed by others.

The strong imaginative interpretative components of sounds can be deduced from auditory experiences, which are not triggered by actual real sounds. We can imagine a continuum, with extreme sounds purely produced by external, physical causes, and on the other side, totally internal, psychological sounds, with no human-independent causes (Bullo & Égré, 2009). If sounds have mixed components, we should be able to find occurrences at all points of such a continuum.

At one extreme of the continuum (left from Figure 2.1) the question is whether we can "hear" sounds without related air or surface vibrations. The simple clinical case of tinnitus— uncontrollable auditory illusions (Møller, 2011)—is enough to assert this fact. Another type of phenomena is interesting here: dreams, which are in principle disconnected from external, physical stimuli. Dreams, which are mainly using traces of daily mnemonic experiences as well as earlier memories to compose the dream work, can also include sounds as material, and so dreams are often reported as sonor (Moorcroft, 2013). Even more, dreams might be musical and research suggests that, even if musicians dream more of musical dreams than other people, everyone does; they can thus contain new, unheard melodies (Uga, Lemut, Zampi, Zolli, & Salzarulo, 2006). Tinnitus has partly physiological causes, but what about musical dreams? Music and sounds in dreams raise a question: if our reaction to music is partly physical, if not visceral, how can music in dreams be moving or "realistic"? Can the body generate internal vibration with their emotional correlate from within? Given what we know from the mind capacity to generate states of the body (e.g., fear, stress, excitement about an event to come, as well psychosomatic illnesses,

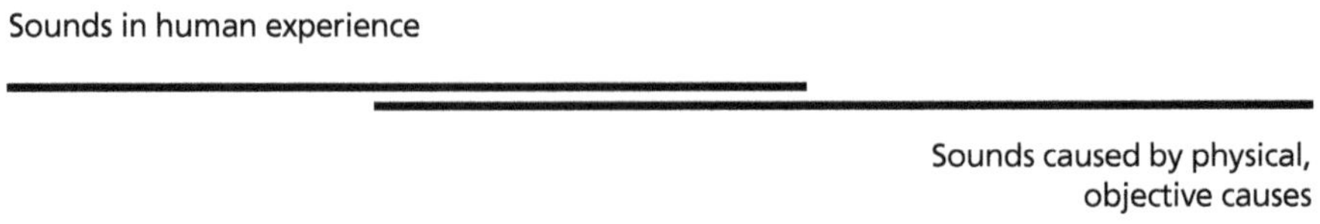

Sounds in human experience

Sounds caused by physical, objective causes

Figure 2.1 Continuum of sounds.

etc.), then this is quite likely. But then, this interrogates the very definition of sounds, as they seem to be hearable without "quick change of pressure."

Further toward the middle of the continuum, it has been long shown that dreams might include various environmental noises—typically, one's morning alarm clock becomes a siren in a dream (also Freud, 1900/2001). Some hallucinatory experiences are likely to have the same properties than dreams: they might be producing purely imaginary sounds, but also, they might be developed around environmental sounds whose meaning is changed.

In the same zone of that continuum, it is quite common that a sound currently heard recreates a whole experiential Gestalt: as Proust's Madeleine, the sound of a morning bird can trigger the memory of being in one's childhood room, or a church bell can remind us of a known street. Hence a physical sound can trigger an imaginary loop oriented toward the past, and that allows such re-experiencing, which might also be multimodal—one might hear a sound, "see" the colors of that room or street, "smell" the morning coffee or the wet pavement associated to that sound, and so on.

In the middle of the continuum are sounds that we usually hear and instantaneously or rapidly interpret as sounds from our environment—the regular noise in the back is the ticking of a clock, the noises far down are people talking in the street, etc. This is the zone where sounds are physically caused by transformation of the air pressure and also semiotic units for which we master various interpretative repertoires.

On the other extreme of that continuum (right in Figure 2.1), there are obviously physical sounds that we do not hear, depending on the physiological limitations of the human ear, but also, on individual differences and losses due to exposures to noise or aging (such as high sounds frequencies). There are then the sounds which we ignore or do not hear because they are not relevant (such as the clicking of a keyboard as we work or the buses in the street), or for issues related to repression (such as when we "ignore" an alarm clock).

Hence, this short exploration suggests that the imaginary component of sounds is at least as important as the physiological one. Drawing on Winnicott (2001), we can distinguish three zones of sonic experiences along this continuum of sounds (Figure 2.2): the zone of inner life (dreams, and

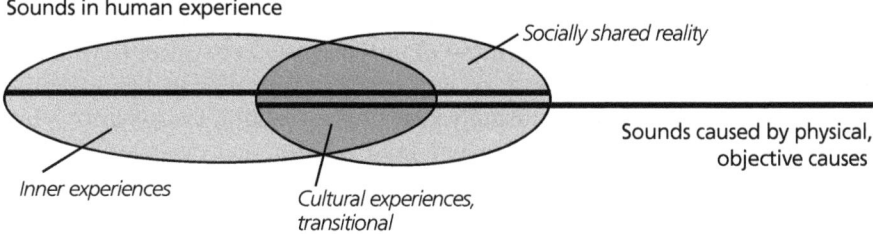

Figure 2.2 Zones of sonic experience on the continuum of sounds.

phantasy) in which sounds are purely generated from within, without actual physical sounds; the zone of our experience with the socially shared reality, in which sounds can be related to their physical origin (something has generated a vibration or air pressure) and that we interpret as due to "real" causes; and the middle zone of so-called transitional phenomena, for which sounds are the departure and playground from imaginary loops, playing, and all cultural experiences, including these to which we now come back, poetic and musical experiences.

Music as Cultural Experiences

Most of what has been said so far applies for sound in general and the particular case of music, as the examples given previously suggest. However, there are important differences in listening to music, however abstract, or to sounds. Sounds and soundscapes are always there, they are in the background of our experience. We normally hardly "hear" the discussion in the street, the far away buzzing of the cars, or even the radio singing next door. Yet there are situations in which we start to pay attention to sounds, or in which sounds forces our attention. Sounds can become noise, and are heard when their volume or nature changes to such a way that they disrupt our other activities. Yet also, sounds become music, or more specifically, musical experiences, when we deliberately engage in listening to them. (Of course there are liminal cases: typically, "elevator music" is meant to belong to the soundscape, often to induce a certain emotional state, without requiring the attention of listening to music.)

The experience of music falls back to the case of cultural experiences. This has various implications. First, listening to music implies the entrance into a specific type of experiences, and for this, thresholds. To enter in a music piece, there needs to be a sort of disjunction of our current flow of experiences, and through an effect of threshold, the acceptance of the specific quality of that experience. The threshold is, in the most ritualized experiences, the entry in a colossal building, the abandonment of one's coat to cloakroom attendants, the pleasure or pain of finding a spot from where to see or hear the coming performance, the perception of the changes of light, they temporary renouncement of judgment so as to enter in whatever experience a musician, a band, or an orchestra will offer us for a definite period of time. There is also usually a closing threshold, for instance when the public loudly manifests his or her gratitude for that experience (hand clapping, whistling, etc.). Such ritual threshold effects are usually so powerful and usually nonreflexive that John Cage—him again—could create a piece of music where only these thresholds were performed, the piece itself consisting of 4 min 33 sec of silence (Cage, 1952). The threshold in and out of the cultural experience of listening music can also be more modest, as when one has a preferred place or position to listen to a record, or the placement of earphones, or any other act that performs the entry into a musical experience. Minimally, it might simply be to decide to turn our attention into an aesthetic experience and decide to listen to all the surroundings sounds *as if* they were music (and so we become absorbed in the symphony of the city streets, or the gurgling of a heating system, or the folly of spring birds chirping).

A second implication of music being a cultural experience is that it occurs midway between the reality of the sounds provoked by instruments or technical objects, and a person's inner experience—precisely in this zone of transitional phenomena, where guided imagination or adult playfulness occurs (Winnicott, 1968, 1971). This brings Winnicott to the following account of enjoying a piece of music:

> Put rather crudely: we go to a concert and I hear a late Beethoven string concert (you see I'm highbrow). This quartet is not just an external fact produced by Beethoven and played by the musicians; and it is not my dream, which as a matter of fact would not have been so good. The experience, coupled with my preparation of myself for it, enables me to create a glorious fact. I enjoy it because I say I created it, I hallucinated it, and it is real and would have been there even if I had been neither conceived of nor conceived. (Winnicott, 1959, pp. 57–58)

For Winnicott, the experience of the Beethoven concert occurs in the zone of transitional phenomena, there where cultural elements come from the sociocultural, shared reality, and are experienced thanks to the person's interiority or subjective experience—dreams, memories and fantasies, and actual skills—the "preparation" required for enjoying such performance.

A third implication of this idea is that a musical experience becomes a specific moment within the time flow; it is anticipated, as just seen; it has duration, and it has an aftermath. It is this very duration that allow elements and sounds to unfold, and thus, to become transformative of the psychological elements awaken by music. This duration and transformative power of music is described by Claude Levi-Strauss as part of his analysis of mythology:

> Every melodic phrase or harmonic development proposes an adventure. The listener entrusts his mind and sensitivity to the composer initiatives. And if at the end tears of joy flow, it is because this adventure, lived from beginning to end in a time much shorter than if it were a real adventure, was successful and ends with a happiness that true adventures more rarely provide. The profile of a melodic phrase which is considered beautiful and moving is such that it appears as homologous with that of an existential phase (probably because

in the act of creation of the composer, the same projection was first reversely performed), easily solving in its own terms difficulties homologous with these others against which life would often stumble and fail.

But then we will be entitled to say that in its own way, music fulfills a role similar to that of mythology. Myth coded in sounds instead of words: the musical work provides a decryption grid, a matrix of relations that filters and organizes the lived experience, replaces it, and gives the comforting illusion that contradictions can be overcome and difficulties solved. . . . Mythology and music have this in common that they invite the listener to a concrete union, with this difference that rather than a pattern of encoded sounds, the myth proposes a scheme coded in images. In both cases, however, it is the listener who invests the scheme with one or more virtual meanings, in such a way that the real unity of myth or the musical work can only be achieved in two, through and with a kind of celebration.

Any attempt to understand music would however stop halfway if it does not account for the deep emotions one feels while listening pieces that bring tears to flow. It can be guessed that the phenomenon is similar to laughter in the sense that, in each case, a certain type of configuration external to the subject—words, actions or sounds—triggers a psycho-physiological mechanism that is in some sense predetermined; but what is it, and what exactly is crying with laughter or joy? This is not all, for as Proust has shown, musical pleasure last longer than a performance. It perhaps even reaches its fullness later; when the silence returns, the listener remains saturated with music, submerged with sense, victim of a kind of invasion that dispossessed of him of his individuality and his being; he had become the location of music, as Condillac's statue has become the smell of roses. (Levi-Strauss, 1971, pp. 585–590, author's translation; see also Levi-Strauss, 1990)

Levi-Strauss's analysis suggests the triple conjunctions of the person's embodied experience, his or her mastery of a semiotic mode, the actual structure and composition of the piece of music, its inscription in a sociocultural context, and the inscription of the experience of listening in a longer duration—not only the duration of the musical experience, but also its aftermath.

In that sense, musical experiences, as any other cultural experiences, are anticipated, have the power to awake personal memories, emotions and experiences, host them into the semiotic construct that is the cultural artifact, and as they unfold, transform these contents, so as to generate new emotional experiences, as documented by Vygotsky (1971) or more recently Tisseron (2000). Musical experiences, like film watching or novel reading, can finally become experiences to which we refer later, to which we come back, and that thus become symbolic resources (Zittoun, 2006). However, we should be careful to preserve, in such analysis, the specificity of music—the fact that it is a complex composition of sounds (and not colors, or words, or shapes).

A SOCIOCULTURAL, EMPIRICAL APPROACH TO MUSIC

This theoretical exploration of course raises the question of the possible developments of a sociocultural psychology accounting for the dynamics explored. In what follows, I propose one of the possible directions of studies, illustrated by an example, before concluding.

Studying Sound and Musical Experiences

Theorizing sounds and music belongs to the project of a sociocultural psychology: it is a deeply human, essentially cultural experience, which is part of the world in which we live. Moreover, as developmental science, psychology can especially be curious of music—an essentially temporal experience. This opens many avenues for the study of sound and music in the life of people and groups.

In my own work, I have found particularly interesting to consider musical experiences in people's life trajectories. When do people engage in them, what for, and what does it change? Beyond their daily uses, musical experiences might in effect have important roles to play in changing or transforming people's life path. Music is listened to by many in periods of transition, as solace, support or mirror, as mean to maintain people who are gone, or to imagine some other futures (Zittoun, 2006, 2007, 2012b). In addition, because musical experiences are complete human experiences, they might themselves trigger ruptures and transformations of people's lives. This is what I illustrate in what follows.

One problem is, however, to accede to people's sound and musical experiences: as all human experiences, they are internal, and can be shared only if one way or another externalized. In that particular case, it demands the translation of one semiotic language—vibrations, tonalities, melodies, rhythms and structures—in other one, dancing, drawing, and generally privileged by psychologists, verbal language. In addition, if some experiences can be documented in almost real time, sound and music can in principle not be. Hence, classically, access to musical experiences is made post-hoc, narrating in the past, or trying to re-experience them, orally or under a written form. An alternative to this has been proposed by Alexandre Diep (Diep, 2011). Inspired by the activity theorist Yves Clot (2002), he filmed musicians rehearsing their pieces; he then edited the films, collecting passages where obviously the musician experienced a rupture—they suspended their activity, or expressed physically some unexpected event. He finally showed these films to the musicians, asking them what they were then experiencing. Thanks to the recording of the music they played, as well as their view of their filmed nonverbal externalization, these musicians were able to re-explore the past flow of their experience of playing, including, for some of them, the imaginary visions and experiences in which they were engaged. Note however that musical experiences are mostly studied in the case of people having strong connections to music—musicians, composers (Holtz, 2009), or fans. The sociocultural of lay people's experiences to music has still to become systematically explored.

An Example of An Adolescent's Musical Experience

To indicate a possible direction for enquiry, a short empirical situation is presented to exemplify our theoretical propositions. The following text, written neither by a musician nor by a "high-brow" author, has been posted at online blog by an anonymous young man. Entitled "My First Staind Concert That Changed My Life," it seems to have been written a few weeks after having assisted to a rock concert:

> My first Staind [a rock band] concert was at XYZ City in UK, I remember being so excited. Staind were really the first band I've felt so attached to. I listened to some really heavy music when I was little (. . .) but Staind had it all for me. I fell in love with the sound of honesty and Aaron's lyrics really helped me to . . . *wind down and mellow out, for the 3/4 minutes however long the song was on for I felt like I was layed on a beach somewhere far far away from any commotion that was going on around me.*
>
> There was something unbelievable about Staind that I couldn't quite get around, what have this band been through to get where they are. Where the hell does Mike's riffs come from? Why is Old Schools harmonized vocals giving me an orgasm? Why would I rather sit at home listening to Johns percussion fills than hang out with my friends and most of all why do Aarons lyrics seem so comforting. *I haven't been through nothing Aaron has so why do they help?* I know a lot of Staind fans say that Aaron's lyrics help, I never understood why until my first Staind concert.
>
> It was after school one Wednesday and I guess my Mum had got me and my partner tickets to see them. My partner . . . Sadie really enjoyed listening to them, she kinda had to . . . seen as though she liked spending time with me. I came home and sat in the living room whilst my Mum got ready and I had butterflies in my stomach. I was so nervous. We got in the car . . . I walked through the door and my Mum told me to text her let her know everything is okay, I text her the second I got in telling her all was all okay haha I was so nervous. . . . I stood there waiting impatiently, I was right it was suffocate, I was stood there mesmerized. Aaron didn't play guitar back then so he was moving around the stage slowly. Song after song I stood there and I took some photos and some videos, I remember they played 'Open Your Eyes' my favorite song off of Break The Cycle and in the second verse when Aarons starts sing-

ing louder and the lyrics change to talking about overpopulation, he looked straight in my eyes . . . I think. *Well it felt like it he did and it felt like he was talking to me, like he was staring at me and telling me to grow the fuck up and start doing things I had always felt never meant much to me. Really pursue my music, Care for my family, Stop drinking so much with friends that didn't no any better and try to introduce them to music. With that one line and stare I felt this rush of excitement and relief.* Who needs heroin or drugs when I have this feeling? They played loads of old songs at that concert which made my night, I mean I love 'Its Been A While,' 'Outside,' 'So Far Away,' 'Zoe Jane,' and the softer side but I loved it when they played 'Crawl,' that chorus is just well to catchy. I was humming it all the way home . . . The concert ended and Aaron ended the concert by telling the fans how much they mean to the band and that they will see us soon. That's all I thought about for about 3 weeks.[4]

How to read this text? Obviously, it is a post-hoc creation of an important experience, probably transformed by memory, previous recall, and narrations, and the very fact of being turned into a public text (Gillespie & Zittoun, 2012; Zittoun & Gillespie, 2012). This being said, this musical experience is something more than an average background radio buzzing, it has a quality of epiphany. As such, it amplifies the processes usually involved in music as cultural experiences, as described previously.

For the young man, the musical experience comes at a very specific period of his adolescent life. The event of listening to music here at a concert, is highly ritualized and framed. Driving to the concert, negotiating with the mum, etc., participate in the construction of the experience. The threshold is suggested by the young man who "stood there waiting impatiently, [he] was right it was suffocate, [he] was stood there mesmerized." This different temporality and quality of the experiences in the daily world and in the musical experiences is also marked in the verbal tense used in the text, which change from past to present when the young man is actually describing the immersion in the music (when Aaron is "talking" to him). The transitional nature of the musical experience itself appears very clearly, whether the young man describes listening to music at home and feels transported on a beach or having an orgasm, or when at the concert, he feels directly addressed by the singer. Interestingly, the imaginary experience is here fed by various semiotic modalities—the melodies and sounds (e.g., the riffs of the guitar, the melody of the chorus) as well as the lyrics (e.g., when it becomes about overpopulation). The transitional nature of the experience also appears in its sociocultural and personal nature: a concert, shared with the young man's partner, in the highly crowded place that is a concert, then discussed on an online public blog, has also an obviously very unique and personal resonance. Many other people might consider these sounds as "noise" more than music, and even so, would not be transported by them. Note again how the most intimate is already social: imagining "lying on a beach" when listening to music at home is already a highly culturally saturated image. This experience is also interesting for highlighting the transformative effects of music. Not only does listening to music change bodily states—relaxation, intense pleasure, excitement and relief —but it also brings the young man to distance himself from his experience, and, through the imagined other that is the singer, question his life, his actions and his goals. Music becomes a symbolic resource, used here to define representations of the future as well as norms to guide one's conduct ("really pursue my music, care for my family, stop drinking so much with friends that didn't matter") (Zittoun, 2006, 2007, 2012b). Finally, here music—and especially a concert—has duration and aftermath. The young man thinks about this concert for the three following weeks, and externalizes this internal vividness of the music by the writing of the blog itself.

This short example is not a proof of or theorization, but is chosen simply for its availability. It shows the heuristic power of considering sounds and music as cultural experience, physical yet imaginary, social and personal, historical and biographical. It also suggests that even "naïve" first person accounts of musical and sound experience can teach us a lot about the microgenesis of musical experiences.

CONCLUDING WORDS

Sounds and music are part of our semiosphere, and with its general ambition, sociocultural psychology has to be able to theorize them. Here, it is via an exploration of sonor and musical experiences that I have tried to contribute to this theoretical adventure. Exploring the continuum and boundaries between noise, sound and music, perception of the world and imagination, culture and minds, I tried to characterize these experiences as temporal and semiotic, actively created. Finally, music itself appears as one of the many miracles of our lives in world of cultures. Even appreciating the most elementary lullaby is already the result of a complex cultivation, and a piece of music can drastically change the course of life.

ACKNOWLEDGMENTS

This chapter is an expansion of a commentary published in *Culture & Psychology* (Zittoun, 2012a), and I thank Jaan Valsiner and Hroar Klempe for offering the possibility of carrying on this exploration. I also thank Jerôme Hentsch for introducing many of the mentioned pieces over the years, and an anonymous blogger for sharing experiences we all may know.

NOTES

1. This has been at times explicitly addressed as a theoretical problem in music, as retraced in Meric (2012), and more informally as pragmatic issue by musicians, such as by the Young Gods (Walther, 2010).
2. http://www.straebel.de/praxis/index.html?/praxis/text/t-urban_circus.htm
3. For example, http://voyard.free.fr/textes_audio/bruitage.htm
4. http://www.staind.com/profiles/blogs/my-first-staind-concert-that, retrieved 03.05.2009. See also Zittoun, Valsiner et al. 2013, p. 335, for another analysis.

REFERENCES

Anzieu, D. (1995). *Le moi-peau* (2nd ed.). Paris, France: Dunod.

Boesch, E. E. (2007). The sound of the violin. In W. J. Lonner & S. A. Hayes (Eds.), *Discovering cultural psychology* (pp. 177–195). Charlotte, NC: Information Age.

Bullot, N. J., & Égré, P. (2009). Editorial: Objects and sound perception. *Review of Philosophy and Psychology, 1*(1), 5–17. http://doi.org/10.1007/s13164-009-0006-3

Cage, J. (1952). *4'33"*. New York, NY: Edition Peters.

Cage, J. (1979). _____, _____ _____ *circus on* _____. New York, NY: Henmar Press.

Chuengsatiansup, K. (1999). Sense, symbol, and soma: Illness experience in the soundscape of everyday life. *Culture, Medicine and Psychiatry, 23*(3), 273–301. doi:10.1023/A:1005556026679

Clot, Y. (2002). *La fonction psychologique du travail* (3rd ed.). Paris, France: Presses Universitaires de France.

Daiute, C. (2010). *Human development and political violence.* New York, NY: Cambridge University Press.

Diep, A. (2011). *On connaît la musique ? Un regard socio-culturel sur le travail des musiciens* (Master's dissertation). Institute of Psychology and Education, University of Neuchâtel, Neuchâtel, Switzerland.

Döblin, A. (2003). *Berlin Alexanderplatz: The story of Franz Biberkopf.* (E. Jolas, Trans.). London, England: Continuum International.

Freud, S. (2001). *The interpretation of dreams* (Original 1900, Vol. 4–5). London, England: Vintage.

Gillespie, A., & Zittoun, T. (2010). Studying the movement of thought. In A. Toomela & J. Valsiner (Eds.), *Methodological thinking in psychology: 60 years gone astray?* (pp. 69–88). Charlotte, NC: Information Age.

Gonseth, M.-O., Knodel, B., Laville, Y., & Mayor, G. (Eds.). (2011). *Bruits: échos du patrimoine immatériel.* Neuchâtel, Switzerland: Musée d'Ethnographie.

Holtz, P. (2009). What's your music? Subjective theories of music-creating artists. *Musicae Scientiae, 13*(2), 207–230.

Kharlamov, N. (2012). The city as a sign: A developmental-experiential approach to spatial life. In J. Valsiner (Ed.), *Handbook of culture and psychology* (pp. 277–302). Oxford, England: Oxford University Press.

Levi-Strauss, C. (1971). *L'Homme nu: Mythologiques 4.* (pp. 585–590) Paris, France: Plon.

Lévi-Strauss, C. (1990). *Mythologiques: The naked man* (Vol. 4). Chicago, IL: University of Chicago Press.

Lotman, Y. M. (1990). *Universe of the mind: A semiotic theory of culture.* (A. Shukman, Trans.). Indianapolis: Indiana University Press.

Märtsin, M., & Mahmoud, H. W. (2012). Never "at-home"?: Migrants between societies. In J. Valsiner (Ed.), *Handbook of culture and psychology* (pp. 730–745). Oxford, England: Oxford University Press.

Maslov, K. (2012). Beyond visible borders: What may we see from the window or what a window may show to us? In *Seeing the blindness: Body and history* (pp. 149–178; doctoral dissertation). University of Tallinn, Tallinn, Estonia.

Meric, R. (2012). *Appréhender l'espace sonore: L'écoute entre perception et imagination.* Paris, France: Editions L'Harmattan.

Møller, A. R. (Ed.). (2011). *Textbook of tinnitus.* New York, NY: Springer Science + Business Media.

Moorcroft, W. H. (2013). Dreams. In W. Moorcroft *Understanding sleep and dreaming* (pp. 143–170). Boston, MA: Springer.

Müller, J. (2012). The sound of history and acoustic memory: Where psychology and history converge. *Culture & Psychology, 18*(4), 443–464. doi:10.1177/1354067X12456716

Procter, P. (Ed.; 1995). *Cambridge international dictionary of English.* Cambridge, England: Cambridge University Press.

Remarque, E. M. (1989). *All quiet on the western front.* (A. W. Wheen, Trans.) New York, NY: Fawcett. (Original German publication, 1928).

Russolo, L. (1913). *The art of noise.* (R. Filliou, Trans.). New York, NY: A Great Bear Pamphlet. (Italian original, 1913; Translation published, 1967). Retrieved from http://www.unknown.nu/futurism/noises.html

Schafer, R. M. (1993). *Soundscape. Our sonic environment and the tuning of the world.* Rochester, VT: Destiny Books. (Original publication, 1977).

Simonds, C. (1988). *Comportement des oiseaux de jardin.* (R. M. Lapierre, Trans.). Montréal, Quebec, Canada: Les Editions Québecor.

Thompson, N. S., LeDoux, K., & Moody, K. (1994). A system for describing bird song units. *Bioacoustics, 5,* 267–279.

Tisseron, S. (2000). *Enfants sous influence. Les écrans rendent-ils les jeunes violents?* Paris, France: Armand Colin.

Uga, V., Lemut, M. C., Zampi, C., Zilli, I., & Salzarulo, P. (2006). Music in dreams. *Consciousness and Cognition, 15*(2), 351–357. doi:10.1016/j.concog.2005.09.003

Valsiner, J. (2007). *Culture in minds and societies: Foundations of cultural psychology.* New Delhi, India: Sage.

Valsiner, J. (2008). Ornamented worlds and textures of feeling: The power of abundance. *Outlines: Critical Social Studies,* (1), 67–78.

Valsiner, J. (2011, March 10). *The visible invisibility: How cultural guidance captures us.* Invited lecture at MAPS/University of Neuchâtel, Neuchâtel, Switzerland.

Vygotsky, L. S. (1971). *The psychology of art.* Cambridge, MA: MIT press.

Walther, C. (Director & writer; 2010). *Lonely pioneers: The young gods* [Documentary]. Swiss National Television.

Werner, H., & Kaplan, B. (1963). *Symbol formation. An organismic-developmental approach to language and the expression of thought.* New York, NY: John Wiley.

Winnicott, D. W. (1959). The fate of the transitional object. In C. Winnicott, R. Shepherd, & M. Davis (Eds.), *Psycho-analytical explorations* (pp. 53–58). Cambridge, MA: Harvard University Press.

Winnicott, D. W. (1968). Playing and culture. A talk given to the imago group, 12 March 1968. In C. Winnicott, R. Shepherd, & M. Davis (Eds). *Psycho-analytical explorations* (pp. 203–206) Cambridge, MA: Harvard University Press.

Winnicott, D. W. (2001). The location of cultural experience. In *Playing and reality* (Original edition 1967, pp. 95–103). London, England: Routledge.

Young, L. M. (1960). *Compositions*, n° 2, 3, 4, 5, 6, 7, 9, 10, 13, 15, œuvres pour performance.

Zittoun, T. (2006). *Transitions: Development through symbolic resources.* Greenwich, CT: Information Age.

Zittoun, T. (2007). Symbolic resources and responsibility in transitions. *Young,* 15(2), 193–211.

Zittoun, T. (2012a). The art of noise: Comment on the sound of silence. *Culture & Psychology, 18*(4), 30–41.

Zittoun, T. (2012b). Les ressources symboliques à l'adolescence: Transition vers le monde adulte. *Langages & Pratiques,* (49), 6–14.

Zittoun, T., & Gillespie, A. (2012). Using diaries and self-writings as data in psychological research. In E. Abbey & S. E. Surgan (Eds.), *Emerging methods in psychology* (pp. 1–26). New Brunswick, NJ: Transaction.

Zittoun, T., Valsiner, J., Vedeler, D., Salgado, J., Gonçalves, M., & Ferring, D. (2013). *Human development in the lifecourse: Melodies of living.* Cambridge, England: Cambridge University Press.

CHAPTER 3

RELIGION, CULTURE, AND MUSIC

A Psychological Exploration

Jacob A. Belzen

*Not conceptual speech, but music rather, is the element
through which we are best spoken to by mystical truth.*
—William James (1902/1982)
The Varieties of Human Experience, pp. 420–421

THE NECESSARY LIMITATION

Anyone who tries to give some account of the relation between music and religion by means of psychology will find, as is always the case when any halfway interesting theme is formulated, that she or he has taken on an enormous task. The problem does not just consist in there being more connections than one imagines between music and religion. The greater problem is above all that the expressions "music," "religion," and "psychology" address utterly heterogeneous realities, each of which in its turn seems to resist efforts at conceptualization. What, for example, is music? If I, as a

Cultural Psychology of Musical Experience, pages 41–67
Copyright © 2016 by Information Age Publishing

representative of psychology of religion who has his roots in cultural psychology, were to stick to areas I know reasonably well, then I would remind the reader that many approaches that some regard as psychology *par excellence* are vehemently rejected by others; look for example at the old quarrel about the status of psychoanalysis. Nor is it very different when we turn to the domain of religion: in spite of centuries of scholarly reflection and even after about a hundred and thirty years of the existence of a "science of religion" (*religionswissenschaft*) as a branch of science, we have not even begun to agree on a definition of what we are to understand by "religion." And things are scarcely different with "music": the fact that one musicologist accepts certain sound combinations as music more or less disqualifies her in the eyes of another. In this chapter I shall not go in the direction of attempts at unambiguous definition, as they seem doomed from the outset.

Nor do I have any desire to lose myself in metaphysical or any other kind of speculations. Wagner's thesis of the identity of religion and art (Loesch, 2003), for instance, is now familiar, but are we then to regard music, too, as a religion, or as a privileged form of it (as with, say, Stockhausen), or as religion in general or as that of the future? These are questions that cannot be answered by psychology, just as the latter has in general to stay silent on the question of what may count as a religion. And psychology (of religion) is just as little entitled to judge whether for example the experience of being deeply moved that some people tell of as an essential part of their experience of music, is religious in itself. In his justly famous *Varieties of Religious Experience*, William James tended in this direction:

> This sense of deeper significance is not confined to rational propositions. Single words, and conjunctions of words, effects of light on land and sea, odors and musical sounds, all bring it when the mind is tuned aright. Most of us can remember the strangely moving power of passages in certain poems read when we were young, irrational doorways as they were through which the mystery of fact, the wildness and the pang of life, stole into our hearts and thrilled them. The words have now perhaps become mere polished surfaces for us; but lyric poetry and music are alive and significant only in proportion as they fetch these vague vistas of a life continuous with our own, beckoning and inviting, yet ever eluding our pursuit. We are alive or dead to the eternal inner message of the arts according as we have lost this mystical susceptibility. (James, 1901/1982, pp. 382–383)

This beautiful passage from James cannot however be seen as representative of psychology of religion, it is altogether more a sign that in the *Varieties* James was in no way speaking as a psychologist (Belzen, 2005). He certainly did not claim any such thing; he himself said he was describing material that he was going to reflect on philosophically in a further book. That James is nevertheless regarded as a psychologist of religion and that his *Varieties* stands as a bestseller in this discipline has been a politically convenient fact for the guild in question, but also from some points of view a historical paradox, especially when one considers that the greatest part of psychology of religion does not at all proceed on the Jamesian model of psychology!

James' conception of religion, and hence that of the many who refer to him, was certainly one-sided and probably apologetically motivated: it takes altogether too little account of aspects of religion that many people nowadays are more inclined to sense as negative. The phenomenology of religion offers, after all, not just beauty, but also terrors: the history of religion is filled with blood and tears, with endless sacrifices of animals as well as humans, of violence against others and oneself, etc. But however religion is to be understood or defined, it is not the task here of psychology (of religion) to show the way. (What is altogether more the case is that many of the deficiencies, especially those of the earlier psychology of religion should be traced back to the fact that the advocates of this discipline were often working with a deficient concept of religion and were above all much too inclined to over-generalizations of their findings; Belzen, 2007.)

Extremely interesting—though as it happens in certain respects too general in their statements about religion "as such" too—are two completely different psychological discussions that have recently been put forward on the connection between music and religion; one of them from the viewpoint of evolutionary psychology, the other based on the findings of pre-natal research. The thoughts that have been presented from an evolutionary perspective by anthropologists and psychologists such as Atran (2002), Boyer (2001), and Kirkpatrick (2005) have brought about some progress in the familiar, though somewhat older discussion about the definition of religion from a substantive as opposed to a functional perspective. If nothing else, they have at least done serious damage to the attempts to explain "religion" from its functions: neither religion nor art (including music), say these authors, can be understood as evolutionary adaptations serving human survival. Religion and art are altogether more by-products of adaptation, they cannot be reduced to a definite function that they are supposed to serve. Religion and music, according to this line of reasoning, do not emerge as a result of adaptations, but result from the interplay of several other psychological adaptations that have developed for other purposes. Take the case of the spandrel, that surface enclosed on three sides that results for example when different arches come together in the ceiling of a gothic cathedral: here some kind of ornament is usually undertaken (a rose, a head, etc.). Religion and music are like this kind of ornament: in themselves without a specific function of their own, they would almost always develop when other elements result in the constellation in question. What Pinker (1997) says about music can *mutatis mutandis* be said about religion as well: Pinker compared music to cheesecake, which most people like, since it suits the preferences we have developed for fats and sugar. Humans, however, do not have any evolved mechanism that makes them prepare or look for cheesecake; rather, the invention of cheesecake is to be traced back to the fact that it exploits such preexisting mechanisms that have evolved for purposes totally unrelated to cheesecake (Kirkpatrick, 2005, p. 236). This argumentation should doubtless be taken seriously but it perhaps speaks too generally about "religion," and there is furthermore still nothing definite about to what extent so-called evolutionary psychology has anything to do with a genuinely psychological perspective (Davies, 2009; Derksen, 2010; Stephenson, Radtke, Jorna, & Stam, 2003).

A quite different discussion, which likewise postulates something in common between music and religion, has been presented by Oberhoff and by Parncutt. Based on the results of prenatal research, they have proposed the thesis that the prenatal perception of the mother as something big and moving and as a voice (Oberhoff, 2005) forms the basis for religion as well as music. The experience of God would so to speak graft itself onto the primal experience of the mother, just as psychoanalysis does indeed demonstrate that particularly the emotional relations to God bear traces of the emotional bonds to the parents and to early significant others as well (Faber, 2010; Rizzuto, 1979). In a similar way, music would graft itself onto the hearing of what happens in the mother's body and the hearing of her voice, which is thus the basis for musical emotion. Music as well as God appear here as a "virtual person" (Parncutt & Kessler, 2007). The thesis appears entirely plausible, although I realize—like the authors themselves—that it may sound speculative to some contemporaries. Apart from that, here too religion is spoken about very generally.

In what follows I would like to try to be as concrete as possible and not to speculate, but rather to set out from a recurring, pretty well-known empirical observation. The modesty that proclaims itself here as it does in the whole of the preceding should not, however, be misunderstood: it shall be seen that even when psychology restricts itself to what is most essential to it, it is not at all simple to give precise and above all tenable answers to interesting questions. We shall at any rate see that modesty is a real prerequisite for getting even some way forward.

THE EMPIRICAL OBSERVATION: DOES MUSIC MAKE RELIGIOUS?

As has been said, the empirical observation that I would like to make the occasion for my discussions is quite familiar. It has been reported to me by interviewees in many studies but I have also often heard it in informal small talk, as well as having seen it acted out in front of me on a number of occasions, and it will not be any different for the readers: many people are at times moved to tears, perhaps even existentially, when they listen to religious music, even when it is to a text that they would dismiss (if not worse) as dreary, stupid or nonsensical if it were not put to music, if they merely read it or heard it declaimed. (Familiar examples from the Western musical tradition would be the many masses, requiems, te deums, passions, etc.) Can psychology help us to understand this phenomenon, or, to put it somewhat pointedly: can psychology help in determining whether music makes people religious? Since the science of religion is best served by doing things as concretely as possible and by being careful from the outset to avoid any sort of overgeneralization, it would be best to limit the question and the argumentation to the contexts in which I encountered the observation described, i.e., the "Western world," and to formulate as follows: is religious music, during the time that it is sounding—or perhaps even longer— capable of leading unbelievers to the Christian faith, or back to it? What contribution can psychology make toward settling this question?

RELIGIOUS MUSIC?

Although certainly not as fascinating as the great perspectives that open from more speculative studies, the trouble taken to investigate a particular problem, of a limited size, can still teach us certain things, even if it is only to deprive some far too general formulations of their misleading air of self-evidence. But to begin with, this empirically oriented way of doing things obliges us to make some further observations. For what is this "religious music" that has so simply been put on stage here? There does without doubt seem to be religious music, the above-mentioned examples (masses set to music from Machaut to Pärt, composers of passions ranging from, e.g., Schütz to Rihm, etc.) can be seen as clear indications, and we can certainly find them under this name in the appropriate shops and catalogues. But is for example Mozart's *Coronation Mass* really religious music? Or is it a case here of music that is a setting of a religious text? Put differently: is it the music, or the text that is set to music, that is religious? I would like to point out to anyone who thinks that it is the music itself that is religious that the melodies that were used by the first Protestants at the time of the Reformation to sing psalms in the vernacular were taken in part from profane European street songs (in the Netherlands called *souterliedekens*; Grijp, 2001, p. 170), which was precisely the reason that these melodies were turned down by other Protestants. Furthermore, it is known that many great and, above all, prolific composers like Bach and Handel often used the same melodies for both religious and profane music.

For centuries Protestants of the Calvinist persuasion—and whether they were or indeed are justified in doing so is once again no question that any psychologist of religion can decide—rejected pieces, and some of them still do, like Mozart's *Coronation Mass* without exception: this, they say, is not religious music, since in their opinion a mass is "idol worship." Still, whether Protestant or not, for many people the genre itself excludes Mozart from the outset because his music would be much too extravagant. For people like this, music such as for example Verdi's *Requiem* or Rossini's *Stabat Mater* does not come into consideration as religious music either, since large parts of these works would be in no way distinguishable from opera; though assuredly musical masterworks, as settings of religious texts they are simply inappropriate. If we widen the circle somewhat beyond the Western world, it will probably become evident even sooner that it is not music as such that is religious: for many people from Western cultural circles chanting, as is to be heard in Hindu temples for example, does not come at all into question as religious music; for many, instruments as they are played in Tibetan monasteries will not produce any "music" at all. Since the author, as may well be the case with the reader, is too unfamiliar with non-Western music, we shall not address such examples in what follows.

Or should we put the question differently, as for example: which music counts under which conditions as religious music? Should we call music religious only if it was composed for a religious, for example liturgical, purpose? But what are we to make of it then if such music is, as is nowadays often the case with most of the technically finest performances of the canon of Western "religious" music, performed in a wholly profane context, for example in a concert hall that costs money to get into?

Or what is the case if music that arouses absolutely no associations with religion is performed for religious purposes? (One thinks for example of a benefit rock concert in aid of a religious charitable campaign.)

Is it when the composer regarded himself as religious that we should speak of religious music? Clearly not all music written by a religious composer is regarded as religious music. (Or is everything that Liszt or Bruckner composed religious in itself?) Or how would it be with the many "religious" works of composers who did not regard themselves as religious, or at least not as their patrons saw it?

Do we get any further if we ask about the interpreters rather than the composer? Once again, it is clear from the outset that not all music, just because it is played by religious musicians, is for that reason to be regarded as religious. Or is it the combination of all the aspects mentioned so far that justifies us in speaking of religious music: hence, if a religious text set to music by a religious composer is played by a religious musician? Verdi was not very engaged in church life but probably regarded himself in some way as religious, since anything else would hardly have been possible in

19th century Italy. Suppose now that his setting of the *Ave Maria* is sung by a religious soprano: is it really religious music if he or she does so not for religious reasons but for professional ones, and in the wholly profane context of Othello?

And what is even more interesting, because more paradoxical: what are we to make of music whose composers and/or performers regard themselves as religious, which is composed and/or performed for religious purposes, but which is rejected as religious music by acknowledged religious leaders? (For example: Pope Benedict XVI rejects all rock and pop music, even if it is a setting of "Christian" texts, as a flight from reality.) So music need not necessarily be religious because it is performed in a religious context? (Think of the many concerts where a church building serves simply as the location for the concert.)

But let us break off. For the purposes of this chapter we may have put enough questions about the term "religious music"; defining this is not our aim after all. The result we seem to reach, is that any music—and let us not start asking what we can regard as music and what we cannot—*can* be religious music, but also that any so-called religious music can lose its religious character. Thus we appear to be getting close to a view according to which religious music is such music as is considered as religious music by whoever calls it religious music, for whatever reason. This formulation sounds suspiciously tautological and hesitant, something like beauty is in the eye of the beholder, but is it wrong?

WHAT IS A RELIGIOUS EXPERIENCE?

The way we have gone about things in the previous section is very like the discussion about the definition of religious experience, or rather the discussion of how to determine any peculiarity it may have. Hence it will hardly be necessary to repeat the kind of exercise we have just been doing, we can therefore be brief: what is specific to a religious experience is its interpretation as religious (Ricken, 2004). One should not make the mistake of thinking that this is too little: in the case of lived-through experience, interpretation is not something that is afterwards added to an experience or even to a certain core of an experience. This fallacy, mostly apologetically motivated, is often to be found in the literature on what is called mysticism: all mysticism, it says, has ultimately the same core, all that distinguishes it, is merely interpretation. In response to this one should argue that in order to experience mystically, the experiencer must be able to apprehend something as mystical. Experience is "always already" (Heidegger) interpreted by the experiencer: there is no core that is untouched by elements dependent on the context. For an experience as experience interpretation is a sine qua non, not something that is added to a somehow a priori and separately existing core (see classics like Hollenback, 1996; Katz, 1978; Proudfoot, 1986). That there are exceptions here, that people can, even if rarely, also come by reflection, including reinterpretation, to the later conclusion that they have had this or that mystical experience, is no counterargument. On the contrary, it is sometimes precisely lifelong reflection on experience that should be regarded as an intrinsic part of a mystical process.

Anyone who wants to, may carry out the thought experiment, but they will eventually come to the conclusion not only that anything can be religious, but also that nothing is only or necessarily religious. The birth of a child, the reading of a poem, the entry into a certain order, a war, a funeral, a journey, a visit to a certain building, nursing the sick, spending time in a certain place, sex, authority, human sacrifice—whatever. At one time or another it has all been regarded as religious or at least claimed to be religious; anything can be interpreted and experienced as religious. And that, conversely, means that anything that is or appears to be religious, may equally seem not to be religious or impossible to be interpreted as religious.

Opinions about what is religious or is to be interpreted as religious certainly diverge completely, not just among the adherents of different religions and denominations of the same religion, but also in different epochs of a religion or a denomination; just as religious commandments and prohibitions are subject to constant change, even if only in the way they are expounded and applied. Somebody who is religious in the sense of tradition A may dispute the religious experiences of tradition B, may deny the religious character of the experiences of a follower of tradition B or regard them as false in the religious sense (either as falsely interpreted, or as idolatry, or as coming from a devil, or whatever). Such running disputes are, however, conducted within the framework of a religious interpretation, and are consequently to be regarded as data to the science of religion that ought to be explained, not as elements of a scientific explanation. For this reason we should not regard exclusively religious or as exclusively religiously to be interpreted even those actions that seem from a certain perspective to belong to the core of religion and that seem only to occur as religious actions: prayer for example is very differently conceptualized, taught, and promoted in different traditions. (Some traditions do not have it at all. As is the case with all religious categories, there is no universal core of prayer "as such.")

For this reason present-day, especially postmodern, theologians call religious interpretation supererogatory (Ploeger, 2009): it is not needed to explain anything in the world, nothing requires religious interpretation to be able to exist, but, put in a Christian way, anything can be interpreted as referring to God.

In the older science of religion, attempts have often been made to define religious experience as a sphere of being peculiar in itself, and indeed in the sense of religious experiences being *sui generis*: they are, it is said, unique, not comparable to anything. In psychology of religion this has led to attempts to identify independent and specific religious emotions: alongside the emotions that had otherwise been distinguished by those from Aristotle to Frijda (2007), there would also exist religious emotions. This again is a fallacy, one that William James had already tried to correct. James determined religious emotions to be "ordinary emotions" that are brought into connection with a religious object. Though in his opinion religious emotions are accordingly to be distinguished from other concrete emotions, "there is no ground for assuming a simple abstract 'religious emotion' to exist as a distinct elementary mental affection by itself, present in every religious experience" (1902/1982, p. 28).

And psychology of religion cannot say it much better today, even if within this subdiscipline ideas are still in circulation about independent religious emotions, attitudes, experiences and a lot besides. What is unique, however, about a religious emotion is the domain or the object to which it relates. (Here many will speak of God. "God", however, is according to classical as well as present-day theology, not a reality like other realities, God does not admit of being rationally demonstrated or being introduced as a factor in a scientific explanation.) It is in fact as we concluded at the end of the previous paragraphs: something is religious in the eye of the beholder, not because something in the intersubjectively experienced reality will necessarily present itself to everyone, always and everywhere, in such a way.

A totally different consideration supports the conclusion that should be drawn from the previous one: present-day sciences of religion offer no systematic concept of religion. On the contrary: "religion" is ever more frequently deconstructed as a concept formed in the West and calibrated on certain phenomena, and wrongly applied to non-Western phenomena and constellations. There is no universally valid concept of religion. Therefore the motto in empirical research must be a general abandonment of the claim to essentialist, normative, or even universally valid statements about "religion." Empirical sciences of religion, such as history, anthropology, economics, psychology, and others, ought to investigate phenomena of a kind that are regarded in a particular, though not necessarily only individual, context as "religious," without going on to maintain that they can thereby make statements about all religious phenomena at all times and places, or that they can even determine what the core of religion is (Belzen, 2010).

WHICH PSYCHOLOGICAL APPROACH TO CHOOSE?

Hopefully it has now become sufficiently clear that the modesty insisted on at the beginning is by no means to be understood as intellectual laziness, but rather as genuine necessity. But even if this ought to be positively valued, it is perhaps frustrating that up till now we seem to be proceeding so slowly towards the major point of this chapter. And there is no end in sight to this frustration! First, however, let us take one small step forward: if everything can count as religious, it surely depends on the subject above all whether or not he or she experiences something as religious. Since music, too, is not in itself religious and does not in and of itself demand religious interpretation, it certainly looks as if we must turn to the human subject to understand why he or she sometimes experiences some music as religious, why for example an atheist can be brought "to the brink of conversion" by a performance of *St. Matthew's Passion* (Witteman, 2010, p. 7). In this way, finally, psychology comes into view as the science of the subject *par excellence*. But just as it has already been with our understandings of (religious) music and of religion (or of religious experience), we must begin by treating the understanding of psychology itself as a problem, even if for somewhat different reasons.

One of the main problems with psychology "as such" is, namely, that probably nobody now knows anymore what it is: there are nowadays an immense number of approaches, all presenting themselves as "psychology," but otherwise seeming to have hardly anything in common. If we now simply restrict ourselves to those that are scientifically recognized (whereby, however, some highly interesting, perhaps indeed utterly relevant ones from non-European cultural spheres will certainly escape our view), this number is certainly reduced, but not the fundamental problem: among psychologists working as scientists there is not only no agreement on what should be regarded as scientific psychology, there are not only quarrels and inherited vendettas, there is what is worse, there is probably no longer anyone who has anything approaching full knowledge of the manifold directions that present themselves as scientific psychology. Although many, even today, repeatedly air a lament over the lack of unity in psychology "as such," one may also interpret the state of affairs in question positively: the object of psychology that the different directions naturally name and conceptualize differently is so complex that by necessity it needs a multiplicity of approaches to understand at least something about it. And when different goals are set, one need not hesitate to apply different approaches (in the study of some aspect or another of perception, for example, one will assuredly have to proceed otherwise than one would in treating some psychopathological syndrome.) Probably all the different approaches in psychology "as such" let a certain aspect of psychic functioning come into view, and all together surely produce a more comprehensive picture. When it comes to exploring a particular object, the most important question in concrete research is not whether one of the many forms of psychology is to be employed, but rather which of them.

In carrying out psychological research on domains like "religion" as well as "music," all the approaches within present-day psychology are applicable in principle. It is clear from the outset that psycho-physiological principles of psychic functioning, for example, are always involved in religious behavior and experiencing, however these are defined. But even if no human being can function without a brain, this does not imply that psychic functioning is to be reduced to brain activity. The *dernier cri* of materialism that provoked such heated discussion in the 19th century is actually a trivial one: it goes without saying that "without phosphorus there are no thoughts" (the critically intended dictum of a Moleschott), but it is not phosphorus that determines thoughts. However important the psycho-physiological level may be in analyzing psychic functioning comprehensively, in order to analyze anything specific about any psychic functioning whatsoever one needs another approach. To clarify this with an example from the area of religions: in a prayer to Allah the same neurological principles are involved as in a prayer to the Virgin Mary; it is consequently more interesting to find out why, for example, somebody who at first venerates Mary at some point begins to pray to Allah, or why somebody who prays to Allah tries to prevent the veneration of Mary, and so on. As has been previously argued, not "prayer" in general should be in the center of concrete research, but rather the specific prayer of a specific person (or a group of people at most).

In order to analyze psychic aspects of concrete phenomena in this sense, there is a need for the kind of psychological approaches that are sometimes described as cultural psychology. In general, to put it perhaps somewhat too simply, cultural psychology tries to understand human beings from their culture, also, and especially, in their psychic functioning (see, for instance, Bornstein, 2010; Ratner, 2002, 2006, 2008, 2012; Straub & Chakkarath, 2010; Valsiner, 2007, 2012). Cultural psychology takes seriously the apparently so trivial observation that people at different times and in different places function differently, and it tries to understand why this is so and how it is possible. Very different approaches can be counted among those employed within cultural psychology, a whole variety of modes of psychoanalytical thinking through socio-psychological approaches such as those presented by Mead, Vygotsky, or Bourdieu, to phenomenological, action theoretical and narrative psychological approaches. Uniting all these very different psychologies is the insight that there would be no subjectivity without a specific subculture in each case constituting, facilitating and regulating psychic functioning. Hence, in its analysis cultural psychology concentrates on the particular culture that has made the subject what she or he is: it inquires into the effect of culture. (And hence not just about the variability of the presupposed psychological universality in whatever is the surrounding culture. These latter questions are asked by so-called cross-cultural psychology, another approach in present-day psychology that also takes "culture" seriously and yet sets out more from the categories of contemporary psychology than the data about the culture to be analyzed.) For an area of human functioning so culturally and historically variable as that of the religious, cultural psychology is of course not the only possible, but certainly one of the preferable approaches (Belzen, 2010). A cultural psychology does after all inquire into the particularity of a subculture and is thus the appropriate partner to discover the possible specificity of a way of living that has been designated as religious.

The now rapidly growing neurologically oriented directions are understandably expanding into the areas not only of the psychology of religion (Bering, 2010), but also of the psychology of music. Neurologists like Blood and Zatorre discovered that the profound emotional effect of music is to be traced to an activation of the limbic system with simultaneous reduction of the activity of the amygdalae, which become activated in fear. Spitzer (2002, in Bolterauer, 2006) summarizes the results as follows:

> Music has the same effect in principle as other biologically exceptionally important stimuli such as for instance nourishment or social signals. It stimulates the body's own reward system, which is also stimulated by sex or intoxicating drugs and is associated with the secretion of dopamine ... and endogenic opioids. Conversely, music that is felt to be pleasant reduces the activation of central nervous structures signaling unpleasant emotions such as fear and aversion. Thus music the hearer likes, has a doubly pleasant effect. In addition to this, music leads to the activation of structures that are important for wakefulness and attention. (pp. 1178–1179)

And in a recent *American Scientific Mind*, the following research results were proudly presented, in which examples of church music are also produced:

> Music has been found to excite brain regions involved in understanding and producing language, including Broca's area and Wernicke's area, both located in the left hemisphere on the surface of the brain. (The majority of people process language mainly in the brain's left hemisphere but encode most aspects of music in the analogous regions on the right.) Thus musical syntax—for instance, the order of chords in a phrase—could have arisen from the mechanisms that evolved to organize and understand grammar.

> But tunes also recruit other brain systems, principally perhaps those governing emotions such as fear, joy and sorrow. For example, damage to the amygdala, the brain's fear hub, impairs a person's ability to feel scared and, in some

studies, sad in response to song. Many modern researchers thus conjecture that music evolved by piggybacking on a unique constellation of brain regions dedicated to language, feelings and other function. (Schrock, 2009, p. 36)

All things found out this way do not amount to nothing, the only trouble is that this approach does not help us even slightly to understand the observation that was the point of departure for our considerations. Hence a more cultural-psychological approach will suit this better, one that sees human subjectivity as the point of intersection between body and culture, both historical entities whose combined effect is consequently a process that varies as much historically as it does culturally. Any at all comprehensive psychological analysis will in fact always call for a historical (or at least biographical) perspective if the goal is to understand why these people experience and act now, thus, and not otherwise. In the question that occupies us in this chapter one has to bear in mind that the physical characteristics alone of the tones or the physiological characteristics as such of the processing brain of the musicians or the hearers do not lead to a religious interpretation; they are necessary but not sufficient conditions for the phenomenon. To understand a subject's producing a religious interpretation, psychology, as tried to explain previously, needs to concentrate on the specificity of the one doing the interpreting, hence on the specificity of the (subcultural) constitution of the interpreting subject and on the specificity of the (subcultural) situation in which the interpretation is made, and also on that of the (subcultural) data that led to this interpretation.

VIEWPOINTS FOR ANALYSIS FROM THE PERSPECTIVE OF CULTURAL PSYCHOLOGY OF RELIGION

Though simply putting together the results of our deliberations will not bring us even close to getting unambiguous answers, we shall no longer face the phenomenon we summoned at the outset with such incomprehension as we seemed to at first. From a cultural psychological perspective, viewpoints can almost certainly be gathered from for example psychoanalysis, sociopsychological attribution theory and other psychological theories. But first let us bear in mind that, as is mostly the case in psychology, we are not dealing with a phenomenon of natural science that could be explained by laws that would have universal validity. We are dealing with phenomena that at best can be interpreted, and mostly only retrospectively, with the aid of different perspectives: even if we could determine all the conditions that are necessary for the phenomenon to appear, the phenomenon would probably not "automatically" let itself be produced if we fulfill these conditions. Even profound believers, let alone an atheist, do not always have a religious experience during, for instance, a divine service of their denomination. And yet the fairly casually framed questions we began with can be answered now in some more definite-sounding tones. On top of that, some justified hypotheses can be set up and the limits of the possibilities of a psychological analysis can be discerned. Let us begin with our notes.

It is not true that music, even music that is, in a certain cultural circle, regarded as religious in the narrower sense by someone experiencing it, can simply make people have a religious experience, or go so far as to bring atheists "to the brink of conversion."

It is also not true that the phenomenon in question is always experienced as a religious phenomenon: being peculiarly moved by "religious music" need not at all be interpreted as religious as such by the one experiencing it, and is very likely often not. (It is not for nothing that Witteman speaks of the "brink of conversion." He was *not* converted.)

We are probably dealing with the phenomenon of the "tearjerker": a text hardly relevant in itself moves listeners peculiarly by being set to music and played. We find this phenomenon in all kinds of nonreligious contexts (from pretty bad poetry, settings of which by, for example, Verdi, Wagner, or the Beatles sound to listeners like articulations of sublime romantic love, to the mass-psychological use of music at mass events like, for example, those organized by the Nazis, at which the odd person who was actually opposed to the regime sang along with raised hand). This occasionally being moved to tears can be as easily interpreted religiously as not religiously.

But however banal the text may be, it still plays a great, in fact decisive role. Music that seems to be able to unfailingly achieve the effect we are talking about here (like some church songs, for example from so-called revivalist movements) is sometimes of really dubious quality, and without the text would never achieve the effect described. (Compare, for example, the so-called Sankey hymns from the English Evangelical field, or also the melodies of a present-day composer like John Rutter, for example his utterly elementary setting of the blessing "The Lord Bless Thee," etc.) Melodies, too, like those of the Geneva Psalter are hardly artistically successful, but often immediately put anyone in whose religious socialization they played a part, into a mood that can be interpreted religiously and that can lead to a religious experience (or in the cases of some people into a mood that can at least remind them of religion, and for that reason is sometimes radically rejected, etc.).

Furthermore, the characteristics of the event and the place are often of crucial significance: someone who puts on Sankey hymns when doing the cleaning has less of a chance of being religiously moved by them than someone who hears them in the setting of divine service or who sings them herself. In a fitness studio you will hardly ever meet anyone who listens to Rutter's music on the cross trainer; but in a Gothic chapel, i.e., one built in a style that for many people north of the Alps continues to be the essence of religious architecture, the chance of religious interpretation is certainly greater. Hence the mindset with which an individual comes to an event at which this music is performed plays an important role. Again, nothing specifically religious plays a part here, but it can become religious. Performances of Wagner and Bach are often attended by ostensibly nonreligious people in what is very close to a solemn mood, which when experiencing a Bach *Passion* can definitely lead one "to the brink of conversion," especially when this mood is subculturally legitimized or actually desired to begin with. Nevertheless for a psychological analysis it would in each case be necessary to look into the biography of an individual listener, especially of someone who experiences religiously. I suspect that in this latter case there will be much religious socialization to be found.

Let us stay for a moment with the example of a Bach *Passion*. It offers a clear example of the importance of the role of the text (but probably also of the limited capacity of psychology to explain the previously mentioned effect of the music). When Matthias Hirsch (2008) explains that in *St. Matthew's Passion* by Johann Sebastian Bach universal dimensions of human life and the connections within it are dramatized in a metaphorical way (especially the fates of the parent-child relationship, object-loss and grieving process, guilt, repentance, forgiveness, etc.), he is doubtless right in doing so, but in this he is primarily naming elements of the text—and by itself the text of the *St. Matthew's Passion* will hardly bring anyone to tears. (With its baroque and pietistic elements it is more likely to daunt some people.) On the other hand, it is not true that the combination of text and its setting as in the *St. Matthew's Passion* is in itself enough to bring someone to tears: only someone who has learned to listen to this music will be able to be moved like this. (Out of enthusiasm or reverence one forgets all too easily that the modern Western person must have learned to "endure" passions or operas: just try to take someone or another from the street and subject him to an hours-long performance of such music!) Many, incidentally, in whom the phenomenon in question appears when they sing Sankey hymns for example, will have no idea what to make of the *St. Matthew's Passion*.

The sentence that has already been quoted several times, namely, that hearing a piece like the *St. Matthew's Passion* could lead "to the brink of conversion," comes from the Dutch book *The Mysteries of the St. Matthew's Passion: The Craftsmanship and Mysticism of a Masterwork* (Dirksen, 2010). This book contains mostly texts appearing between the years 2000 and 2010 in the programs of performances of the *St. Matthew Passion* in the beautiful Dutch fortress city of Naarden. In little Holland, these performances have a certain social similarity to the Wagner Festival in Bayreuth: they are a society event. Tickets are almost impossible to get, performances are usually attended by the country's leading figures exclusively, the entire cabinet is sometimes to be found here in rapt attendance. The introduction to the previously named book was written by Paul Witteman, one of the best-known journalists in the Netherlands, who presents a top-rated political talk show several times a week. He is one of the regular guests of the Naarden performances. He makes no bones about being an atheist (one who has not been converted by the performances either), but who—differently from all the other authors in the book— lets us have an insight into why the *St. Matthew's Passion* is so able to move him in that place. The whole setting is certainly crucial: one is practically expected to be there in solemnity and to be peculiarly moved (he reports the "aimless walk" in the interval: "we remain silent, any word would be too much"; Witteman, 2010, p. 7). But what must be at least as important: at the age of only six, Witteman was brought by his mother to a performance of *St. Matthew's Passion* in the concert hall in Harlem and there he experienced the solemn mood, especially that of his mother. She was totally concentrated, she followed the music in the piano score. "At the first bars her eyes moistened. I looked shyly straight ahead, my mother was not accustomed to showing her emotions. Only the music of Bach, she told me later, could move her to tears" (Witteman, 2010, p. 8; author's translation). Since that time, the *St. Matthew's Passion* has evidently become an entry for Witteman into a singularly intimate closeness with his mother, even after her death.

> The CD . . . is always to hand. The piano score was left to me by my mother, on Palm Sunday it rests on my lap when I am in the church in Naarden. When the music begins I follow it from the score, not from sentimentality, but to think of my mother, who introduced me silently and with brimming eyes to the most important man in my life, to Johann Sebastian Bach. (Witteman, 2010, p. 8)

It may in itself be moving to read this account by a journalist who enjoys such a "hard" reputation. But what matters here is this: what he tells will not surprise anyone who is even somewhat familiar with psychoanalytical points of view. Witteman finds access to the longed for, once (and perhaps too little?) experienced closeness to his primary attachment figure, he finds access to a yearning that lasts an entire lifetime and can be satisfied in the most different forms. His reminiscences of his mother are an intrinsic part of his (not religiously interpreted) experience of the performance of the *St. Matthew's Passion.*

This and other similar constellations in the subjectivity of an individual listener must necessarily be taken into account if we are to achieve some understanding of these effects of music. For with all due respect to this master-work of Western musical history, in and of itself the work does not explain such an effect. One must already have been socialized in a particular way to be able to be thus moved by this and other "great" music.

Hence the question remains, why it is precisely this setting of the words that succeeds in moving the listener so particularly? One could perhaps conjecture that the music succeeds in (again) bringing the listener into contact with fantasies of a kind that he or she regards as actually having grown out of, and as an adult has perhaps even become ashamed of: a grown-up person, says the general opinion, should be in a position to stand up manfully to the adversities of life, to challenge destiny, to deny one-self childish or indeed narcissistic fantasies that one is the only, the most important, the uniquely loved one, the especially protected one, etc. The only trouble is, as we know, that this kind of self-denial is not so simple, and the yearnings articulated in such fantasies do not go out of existence just by swearing off them and no longer admitting them to oneself even. The psychic censorship that an adult always imposes on himself is circumvented in art, whose effect principally goes back to its similarity to primary processes, and it is precisely music that seems to be able to put the listener in a state that enables "unconscious impulses to penetrate into consciousness." Already in the older literature, Teller advanced the hypothesis that it was precisely being brought to tears that could be traced back to the fact that through the forceful elimination of the psychic resistances "the cathectic energy used in inhibition" (Freud) is being discharged (1917/2002, p, 52) and hence one gains access to what had been displaced.

One should not, however, interpret this phenomenon only as regression, and certainly not in the pathological sense. In aesthetic experience, for example in the experience of music, there is the possibility of entering a different mode of being in the world than the one of active providing (*besorgen*). The adult human is distinguished precisely by his or her being active: by goal-directed, rational, and creative action. In the view of Western culture, it is characteristic of the adult to achieve, to create, and to conquer, manipulate, and subjugate the world. The care (*sorge*) that characterizes human existence according to Heidegger is, for the adult, that of providing (*besorgen*). But there are other ways of relating to the world too: the tree that one can fell and use for building a house can also be gazed at so as to delight in its beauty, or playfully climb on it from branch to branch. One of these ways will suit one situation, another will suit another situation. The play mode will be more familiar to one individual, the use mode to another, and the contemplative mode to yet another.

Numberless are the modes of being human that have been distinguished in the course of the history of culture; and ever more differentiated too, the phases into which the course of a human life is divided. Hence, if I merely distinguish between youth, maturity, and old age, I am not saying anything unusual, not even if I put modes of being such as play, creative achieving, and contemplation on an equal footing with them. In nearly every theory of development, be it psychological or rather anthropological, one presumes that development consists in reaching a further stage or level, although maintaining access to levels already attained to. In nearly all reasonably well-elaborated developmental psychologies, such phases are distinguished according to ideal types. The individual can accordingly be assigned to a phase on the basis of some or more criteria, but an individual will in fact nearly always fulfill criteria of different phases. In which phase the individual is located, will depend on the aims set for the analysis. Characteristics of an earlier phase are often taken over transformed into a later phase; therefore, if such characteristics come to light in behavior this is no regression, and even if ways of behavior from an earlier phase appear, the regression does not need to be morbid. Play, for example, as a mode of relating to reality is not lost to the adult, he will just play differently from a child. (If an adult plays with dolls, again this might be dubious behavior; if one plays chess, one will be regarded as intelligent; if one is able to maintain so playful a way of dealing with one's surroundings that one can design entire cities, that person may star as an architect, etc.)

Excessively familiar as all this may be, there are in this connection two further relevant considerations: (a) people in general have at their disposal all the three modes of being distinguished here. Active providing assuredly does characterize the adult, as does passive contemplation more the old person. Even though youth does not yet have complete success in creation and lacks wisdom entirely, the old person still has access to play and she is even still capable of making creative contributions. Playing, creatively providing and contemplating, all three belong to the normal human functioning that is at the disposal of every fully grown person. In the experiencing of music, many people attain access to another mode of being than the everyday one characterizing their lives as provident, creative persons: one becomes quiet, passive, receptive; fantasy and creativity become possible; one comes literally to rest (even though as a musician one may have to be extremely active) and to other thoughts. This is not simply, and certainly not necessarily, a regression to an earlier level of psychic functioning; although on the one hand an earlier world of experience can certainly be recalled by means of music (compare Witteman's account of his closeness to his mother), on the other hand also the other mode of being in the world, associated not with "earlier" but rather with "later," is made accessible, a mode that is more readily evoked by words such as pausing, contemplating, and wisdom. In the experience of music, as in that of art in general, the world becomes present as a symbol to the usually rationalist adult. (If in this mode of being one becomes responsive to an ethical appeal, as is for example described by Levinas, this is certainly not a regression to an earlier functioning.) Hence instead of speaking here of regression to an earlier phase one should perhaps speak of transition to another mode of being? And (b) as I have tried to explain shortly, nothing is religious in itself, not even any of the modes of being that were briefly touched upon here. It is more like prejudice than comprehensive knowledge to want to identify religion with one or the other, the mode of play or that of wisdom. There is certainly a childish way of being religious, one that is to be found not just with children, but also with adults; to dismiss all religiosity as childish or to reduce it to childish functioning is inadequate. All great religions possess an extensive wisdom literature, which aims to urge and bring up adherents to let go of childishness and to progress to adult forms of religiosity. (Far from confirming their followers in their relating to God as nothing but an elevated father, many mystics insist on their jettisoning all images of God, taking back their projections and not living out their own longings in religion. Whether they have much success in this is another question entirely; what we are here concerned with is to remember that not all religiosity bears childish traits only.) For many who nowadays want to be open to religion, positively regarded attitudes and comportment such as openness, passivity, calmness, receptivity, and many others in themselves count as religious. This, however, is just as much of a prejudice, although with reversed signs, as the one we have just been talking about: wisdom, composure, patience, and other possible virtues *could*, but do not have to be religiously embedded. As always, only interpretation as religious will make them appear religious, no matter how trivial this may sound. Religious functioning can express itself in the mode of play as well as in that of providing and that of composure, it manifests itself as childish and naïve, as assiduous and performative, as wise and patient; no mode of being human, understood in this sense, is in and of itself or necessarily to be seen as religious, and conversely a characterization as religious still does not at all allow any conclusion about the manner of psychic functioning.

So, again this means that a psychological analysis of religious phenomena dare not allow itself be seduced into generalities: if someone reports the experience mentioned at the outset (becoming particularly moved by a setting of a text to which he actually has a dismissive attitude), this can be a religious experience, one which certainly can have a regressive character, but does not have to have. As is nearly always the case, the observing psychologist will have to immerse herself in the individual's biography in order to be able to understand and interpret any phenomenon: just as for example a certain degree of professional engagement can be neurotically structured, but does not have to be, a religious attitude found in any one person cannot be judged psychologically without further knowledge. (If someone does not enthusiastically greet every innovation at her work or throw herself into activity, is she wise, then, or at least calm, or is she, rather, job-tired or even resigned? Having to investigate this, if called upon to, is psychology's task, not to make ethical or religious judgments on this attitude.) When in his now quite well-known correspondence with Jacques

Wirion, Hermann Kurzke gives a striking example of the previously mentioned phenomenon, psychology cannot say all that much about it without having gathered further data in a specific study. On May 10, 2004, literature professor Kurzke told his friend Wirion about a

> heart-rending nostalgia that often seizes me when I hear church bells. Come home, call the bells with sweet siren voices; reason may object what it will. The cool power of holy water only opens itself to the humble that do without the modern drivel of superstition.... The water comes into my eyes when I join in Claudius' Evening Song: "And when Thou hast taken us, let us come to Heaven, Thou our Lord and our God." It would be so much easier intellectually to be an atheist! But feelings do not go along with this. (Kurzke & Wirion, 2005, p. 193)

Kurzke reports exactly what, as an observation, gave occasion for this chapter: he is struggling to maintain his attitude toward the Christian faith. As a highly educated man, his reason rejects tenets of belief provided by the church, but if he hears the concepts in question sung or even goes so far as to join in himself, he is moved to tears. Are we dealing with a religious experience here? Psychology of religion cannot tell us: Kurzke or a religious institution such as a Christian denomination can perhaps do it, but not a scientific discipline like psychology. The latter has to analyze, apply its categories, and interpret. The question whether the experience described by Kurzke is a regression can only be answered with the question of why this is to be suspected: nothing in the words quoted obliges us to assume a regression, Kurzke provides us with no associations with an earlier world of experience (which Witteman at least did), not a single indication of lower phases of psychic functioning. One would have to know considerably more about him to come out with any explanation of his experience that would come even near to being psychologically justified. Certainly when he pauses to listen to the sound of bells, he no longer seems to be in the mode of activity and creating, scientific or otherwise, no longer to be manipulating the world but rather to be letting it, particularly its sounds, talk to him. But that they talk to him of a "homecoming" is something that they can only do because Kurzke, in an earlier phase of his life, was religiously socialized: he learned to connect the sound of the bells with church and faith. (In itself the sound of bells has nothing to do with religion and will not evoke religious experience; in Amsterdam, nonreligious, especially American tourists tell me of their irritation when on Sunday mornings they are woken against their will by the to them incomprehensible pealing from the many old church towers.) Through these sounds, however, Kurzke is put into a mode that provides him with a different access to the world: not that of rational analysis, but of contemplative lingering that might turn out to be able to express itself as religious reverence but does not have to. For

Kurzke the entry into this mode by means of "religious music" seems to be deeply ambivalent: he is ashamed of his religious associations, he does not (yet) interpret this being particularly moved as religious. (Whether or not he ought to do this is not for psychology to decide. Here many in present-day psychology of religion, in the United States above all, make a crucial mistake: they think, in psychotherapy for instance, that they have to help bring to faith, not least because there are at present so many publications that "demonstrate" a positive relation between religiosity and psychic well-being, see Koenig [1998] or Pargament [2007]. The old master of the psychological critique of religion dealt more carefully with the boundaries of his professional competence: he granted both critics and defenders equal use of psychoanalysis and, against the popular opinion, there is no known case in which Freud deprived a patient of his faith [Belzen, 2009].)

FINAL WORDS

The results that we have obtained after our deliberations seem to be modest indeed: the psychological viewpoint has no more than a limited validity, there are only certain kinds of questions to which psychological approaches are able to contribute towards an answer. Psychology teaches us to have regard to the particularity of the person investigated, it obliges us to situate in different contexts the behaving and experiencing, attitudes and emotions, and all the other things it studies, of the individual or of small numbers of persons; in this it does not just consider contexts such as the premises or what takes place in them, but above all the personal, individually biographical context, in order to establish which significances have emerged in which way. It is right for psychology of religion as it is for psychology of music to take the same path as so many other psychologies of a certain object or field: on the basis of a more or less elaborated psychological theory, for example a cognitive psychological or a psychodynamic theory, certain subsidiary questions can be posed and perhaps answered, but never in general, never with a claim to have said everything about everything. One psychological theory will put socialization at the center of consideration, another cognitive development, yet another other group dynamic aspects, depending on what the theory in question aims to capitalize on. Why some people are moved to tears by hearing music, although they would in part dismiss out of hand the texts to which it is a setting, is something that cannot be answered there and then or universally: one must go and, through an empirical study, ask people who can report from their own experience on the phenomenon in question (as soon as possible after the appearance of the phenomenon). It shall be seen that in each case it is a specific combination of event, place

and musical as well as religious biography, including the dispositions resulting from it, that facilitates the appearance of the phenomenon.

The modesty of these truly general conclusions is especially frustrating in
view of the observation that it is after all certain pieces of music that achieve
the effect in question, even if it is among a select group of people. Though
it may not be the text of the *St. Matthew's Passion* in itself that moves to tears,
or it may not be the melodies of Bach in themselves (his aria "Edifying Reflections of a Tobacco Smoker" [BWV 515], for example, does not do it), it
will not be the attendance at a performance of *St. Matthew's Passion* in itself
that does it, however solemn the mood may be, and it will not be every, for
example, narcissistically deprived, religiously ambivalent, or whatever kind
of person who is going to be moved by hearing the *St. Matthew's Passion*.
And yet the effect in question probably comes about—it really should be
more precisely established whether this is true—more readily by listening
to this music than to any other. So have certain pieces of music specific
psychic consequences, at least potentially? The question is understandable,
but ends up suspiciously near to an older aesthetic view of invariable reactions to colors or their combination, especially of universal significances of
sound combinations; these views, however, have long been quite sufficiently
deconstructed (Chandler, 1934, pp. 114–115; Suppan, 1984, p. 28).

But however meager our results may seem are they wrong for this very
reason? Could one have expected anything more or anything different?
Progress is made slowly in the humanities, also in their application in research on religion, and also in particular psychological areas of the latter.
Other than do their colleagues in the natural sciences, scholars in the humanities come up with no discoveries or inventions; they certainly arrive
at new thoughts (even if not very often), and a large part of their work
consists in thinking through the peculiar nature of a perspective arrived at
and often protecting it from over estimation and, especially, being pirated.
The history of the psychology of religion shows this clearly: it is filled with
misunderstandings, even among its practitioners (when, for example, these
think that—for instance, on the basis of their having determined a function that, they say, is served by "religion"—that they would have grasped
the "essence of [all] religion"). It is constantly confronted by prejudices as
if it would harm the Christian faith or indeed be useful to it, whereas it is
not psychology of religion "as such" that brings harm or benefits to faith
"as such," but it is always only a specific application of the psychology (of
religion) that intends to do harm or to be of benefit. Much of what is seen
as psychology of religion is nothing of the kind, it is only the private opinion of one of its practitioners, etc. For this reason, psychology of religion
is already making a contribution if it insists that scientific precision should
prevail in the work of defining (or declining to define) concepts, both in
empirical research and in its interpretation. Proceeding in this way teaches

us a certain amount, even if it is only to occasion correction. Hence the familiar quotation from James prefacing this contribution as a motto: "Not conceptual speech, but music rather, is the element through which we are best spoken to by mystical truth" (James, 1902/1982, pp. 420–421) must, after the considerations so far presented, be deemed wrong, and that for several reasons. For anyone who has not learned to listen to certain music will not be moved by it, not even in the general aesthetic sense. And it is just the same with all the experiences that are designated as "mysticism": one has to have learned to call them mystical to be able to experience them as mystical and to report them as mystical. (Although James is often counted as part of the phenomenological tradition [Spiegelberg, 1972, 1982], his procedure is still far removed from phenomenologies like those of Husserl, Heidegger, or Merleau-Ponty, who gave much more thought to the world in which the subject comes to himself.)

Yet compared to many other ways of viewing it, we have perhaps still made a certain amount of progress. In his thoroughly nuanced and engaging treatment, *The Aesthetic: A Path to Belief?* the Dutchman Hoenderdaal formulates a clear "no" in answer to the question we started with. He properly distinguishes between religious and aesthetic experience, but emphasizes in spite of his great interest in aesthetics that "by its nature, the aesthetic" could become "an enemy of our faith" (Hoenderdaal, 1982, p. 89). As a theologian and articulator of a certain kind of Christian faith, he is of course free to form an opinion, but it is neither scientifically nor philosophically tenable. Behind this—Hoenderdaal mentions him in his book—is probably Kierkegaard. Kierkegaard, who was certainly also a great psychologist, drew, as is known, a distinction between an aesthetic, an ethical, and a religious stage (the latter again divided into religion A and religion B), but in doing so he undertook distinctions that are religious in nature, distinctions that can only be undertaken from the perspective (of a variant) of the Christian faith. From the Kierkegaardian perspective, which thus wants to lead people to a certain kind of Christian faith (religion B), it may be entirely true that experiences such as those at the center of this chapter are too "noncommittal," merely an "ephemeral side effect" (Hoenderdaal); Kierkegaard demands a self-abandonment to God that goes beyond the "level" of ethics he distinguished, and *a fortiori* of aesthetics. Once again: it is not the business of psychology as a science to make such judgments. Psychology is religiously abstinent and in no way normative; it does not know whether experiences such as those reported by Witteman or Kurzke are religious or not, whether if they are religious they are the right kind of religious experiences, whether they are intermediate stages on the way to the right faith, or whatever may most deeply concern theologians as representatives of the Christian faith. Neither is psychology of religion able to judge the content of the kinds of religiosity, between which kinds an insufficient distinction has already been made: it does not know whether belief should be childish, manly, or ripe (The most it would be able to establish is whether there are correlations with life phases, and it would do better to try to study how religiosity, of whatever kind, lies embedded in the broader psychic functioning of the believer in question.) In light of the considerations presented so far, however, psychology would very likely be inclined to amend Kierkegaard at least to the extent that the aesthetic and ethical stage could also be named and experienced as religious (even if in themselves they may not be ideal from a certain religious perspective). Whether a development from one stage to another (say from aesthetics to religion A) is to be judged as an advance, is not something for psychology to judge. (And an empirical investigation of whether and when such developments are in evidence would not be a psychological but rather a practical-theological one.) As an empirical science, psychology would to begin with leave it to Witteman and Kurzke themselves to judge whether or not their experiences are (or have been) religious, establishing this is not the proprium of science. To establish why they interpret their experiences as religious or as not religious would be much more regarded as an object of psychological investigation.

Psychology of religion must proceed cautiously, not let itself be taken over religiously (including atheistically) or theologically, and it must above all be precise in its analyses if it is to be able to make statements that are anyway significant. Though in studying religious phenomena, the scientific approach has to be modest in general, if one proceeds in this fashion one does get a step beyond all too generalized statements or hasty judgments. From the nonnormative observation point of psychology, the answer to Hoenderdaal's question is not "no," but rather it could be so, but in each individual case it must be settled whether and to what extent "the aesthetic" was or could be "a path to faith," or whether it leads away from it. As a clear example one could also refer here to Augustine, hence to precisely that doctor of the church who almost certainly inspired Kierkegaard's skepticism about "the aesthetic." In spite of all his personal pleasure in sung music, this great psychologist of late antiquity pointed out that it is possible to lose oneself in the aesthetic enjoyment of music at the cost of the religious dimension. He was however more realistic or at least more differentiated than was Hoenderdaal with his negative answer to his own question: in this same passage Augustine (1987) also describes how, even though the words were later more important to him than the setting, the setting of religious texts had been a real help to him on the path to faith and in his initial faith (*Confessions,* 33:50).

Thus present-day psychology as science of the human being can at times contribute to (newly) discovering nuances and to reflection on what we are to make of those who are led (back) to the Christian faith by music, even though its share remains a modest one when it comes to finding the answer to the question set by this chapter.

REFERENCES

Atran, S. (2002). *In gods we trust. The evolutionary landscape of religion.* Oxford, England: Oxford University Press.

Augustine. (1987). *Bekennisse.* Munich, Germany: Insel.

Belzen, J. A. (2005). The varieties, the principles and psychology of religion: Unremitting inspiration from a different source. In J. Carrette (Ed.), *William James and the varieties of religious experience: A centenary celebration* (pp. 58–78). New York, NY: Routledge.

Belzen, J. A. (2007). *Psychologie en het raadsel van de religie.* (Psychology and the riddle of religion). Amsterdam, the Netherlands: Boom.

Belzen, J. A. (2009). *Changing the scientific study of religion: Beyond Freud? Theoretical, empirical and clinical studies from psychoanalytic perspectives.* New York, NY: Springer.

Belzen, J. A. (2010). *Towards cultural psychology of religion. Principles, problems, applications.* New York, NY: Springer.

Bering, J. (2010). *The God instinct: The psychology of souls, destiny and the meaning of life.* London, England: Nicholas Brealey.

Bolterauer, J. (2006). Die macht der musik: Psychoanalytische überlegungen zur wirkungsweise von musik und ihren wurzeln in der frühkindlichen entwicklung. *Psyche, 60,* 1173–1204.

Bornstein, M. H. (2010). *Handbook of cultural developmental science.* New York, NY: Psychology Press.

Boyer, P. (2001). *Religion explained: The evolutionary origins of religious thought.* New York, NY: Basic Books.

Chandler, A. R. (1934). *Beauty and human nature: Elements of psychological aesthetics.* New York, NY: Appleton.

Davies, P. S. (2009). Some evolutionary model or other: Aspirations and evidence in evolutionary psychology. *Philosophical Psychology, 22*(1), 83–97.

Derksen, M. (2010). Realism, relativism and evolutionary psychology. *Theory & Psychology, 20,* 467–487.

Faber, M. D. (2010). *Becoming God's children: Religion's infantilizing process.* Santa Barbara, CA: Praeger.

Frijda, N. H. (2007). *The laws of emotion.* Mahwah, NJ: Erlbaum.

Grijp, L. P. (2001). De honger naar psalmen en schriftuurlijke liederen tijdens de reformatie (The hunger for psalms and other songs from scripture). In L.P. Grijp (Ed.), *Een muziekgeschiedenis der Nederlanden* (A music history of the Netherlands; pp. 168–173). Amsterdam, the Netherlands: Amsterdam University Press.

Hirsch, M. 2008). *Die Matthäus-Passion Johann Sebastian Bachs. Ein psychoanalytischer musikführer.* Giessen, Germany: Psychosozial Verlag.

Hoenderdaal, G. J. (1982). *Het esthetische: Een weg tot geloof?* (The aesthetic: A path to faith?). Baarn, the Netherlands: Ten Have.

Hollenback, J. (1996). *Mysticism: Experience, response, and empowerment.* University Park, PA: Pennsylvania State University Press.

James, W. (1902/1982). *The varieties of religious experience: A study in human nature.* Hammondsworth, England: Penguin.

Katz, S. T. (1978). Language, epistemology, and mysticism. In S. T. Katz (Ed.), *Mysticism and philosophical analysis* (pp. 22–74). New York, NY: Oxford University Press.

Kirkpatrick, L. A. (2005). *Attachment, evolution and the psychology of religion.* New York, NY: Guilford.

Koenig, H. G. (Ed.). (1998). *Handbook of religion and mental health.* San Diego, CA: Academic Press.

Kurzke, H., & Wirion, J. (2005). *Unglaubensgespräch: Vom nutzen und nachteil der religion für das leben.* Munich, Germany: Beck.

Loesch, H. (2003). Kunst als religion und religion als kunst: Zur kunst- und religionsphilosophie Richard Wagners. In H. de la Motte-Haber (Ed.), *Musik und religion* (pp. 187–208). Laaber, Germany: Laaber-Verlag.

Oberhoff, B. (2005). Die fötalen wurzeln der musik: Musik als 'das große bewegende' und 'die göttliche stimme.' In B. Oberhoff (Ed.), *Die seelischen wurzeln der musik: Psychoanalytische erkundungen* (pp. 41–63). Giessen, Germany: Psychosozial Verlag.

Pargament, K. I. (2007). *Spiritually integrated psychotherapy. Understanding and addressing the sacred.* New York, NY: Guilford Press.

Parncutt, R., & Kessler, A. (2007). Musik als virtuelle person. In B. Oberhoff & S. Leikert (Eds.), *Die psyche im spiegel der musik: Musikpsychoanalytische beiträge* (pp. 203–251). Giessen, Germany: Psychosozial Verlag.

Pinker, S. (1997). *How the mind works.* New York, NY: Norton.

Ploeger, M. (2009). Op zoek naar een christelijke theologie van de muziek. (Searching for a Christian theology of music) In: M. Hoondert, A. de Heer, & J. D. van Laar (Eds.), *Elke muziek heeft haar hemel: De religieuze betekenis van muziek* (Each music has its heaven; The religious meaning of music; pp. 78–104). Budel, the Netherlands: Damon.

Proudfoot, W. (1986). *Religious experience.* Berkeley, CA: University of California Press.

Ratner, C. (2002). *Cultural psychology: Theory and method.* New York, NY: Kluwer/Plenum.

Ratner, C. (2006). *Cultural psychology: A perspective on psychological functioning and social reform.* Mahwah, NJ: Erlbaum.

Ratner, C. (2008). *Cultural psychology, cross-cultural psychology and indigenous psychology.* Hauppage, NY: Nova.

Ratner, C. (2012). *Macro cultural psychology: A political philosophy of mind.* New York, NY: Oxford University Press.

Ricken, F. (Ed.) (2004). *Religiöse erfahrung: Ein interdisziplinärer klärungsversuch.* Stuttgart, Germany: Kohlhammer.

Rizzuto, A.M. (1979). *The birth of the living God: A psychoanalytic study.* Chicago, IL: University of Chicago Press.

Schrock, K. (2009, July/August). Why music moves us? *Scientific American Mind,* pp. 32–37.

Spiegelberg, H. (1972). *Phenomenology in psychology and psychiatry.* Evanston, IL: Northwestern University Press.

Spiegelberg, H. (1982). *The phenomenological movement: A historical introduction.* Den Haag, the Netherlands: Mouton.

Spitzer, M. (2002). *Musik im kopf.* Stuttgart, Germany: Schattauer.

Stephenson, N., Radtke, H. L., Jorna, R., & Stam, H. J. (Eds.). (2003). *Theoretical psychology: Critical contributions.* Calgary, Alberta, Canada: Captus University Publications.

Straub, J., & Chakkarath, P. (2010). Kulturpsychologie. In G. Mey & K. Mruck (Eds.) *Qualitative forschung in der psychologie* (pp. 191–205). Konstanz, Germany: Verlag für Sozialwissenschaften.

Suppan, W. (1984). *Musikpädagogik. Forschung und lehre. Band 10. Der musizierende mensch. Eine anthropologie der musik.* Mainz, Germany: Schott.

Teller, F. (1917/2002). Musikgenuss und phantasie. In B. Oberhoff (Ed.), *Psycho-analyse und musik: Eine bestandsaufnahme* (pp. 47–56). Giessen, Germany: Psychosozial-Verlag.

Valsiner, J. (2007). *Culture in minds and societies.* New Delhi, India: Sage.

Valsiner, J. (Ed.). (2012). *The Oxford handbook of culture and psychology.* New York, NY: Oxford University Press.

Witteman, P. (2010). Bach en mijn moeder (Bach and my mother). In P. Dirksen (Ed.), *De geheimen van de Matthäus-Passion: Ambacht en mystiek van een meesterwerk* (The secrets of the St. Matthew-Passion: Craft and mysticism of a masterpiece; pp. 7–8). Amsterdam, the Netherlands: Balans.

PART II

MUSICAL SENSATIONS

CHAPTER 4

THE "UNATTAINABLE VIBRATION"

Julia Kristeva, the Opera, and Psychic Life in a Mexican City

Karen Rodríguez

Psychoanalyst Julia Kristeva has consistently woven references to music through her oeuvre, a body of work that now spans half a century, several genres (including theory, novel, and biography), and a wide range of themes such as otherness, sexuality and maternity, religion, literature, and art. Her musical references are light-handed: some are metaphorical, and others form part of a character's aesthetic preferences. As a consequence, they can be easy to miss within the density of her ideas and prose, which seem to take us in other directions. Nonetheless, there is a definite musical presence in Kristeva's work. She locates musicality within our most archaic psychic makeup, arguing that musicality forms part of our semiotic disposition and sensory capacity, both of which should be harnessed to interrupt the spectacle in which we find ourselves currently immersed. Read this way, as a trans linguistic form of expression tied to the body along with the drives

Cultural Psychology of Musical Experience, pages 71–87
Copyright © 2016 by Information Age Publishing
All rights of reproduction in any form reserved.

and affects, musicality may help us to reconnect with both our affective, corporal selves and our others.

While this could and should be examined in relation to the human subject, this essay explores Kristeva's position on music within an example taken from a city subject. I posit the small Mexican city of Guanajuato, located in central Mexico, as a sensing, listening subject that, like its human and its global-city counterparts, finds itself in constant contact with a range of cultural others to whom it must respond (Rodríguez, 2012). In this piece, I show how the city enlists its sensory resources, and in particular music, to dialogue with an aural other. The other in question was an opera performance introduced into the city's most interior, domestic space of self, the main market, during an arts festival that occasionally threatens to convert the city into a tourist spectacle. Following Kristeva's theory, I trace the contours and the effects of this encounter to argue that the psychically healthy city is one that can mobilize its sensory resources to respond creatively to the other and to the spectacle—whether to question, to rebel or to accommodate difference on more equal terms. Understood this way, music may lead to nothing less than urban regeneration at both the spatial and the psychic level.

MUSIC AND PSYCHOANALYSIS

Despite Sigmund Freud himself, who is oft quoted for having expressed an inability to feel anything when listening to music, many subsequent analysts have noted a pronounced musical inclination within their profession. Brett Kahr, for example, comments on psychoanalysts' proclivity toward music, citing their tendencies to play instruments informally or professionally, to attend musical performances on a regular basis, and even to marry musicians (2007, p. 95). He goes on to note that:

> Perhaps psychological workers have a natural affinity for music because both mental health professionals and musicians have an acutely developed auditory capacity, a heightened sensitivity to sound and its importance.

Julie Jaffee Nagel, a psychoanalyst who trained as a musician at Julliard before becoming an analyst, says something similar, pointing out that, "Both music and psychoanalysis involve careful listening, uniting them as aural experiences. Psychoanalysis is concerned with a symbolic verbal world; music is embedded in a symbolic sonic world" (Nagel, 2008, p. 517).

This psychoanalytical sensitivity to sound, voice, and music has been brought out in a wide body of work. Much of this research references Didier Anzieu's concepts: Anzieu posited a sonorous envelope or sound bath that contains the infant within the aural maternal realm both before and after birth, as well as an *acoustic* mirror stage (following Lacan) in which the infant recognizes himself in the voice of the mother who he imitates, identifies with, and then gradually perceives as separate from his own emerging, sound-producing self (1976; 1985). This work has been elaborated upon by Kaja Silverman in her study on voice in cinema (1988), in David Schwarz's studies of music (1997; 2006), and in Guy Rosolato's studies (1974), among others. Bearing some similarity to the sonorous envelope is Kristeva's (1984) concept of the *chora* (an unlocatable structure and space of unity with the mother); like Guy Rosolato's "sonorous womb, a murmuring house" (1974, p. 81), Kristeva's chora is a site of musicality. It is where she locates what she terms our semiotic disposition—the drives, affects, and other energies—which are discharged into language in the form of an excess that we hear in such translinguistic aspects as alliteration, intonation and other not-quite-verbal elements of communication that give our words a singular, bodily and emotional charge, which in turn, produce our creativity and uniqueness.

Through these diverse concepts, scholars emphasize the importance of sound and voice in the constitution of the subject and in the relationship of a subject to language, others and the larger social context, as sound is used to both join and separate. Psychoanalyst Alexander Stein expresses the shared view that:

> A study of the consilience between music and mental functioning offers unrivaled access to the prerepresentational, preverbal, and nonlinguistic derivatives and elaborations of archaic experiences, primitive fantasies, and primary process affects and impulses. In this view, music gives auditory tangibility to the incipient music of early life. (2007, p. 60)

Within these shared interests in music and psychic life, psychoanalysts have studied diverse musical pieces and particular composers' lives for their psychic meanings. They have explored compositions ranging from Leonard Bernstein's show tunes (Nagel) to youth music (jan jagodzinski), from classical music to the Beatles (David Schwarz), and opera (Zizek & Dolar, 2002; Nagel). Respectively, they have read music as it conveys psychic polyphony; youth fantasies, hysteria, and perversion; abjection, horror, and fantasies of the sonorous envelope; universally felt affect; mental conflict, shame and guilt. Similarly, studies of the psychic lives of composers have also revealed the connections between affect and sound, with perhaps the earliest psycho-biographical study coming from Herbert Graf, a musicologist who was a member of Freud's Wednesday Society (and father of "Little Hans"). Graf (1951) wrote about several psychic aspects of Wagner's creative process and then went on to examine psychoanalytical themes in the work of Beethoven and Mozart as well. More recently, psychoanalyst Stuart Feder studied the deep emotional links between composer Charles Ives and his father as they affected his music (*The Life of Charles Ives*, 1999) as well as the affective dissonances in Gustav Mahler's family and marital relationships which similarly left traces in his work (*Gustav Mahler: A Life in Crisis*, 2004). Emphasizing music's potential to contain/represent affect, Feder quotes Mahler as saying, "My whole life is contained in my first two symphonies. . . . To anyone who knows how to listen, my whole life will become clear" (p. 7).

What Mahler alludes to is the capacity of music to carry affect and experience. The musicality of our discourse, the importance of the non- or trans verbal sounds in what is said during the analytic process, has been emphatically underlined by analysts from most if not all theoretical persuasions, and indeed, makes up a significant part of good listening. Often a patient cannot articulate an emotion in words, and the trans verbal is what will offer more meaning to the analyst.

> Just as often, there are no such linguistic indicators; only silence, wordless metaphors, sounds, somatizations, symptoms, kinetic and sonoric gestures or enactments, primary and primitive affective utterances. I believe such moments present the analyst with a symbolic sound world that is, in its own terms, music. (Stein, 2007, p. 61)

It is Nagel, perhaps, who has most directly called for an examination of music as psychoanalytic data (2007, 2013). She has argued that music, like dreams, has both specific and over-determined meanings, and is equally capable of representing psychic affect, which permits music to function as a "point of entry to affect and the unconscious" (2008, p. 508). Furthermore, she finds that music's formal elements embody psychic conflicts since music can include and convey "tension/release, tempo/rhythm, silence, ambiguity, and multiple function," as well as "elaborations, dissonances, paradoxes, disruptions" (pp. 518–519). "As such, these sonic signifiers have the capacity to evoke latent fantasies, screen memories, and bodily memories, which in turn have the potential to link psychic past with present, affect with idea, feeling with meaning," accomplishing something uncannily similar to what psychoanalysis attempts to do (p. 520).

Referring to sound, music, and the musicality of our discourse, Stein affirms that "One of the accomplishments of psychoanalysis has been to rescue a host of meanings from the aural meaninglessness of everyday noises and to redefine these noises as unconscious signs" (Stein, p. 79). Combined with earlier work that brought out the role of music and sound in the establishment of subjectivity and relationship of the subject to others and the external world, it is clear that music is anything but an aesthetic aside in our lives.

For those with musical preparation, there is no shortage of material to analyze, but for those of us who are not musicians, clear and unsurpassable methodological difficulties arise. Without being skilled readers of musical notation and/or without a trained ear, our analyses tend toward to the metaphorical or theoretical, which undoubtedly leaves certain types or aspects of musical data unanalyzed. Notwithstanding, because musicality is not strictly limited to the formal characteristics of music per se, there is room to think about the role of music in our relationships of self and other in both individual and broader cultural context. Julia Kristeva herself claims not to have any musical talent, although she has always been surrounded by it, mentioning her father who sang at the church in her native Bulgaria, her sister who plays the cello, and both her husband ("the most musical person I know") and son who "has a perfect ear" (2011, p. 299). Yet despite her self-positioning at the margins of musical talent or performance, her work highlights a unique link between music and a larger sensory crisis, which stems from her central interest in the contemporary society of the spectacle as posited by Guy Debord (1968/1994). The rest of this essay will draw out these links to show how music can renovate the alienated subject and facilitate a reconnection with both self and other.

KRISTEVA'S SENSORY CRISIS AND MUSICAL CURE

Without labeling it directly as such, Kristeva follows Debord's work on the spectacle to posit a sensory crisis. In 1967, Debord advanced the idea that modern life had become a spectacle, a situation that critics agree has only deepened as the spectacle went virtual, and mass media exploded in seemingly infinite directions. Debord contends that society values representations more than the real things being signified. Images represent other images which represent still other images, and what is bodily, physical, or phenomenological, becomes alienated. He finds that the images and representations now mediate social relationships between contemporary subjects. As a result, the quality of life declines, and people lose the ability to think creatively as images step in to do this work for them. Our creative potential, which enables us to respond, imagine alternatives, question, or protest, thus finds itself at risk.

Kristeva elaborates upon Debord's work to map the devastating psychic effects of the spectacle. Indeed, she posits this as the fundamental cause of contemporary discontent, arguing that mass-produced imagery, TV slogans, and the constant information overflow takes away our capacity to think and feel. This bombardment anesthetizes to the point where the contemporary subject becomes disconnected from his senses, affects, and lived bodily experiences, adrift in a "cascade of false images" (1987, p. 373). In Kristevan terms, his semiotic disposition, that part of both language and the subject, which includes the drives, affect, musicality and other playful aspects, is no longer accessible to him, as the spectacle society closes off all sites into which these elements used to be discharged. In short, he is left "senseless."

Like Narcissus, the contemporary subject is stuck staring into a void filled only by idealized images he can neither be nor possess, lacking the ability to look away and move toward language, questioning, and others.

Alongside their human counterparts, cities too find themselves adrift in a spectacle of images. Kristeva makes several key references to cities' crises, noting that the contemporary city is one of "skyscrapers only reflecting emptiness" (1998, p. 15), of pure superficiality and meaningless images. Aggravating this is the fact that small and large cities face increasing pressures to brand themselves to attract tourists, businesses or Richard Florida's (2002) "creative class," thus heightening the risk of becoming transformed into images versus sensing, emotional, corporal and singular entities. Cities who brand and slogan themselves to meet tourist or other desires find themselves not only creating a particular sort of discourse about themselves, but also forging a city body that supports this discourse with very particular soundscapes, tastescapes, smellscapes and so on that are not connected to their original bodily realities and histories.

In particular, cities that are designated as UNESCO patrimony sites, which tend to go hand in hand with tourism-based economic interests, receive considerable amounts of funding attached to preserving and refortifying an established set of signifiers. Therefore, if Kristeva finds that the contemporary subject is a "patrimonial person," someone who thinks of his own body and organs as commodities and someone who is "barely free enough to use a remote control to choose his channel" (2002, p. 4), patrimonial *cities,* like the UNESCO-protected Guanajuato in the example I will use shortly, might find themselves in much the same quandary. Awash in tourist imagery that extends into the sonic, gastronomic, and other sensory realms, the city can lose not only its ability to respond, but its very "sense of self" as local discourse becomes increasingly disconnected from a city's sensory, emotional, and physical history and as the local body becomes a commodity for tourist consumption.

What is the remedy, then, for this sensory crisis in which humans and cities find themselves immersed? The alternative to the "robotizing and spectacular society," writes Kristeva, "is, quite simply, sensory intimacy," and she calls for nothing less than the "rehabilitation of the sensory" (2002, p. 5). Because so much of her work has focused on pre-Oedipal processes and the maternal, it is not surprising that she comments:

> The emphasis placed on language as the organizer of psychic life, though judicious, has too often prevented us from fully appreciating the sensory (pre-linguistic or trans linguistic) experience. (2000a, p. 99)

In order to rehabilitate our depleted sensory capacities and revitalize the imagination, which is what is needed to respond to the spectacle, Kristeva calls for a return to the chora, a return to the sensory, musical, poetic and drive-based energies. It is within this call that she emphasizes the importance of sound:

> As for the image making up this "imagination," it should not be conceived as simply visual but as a representation activating various facilitations corresponding to the entire gamut of perceptions, especially the *sonorous* ones; this because of their precocious appearance in the domain of neuropsychological maturation, but also because of their dominant function in speech. (1987, p. 40)

In keeping with her call to pay particular attention to sonority, Kristeva makes myriad references to ears, listening, and musicality in her different essays and books. In the introduction to *Tales of Love*, she processes her own thoughts in her "inner ear" (1987, p. 3), and in *Strangers to Ourselves*, she reminds us that "The ear is receptive to conflicts only if the body loses its footing" (1991, p. 17). In *Stabat Mater*, she writes of the Virgin Mary whose "sexed body" was replaced "with the ear of understanding" (1987, p. 257), which then underlines her attempts to bring back the sexed body to the existing discourse about maternity. And in *Possessions*, she cries, "There's nothing to see! Open your ears instead, if they're not too sensitive" (1998, p. 8). The ear is thus many things—a way to reach others, a patriarchal reduction of the sexual feminine to the asexual maternal, and a symbol of opening up to the interruptions the other may provoke.

Kristeva also speaks frequently of the musicality of language and, specifically, of one's accent in a foreign language. She points to the sonority of Bulgarian, her native language, describing its semiotic presence beneath her own second language of French as: "a surge that is not made up of words but has a music all its own [and which] imposes an awkward syntax on me..." (2000b, p. 167). She remarks upon a "maternal memory" filled with Gregorian music, "jolts of an early music coiled around a memory that is still vigilant" (p. 167). She also acknowledges the dissonance of one's foreign accent, which disturbs the dominant language's symbolic order (1991). Once again, sound binds us to others only to interrupt and separate us again, which makes being bilingual "a matter of sonority" and "monstrous intimacy" (2002, p. 252).

Consistently, the characters in her novels are avid music fans. Septicus, in *The Old Man and the Wolves*, listens to Billy Holliday, and sings with protagonist Stephanie's father: "They were celebrating the marriage of discourse and music—their osmosis, the limits beyond which they are no longer separate" (p. 152). In *Possessions* and *Murder in Byzantium*, Stephanie and Detective Rilsky listen to classical music: separately and more often together, they listen to Vivaldi, to violinist Yehudi Menuhin, Scott Ross's "Scarlatti," and Bach's "Concerto for Two Violins and Orchestra." And Rilsky, as a detective, is referred to as a "connoisseur of both music and nausea," (1998, p. 74), a "music lover" (p. 107) "with a typical music-lover's voice" (p. 14), a "violin-playing captain" (p. 209) who tears up at concerts (p. 74), whose father had conducted the philharmonic in another city and whose mother was a piano teacher. In *Murder in Byzantium*, Rilsky's family history with music is elaborated upon, and in his feelings for Stephanie, "love is more a kind of music than a bond" (p. 52). Anna Comnena is educated in music, Xiao Chang protects himself behind a Walkman and calls Bach a "purifier" (p. 207), Sebastian Chrest-Jones cannot bear a Pergolesi variation of the "Salve Regina" at Le Puy, and Jerry's way of being is likened to music (p. 237) as well. Almost all of the characters have some relationship with music.

Clearly, we can track a certain musical motif through Kristeva's work. Yet, despite her aural leanings and a particularly provocative invitation to listen to music in her essay "Stabat Mater" (1987), Kristeva does *not* explicitly detail how a sensory/musical response to the spectacle might play out. Her musical allusions tend to remain in the background of the texts. The rest of this essay will show how the city of Guanajuato mobilizes aurality in conjunction with the other senses in order to reclaim both psychic and physical space within the context of a local festival that has become increasingly other to the city, refortifying the connection with self and other at once.

GUANAJUATO: THE EAR-SHAPED CITY WITH A NOISY FESTIVAL

Guanajuato is a small provincial city of about 160,000 located in central Mexico. Along with the rest of *provincia*, it tends to be characterized as change-averse, traditional, and reserved, sometimes held up as a bucolic and nostalgic paradise, sometimes disparaged as close-minded and resistant to change. The city's topography, however, differentiates it from other sites: the city rests in a bowl-like hollow between mountains, but the inside of the bowl, the terrain is fabulously dented and twisted. It is not far-fetched to see the concave city as ear-like because it follows the same soft and errant lines of the human ear, and because sound also ripples around these contours at multiple levels (Rodríguez, 2010). Underneath the crinkly surface are layers of equally twisting tunnels, a first level for the cars and pedestrians, and a deeper level of mining tunnels that link the silver mines up beyond the northern end of the city all the way down to its southern extremes. These dark channels are flooded with an array of eerie sounds.

Shaped like an ear, this concave city overflows with myriad others as tourists pour in at different points of the year. As a UNESCO patrimony site, Guanajuato receives tourist influx all year, thanks to the draw of the tunnels, the silver mines, its bizarre mummy museum, and the well-preserved baroque and churrigueresque architecture from the 16th to 18th centuries. But the peak tourist moment occurs in October, which marks the annual Cervantino Festival, or "FIC," its Spanish acronym. The FIC is an arts festival that lasts between three to four weeks and represents important cultural capital, bringing in domestic and foreign tourists in large numbers: typically, up to 90,000 extra people on weekends. The FIC began in the 1960s when a university theater group began to perform Miguel de Cervantes Saavedra's short plays (*entremeses*) in the small public plaza of San Roque. These were local events, obviously enacted in Spanish. In 1972, other performances were added to create the festival and to attract not only domestic but also international tourists. Now the festival's "best" (most prestigious) performances tend to be indoors and/or in ticket-accessed areas; and the shows are often performed in foreign languages, flaunting exotic instruments and costumes as different countries from around the world are featured each year.

While the city's public spaces are still used for impromptu street performances, the locales of the intimate/everyday city are increasingly disconnected from the higher-class festival events. Tourist brochures and posters advertising the FIC pay little attention to these sites, and about a decade ago, there was a concerted effort to clean up and regulate the festival's informal elements, which had eased into what was perceived as a scandalous level of public debauchery (festival goers at the lower economic end were drinking, vomiting, urinating, and sleeping in the public spaces during these three weeks). As a result of the cleanup, popular sites find few openings in the festival's symbolic into which their singular experiences, affects, desires, and anxieties can be discharged. Oddly, and in keeping with Kristeva's understandings of the effects of the spectacle, the festival has come to signify the city, but these most crucial popular sites where city life still unfolds have been relegated to the role of passive observers. The "city-popular"—those areas and aspects of the city not involved in the cultural and economic benefits of the festival—provides us with an example of the numbed, alienated subject observing the spectacle without any opportunity to participate or question.

In October 2010, however, one performance interrupted this aural-slash-spatial separation of the popular and elite. The opera came to the main market. Created by local-born César Piña, a stage director now living in Mexico City and performing around the world, the Opéra en el Mercado Hidalgo intervened into the festival's "usual" way of using space.

THE OPERA IN MEXICO AND GUANAJUATO

Opera, while European in origin, is hardly new to Mexico. Leonora Saavedra comments on the "predominance of opera in Mexico's musical history in the 19th century" (2007, p. 2). She notes that:

Of all the colonizations and invasions of Mexican culture and territory by foreign powers, the one performed by Italian opera has been the gentlest. Audiences loved Italian opera from the beginning of Mexico's independent life, and composers followed suit. Operatic troupes were hosted in all manner of venues, the productions were enjoyed regardless of their quality, and, for those who could not attend a performance, the many wind and military bands performed overtures, marchers, and instrumental medleys of well-loved operatic arias every Sunday on the kiosk of the central plaza. (2007, p. 18)

Despite this initial popularity, Saavedra notes that formal opera as such has always remained foreign; efforts mid century and since to launch a Mexican opera with nationalistic themes and domestic musical elements have been somewhat erratic with limited success. Furthermore, opera continues to be considered to be the purview of the upper class. Nancy Vogeley (1995), in a study of opera's role in 19th century Mexico, argues that the new nation used opera performances to affirm its status as a sophisticated society, thus joining with Europe, while also preferring performances in Italian over Spanish, which underlined Mexico's definitive separation from Spain. Once again, music was used to assert a sense of national identity both related to and separate from other aural subjects.

In the case of the city of Guanajuato, opera's most notable early performance occurred at the inauguration of the opulent Teatro Juárez on October 27, 1903. The Italian company Empresa Ettore Drog y Cía, directed by Georgio Polaco and Napoleón Sieni, was brought in to perform Guiseppe Verdi's *Aida* to an elite public drawn from the local and Mexico City bourgeoisie, including the then-dictator, Porfirio Díaz himself. The Ethiopian setting of the opera's narrative, the Italian company that performed it, the aristocratic desires of the invited public, and the classic style of the theater, all reinforced the outsider/exotic nature of the opera. However, in the decades that followed over the course of the 20th century, opera did not evolve into a commonplace event, and needless to say, the market was never considered as a venue for an opera performance.

THE OPERA COMES TO THE MARKET

The physical distance between the city's Teatro Juárez and its main market, the Mercado Hidalgo, is only about five blocks. Unlike the extravagant theater, however, the Mercado Hidalgo (hereafter, the Market) constitutes one of the city's most intimate, interior, and domestic of spaces. It boasts a unique tube-like shape and an elaborate, French-influenced exterior; the inside shows exposed scaffolding and is hollow and cavernous. It is an everyday site through which flow, as one historian observes, not only crowds of shoppers and sellers, but also tradition, culture, identity, and life (Villalobos, Castillo, & Moye, 2010, p. 11).

While people from any class can and do buy produce at the Market, it is, nonetheless, a highly popular site with its own recognized subculture. It is associated with several key families, and it has its own adolescent "queen of the market" chosen each year. Yet, unlike the queens of university departments or service organizations, the market queen is taken to represent the popular class, and indeed the average educational level of market vendors tends to primary and secondary schooling only (although this is rapidly changing). As the local newspaper occasionally reports, the food that is presented at its open stands is of questionable hygienic quality, although that does not deter residents of many class levels from appreciating the flavorful snacks and meals sold there. Overall, the atmosphere is one of sensory chaos across the five senses. Pirated CDs blare from all four corners, ranging from traditional *mariachi*, to popular *grupera*, to the *punchis punchis* beat of dance music. The smells include both the raw and the cooked, the served and the discarded, the sweet and the spicy. One can see (and smell) hanging cow carcasses at the butcher stalls and a cornucopia of colorful fruits and vegetables, intermingled with sweat, perfume, soap, and soup. There is a prominent image of the Virgin Mary on the staircase to the balcony level who protects the market vendors, shoppers, and tourists alike.

One would think that amidst the sensory cacophony of the Market, something as foreign as opera music would be unfathomable. The market is *not* the "city of romance" or "city of legend" promised in the city's formal tourist brochures and slogans. Indeed, the Market's role in the FIC is practically nil, with the only sign of tourism being the sale of T-shirts and cheap trinkets on the wraparound second floor balcony that looks over the main floor. Confronted with the aural other of such a distant musical genre as opera, one might have expected the market to retreat into its own noisy and narcissistic "sound bath" of self, to use Didier Anzieu's term, to block out this external source of dissonance. One might also have expected the market to make more noise to form what Esther Bick (1968) labels a defensive "second skin" of sound, to contain the self and keep out the opera all together. Yet this popular city site did not close itself off, nor was it thrown into abjection and shattered by this internal yet foreign sound that came out from its very core; nor was the market colonized by the foreign aurality. Rather, the Market fell in love, thanks to a sense-based response attuned to its own singularity.

The opera performance was launched amidst full weekend bustle. Against a backdrop of nonstop blenders, the hammering sound of beef and pork being pounded into thin steaks, and the din of shoppers and breakfasters interacting with the vendors, an apron-clad opera singer emerged from "Mariscos Pancho" (a seafood stand) and began to sing Rossini's

Barber of Seville. A full 45 minutes of arias ensued, including music by Verdi, Puccini, Bizet, and Donizetti.

What occurred in the aural and general sensory encounter that resulted was rather astounding. First, both singers and Market vendors and goers recovered an unexpected sense of play. While several stands had been wired for speakers, the singers, who were from Mexico City, had to improvise as other stands joined in spontaneously. As the stage director noted in a later interview, the whole performance became a game as no one knew exactly what might occur or how the attendees, equally surprised by the music, might respond. The Market also played along as well from its own sound base—the pounding of the meat, the whir of the blenders. At one point, a little girl got up on a stand and pretended to direct part of *La Bohème.* And at the end of the performance, the singers began handing out fruit and flowers, transformed into pretend vendors, both of music and goods.

What one could observe happening was the city-popular—the Market— meeting the opera from a place situated in its own singularity. As the market goers listened to the opera arias, they were eating *tacos de carnitas* in *salsa borracha,* and they were shopping for avocado, mango and chile. And when local spectators spontaneously began toasting the singers at the end, they raised clay cups filled with *rompope,* a local eggnog-ish alcohol. This can be compared with the opera as it was performed earlier in a market in La Valenciana, Spain, in which the reaction was completely distinct: the crowd was clearly familiar with opera, often singing along, opening up the space and ceasing their usual activities, and enacting a final toast with wine (http://www.youtube.com/watch?v=Ds8ryWd5aFw). The Market in Guanajuato clearly responded on its own sensory terms, from its own sensory self.

What emerged was a tremendous two-way discharge of the sensory and the affective (the city's semiotic) into public space, interrupting normal FIC discourse. It showed that despite what people thought, the FIC could include the popular sector and popular spaces, without compromising the festival's commitment to bring in international content. The singers interviewed after said that they finished emotionally overwhelmed, spent, beyond what a normal performance would have exacted from them. Here we see (or hear) the jouissance of excess: in the televised interview, the stage director of the opera César Piña stated that what he witnessed was a "complete emotion," which seems to signify for him this polyvalent, orgasmic coming together of the city and the festival. Indeed, there were intense emotions and a palpable "vibration" running through the market, as the director noted (Fuentes, Oct.–Nov., 2011).

Grounded into their senses and situated in their own space, the Market vendors and patrons opened up their ears to something new and took a risk. For Kristeva, the assumption of risk is the willingness to still question and revolt, and rather uncannily, director Piña used the word "risk" as well:

for the Market, he said, listening to opera risked exposing oneself to boredom (the stereotype that opera is boring) and therefore demanded giving oneself up to the unknown. But by engaging in this risky listening, the popular city site took back authority and authorship. It transgressed by discharging its own sounds, textures, smells, and tastes into the spectacle. At the end of the performance, hand-painted signs were raised in the crowd, and they asked, in the particular vernacular of the market inhabitants, "*¿No que no te gustaba la* ópera?" "*Cómo que no, la* ópera *es la* ópera." (Didn't you say you didn't like the opera? Of course not, opera is opera.)

If the depressed subject is one for whom language and the system are dead, the empty language of the tourism brochures and FIC promotion similarly tends to foreclose any participation by the city-popular. However, the opera-in-the-market allowed the popular side of the city to discharge its senses and to sublimate its feelings, a process that Kristeva notes "weaves a hypersign around and with the depressive void" (1987, p. 99). In other words, the symbolic system of this heavily external arts festival was opened up to new questions and new participation. And the empty nothingness of FIC discourse was transformed, made meaningful and even beautiful.

Within this beauty, one can say that the Market fell in love with the opera. The subject in love, Kristeva writes, is paradoxically possessed by the other and at the "zenith of subjectivity" at once (1987, p. 5). As another scholar puts it, "While two in love remain two, one in love does not remain one but becomes many in truly polymorphic, 'perverse' fashion" (Schultz, 1994, p. 194.) Two polyphonic subjects encountered each other from a heterogenic stance based on their intimate singularities: one of musical complexity (a range of arias from different composers) and the other of sensory abundance. Their encounter is one of aurality, love, and imagination, each of which, in its own way, constitutes a transference and a return to a moment of play and openness. The performance allowed for the reorganization of emotions as listeners and performers integrated the competing "sonic signifiers" at hand with their memories, lived sensory and bodily experiences, and emotions (Nagel, 2008; 2010). These flights of imagination and feelings of love similarly transferred meanings to sites where there was none. The multiple displacements experienced here produced what Kristeva labels as "tiny revolts," a jouissance "that proves indispensable to keeping the psyche alive, indispensable to the faculty of representation and questioning that specifies the human being" (2002, p. 7).

The opera allowed the city to create an aural narrative that connected festival, the sensing body and affect, a process that in turn let this popular site forgive and sublimate the trauma of having been "displaced," in the negative spatial sense, from the FIC. This resulted in nothing short of a rebirth. By connecting with its sensory, intimate, and singular nature, the city-popular thus rescued and recuperated both psychic and public space, which is the very definition of Kristevan transgression. And en route, this aspect of the city achieved the sensory rehabilitation that Kristeva finds so urgent. The Market found its own voice and response with which to carve out spaces of freedom within an experience created from without, thus simultaneously re-igniting its own sensory singularity while symbolizing with and for others.

MUSIC, SUBLIMATION, AND CONNECTION

Kristeva places music at the core of our psychic makeup along with the affects and drives in the not-locatable site of the chora. To access these elements is to access one's own heterogeneous nature, one's maternal origins, those parts of us we can know, and those we cannot. This psychic material can then be fruitfully displaced/transferred/represented for another within the larger symbolic world, which allows the subject to both join and interrupt the world at once, resisting the spectacle that would make subjects into passive observers or passive listeners.

In an essay entitled "The Impudence of Uttering," Kristeva argues that language is a sublimatory process that occurs as the infant transforms his needs and desires for unity with the mother into words, which produce or carry this semiotic excess into the world of others. In later life, playing, making art, writing literature, and crafting other creative projects also constitute sublimatory acts, which move the drives and affects into a symbolic form; however, for Kristeva, music is the highest form of sublimation:

> At the extreme of this sublimatory desire of forms lies, of course, music. In a Mozart opera or in a Bach fugue, the "object" is the musical language itself. This language is essentially a parallel world, independent of amorous intrigues, even of the divine exaltation that it celebrates. Would music as an "artificial paradise," a paroxysmal working through of the drive in pure *jouissance* and with no other aim but its own construction, be therefore the supreme "impudence of uttering?" (2010, p. 683)

By impudence, she is referring to the semiotic, which interrupts the spectacle society, and she argues that music can do or be just this. Furthermore, and more personally, in *Hatred and Forgiveness*, Kristeva says:

> As for me, when I listen to music, or when I think I am integrating it into my thought, my writing, I see a perpetual framing of vital excitation: breathing, the beating of the heart, the pulse of sexual pleasure....Sound that is thought...composed by the human voice or an instrument— seems to me the ultimate sublimation of the sexual relationship, its absolute transposition into human history as well as into the inhuman flesh of the world. (2011, p. 300)

She concludes: "I see music as a sublimated vital sharing, in modest and the greatest detachment" (p. 300). This is the basic argument she sustains throughout her oeuvre and brings out most clearly in this recent work. In the search to maintain subjectivity when confronted with (aural or other) others who challenge us, whether by provoking love or hatred, the subject must find a way to be together with difference. Sublimatory processes permit the subject to release his amorous or passionate desires to possess, control and contain. By naming desire (by bringing the affects and drives into symbolic form), the subject detaches and shares at once. For Kristeva, this is essential psychic work which permits the subject to maintain relationships with others.

> Our access to what other people experience, whether they're men or women, living or dead, is bound to be fragmentary, limited to the vestiges they leave behind in colors, sounds, or words. We can't apprehend them unless we're lucky enough to be able to forget our own preoccupations, large or small, and to touch not another body, nor even another name hiding in—or outside ourselves, but a vibration that's usually unattainable [author's emphasis] and that no personal pronoun can convey. (1998, p. 35)

As the opera director noted, these "vibrations" were palpable in the staging of the opera in the Market, and both performers and spectators underwent this emotional, transverbal experience. What this seems to suggest is that music serves as a between space; like the semiotic musical presence of an accent or original syntax in a second language, or like a person in flight between two countries, music provides a between space between self and other where things can be reopened and renegotiated without losing oneself or forcing the other to assimilate. As Stephanie Delacour, a recurring protagonist in Kristeva's novels, muses in the company of Detective Rilsky, her colleague and lover, "We were both in shock, and thus together, but differently, 'at home'" (p. 34). The Market and the opera were probably also in a good bit of shock caused by their respective aural differences, but they found a way to be temporarily "at home" within their difference as they listened together. Referring again to Rilsky, Stephanie observes, "Music contained the only beauty he believed in, and then only if it could be shared. 'Music ought to be listened together,' he always told me" (1998, p. 12). The case of the Market and the opera would seem to support this.

In an article on the experience of opera, Scott Pratt cites John Dewey's statement that occasionally, "the organism falls out of step with the march of surrounding things and then recovers unison with it—either through effort or by some happy chance" (2009, p. 80). In this example, the popular-city had fallen out of step with the dominant aspects of the city and the many aural others coming into town. Music provided an unexpected way to recover a sense of connection between self, other, and context. This would probably not surprise Julia Kristeva, who has asserted that, "Sense takes root in the sensory" (2004, p. 422). To think creatively, to imagine, and to question depends upon this connection between language and the sensory or bodily. As cities are pressured to brand themselves by making over their sensing, bodied selves in response to tourist and other capitalist spectacle desires, I believe that sensory texts—pieces of music, types of foods, smells and tactical experiences—will be at the heart of the struggle over urban subjectivity processes. Kristeva's work leads us to recognize that music has a particular power to induce an affective encounter with others in a polyphonic, "safe space." As Guanajuato plans new public operas for subsequent FIC celebrations, one suspects that music will continue to offer these unexpected routes to psychic and spatial regeneration.

ACKNOWLEDGMENT

The author would like to acknowledge the late Professor Hernán Ferro of the Universidad de Guanajuato for his kind assistance in obtaining recorded interviews with César Piña and Rodopi Press as this paper expands upon the opera example used in my book (2012).

REFERENCES

Anzieu, D. (1976). L'Enveloppe du soi. *Nouvelle revue de psychoanalyze, 13*, 161–179.

Anzieu, D. (1985). *Le moi-peau.* Paris: Dunod

Bick, E. (1968). The experience of the skin in early object relations. *International Journal of Psycho-Analysis, 49*, 484–486.

Debord, G. (1968/1994). *Society of the spectacle.* New York, NY: Zone Books.

Feder, S. (1999). *The life of Charles Ives.* Cambridge, England: Cambridge University Press.

Feder, S. (2004). *Gustav Mahler: A life in crisis.* New Haven, CT: Yale University Press.

Florida, R. L. (2002). *The rise of the creative class: And how it's transforming work leisure, community and everyday life.* Cambridge, England: Cambridge University Press.

Fuentes, G. (Oct.–Nov. 2011). Televised interview. *Voz ciudadana.* Guanajuato, Mexico.

Graf, H. (1951). *Opera for the people.* Minneapolis: University of Minnesota Press.

Kahr, B. (2007). Musings of a musicophiliac. *American Imago, 64*(1), 95–107.

Kristeva, J. (1984). *Revolution in poetic language.* (M. Waller, Trans.). New York, NY: Columbia University Press.

Kristeva, J. (1987). *Tales of love.* (L. Roudiez, Trans.). New York, NY: Columbia University Press.

Kristeva, J. (1991). *Strangers to ourselves.* (L. Roudiez, Trans.). New York, NY: Columbia University Press.

Kristeva, J. (1998). *Possessions: A novel.* (B. Bray, Trans.). New York, NY: Columbia University Press.

Kristeva, J. (2000a). *The sense and non-sense of revolt: The powers and limits of psychoanalysis* (J. Herman, Trans.). New York, NY: Columbia University Press.

Kristeva, J. (2000b). *Bulgaria, my suffering: Crisis of the European subject.* (S. Fairfield, Trans.). New York, NY: The Other Press.

Kristeva, J. (2002). *Intimate revolt.* (J. Herman, Trans.). New York, NY: Columbia University Press.

Kristeva, J. (2004). *Colette.* (J. M.Todd, Trans.). New York, NY: Columbia University Press.

Kristeva, J. (2010). The impudence of uttering. (P. Vieira & M. Marder, Trans.) *Psychoanalytic Review, 97,* 679–694.

Kristeva, J. (2011). *Hatred and forgiveness.* (J. Herman, Trans.). New York, NY: Columbia University Press.

Nagel, J. J. (2007). Melodies of the mind: Mozart in 1778. *American Imago, 64*(1), 23–36.

Nagel, J.J. (2008). Psychoanalytic perspectives on music: An intersection on the oral and aural road. *Psychoanalytic Quarterly, 77*(2), 507–529.

Nagel, J. J. (2010). Psychoanalytic and musical ambiguity: The tritone in "Gee, Office Krupke." *Journal of the American Psychoanalytic Association, 58*(1), 9–25.

Nagel, J. J. (2013), *Melodies of the mind: Connections between psychoanalysis and music.* New York, NY: Routledge.

Pratt, S. (2009). Opera as experience. *Journal of Aesthetic Education, 43,* 74–87.

Rodríguez, K. (2012). *Small city on a big couch.* Amsterdam, the Netherlands: Rodopi.

Rodríguez, K. (2010). Audiotopia: La ciudad provinciana como oreja. *Delaware Review of Latin American Studies, 11*(1).

Rosolato, G. (1974). La voix: Entre corps et langage. *Revue française de psychoanalyse, 37,* 75–94.

Saavedra, L. (2007). Staging the nation: Race, religion, and history in Mexican opera of the 1940s. *The Opera Quarterly, 23,* 1–21.

Schultz, K. (1994). In defense of Narcissus: Lou Andreas-Salomé and Julia Kristeva. *The German Quarterly, 67,* 185–196.

Schwarz, D. (1997). *Listening subjects: Music psychoanalysis, culture.* Durham, NC: Duke University Press.

Silverman, K. (1988). *The acoustic mirror: The female voice in psychoanalysis and cinema.* Bloomington: Indiana University Press.

Stein, A. (2007). Sound of memory: Music and acoustic origins. *American Imago, 64,* 59–85.

Villalobos, L., Castillo, O., & Moye, A. C. (2010). *Market Hidalgo: Un momento centenario.* Guanajuato, Mexico: Ediciones La Rana.

Vogeley, N. (1995). Turks and Indians: Orientalist discourse in postcolonial Mexico. *Diacritics, 25,* 2–20 (Latin American issue).

Zizek, S., & Dolar, M. (2002). *Opera's second death.* New York, NY: Routledge.

CHAPTER 5

THE MUSICALIZATION
OF "REALITY"

Reality, Rap, and Rap Reality
on Public Enemy's *Fear of a Black Planet*

Anne Danielsen

The "mainstreaming" of rap music has given Black music culture more global visibility than ever before. As Bakari Kitwana, former editor of *The Source*, points out, we do not yet know the consequences of the acceptance of hip-hop as mainstream popular culture, or how this may have "altered the racial landscape" (Kitwana, 2005, p. 12). Even though rap's popularity to some extent has been achieved through confirming a primitivist representation of African American culture, this ongoing process has led to what Cornel West more than 10 years ago described as an "Afro-Americanization of white youth" (West, 1994, p. 127).

An interesting part of this process is the genre "reality rap," which earned its name from its attempts to portray the soundscapes and difficult sociopolitical realities of North American inner cities. Reality rap's prehistory is located in the early 1980s, when several artists addressed the problems

Cultural Psychology of Musical Experience, pages 89–105
Copyright © 2016 by Information Age Publishing
89

and issues linked to unemployment, poverty, the underground economy, and drug abuse in inner-city communities. Grandmaster Flash and the Furious Five were among the first to introduce such social statement into rap through their song "The Message" (1982), which commented on New York City's deteriorating conditions. The genre peaked with the commercial breakthrough of groups like Public Enemy and Niggas With Attitude (NWA) at the end of the 1980s, then declined with the larger shift to the more stripped-down, minimalistic sound of gangsta rap.

Reality rap brought about a representation of the situation in inner-city communities that has become inextricably linked with rap as a genre. The aim of the present article is to get a better understanding of the processes at work in this two-way exchange between music and reality in reality rap through an investigation of Public Enemy's music. My analytical focus is on *Fear of a Black Planet* (Public Enemy, 1990). I have chosen this album both because it is an outstanding example of their sonic output at the time and because my topic requires an in-depth reading of one album rather than a survey of several. A starting point was the experience that the political and musical dimensions of Public Enemy's work intertwine to an extreme degree; it is almost impossible, in fact, to say where the one ends and the other begins. As a consequence, their songs appear to actually report on reality—their music does not present itself as a separate musical world in which events unfold according to abstract musical rules, but is rather perceived as relating to and dealing with life outside of music. In the following, I will discuss some features of this process, focusing on how their music manages to produce "reality effects" as well as on its documentary aspects in relation to "real life," the latter of which recalls the relationship between image and reality in documentary film.

The reality effects and documentary aspects of Public Enemy's music are part of a larger picture of how identity formation in hip-hop in general is strongly linked to place. In his book *The 'Hood Comes First: Race, Space and Place in Rap and Hip-Hop* (2002), Murray Forman links the importance of dimensions such as space and place to articulations of Blackness. According to Forman, an important aspect of the process of making spatial sites significant—of transforming space to place—is the attribution of meanings to components of the socially constructed environment. In this "reiterative process," certain practices of everyday life or otherwise subordinated details of the immediate environment are rendered explicit and in turn loaded with value (Forman, 2002, p. 28). Making sonic samples of such practices and environments part of one's music contributes to this reiterative process of meaning investment, since lifting sonic elements and details out of a pragmatic context and making them part of a musical one is in itself a way of investing symbolic value into the elements used.

I begin with a discussion of the notion of "documentary" as applied to music based on the theorizing of documentary film that has taken place within media studies in the last 10 to 15 years. I then proceed to a discussion of selected songs on the album *Fear of a Black Planet*, using different contributions from linguistics as my own theoretical point of view. I will only deal with the auditory output of Public Enemy's production. Even though I acknowledge that music videos and other related images influence how I interpret their music, my aim here is to focus on how an exchange of art and reality may be staged inside a *sonic* world. I pay specific attention to Public Enemy's use of samples from "real life" locations, their inclusion of mass media debates, and their use of sonic montage, all now trademarks of Public Enemy's production style.

THE RELATIONSHIP OF RECORDING AND REALITY

In the theory of documentary film, the relationship between image and reality is a recurring theme. As Bill Nichols points out in his 1991 book *Representing Reality*, there is a distinctive bond between a photographic image and that which it depicts: "Something of reality itself seems to pass through the lens and remain embedded in the photographic emulsion" (Nichols, 1991, p. 5). Michael Renov also stresses the documentary film's relation to a historical world. In the introduction to the anthology *Theorizing Documentary* (1993a), he states:

> At the level of the sign, it is the differing historical status of the referent that distinguishes documentary from its fictional counterpart, not the formal relations among signifier, signified, and referent. . . . Is the referent a piece of the world, drawn from the domain of lived experience, or, instead, do the people and objects placed before the camera yield to the demands of creative vision? (Renov, 1993a, p. 2)

We might also say that the image or documentary bears an *indexical* relation to the historical world (Nichols, 199, p. 27). This description relies on Charles S. Peirce's semiotic theory of three different classes of signs: icons, indexes, and symbols (Peirce, 1960). While "icon" points to a certain likeness between the sign and its referent, "index" is a sign because there is or once was a causal connection between the sign and its referent—"An *Index* is a sign which refers to the Object that it denotes by virtue of being really affected by that Object" (Peirce, 1960, p. 143). Symbols, finally, become signs by way of convention (Peirce, 1960, p. 165). For example, in the case of a word there is a rule determining the otherwise arbitrary relation between the sign—which may vary from language to language (cat, Katz, chat)—and its referent (cat). The rule determining the relation between the sign and its referent is in the case of symbols thus derived from practice and not from an initially physical connection or correspondence in features by way of similarity or analogy. An index differs from this by being a sign or representation that

> refers to its object not so much because of any similarity or analogy with it, nor because it is associated with general characters which that object happens to possess, as because it is in dynamical (including spatial) connection both with the individual object, on the one hand, and with the senses or memory of the person for whom it serves as a sign, on the other hand. (Peirce, 1960, p. 170)

This resonates with Renov's emphasis on documentary's reliance on the historical status of the referent. Documentary (the sign) is also based on a perceived connection with events or objects belonging to a historical or present world (referent) as well as on the perceiver experiencing such a relationship.

The importance of indexical signification in documentary does not mean that documentary does not involve fictional strategies, or that documentary is necessarily truer than fiction. Following Derrida, one might say that there is an irreducible difference between reality and truth. While reality simply *is*, truth has to be 'unveiled' through an act of inscription.[1] The presence of an indexical relation to reality is thus no guarantee of truth, since telling the truth, or nonfiction, in fact relies on the very structure of fiction. In keeping with Derrida, Renov holds all discursive forms—documentary included—to be, if not fictional, at least *fictive*, "this by virtue of their tropic character" (their recourse to tropes or rhetorical figures; Renov, 1993a, p. 7). Moreover, according to Renov, there is nothing inherently less creative about nonfictional representations, and both fiction and nonfiction may create a "truth" with their text. What differs between them, however, "is the extent to which the referent of the documentary sign may be considered as a piece of the world plucked from its everyday context rather than fabricated for the screen" (Renov, 1993a, p. 7). In line with this, documentary may be described as an artistic practice of plucking and recontextualizing prefilmic elements in a filmic discourse.[2] As Renov points out, such an act of plucking elements from a culturally specific context and using them within a documentary may be a kind of "violence," and the question then arises quite forcefully about the adequacy of a representational system as "a stand-in for lived experience" (I will return to this later).

Although the presence of indexical traces of the real or historical world is considerably greater in a traditional cinematic documentary, Public Enemy's style of musical production—for example, their samples from "real-life" locations or inclusion of mass-media debates—merits examination in relation to indexical signification. These nonmusical, or to borrow from Renov, "premusical," elements likewise carry with them indexical traces of a world outside music and thus act as documentary material within it.

Soundscapes made up of obviously manufactured sonic elements may also lead to a strengthening of this music's bond with reality, producing certain reality effects and thereby raising the listener's expectations about the authenticity of the representation. This in fact parallels the paradigm of realism in film. In some cases, such as the docudramas *Schindler's List* (1993) or *Sophie Scholl: The Final Days* (2005), the claim of authentic representation is essential to their viability. In his writings on historical discourse and realism in literature, Roland Barthes has argued that "the real" in such cases "is never anything but an unformulated signified, sheltered behind the omnipotence of the referent. This situation defines what we might call the 'reality effect'" (Barthes, 1986, p. 139). According to Barthes, historical discourse's extrusion of the signified outside any "objective" discourse, by way of a repeated "this happened" produces a new meaning: reality itself. Furthermore, realism in literature relies on a referential illusion. The exactitude of realism—its meticulous descriptions of things or interiors, for example—works to signify the "real," in the sense that the apparent absence of interpretational activity becomes the very signifier of realism, as if the act of attending to the meticulous descriptions defers the production of a traditional signified. (Barthes, 1986, p. 148).

Both documentary effects and reality effects—the latter in the form of "docudramatic realism," a manufactured realism that tries to represent a historical or contemporary reality authentically—may be said to be present in Public Enemy's music. However, in the age of digital reproduction the dividing line between these two modes of signification is hard to draw. Today's software makes it possible to digitally record any sound (or image) and then manipulate it in different ways: it can be filtered, stretched, inverted, morphed or combined with other recordings, and so on. This means that a documentary sound, for example a recording of voices from mass media, can be manipulated to sound inauthentic through various forms of digital signal processing. At the same time a constructed realistic soundscape may sound more authentic than a recording of a similar real soundscape. In short, there are now many new and perhaps historic technological possibilities for the manipulation, as well as blurring, of musical and nonmusical sounds.[3]

We are thus definitely beyond the era described by Nichols, among others, during which the phonographic recording (or the photographic document) could be trusted to be a reliable representation of what it was a record of. However, indexical signification has not outlived its role, and indexical traces as mediators between an artistic and a "real" world are no less important. On the contrary, our desire for the "real" seems to have only increased, in the sense that the circulation of indexical signs continues to accelerate. Hal Foster, for example, has discussed certain trends of visual art in the last 20 years as a "return of the real" (Foster, 1996, Chapter 5).

Moreover, in their book *Remediation: Understanding New Media* (1999), Bolter and Grusin describe the contradiction at play concerning the real in contemporary media, referring to "our culture's contradictory imperatives for immediacy and hypermediacy. . . . Our culture wants both to multiply its media and to erase all traces of mediation: ideally, it wants to erase its media in the very act of multiplying them" (Bolter & Grusin, 1999, p. 5). Certainly it is arguable that people maintain a desire for the real in the sense of indexical signification. Perhaps it is thus only the status of the documentary as evidence—as a real trace of an initial indexical relationship with reality— that has become more problematic (or less important). The authenticity of their relationship is now strained, to say the least. We are in an era where the possibilities for manipulating the duality of fiction and nonfiction in documentary material are richer than ever before. Or as Renov states in his introduction, following Trinh T. Minh, one of the contributors in *Theorizing Documentary*, perhaps "it is toward the 'interval' between those two terms [fiction and nonfiction] rather than to their identity or dichotomization that our fullest attention should be given" (Renov, 1993a, p. 11).

THREE WAYS OF MUSICALIZING REALITY

A striking aspect of rap music is the way fragments of other songs or sounds are recirculated and reused in a new musical context via sampling. This recirculation takes place on two levels. Firstly, the choice of samples serves musical aims, such as the need for raw material in designing a sound or a particular rhythmic event. In this respect the sound quality and feel of 1960s and 1970s soul and funk are, in Tricia Rose's words, "as important to hip hop's sound as the machines that deconstruct and reformulate them" (Rose, 1994, p. 78). On another level, the sample, musical or nonmusical, obviously has more to it than its sound as such: it includes a history and symbolic value as well. The musical era of the classic Public Enemy albums had fewer options for manipulating recorded sound; nevertheless, the sampler, combined with sequencing equipment, was central to the development of the signature multilayered sound collages of the Bomb Squad, Public Enemy's production team. One important aspect of their technique was the linking of musical recordings with certain sociopolitical realities.

Situating the Musical Event

On the album *Fear of a Black Planet* (1990), both indexical signification and reality effects are used to establish a connection to the real. In the tune "911 Is a Joke," for example, such techniques locate the music in time

and space. The eight-bar intro immediately evokes an emergency in an inner-city environment. The atmosphere is urgent: There is hectic, chaotic
engagement among several voices talking over one another. Some sort of
authority repeatedly states "There is not a minute to spare!" while another
repeats "Don't worry!" Far behind we hear the sound of a megaphone,
and running throughout is an oscillating, enervating synthetic sound with
a siren-like melodic movement.

As the rap itself starts, this act of sonic location retreats to the back of
the mix and the sound dries up. The lead rapper enters the scene, establishing a communicative focus similar to the live report of a journalist on
television. In the rap's "chorus," however, the soundscape recalls the intro.
Once again it is crammed with emergency sounds and distinct utterances
of different kinds, some shared with the intro. Yet the overall impression
of the chorus is significantly different. This is partly due to the fact that the
lead rapper remains the focus here. However, there are also important differences regarding the underlying rhythmic collage. In general, the soundscape of the chorus is less dense and chaotic; a few elements have been
removed, including the voices uttering the various "emergency statements"
and the siren-like synthetic sound. The one added element, a sample that
fills the musical role of a horn section (though it does not sound like one),
manages to tug the soundscape in the direction of musical signification. As
a consequence, the samples forming the original location, such as the buzz
of voices in the background, trade much of their original contextual function for a musical function, emerging as significant timbral and textural
aspects of the groove as a whole.

This becomes even clearer with the arrival, after the chorus, of the in-
terlude before the second verse, which returns to the location sounds of
the intro, thereby refocusing on the urgency of the inner-city environment
through the reality effects of the samples. This time, though, there is a
distinct strain of evil added to the situation in the form of sarcastic, raw
laughter. This change in atmosphere underlines the message of the rap itself: even though the emergency service was called upon a "long time ago,"
as lead rapper Chuck D. states, no help arrives: "911 is a joke in this town."

The relatively small alterations in sonic texture described above result
in the profound shift from informational to musical signification and back
again: the sign moves between a primarily pragmatic function and a primarily aesthetic one. The close relation between the pragmatic and the aesthetic functions of language, interestingly, is a recurring theme of what is called
the Prague school of linguistics, whose body of theory specifically includes
language's poetic qualities among its "normal" usages: aesthetic functions
are not isolated in a separate realm but incorporated among language's
practical, everyday purposes. Jan Mukarovsky investigates the exact relationship between pragmatic and aesthetic functions through a discussion

of what he calls poetic reference, or "every reference appearing in a text which has a dominant aesthetic function" (Mukarovsky, 1976, p. 155). According to Mukarovsky, poetic reference is not determined by qualities in the sign itself. Nor is it the relationship (or lack thereof) to the reality indicated that is decisive. Poetic reference is instead primarily determined by the way it is set into the verbal context:

> In poetry as against informal language, there is a reversal in the hierarchy of relations: in the latter attention is focused above all on the relation, important from the practical point of view, between reference and reality, whereas for the former, it is the relationship between the reference and the context incorporating it that stands to the fore. (Mukarovsky, 1976, p. 157)

Put differently, one might say that this "shift in the center of gravity" concerns whether the sign and the signifyin(g) chain point outward, toward an object or reality, or inward, toward the sounding work of art. In a tune like "911 Is a Joke," the possibility of such a shift is used to make a sample balance on the edge between musical and informational signification. One moment a sampled element may direct our attention towards the relation between the sample and a certain extra-musical reality, while in the next to act primarily as a musical feature: the musical qualities of the sampled element and the (musical) context incorporating it come to the fore. This shift is achieved by small alterations in the texture. In line with Mukarovsky, such minor changes could be seen as an awakening of the aesthetic potential in any "real" sound.

Signifyin(g) on the Public Debate

As Mukarovsky points out, the boundary separating the aesthetic from the practical is not always apparent and in fact seldom coincides with the boundary between art and other human activities (Mukarovsky, 1976, p. 157). Public Enemy fully exploits this ambiguity when they pick their samples from mass media, in this case from the debate on the relation between rap, race, crime, and violence in American inner-city ghettos. "Incident at 66.6 FM," also from *Fear of a Black Planet*, is an example of how such mass-media fragments can be musicalized while simultaneously evoking the public discourse surrounding the music. This "instrumental" song—there is no rap in it—is almost completely based on sonic material from a New York radio call-in program devoted to Chuck D. and Public Enemy's music.[4] The tune is a patchwork of different samples, many of them phoned-in snippets such as "Go back to Africa!" "They are the most appalling things I have ever seen," and "Chuck D. represents the frustrations of the majority of Black people out there today." These verbal utterances are combined with other sampled sounds, among them a telephone's characteristic keypad tone. Together they form a collage-like but steady rhythmic pattern.

In this tune, documentary sounds are taken out of their original context and used as music; their aesthetic role overrides their original semantic meanings. The effect parallels Renov's fourth mode of documentary in his poetics of documentary, namely the "expressive." "The documenting eye is necessarily transformational in a thousand ways." he states. About the photographs of Paul Strand, he continues, "Strand's mutations of the visible world foreground the singularity of his vision as against the familiarity of his object source" (Renov, 1993b, p. 33). In more general terms, one might say that Strand's photographs foreground his mediation at the expense of the mediated object's familiarity. As a consequence, the bond between the situation and the image's portrayal of it is weakened. Likewise, in Public Enemy's "Incident at 66.6 FM" the referential bonds of the samples to the original talk radio show are loosened. In the very same moment, however, these samples start to speak again: as they are transformed into music, they acquire new semantic meanings. They cease to form arguments in a debate on crime and disorder in North American urban areas—a debate that ran nonstop in the American mass media after rap exploded in the late 1980s— and start to act as powerful examples of the common prejudices and opinions about both Public Enemy and Black rap in general at the time.

This means of reusing and at the same time commenting upon historical material evokes the act of signifyin(g) as described by Henry L. Gates Jr. in his pioneering book *The Signifying Monkey* (1988). In general terms, signifyin(g) can be described as repetition and revision in one and the same maneuver: to signify upon something is to repeat with a difference (Gates, 1988, pp. 19–25). According to Gates, such rhetorical skills are highly regarded in African American communities, and he quotes Roger D. Abrahams's definition from 1962: "The name 'Signifying Monkey' shows the hero to be a trickster, 'signifyin(g)' being the language of trickery, that set of words or gestures which arrives at 'direction through indirection'" (Abrahams, 1962, p. 125, quoted in Gates, 1988, p. 74). Signifyin(g) is, among other things, a means of communication to which one may assign messages that are undeliverable via literal language.[5] In line with this, we might say that Public Enemy, by repeating (and revising) the White establishment's public debate, manages to comment upon these arguments in a rather subtle way. When combined with the soundscape of the reality Public Enemy want to address, the tone of these statements on rap, race, crime, and the situation in the inner-city ghettos, which are usually uttered from a position of power and authority, is significantly changed. They become somehow ridiculous, even comic.

Following Mukarovsky, we can observe that when documentary material is used musically, indexical signification must to some extent give way.

Throughout this process the original meaning is transformed and displaced, and verbal utterances are deverbalized: sometimes speech even becomes pure sound. In fact, the very distinction between documentary and musical meaning becomes difficult to maintain. The close relation and frequent shifts between the two modes of signification (like the interweaving of fiction and non-fiction in documentary) make the patchwork of sampled sounds act almost simultaneously on two levels.

Roman Jakobson, another writer of the Prague school, theorized this borderland between aesthetic and pragmatic functions as a borderland between signs and things (see Jakobson, 1976a). As an example he used the difference between the effect of a painted dog and a filmed (real) dog on a real dog: "A dog does not recognize a painted dog, since a painting is wholly a sign. However, a dog barks at dogs on film because the material of the cinema is a real thing, but he remains blind to the montage, to the semiotic interrelation of things he sees on the screen" (Jakobson, 1976a, p. 147). Jakobson claims that it is precisely such real things (visual and auditory) transformed into signs that are the specific material of cinematic art. Similarly, in the music of Public Enemy, many of the sounds, like the keypad tone or the phone-ins from the radio program, belong to the world outside of the musical "screen" and are thus things transformed into signs. But just like in a film, they are "things" that have become part of a new context, a musical montage that promptly generates new perspectives.

Nevertheless, much of the expressive power of their music results from how they *retain* some indexical signification in it. This means that while things have become signs, they still (vitally) "bear an indexical relation to the historical world" (Nichols, 1991, p. 27). It is important that the statements in "Incident at 66.6 FM" still point to their original context. In this way, not only is speech transformed into music but music also becomes "speech." The samples are reactivated: the documentary material points to an actual reality while commenting on it in an act of signifyin(g).

Association by Contiguity: The Sonic Montage

Public Enemy's sonic montages combine glimpses of reality (so as to launch virtual landslides of recognition and meaningfulness) with an equally crucial musical role. The use of montage is a familiar rhetorical device in visual documentary, and in particular the mode described by Renov as "analytical" or "interrogatory": "The analytical documentary is likely to acknowledge that mediational structures are formative rather than mere embellishments. . . . A process of interrogation is thus undertaken through the layering and resonance of heterogeneous elements" (Renov, 1993b, pp. 31–32). Nichols also points out how a documentary film can sustain gaps, fissures, cracks, and jumps in the visual representation of reality, because, he says, "Leaps in time and space and the placement of characters become relatively unimportant compared to the sense of flow of evidence" (Nichols, 1991, p. 18).

The transition from track 4, "Incident at 66.6 FM," to track 5, "Welcome to the Terrordome," on *Fear of a Black Planet* demonstrates Public Enemy's exploitation of sonic montage. The last 17 seconds of "Incident at 66.6 FM" include the following dialogue:

> **Listener:** I think that White people have difficulty understanding that Chuck D represents the frustrations to the majority of Black youth out there today.
> **Host:** I do understand that.
> **Listener:** But before he came on you were blaming...
> **Host:** If you had read the stuff I've read about them, you know the way he [Chuck D.] has been portrayed in the American press.

The conversation ends abruptly, and after a moment of silence a sample of a strongly syncopated riff is played in unison by a synthetic "horn section." This sample lasts for two or three seconds, evoking a radio jingle or a commercial break. A cacophony of sounds lasting for another second or so in turn introduces the next "groove"—the oscillating, enervating, chaotic soundtrack of the journey to the "Terrordome."

In this very short and, in terms of composition, quite simple montage, both the contrasts in texture between the radio conversation, the synthetic horn section and the cacophonic introduction to "Welcome to the Terrordrome," and the timing are relevant to how the combination of the different elements in the montage suddenly emerges as a distinct and meaningful constellation. This meaningfulness is, however, rather elusive in character, since it is a quality linked to the temporal nature of music. Even though we could disassemble the montage and catalogue its different aspects—the chronology of the elements, their timbral relations, their relative durations, the intervals between arrivals, and so on—a constellation such as this can hardly be reproduced via such structural data.

Interesting to us here is less the montage's musical success than its potential for communication. As mentioned previously, both Renov and Nichols refer to the editing of documentary as devoted to creating "a flow of evidence." Instead of organizing cuts within a scene according to a narrative logic—to present a sense of a single, unified time and place, for example—the "documentary organizes cuts within a scene to present the impression of a single, convincing argument in which we can locate a logic" (Nichols, 1991, p. 18). Even though the montages in Public Enemy's music do not form "arguments" like a traditional documentary, partly because of their very limited duration, the different montage elements create a similar flow of evidence. As a result Public Enemy uses the expressivity of the successful montage to communicate something about power relations and inequality in American society that is fundamentally richer than any exclusively verbal text could manage. Moreover, the "knowledge" transmitted by the sonic montage is located less in the indexical traces of the elements used than in the way these elements are combined—that is, in the breaks, the timbral contrasts, and the timing.

How do these sonic montages convey so much "information" in such a short period of time? The concept of metonymy contributes something here. A montage establishes what Jakobson has described as "forced" metonymical relations. While metaphors operate through creative association by similarity and contrast, metonymical relations rely upon association by contiguity. Both means of association open up new ways of understanding the usual order of things. In the essay "The Contours of *The Safe Conduct*," Jakobson writes:

> The essence of poetic tropes is not simply to record the multifarious connections between things but also to displace the usual relationships. The greater the stress under which metaphor operates in a given poetic structure, the more violently are traditional classifications disrupted, while things are redistributed on the basis of new generic traits. (Jakobson, 1976b, p. 192)

As Jakobson points out, metonymy may involve the decomposition or mutual interpenetration of objects. This is clearly the case in the transition from "Incident at 66.6 FM" to "Welcome to the Terrordome" described previously, which includes elements from very different social and cultural spheres (or "planes of reality," to quote Jakobson). These different excerpts from the world are combined in a way that evokes new meanings; the natural contiguities and distances between the different elements change, and so do their dimensions.

REALITY RAP AND RAP REALITY— A TWO-WAY EXCHANGE

The notion of "documentary authenticity" developed, according to Andre Bazin (quoted in Renov, 1993b, p. 23), with the wealth of objective reporting following World War II. This work defined the documentary "look"—the shaky camera, grainy black-and-white images, and so on. Today, as Renov points out, "the technically flawed depiction of a purported reality no longer suffices as a visual guarantee of authenticity. It is simply understood as yet another artifice" (Renov, 1993b: 23). Nevertheless, such techniques—albeit no longer comprising a guarantee of factual documentary authenticity—still signify a documentary. Likewise, the construction of imaginary urban locations, the use of documentary material, the sonic montage, and the inclusion of noise and an overall edgy, fragmentary sound contribute to establishing Public Enemy's "documentary" sound, linking their music to a certain post-industrial urban sphere. Even though we know that the reality effects conveyed by such expressive means provide no guarantee for a one-to-one relationship between music and reality, the songs still manage to convey the impression of an unusually close relation between music and reality.

The documentary impulse of reality rap is also striking in rap films from the same era, blurring even further the place of art relative to reality. As Michele Wallace, bell hooks, and Valerie Smith have pointed out regarding the film *Boyz n the Hood* (1991), this blurring can encourage undesirable stereotypes regarding, for example, the role of Black single mothers in the problems of inner-city children, because the documentary aura sustains the illusion that the film occupies "an intimate, if not contiguous, relation to an externally verifiable reality" (Smith, 1992, p. 60; see also Wallace, 1992; hooks, 1992). In his discussion of hip-hop films, Guthrie P. Ramsey, Jr., touches upon the same issue, reminding us that there is no one-to-one homology between lived experience and its representations.

The naïve realism Smith, Wallace, hooks, and Ramsey warn us against is clearly problematic. At the same time, however, there persists some kind of relation between reality and its musical (or documentary) representation. As Ramsey points out, "We should keep in mind that the social energy that sustains ideologies like misogyny and other forms of discrimination also circulates in these films. In other words, these directors didn't invent misogyny, but they help to reproduce it" (Ramsey, 2003, p. 169; see also Lindberg, 1995). In the case of the music of Public Enemy we also face a situation where "the work" is nurtured by the sounds and symbolic capital of a certain sociopolitical environment. This does not mean that there is a one-to-one relationship between their representation of reality and reality itself, but rather that their music succeeds in establishing a link between the two. In fact, the reality effects of Public Enemy's music ultimately rely on listeners experiencing just such a link.

Public Enemy's hybrid of art, politics, and social reality was a success in crossover markets, which was surprising for several reasons. First of all, Public Enemy was a Black hip-hop group with a Black nationalist agenda.[6] Second, as Robert Walser has pointed out, Public Enemy's music is characterized by a multilinear, repetitive, rhythmic organization and the use of polyrhythm and clashing rhythmic accents (Walser, 1995); this, together with the high density of musical events and the heterogeneous sound, links their music to what have been conceived as Africanisms in the African American musical tradition (see Maultsby, 1990; Wilson, 1974; Wilson, 1983). We might well expect, then, that this musical "otherness" would distance them from a traditional White rock audience, who might be prone to hearing such groove-based musical forms as lacking traditional song structure and melody (see, for example, Danielsen, 2006, Chapter 9). One explanation for Public Enemy's crossover success may be exactly their raw, noisy, "documentary" sound, however, which aligns with what Simon Frith claims to be "the continuing core of the ideology of rock," namely that "raw sounds are more authentic than cooked [sounds]" (Frith, 1986, p. 266). Nelson George also points to how well rap music, via its reinforcement of anti-establishment, rebellious attitudes, ties in with some central values of rock (George, 1998, pp. 86–87).

In such a perspective, reality rap was just another episode in the century-long cultural exchange between Black music cultures and White audiences, of Black musicians providing musical hipness and exotic, stylish attitudes to a thrilled, White audience.[7] A spinoff effect of Public Enemy's sonic strategies was, however, that audiences all over the world were exposed not only to the style, music, and values of Black urban communities, but also to a particularly powerful representation of a sociopolitical reality that, according to Kitwana, shaped what he calls the hip-hop generation (Kitwana, 2002). As has been demonstrated above, the potential "didactic effect" of such a musical practice is not achieved simply by the presence of reality effects and documentary aspects, but by the exploitation of the potential *aesthetic* function inherent in this sonic material. This has consequences for the kind of "knowledge" transmitted, since while the informational function of documentary material—both mimed and real—tends toward the pole of immediate relationships between signs and the world, the aesthetic function tends toward, in Mukarovsky's words, "the pole of global relationships": it is precisely the possible *weakness* of the relationship between the sign and the reality it denotes that makes poetry and music capable of affecting our way of ordering and understanding the world. Along these lines, one might say that Public Enemy, through their different ways of musicalizing reality, achieves a referential "weakness" that allows each track, and ultimately the whole album, to in turn create a coherent context that influences all of the references in the entire "work." This weakness does not exclude but rather supports the existence of a relationship between music and the world. The relationship is, however, of a different sort than the traditionally informational, because the global reference affects our way of ordering reality. It allows for what might be called a *critical versioning of the world.*

In order for Public Enemy's music to have this effect, however, the global reference has to be counterbalanced by informational referencing. The power of Public Enemy's sonic output—in the realms of both music and politics—lies in their ability to get this balance right. The group's purpose was not to eliminate the informational function and make the music turn back on itself. Contrary to much avant-garde art, balanced on the line between art and reality, Public Enemy did not primarily aim at pointing out the aesthetic qualities of our lifeworld or questioning the limits of art. They sought rather to work with that very line, asserting a two-way exchange between music and reality, where a certain lifeworld enhances the expressive power of music and the musicalization of reality makes new meanings possible in an informational sense as well.

ACKNOWLEDGMENT

This chapter was first published in *European Journal of Cultural Studies 11*(4), 2008, 305–321. Reprinted with permission.

NOTES

1. Paradoxically, an act of unveiling truth such as this, at the same time, unavoidably veils truth's underlying reality. This is addressed in the philosophy of the later Heidegger (1971) and also by Derrida in his essay «Le facteur de la verité» (1987), one of Renov's references in his discussion of the relation of truth and reality in the introduction to *Theorizing Documentary* (Renov, 1993a, pp. 1, 6–7).
2. According to both Renov and Nichols, the constitutive character of the fictional elements—and, one might add, of the aesthetic aspects in general—in non-fictional forms has been severely understated. Renov writes: "The expressive capabilities of nonfiction forms, too frequently overlooked, account for an aesthetic dimension which is—on historical as well as conceptual grounds—constitutive" (Renov, 1993a, p. 5).
3. The use of nonmusical sounds in musical contexts has a prominent prehistory in the electro-acoustic tradition of contemporary art music. In the late 1940s and 1950s, Pierre Schaeffer, for example, encouraged by developments in recording technology, created *musique concrète,* using the magnetic tape recorder and microphones to record and edit fragments of natural and industrial sounds into a «musical» whole.
4. In an interview with Davey D from the time of the release of the record, published at the website Davey D's Hip Hop Corner, Chuck D. explains the background of the track as follows: «'66.6 FM' deals with me being the topic of discussion on a radio program in New York (a WNBC program hosted by Alan Colmes). Note the 666, which means collectively the media is the devil, especially until we pick up some counterbalance against the same forces that worked against us. In order for us to offset radio. In order to offset television, we must control some sort of television. In order for us to offset movies, we must have some movies» (Retrieved June 10, 2005, from http://www.daveyd. com/peterrord.html).
5. In *Talking Black,* Abrahams defines signifyin(g) as "a wide variety of verbal techniques united by the single strategy of verbal manipulation through indirection" (Abrahams, 1976, pp. 50–51).

6. According to Adam Krims, the complex layering and sampling techniques of the Bomb Squad came, in the late 1980s, to mark out the new musical space of rap "hardcore." In line with this, Krims interprets the collaboration between the Bomb Squad and Ice Cube on the latter's solo album *AmeriKKKas Most Wanted* (Priority, 1990) as a means of fortifying—consciously or unconsciously—Ice Cube's Black revolutionary identity (Krims, 2000, p. 96).

7. For a discussion of this cultural exchange in connection with the meeting of Black dance music and the international, mostly White pop/rock audiences in the late 1960s and 1970s, see Danielsen (2006). For a discussion of the relationship between Black culture and White audiences in early North American popular culture, see Eric Lott's seminal study of Black minstrelsy (Lott, 1993), and Christopher Small's discussions of the same issue in Small, 1987, Chapter 5.

REFERENCES

Abrahams, R. D. (1962). The changing concept of the Negro hero. In M. C. Boatright, W. M. Hudson, & A. Maxwell (Eds.), *The golden log* (pp. 119–134). Dallas, TX: Southern Methodist University Press.

Abrahams, R. D. (1976). *Talking Black.* Rowley, MA: Newbury House.

Barthes, R. (1986). *The rustle of language.* New York, NY: Hill and Wang.

Bolter, J. D., & Grusin, R. (1999) *Remediation: Understanding new media.* Cambridge, MA: MIT Press.

Danielsen, A. (2006). *Presence & pleasure: The funk grooves of James Brown and Parliament.* Middletown, CT: Wesleyan University Press.

Derrida, J. (1987). *The post card: From Socrates to Freud and beyond.* Chicago, IL: University of Chicago Press.

Forman, M. (2002). *The 'hood comes first: Race, space, and place in rap and hip-hop.* Middletown, CT: Wesleyan University Press.

Foster, H. (1996). *The return of the real: The avant-garde at the end of the century.* Cambridge, MA: MIT Press.

Frith, S. (1986). Art versus technology: The strange case of popular music. *Media, Culture and Society, 8,* 263–279.

Gates, H. L. (1988). *The signifying monkey: A theory of Afro-American literary criticism.* New York, NY: Oxford University Press.

George, N. (1998). *Hip-hop America.* London, England: Penguin.

Heidegger, M. (1971). *Poetry, language, thought.* New York, NY: Harper & Row.

hooks, b. (1992). Dialectically down with the critical program. In G. Dent & M. Wallace (Eds.), *Black popular culture,* (pp. 48–55). Seattle, WA: Bay Press.

Jakobson, R. (1976a). Is the cinema in decline? In L. Matejka & I. R. Titunik (Eds.), *Semiotics of art: Prague School contributions,* (pp. 145–152). Cambridge, MA: MIT Press.

Jakobson, R. (1976b). The contours of *The Safe Conduct.* In L. Matejka & I. R. Titunik (Eds.), *Semiotics of art: Prague School contributions,* (pp. 188–196). Cambridge, MA: MIT Press.

Kitwana, B. (2002). *The hip-hop generation: Young Blacks and the crisis in African American culture.* New York, NY: Basic Civitas Books.

Kitwana, B. (2005). *Why White kids love hip-hop. Wankstas, wiggers and wannabes and the reality of race in America.* New York, NY: Basic Civitas Books.

Krims, A. (2000). *Rap music and the poetics of identity.* Cambridge, MA: Cambridge University Press.

Lindberg, U. (1995). *Rockens text: Ord, musik och mening.* Stockholm, Sweden: Brutus Östlings bokförlag Symposion.

Lott, E. (1993). *Love and theft. Blackface minstrelsy and the American working class.* Oxford, England: Oxford University Press.

Maultsby, P. K. (1990). Africanisms in African-American music. In J. E. Holloway (Ed.), *Africanisms in American culture,* (pp. 185–210). Bloomington: Indiana University Press.

Mukarovsky, J. (1976). Poetic reference. In L. Matejka & I. R. Titunik (Eds.), *Semiotics of ART: Prague School contributions,* (pp. 155–163). Cambridge, MA: MIT Press.

Nichols, B. (1991). *Representing reality: Issues and concepts in documentary.* Bloomington, IN: Indiana University Press.

Peirce, C. S. (1960). *Collected papers of Charles Sanders Pierce* (Vol. 2): *Elements of logic.* Cambridge, MA: Belknap Press.

Public Enemy. (1990). *Fear of a Black Planet.* [Audio recording]. New York, NY: Def Jam Recordings.

Ramsey, G. P. (2003). *Race music: Black cultures from bebop to hip-hop.* Berkeley, CA: University of California Press

Renov, M. (1993a). Introduction. In M. Renov (Ed.), *Theorizing documentary,* (pp. 1–11). New York, NY: Routledge.

Renov, M. (1993b). Toward a poetics of documentary. In M. Renov (Ed.), *Theorizing documentary,* (pp. 12–36). New York, NY: Routledge.

Rose, T. (1994). *Black noise: Rap music and Black culture in contemporary America.* Middletown, CT: Wesleyan University Press.

Small, C. (1987). *Music of the common tongue: Survival and celebration in Afro-American music.* London, England: Calder/Riverrun Press.

Smith, V. (1992). The documentary impulse in contemporary U.S. African-American film. In G. Dent & M. Wallace (Eds.), *Black popular culture,* (pp. 56–64). Seattle, WA: Bay Press.

Wallace, M. (1992). Boyz n the Hood and Jungle Fever. In G. Dent & M. Wallace (Eds.), *Black popular culture,* (pp. 123–131). Seattle, WA: Bay Press.

Walser, R. (1995). Rhythm, rhyme, and rhetoric in the music of Public Enemy. *Ethnomusicology 39*(2), 193–217.

West, C. (1994). *Race matters.* New York, NY: Vintage Books.

Wilson, O. (1974). The significance of the relationship between Afro-American music and West African music. *The Black Perspective in Music 2*(1), 3–22.

Wilson, O. (1983). Black music as an art form. *Black Music Research Journal 3*, 1–22.

CHAPTER 6

MUSIC, LANGUAGE, AND AMBIGUITY

Sven Hroar Klempe

Music is no doubt a rational system. However, compared to language it may appear as quite irrational though. In this sense music emerges as ambiguous. Yet this is very much a question about defining rationality. One definition that may clear up this dilemma is to define rationality as "the instrumentally efficient pursuit for a given end" (Elster, 1999, p. 102). In line with this definition music is rational when the purpose is, for example, to have an auditory experience loaded with emotions. Or, to be circular, music is a rational choice of device if the purpose is to have a musical experience. However, if the aim were to make an agreement about how to deal with some practical issues in everyday life, like who is going to pick up the children in the kindergarten, for example, it would be highly irrational to communicate through music, especially if just one of the spouses communicates through music. Thus music is rational if it is applied due to its characteristics, but irrational if not.

However, to define rational communication is probably not that easy either. Sometimes a deep conversation is experienced as both meaningful and rational, albeit the words might be quite superficial or even tend to be meaningless. This might be true when two lovers are sharing their fascinations of

Cultural Psychology of Musical Experience, pages 107–119
Copyright © 2016 by Information Age Publishing

each other. The verbal repertoire might be filled with clichés, but sometimes just meaningless sounds as well. This is why poetry may serve the function, too. Poetry is also about composing words with certain sounds in order to get a proper rhyme or to build up a certain structure to get a proper form. In this sense reviewers often apply "musical" as an honorary term in their description of poetry. Yet there are not only clichés and poetry that are touching the musical domain. Some philosophers would even regard music as something that brings in the real depth in philosophy, like Arthur Schopenhauer, for example. He regards music as something that immediately presents "the will itself'" (Schopenhauer, 1977, p. 527). Some would even go further by saying that music is the real philosophy (Jankelevitch, 1974). An objection to this would of course be that this is irrational talk, highly supported by Elster's definition of rationality. Yet current tendencies in philosophy underline that language is not sufficient to provide rationality in regard to certain topics. This is very much the content of Derrida's deconstruction strategy. In this respect it is interesting how Roland Barthes in his late poststructuralistic phase was very much pointing at musical aspects of language, and how language subverts itself by this, but still appears as a meaningful form of expression though (Barthes, 1977; Barthes & Leger, 2011).

Anyway, the aspect of ambiguity in these examples in which language is touching music do have something in common with ambiguity in human life as well. In a discussion of culture in minds and societies, Jaan Valsiner states, "belonging to a community, and participating in a society, is a process of inevitable ambivalence" (Valsiner, 2007, p. 93). The argument for this statement is first of all that the individual can be regarded from at least two different perspectives, as a member of the community and as a part of the society. Although the two perspectives do no contradict each other, they generate different consequences and narratives related to the same person. Sometimes the identity is related to the community and sometimes to the society, and in certain situations they may contradict each other, or at least be experienced very differently. This was probably what the composer Gustav Mahler thought when he had a slight feeling of homelessness by being a German spoken Jew in Bohemia. Consequently, these labels of group identification, like community, society, people, language, and nation, do make differences and borders, but at the same time they are also unifying. This is the fundamental ambiguity, and Valsiner quotes the German sociologist Ferdinand Tönnies, who concludes "every such relationship represents unity in plurality and plurality in unity" (Valsiner, 2007, p. 92). Thus this may appear as a paradox, or even a contradiction in terms, because plurality cannot be the same as unity, or vice versa. Nevertheless we may accept under certain circumstances such paradoxes and contradictions, and the fundamental question would be: on what basis? If rational uses of language contradict these types of ambiguities and paradoxes, are there any other areas in which the human mind seems to show immediate acceptance for them? Yet to get an idea of what this is about, it has to be put into a certain framework, which both includes some technical aspects of the musical system, but also to see them in a broader context.

In this paper, therefore, I will pursue this intriguing but problematic borderline between music and language. I will start with an example from Freud, which demonstrates how natural irrational use of language actually can be. This will be contrasted with how ideals of rationality are embedded in our understanding of language. At this point, it will also be natural to bring in some aspects of the musical system, in which the aspects of chords, polyphony, and harmony open up for dimensions that characterize music, in contrast to the linguistic system. These aspects open up for a sort of embedded ambiguity or multidimensionality, which provides the dynamism in the musical system. And finally, I will demonstrate how the Freudian irrational use of language has its direct parallel to a rational use of the musical system. In other words, the aim is to demonstrate how musical and linguistic systems merge in our daily communication and by this how ambiguity can be regarded as a fundamental aspect of our way of thinking, not in terms of language, but in terms of music.

AN EXAMPLE FROM FREUD

In *Jokes and Their Relation to the Unconscious* from 1905, Freud is analyzing the nature of the jokes (Freud, 1960). Yet one of the most illustrating examples he is referring to in the very beginning includes what is usually called a portmanteau or a linguistic blend:

> In the part of his *Reisebilder* entitled "Die Bäder von Lucca" [The Baths of Lucca], Heine introduces the delightful figure of the lottery agent and extractor of corns, Hirsch-Hyacinth of Hamburg, who boasts to the poet of his relations with the wealthy Baron Rotschild, and finally says: "And, as true as God shall grant me all good things, Doctor, I sat beside Salomon Rotschild and he treated me quite as his equal—quite famillionairely." (Freud, 1960, p. 14)

Freud gives this a "diagrammatic picture" by visually stacking the two words upon each other, and by this demonstrating how the two words are blended. However this is more obvious in the original German than in English, so also the English translation sticks to German in this case (Freud, 1960, p. 18):

```
FAMILI  AR
  MILIONAR
FAMILIONAR
```

Due to his theory about the unconscious, he describes this linguistic phenomenon as a "process of condensation, accompanied by the formation of a substitute by means of a composite word" (Freud, 1960, p. 19). The result of this is that two words with relative clear meanings are transformed into one with a higher degree of ambiguity. Freud is not referring to music, primarily because of his lack of interest in music. Yet the psychiatrist Daniel Sabbeth published in 1979 an article in which he confesses that he had "come to notice a number of similarities between certain verbal and musical pleasure-producing mechanisms" (Sabbeth, 1990, p. 49). As an example of this, he is referring to the famillionairely example from Freud. The two words that are united have no logical connections, just the sounds "mili" and "är." This is what makes Sabbeth to bring in music. "This multiple use of sound materials is a facet of the joke technique that is also important in music" (Sabbeth, 1990, p. 51). Sabbeth's point is that just the repetition of a certain sound in the two words is sufficient to direct our associations towards music. Interestingly, this coincides very much with the composer Edgar Varése's definition of music, which has been adopted and recirculated as a definition of music among musicologists for the last 50 years, specifically that music is to be defined in terms of organized sound (Varése, 1966). Yet this tells us also something about some musical aspects of poetry, certainly when it is embedded with rhymes, which also are about repeating certain sound patterns.

Although Freud applies this example of portmanteau or blending (Gries, 2004) as an illustration of how the unconscious is working, it seems to point out much further. Blending is on the one hand a linguistic phenomenon, which is widespread in use. Yet on the other hand, it represents a deviation, which is hard to explain from a linguistic perspective. Unless the blended words become adopted into everyday language, like "smog" for example, they appear as ambiguous. Smog is referring to both smoke and fog, and has got a clear denotation in the sense that pollution has become permanent in a geographical region and appears like a fog. "Famillionaire" is not a term that has been adopted into everyday language, and the ambiguity is generated from the two terms familiar and millionaire, which have nothing in common, but some coinciding sounds. In this perspective, linguistic blending might be regarded as an intermediating level between music and language.

Two Types of Ambiguity

Building on this, we may talk about two different types of ambiguity. One is the more open and unspecified definition, which the term "famillionaire-ly" may count as an example. The term combines two different areas, but it is not exactly clear what they may have in common. Thus the ambiguity in this case is unspecified, and it may evoke a lot of feelings and emotions, because the two terms point in different directions and the combination of them leaves a sort of confuse. This is a weaker definition of ambiguity because the two terms may be united in a meaningful way, but not necessarily.

The other type of ambiguity may probably be exemplified with the term "smog," which is rather specific. It consists of two very different denotations as well. Smoke points in one direction and fog points in another. Yet smog points in a third, but quite specified direction, which imply a combination of visible pollution of the air, like smoke, but without any definable source, and as ubiquitous and stable as the fog. If we can talk about ambiguity in this case, it stands in opposition to the former. There is an aspect of embedded ambiguity in the sense that it consists of two underlying terms that point in two different directions. This may indicate a strong type of ambiguity. However when they merge into a specified new term with a clear reference, the ambiguity may also disappear at the same time. If we compare it with the first type, we will see that the two types coincide when it comes to having two underlying terms that point in different directions. In this respect they both actually represent a strong type of ambiguity. Yet the blended outcomes are different in the sense that famillionairely still becomes ambiguous by having an unspecified and open meaning, whereas smog has a clear denotation. Since the latter type of ambiguity is characterized by specificity, in the sense that two oppositions merge into something third that can be specified, one may ask if this represents any kind of ambiguity at all, but if so, it is different from the former. In the first case, the meaning is unclear and the term famillionairely represents rather bad and funny English, whereas the term smog might be included in a proper English discourse without too many hesitations. Consequently, the outcome of a blending may represent at the best a weak type of ambiguity, whereas the underlying two terms may have the potentiality to form a strong type of ambiguity.

It is hard to bring this distinction further, so we just leave it here. But one of the conclusions we may draw is that we see how feelings, emotions, and even ambiguity might be irreconcilable with a correct use of language. In this context, it is appropriate to underline the Chomskian aspect of competence and the Saussurian aspect of system (langue), in which both are pointing at some unequivocal aspects of language. Behind competence, there is a human capacity of sorting out the proper meaning of a sentence or a word. According to Chomsky, logic is governing this capacity of ending up with a clear understanding of what is said (Chomsky, 1965/1976). The Saussurian concept of system does not go that far in obtaining unequivocal statements, although the elements and smallest units in a system presuppose that they are discernible in an unequivocal way (Saussure, 2011).

This brings us back to what could be the stronger definition of ambiguity, specifically that one and the same term generates two discernible or even contradictory meanings. This seems to be difficult to combine with an ideal use of language, in which the achievement of clearness and exactness is normally the ultimate and rational goal for applying language. Although the use of language is not excluded from being both unclear and diffuse, Chomsky and Saussure make both a distinction between the actual and the ideal use of language by applying the terms performance and competence (Chomsky), and parole and langue (Saussure). Yet by these terms they have clearly signalized that the actual use does not necessarily represent the ideal aspects of language. It is therefore appropriate to make a distinction between ambiguity given on the systemic and theoretical level, which seems to be hard to find in language, and ambiguity given as an outcome in practice, and represents a weak type of ambiguity based on an inappropriate use of language. On this basis it is time to stick to music and see if it represents something else when it comes to ambiguity on a systemic level.

AMBIGUITY IN MUSIC

One may find different types of ambiguities in music. One is the fact that it can be understood in terms of numbers or as if it is a language. Another is the inconsistency in the musical system, which Vincenzo Galilei (the father of Galileo) highlighted. Yet these examples presuppose that ambiguity is more or less associated with a sort of incompleteness. To understand music in terms of numbers appears as incomplete, the same does the understanding of music as language. This aspect of incompleteness is also true when it is referring to inconsistencies. However, there is a third perspective on music, which may avoid this problem. If ambiguity is exposed as an embedded part of the musical system, it is not to the same degree associated with incompleteness. And there actually are some examples in music that is highly related to ambiguity, but at the same time seems to be generated from the musical system itself.

Despite the fact that many aspects of the musical system have changed during the history, some of them have exposed a quite stable position. The fundamental roles of the perfect consonances, i.e., the prim, octave, fifth and fourth, belong to this group of stable events in music. Although their role was highly threatened in the 18th century, they survived, not least by means of Rameau's thesis from 1722. He managed to unite the old harmonic perspective with the new melodic perspective. This is expressed through the key term *basse fondamentale*—not to be confused with thoroughbass, though. Whereas the latter refers to the notated bass line, the term basse fondamentale refers to an imaginary bass line. In C-major, the fundamental bass tones would be the C, the F (fourth), the G (fifth), and the C (octave/prim), and the point is that all the chords applied can be referred back to these tones, either directly or indirectly.

In almost all tonal music after 1600, one may say these four chords form the underlying pattern. In abstract terms and independently from the key, it is called the tonic, subdominant, dominant, tonic—or, in roman numerals: I, IV, V, I, which are ordinal numbers indicating the order in which of the bass tone in the chord in the scale applied. We are now talking about the order of chords, which is not the same as the order of a melody. Since a chord consists of an abundance of notes, mostly three or four, the melodic aspect of a chord opens up for a lot of possibilities. In C-major, the tonic (I) will consist of the tones c-e-g, the subdominant (IV) of f-a-c, and the dominant (V) of at least g-b-d. Yet, and to get rid of all doubts about which is the next chord, namely the tonic, the f has to be added to obtain the satisfying tension between b and f, from which the b necessarily leads to c and f to e. Then we are back in the tonic again. This is what is called a complete cadence in tonal music. This is characterized by a start (I), a movement (I–IV–V^7) and a satisfying complete ending (V^7–I).

There are two aspects of these three chords Rameau was focusing on (Rameau, 1722/1992). One is related to the fact that these three chords generate all the tones in the adhering scale. This implies that all these tones may also appear in the bass line. Despite the fact that the chords do not necessarily appear in their root position (i.e., chords just based on thirds) they can nevertheless be traced back to their root position. This implies that there can be one actual row of chords, like: [g-c-e], [f-a-c], [f-g-b-d], [e-g-c], [d-f-g-b], [c-e-g]. The bolded letters indicate the bass line, which forms a stepwise melody in the bass. Although there are actual six different chords in this sequence, they can be reduced to three by ordering each one of them in root position. Thus the same sequence is imaginary following this chord pattern: [c-e-g], [f-a-c], [g-b-d-f], [c-e-g], [g-b-d-f], [c-e-g]. In generic terms this row contains: tonic, subdominant, dominant-seven, tonic, dominant-seven, tonic; or in Roman numeral analysis: I, IV, V^7, I, V^7, I.

This form of reduction is not related to ambiguity, but rather the opposite: to unity. Tracing all chords back to the four main chords in the distance of fifths or fourths rescued the ancient thesis about these intervals as the most fundamental in tonal music. However, Rameau wanted to bring this a step further, which is the second aspect he was focusing on. The most perfect unity between these chords should be that the fifth or fourth should form the distance, not only related to the tonic, but also between each one of them. Yet the problem was the transition between the subdominant and the dominant is a second, which is not a harmonic interval. The solution Rameau found was to add a sixth to the subdominant, the so-called *sixte ajoutée*. In C-major this is a chord consisting of the notes f-a-c-d. By listening to this chord, one realizes soon that its function appears to be similar to the dominant with an added seven. Because of its embedded tension, it leads to the next chord, which in this case is the dominant. Yet this is not the most important part. If we put the tones it consists of in a different order and with the d at the bottom [**d**-f-a-c], we do get another chord. This is a d-minor seven chord, and D major seven is the dominant seven to the G. In other words, by adding a sixth to the subdominant (IV), the chord is immediately transformed into two different functions at the same time. It is both the subsequent to the tonic in fourth distance, but it also precedes the dominant in fourth distance, despite the fact that the subsequent to the tonic is in a second distance to the dominant. This is ambiguity in a strong sense; specifically that one event can appear as two different entities at the same time. The best way to illustrate this visually is that there have to be two layers in which each one of them has different meanings.

$$
\begin{array}{lll}
\text{C–F}^6 & & \text{I–IV}^6 \\
\quad\quad\quad\quad\text{or formulated generally in Roman numerals:} & \\
\text{d}^7\text{–G}^7\text{–C} & & \text{ii}^7\text{–V}^7\text{–I}
\end{array}
$$

The F^6 (IV^6) and d^7 (ii^7) are the one and the same chord, however the chord may have two different interpretations. This ambiguity in music is deeply embedded into the musical system. Yet it is first of all a consequence of the harmony. As long as there is just one pitch at the time, it is not natural to talk about ambiguity, despite the fact that each tone also may have different functions and meanings. Yet this tells us also that our conception of ambiguity is closely related to unity, too. Even when it comes to the ambiguous F^6/d^7, there is an aspect of unity in the sense that the two chords are experienced as one and the function of the two is to unite the harmonic sequence by a continuous bass line consisting of steps in fourths or fifths, which form the *basse fondamentale*. Rameau's purpose by introducing the *sixte ajoutée* was certainly not to underline the ambiguity it caused, but rather the opposite, to create unity in the harmonic progression. Nevertheless the fact that F^6 immediately is to be transformed into a d^7, which is actually another chord, is without question an expression of ambiguity, and must be said to represent the strong type of ambiguity.

STRONG AMBIGUITY IN MUSIC

Unity by means of the two intervals fourth and fifth characterizes a complete cadence. This premise forms our expectations. As far as something emerges as expected, it is perceived and understood as unambiguous. In this sense the normal complete cadence [I–IV–V^7–I] is as expected, and this does not cause any immediate experiences of ambiguity. The experienced ambiguity appears when at least one of the elements turns out to be something nonexpected. This is exactly what happens when the IV^6 suddenly turns out to be understood as an ii^7 instead. Yet there is also a factor of time included. The aspect of the sudden is not of the sequential type. The IV^6 is *at the same time* an ii^7. Thus strongly spoken, ambiguity is something that comes up when the one *appears as* the other at the same time, which is explicitly expressed in the musical system by means of the Roman numerals:

I–IV^6

ii^7–V^7–I

The ambiguity expressed in this way is challenging our ideas of unity. Although the aim of Rameau was to create unity, it was by means of a statement that clearly demonstrates ambiguity. This statement may even violate the Aristotelian principle of contradiction, which says: "the same attribute cannot at the same time belong and not belong to the same subject and in the same respect" (Aristotle, 350). The quality of the subdominant with an added sixth cannot at the same time both be and not be quality of the dominant with an added seventh. However, this is not exactly what the notation for the harmonic progression says either. It rather says that the quality of the subdominant with an added sixth (IV^6) may in addition include the quality of a dominant with an added seventh (ii^7). This is the difference between "not" as a negation in a logical sense and "not" as indicating a difference. The principle of contradiction refers to negation in a logical sense, whereas there is just a difference between the subdominant with an added sixth (IV^6) and a dominant with an added seventh (ii^7).

If one harmonic sequence ends up in something that is reinterpreted and by this forms the beginning of a new one, we have an overlap. In music this appears in many different situations. The most obvious situation is probably related to modulations, in which the movement turns from one key to another. A tonic in, for example, C-major may easily well be reinterpreted and turned into be a subdominant in G-major at the same time. If so, the key smoothly changes from C-major to G-major without violating the musical flow. The musicologist Hugo Riemann indicates almost all the examples of modulations he is presenting in his catechism of harmony and modulation, with an overlap structure in the notation (Riemann, 1905, p. 158, Example 8).

This is also done in more modern handbooks in harmony (Gauldin, 1997, p. 261, Example 9).

Overlap structures may also appear in the melodic line. This is primarily described in the generative theory of tonal music (Lerdahl & Jackendoff, 1983; Klempe, 1999), albeit this theory regards overlaps as deviations. According to this theory, there are two versions of overlaps. One is grouping overlap, in which the ending tone in the first phrase turn to be the beginning tone in the next phrase (Klempe, 1999, p. 73, Example 4.14). The other is grouping elision, in which the ending tone in the first phrase is cut off and replaced by just the beginning tone in the next phrase (Klempe, 1999, p. 75, Example 4.18). Both situations imply ambiguity and coincide very much with the harmonic overlaps demonstrated above. The intriguing question therefore is to what extent these events have to be regarded as deviations in music or not.

AMBIGUITY IN LANGUAGE AND MUSIC

The fact that the two different chords, IV^6 and ii^7, can be regarded as the one and the same, is an expression for strong ambiguity. Or more precisely, when it comes to ambiguity, the order is rather the opposite: a certain group of pitches can at the same time be interpreted as two different chords, in this case either as IV^6 or ii^7. Although IV^6 or ii^7 consist of the same pitches, they are different because the fundamental tones are not the same. In C-major the basic position of IV^6 will be [f, a, c, d] from the bottom to the top. The basic position for ii^7 would be [d, f, a, c]. However, every chord can be inverted, which is the premise for Rameau's conception of the *basse fondamentale*.

Yet ambiguity is highly related to the unexpected. By listening to a chord consisting of the pitches [d, f, a, c] the immediate reaction is that this must be a d-minor seven (ii^7). Information saying that this is also an F-major with an added sixth (IV^6) will therefore be regarded as unexpected. Hence our expectations tend to go for univocality and rather sort out ambiguity as an option. This can be turned around, which says that appearances of the unexpected imply ambiguity, which very often is the case. The best way to illustrate this is to refer to the musicologist Leonard B. Meyer's theory on meaning in music (Meyer, 1956). According to him the meaning in music is produced when expectations are not met. He refers to a cadence in C-major, but without completing it by omitting the expected tonic at the end: I, IV^6, V$^6_4$, V (Meyer, 1956, p. 25). The point is that if for example a-minor (vi) appears instead of C-major (I), the cadence would produce more meaning than ending with the expected C-major. Thus meaning is defined in terms of emotions, and "more meaning" implies stronger emotions. C-major is expected, but the a-minor is not, and the appearance of the a-minor generates an understatement of ambiguity.

The psychologist George Mandler admits that his interruption theory of emotions has very much in common with Meyer's conflict theory (Mandler, 1985). He even points out that Meyer had understood more than very many other scholars in the field of what a psychology of emotions is about. "Leonard B. Meyer was a conflict theorist who, in contrast to many other such theorists, had read and understood the literature" (Mandler, 1985, p. 44.) Although neither Mandler nor Meyer refer to Wundt, his expansion of the emotional repertoire to include what in English has been translated into "strain and relaxation" (Wundt, 1902, p. 92) is very much related to music. In German the terms are *spannung und lösung* (Wundt, 1900, p. 341), which probably could also be translated as tension and relaxation. Wundt illustrates this by referring to music, especially variations in tempo. The point is that the tension represents the more enjoyable and interesting part, although it has to find its final release by relaxation. It is the same with the disappointing replacement of the tonic (I) with its substitute (vi). This is exactly what creates meaning in music, and in very many sentimental songs this replacement has become a stylistic trait.

Mandler asks rhetorically: "Is there a cohesive psychology of emotion?" (Mandler, 1985, p. 16.) He pursued this question extensively, he says, and the conclusion was "that there is no commonly, even superficially, acceptable definition of what a psychology of emotion is about" (Mandler, 1985). However by going further back in the history, and by presupposing that emotion and feeling are synonyms (James, 1884), Immanuel Kant formulated a statement on which a psychology of emotion can be based: "We shall call that which must always remain merely subjective, and can constitute absolutely no representation of an object, by the ordinary term 'feeling'" (Kant, 1790/1972, p. 40). Feelings are here understood as the bodily reaction of the subject when the one encounters the unidentified other. As long as sensation constitutes the situation in which the one is encountering the more or less unidentified other, feelings are the inevitable bodily reaction to sensation. Although William James distanced himself from Wundt by not regarding the articulated feeling as primary, but rather the bodily reaction, they were nonetheless united in relating feelings and bodily reactions to an immediate and inevitable response to a sensation. Since Wundt also regarded feelings as an "unanalyzable and simple process corresponding to a sensation" (Mandler, 1985, p. 17), he is also pointing out the problems in finding adequately corresponding concepts to feelings. In other words Kant, Wundt and James seem all three to agree upon the fact that feelings and emotions are inevitably related to sensation, and that the sensational process that arouses emotions and feelings contradicts clearly definable representations.

CONCLUSIONS

According to Mandler and a long philosophical tradition, therefore, feelings and emotions can be regarded as a state that goes beyond language, but nevertheless is highly influential on thinking and cognition. As long as they are defined in terms of conflict, they are at the same time the clearest example of how fundamental dilemmas and ambiguities are in human life. Yet they cannot be regarded as completely rational, and the aim of this investigation was to find out to what extent ambiguity may appear as a part of our rational thinking. As long as we can talk about rationality in the musical system, we have seen that ambiguity in a strong sense is highly embedded in the musical system. This is revealed on a variety of aspects of the musical system. In this paper it has been focused primarily on Rameau's understanding of the complete tonal cadence, in which the second chord (the subdominant/IV), can be regarded from two very different perspectives if an extra sixth is added to the triad. It appears as two different chords at the same time, and the musical system may easily require this ambiguity to be complete. However this example is just one out of many in which a strong type of ambiguity is embedded in the musical system. All modulations in music represent another type of strong ambiguity, and overlapping structures in musical phrases represent a third type. However in all these types of ambiguities in music, we see that an aspect of verticality is the uniting factor: The ambiguity referred to is characterized by articulating two or more musical statements at the same time. These could be different pitches, which then form a chord, or they could be phrases, which form a polyphonic texture. In other words, if we look at the rationality in music, we see that the human mind is not alien to ambiguity as an acceptable factor. Yet what is also demonstrated here is that this is not restricted to the musical system, but may appear also in language, especially when we apply portmanteaus or blended words. It is hard to avoid that portmanteaus may violate the linguistic system, but sometimes they are definitely acceptable. Yet the main statement here is that we accept them because our minds are used to other patterns of thinking, which have no problem with accepting ambiguities. On this basis it is no problem for an individual to accept that he or she belongs at the same time to both a community and a society, because this is the way we get order in our lives by creating "unity in plurality" but also growth and development by creating "plurality in unity."

REFERENCES

Aristotle. (350). *Metaphysics, book 4, part 3.* (W. D. Ross, Trans.). Retrieved from http://classics.mit.edu//Aristotle/metaphysics.html
Barthes, R. (1977). *Image, music, text.* Glasgow, Scotland: Fontana/Collins.
Barthes, R., & Léger, N. (2011). *The preparation of the novel: Lecture courses and seminars at the Collège de France, 1978–1979 and 1979–1980.* New York, NY: Columbia University Press.
Chomsky, N. (1965/1976). *The aspects of the theory of syntax.* Cambridge, MA: MIT Press.
De Saussure, F. (2011). *Course in general linguistics* (W. Baskin, Trans.). New York, NY: Columbia University Press.

Elster, J. (1999). *The alchemies of the mind: Rationality and the emotions.* Cambridge, England: Cambridge University Press.

Freud, S. (1960). *Jokes and their relation to the unconscious.* London, England: W. W. Norton.

Gauldin, R. (1997). *Harmonic practice in tonal music,* London, England: W. W. Norton.

Gries, S. Th. (2004). Shouldn't it be *breakfunch?* A quantitative analysis of blend structure in English. *Linguistics, 42*(3), 639–667.

Jankelevitch, V. (1974). *De la musique au silence: 1 Fauré et l'inexprimable.* Paris, France: Plon.

Kant, I. (1790/1972). *The critique of judgment* (J. H. Bernard, Trans.). New York, NY: Hafner.

Klempe, H. (1999). *Generative teorier i musikalsk analyse.* Oslo, Norway: Spartacus.

Lerdahl, F., & Jackendoff, R. S. (1983). *A generative theory of tonal music.* Cambridge, MA: MIT Press.

Mandler, G. (1985). *Mind and body. Psychology of emotion and stress.* New York, NY: Norton.

Meyer, L. B. (1956). *Emotion and meaning in music.* Chicago, IL: University of Chicago Press.

Rameau, J. (1722/1992). *Traité de l'harmonie réduite à ses principes naturels,* Genève, Switzerland: Slatkine Reprints.

Riemann, H. (1905). *Katechismus der harmonie- und modulationslehre.* Leipzig, Germany: Max Hesses Verlag.

Sabbeth, D. (1990). Freud's theory of jokes and the linear-analytic approach to music: A few points in common. In S. Feder, R. Karmel, & G. Pollock (Eds.), *Psychoanalytic Explorations in Music.* Madison, CT: International Universities Press.

Schopenhauer, A. (1977). *Die welt als wille und vorstellung ii, zweiter teilband. Werke in zehn bänden. Band IV.* Zürich, Switzerland: Diogenes Verlag.

Valsiner, J. (2007). *Culture in minds and societies: Foundation of cultural psychology.* Los Angeles, CA: Sage.

Varése, E. (1966). The liberation of sound. *Perspectives of New Music, 5*(1), 11–19.

Wundt, W. (1900). Bemerkung zur theorie der gefühle. In W. Wundt, (1983), *Ausgewählte psychologische schriften: Abhandlungen, aufsätze, reden. band 2 (1891–1913).* Leipzig, Germany: Zentralantiquariat der Deutschen Demokratischen Republik.

Wundt, W. (1902). *Outlines of psychology.* New York, NY: Wilhelm Engelmann.

PART III

MUSICAL EXPERIENCES

CHAPTER 7

I'LL TAKE YOU THERE

Tuning Into Emotions
With Mobile Music Technology

Arild Bergh

Over the past decade and a half we have witnessed a move in the different fields of music research from looking at music in isolation to researching, analyzing, using, and discussing music in "everyday life" (Sloboda, 2011). Thus the role of music as an important cultural component of social interactions in a variety of settings have come more into focus (Batt-Rawden, Trythall, & DeNora, 2007; Crafts, Cavicchi, & Keil, 1993; DeNora 2000; Hara 2011). This period also corresponds to a period where our means of interacting with recorded music, and our access to such music has changed dramatically (especially in quantitative terms). What I am thinking of here is of course the changes in technology that has occurred since the late 1990s. This includes digital music access via mobile means, eg. iPod and mobile phones, and via various Internet related means, for example YouTube and online music streaming (Levy, 2011). These new ways of accessing music have been researched in a number of ways (Bull, 2000; Bull, 2007; Chen, 1998; Hosokawa, 1984; Katz, Lever, & Chen, 2008; Simun, 2009; Williams,

Cultural Psychology of Musical Experience, pages 123–141

2004; Yaksich, 2007). Here I will focus on an area that has received less attention: the use of mobile music among adolescents, in particular how they use music to "tune in" to their emotions, alone or together with others.

The data for this paper comes from ethnographic fieldwork on the use of mobile music (and related technologies) among young adolescents in a British town. The key findings from this research (Bergh, DeNora, & Bergh, 2014) was that mobile music was often used in a very socially inclusive way through three new and specific conveniences: physical, exploratory, and storage conveniences, each of which affords easier and more powerful ways of interacting with music. These conveniences are only available in technology that has emerged with the newer, Internet connected, mobile music players. Furthermore, mobile music is now a ubiquitous element of everyday life, and whereas for the older generation it often feels "new" it is "not a big deal" for these adolescents. Thus for the young people in our sample, it is a social rather than a cocooning part of their life, although the switching between personal and social use of music is more seamless than before. Another aspect, which I will investigate further in this paper, was that mobile music provided a means for young people to explore (rather than define) and tune in to their emotional states that is facilitated in ways that are very different to what was possible prior to the late 1990s.

One of the informants, Andrew,[1] explained at length how this tuning in takes place in everyday situations:

> I use music for lots of different things, I use it to kind of prompt emotions, like I'll listen to [pause] you know, thick music or thin music[2] [Interviewer: yeah] cause it makes me feel that way and I want to feel that way. [2 minutes later:] But then stuff like, if I'm cycling to a party, I'll listen to fast music to kind of, you know, [yeah], If I haven't already been... quite often I'll go to a party without already feeling quite kind of revved up. And also, it's not just things like that, it's also like, like I said, when I cycle home, I like to listen to Pink Floyd and things like that, and kind of "bassy" thick music. But quite often I'll start cycling home, and I won't already feel that way, and I'll put music on and the music will kind of, will build my mood up until it kind of reaches a climax just as I'm [at a particular part of the route], because I always go the same route home.

Here we see a number of issues raised that I want to focus on in this paper: how young people deliberately *use* music; how they are very aware of its relationship to their emotions; the fact that they use it to tune in to emotions, i.e., emotions are not a static entity to be invoked by playing a particular piece of music, rather it is a mutual exploration that goes on, where music is half teleprompter, half mirror; and how the social and private are seamlessly switched between using music. In short, young people are deliberately using the new affordances arising from recent technology changes to access music as a shared cultural material to help them tune into different emotions. We will explore here how this tuning in allows them to access or develop shared moments, even if only for a brief period, what this achieves and whether these periods of shared emotions can be considered momentary group identities.

At this stage, findings and suggestions are highly tentative and obviously based on a very specific demographic. I hope to raise a few interesting issues related to how new qualitative ways of interacting with and through music have emerged as a result of quantitative changes such as in music access (i.e., the variety of music we access with increased speed). In particular I want to highlight and consider how this affects our understanding of everyday emotional work.

RESEARCH BACKGROUND AND METHODS

The research discussed here is concerned with learning more about the everyday practices and meanings of young people's mobile music use, which had not (at the time) been subject to systematic investigation. This gap in the literature may partly arise from a "knowledge gap" between young people and older people (i.e., parents or teachers) in relation to mobile music practices. But it was also felt that this was linked to those who research mobile music: when most researchers are middle aged, the young and the old are often not party to the process of research design and analysis. This in turn has meant that young users and the practices they engage in have been underrepresented in the literature.

To redress this bias, we[3] wanted to examine young teenagers' mobile music practices from the point of view of, and in collaboration with, a young person. This was done by enrolling the help of Maia Bergh (age 15 at the time of the interviews in autumn 2009) who is the daughter of the author. As well as performing all the interviews for this chapter, Ms. Bergh's views informed the project design and analysis phase.[4] Opportunistic sampling was used to choose informants to include both genders from among Ms. Bergh's friends, who were all in the same cohort at a secondary school in a small city in England that we will call Christchurch. Their age range was from 15 to 16 years.

The decision to involve a young person in the research was taken after careful consideration and consultation of the literature on this topic, both the idea that promotes the importance of "hearing from" children themselves (Harden, Backett-Milburn, Scott, & Jackson, 2000) and the discussions around the advantages, disadvantages, and ethical issues associated with employing young people as peer interviewers for this task (Harden, Scott, Backett-Milburn, & Jackson, S., 2000).[5] Involving young people on both "sides" of the research, i.e., in the design and implementation of the research on the one hand, and as respondents on the other, also allowed us to tap and explore lay expertise and participant empowerment in our research.

The chosen interview format (peer to peer) gave an air of informality to the interviews that overall proved fruitful for eliciting data. The researcher and respondents (who had been told that this was for research done by the parent of the interviewer) alike were obviously relaxed in the interview situation, greatly helped by the fact that the interviewer allowed her professional demeanor to slip now and again as she moved flexibly between the "adult" role of researcher and her usual role of early teen and friend.

TUNING IN TO EMOTIONS

Before we continue, it will be useful to define what we exactly mean by "tuning in to your emotions." Most people who engage with music in one way or another would agree to the relatively commonsensical view that music affects and/or interacts with emotions at least some of the time. But beyond this fairly general view we immediately encounter difficulties, not least agreeing on what emotions are. For a working definition I will follow Meyer (1956) and Sloboda's (2005) suggestion that emotions are short lived, whereas more long-term feelings would be considered moods. Furthermore, emotions require us to acknowledge the feelings to be what we deem to be an emotion, so a language must exist for us to express them (Wierzbicka, 2003).

The term *tuning in* originates in the tuning of an instrument to the correct pitch, later meaning the action of finding a radio (or TV) station by turning a dial on a receiving device until you hit the exact spot on the dial where the transmission signal was clearest. When using this term here I refer to the (internal or external) negotiations that occur when someone is trying to determine whether the music they hear accurately represent the emotional state they (a) are in, or (b) would like to be in. DeNora (1986) and Sloboda (2000) have both suggested that music impacts us emotionally by acting as a Rorschach ink blot; because music is open to interpretation on the emotional level, we see in it what satisfies us the most, although this is affected by our personal and social biographies as well as cues linked to the music (DeNora, 1999; Sloboda, 2005, p. 208). In other words, emotions are not auto-generated by music, but by people engaging in a back-and-forth manner with music and within the spaces afforded by music and a network that includes other people, objects, and situations as DeNora (2001) and Gomart and Hennion (1999) have suggested. By describing music as a Rorschach ink blot, we allow for considerable agency on behalf of the listener when it comes to emotions. This freedom to project, interpret, and engage in emotional work is what I refer to as tuning in, and is also why music listening is an activity in itself (Bergh & DeNora, 2009). By using the term tuning in to describe how the informants use music to explore their emotions, we also agree with Sloboda's suggestion that music does not work on a person as if they were a tabula rasa, "rather it allows a person access to the experience of emotions that are somehow already 'on the agenda' for that person." (2005, p. 204). Furthermore, this tuning in can go in the direction of music to emotion or emotion to music, thus it is an interplay between the two, rather than a simple cause and effect from one to the other. Finally, tuning in does not indicate emotions that are on the level of peak experiences (Gabrielson, 2001; Maslow, 1994), but rather everyday emotions related to common activities and relationships.

Returning to how the informants viewed mobile music, Marcia explained that

> I have this thing on my MP3 [player] which, a way you can like shuffle through albums, and I really like that, 'cause it is not shuffling through one song, and it's not really like mismatched, but it's kind of finding the mood you're in, and then listening to all of the music that you're in the mood for, and like fits together, I really like that setting. [Interviewer: Why do you think you do that?] Because I don't know what like mood I am in for which music, so I can't choose what I am listening to, so I just randomly go through it, and if a track feels right… [Interviewer: Do you think that's really useful?] Yeah I think so, yeah I use it a lot I think.

Here Marcia gives us a very succinct insight into how recent technology allows new ways of exploring emotions that were previously not possible. With prior technology we would either access music through (a) a physical media collection or (b) through broadcast media. The former would require a break in our listening prompted by the physical necessity of switching to another CD/tape/LP, which in turn would disrupt our emotional "flow." As a result, people would often prepare sessions of music listening (Gomart & Hennion, 1999; Hennion, 2001) which would be more about getting into a predefined mood, rather than exploring. Broadcast media on the other hand left little choice in what you were listening to. On the one hand this could lead to interesting discoveries and when music did gel with your emotions it would have a certain "magical" quality to it, because you had not chosen the music, but on the other hand it required a certain emotional submission unless the music would jar with your own emotional state at that point.

As Bull (2000, 2007) has discussed, the ability to use music nonstationary from the Walkman onwards gives us complete control of our soundscape as we move around, and by extension we can manage and control (to some extent) our interior feelings. The earlier quote from Andrew also illustrated how music that does not require us to be stationary allows a tuning in process that is more continuous and seamlessly integrated into our other activities, whereas before we literally took time out to deal with our emotions in a musical setting. This continuous musical backdrop is in some ways like the Muzak of earlier times (Lanza, 2004), but this time under our personal control. Overall this means that we are more likely to *use* music deliberately (as the informants discussed repeatedly), and less likely to consider any emotional benefits as "magical" or mysterious. In other words, the ubiquity of a vast array of musical choices has altered our perceptions of what music is, and put more power (quite literally) into our hands when it comes to exploring emotions through music.

The moods and emotions that were tuned into by the respondents ranged from the public and light hearted to more private and serious. Preparing for planned events, whether attending school or going to a party, was one frequent use of music. Wayne told us that

> especially if you are on your own, . . . when you get home it can shape how you feel, it depends on what sort of music you want to listen to. For example, if you are excited about going out, you listen to some exciting music and it will better your mood or something. So I think it does play a big part in changing my mood at least. [Interviewer: Why do you think that is?] Dunno, just has a sort of control of me in a way, I'm not someone who pretends it will completely shape my mood, but it is something which can just, . . . it controls me sort of.

And as we saw earlier, Andrew also used music before and after parties to tune into certain moods, and other informants would also do this together, often using portable speakers or playing loud from a mobile phone (colloquially known as "sodcasting" [Redpath Cole, 2011]). Marcia discussed how she preferred to use pop music when with friends (at a sleepover or at a party) "Because it is fun, everyone knows the words, you don't have to concentrate on it that much, because it is simple music, but it is fun and you can dance to it." This ties in with Sloboda's suggestion that music is appreciated for its ability to "evoke or enhance valued emotional states" (2005, p. 215).

The overall picture the informants provided was that music could be used both to move toward certain desirable emotions/moods, as was the case when going to or from a party, but also to avoid certain emotions, the latter particularly prevalent when discussing mobile music and school. For example, Thomas said that

> [Music] can be a distraction sometimes, or it can sort of, I don't know, get you into a different frame of mind . . . distract you from having to think of other things at times. [Interviewer: Why do you think a distraction is a good thing?] Sometimes, like, with all the stresses of school and relationships with friends and just sort of general life, it's good to get your mind off and it's sometimes easier not to have to think all the time.

Similar attitudes were echoed by other informants who would use music to avoid boredom at school or "psych" themselves up in the morning to get ready for school, like Thomas.

However, the music/emotion relationships discussed by our respondents were not only related to regular events in their lives. One of the informants, Heather, discussed a sad occasion (her description) when she had lost her grandfather and was making a video of his life for her grandmother. Doing this she was listening to the song "Hallelujah,"[6] which is a slow song with a rather downbeat mood occasionally punctuated by more upbeat/strident sections. It is just voice and piano, and the lyrics have a somewhat religious aspect to them. When asked if she thought the music had anything to do with how she felt at that moment, she explained: "Yeah, it kind of just like [pause] [Interviewer: Captured your emotion?] Yeah, it captured my emotions, but it didn't . . . it kind of familiarized me with how I was feeling rather than making me upset. It was like what I was feeling."

In the above quotes we repeatedly see how the informants shy away from describing music as something that simply dictates their emotions, and that in no way do they feel that it overpowers them with predefined feelings. Rather it is seen as something that suggests moods and aids emotional work of different kinds. Whether it is used deliberately or incidentally, it is clear that music for these young adolescents is there to suggest emotions that they (at their own volition) then explore and engage with, in short, it helps them tune in to their emotions. Such use of music through MP3 players to work with your emotions has been discussed by Skånland (2009) in terms of self-regulation, and DeNora (1999) has explored the idea of music as a technology of the self (expanding on ideas by Foucault), and more broadly certain music therapy techniques are concerned with a form of tuning in to emotions and issues by client and therapist playing improvised music together (Bonny, 1997). What we see here is a specific subset of these ideas, albeit with recorded rather than live music, being enacted through young adolescents' use of modern music technologies.

Among the informants, there was also an appreciation of how different technologies were useful in different circumstances, depending on their needs. Thomas, for example, preferred to listen to music on a laptop using iTunes[7] because "you can organize it quite easily, and you don't have to like, on an iPod you have to scroll through the menus and do all that, but it's a lot easier to just find the exact song you want on the computer, you can just use searches." This exploratory convenience of direct searches that leads to a particular song/artist/album/genre contrasts with the shuffle mode that was discussed earlier, and shows how the different modes of interacting with your music collection is useful for different ways of tuning in to your emotions. A search is more likely to pinpoint a particular song, thus it most likely reflects a fixed idea of what that song will "do" for you. The shuffle mode, however, as discussed above, is more about exploring music until "chancing" upon something that reflects your mood.

CHOICE, ACCESS, SHARING, AND EMOTIONS

The new (and still emerging) technologies related to music listening are not only about our ability to listen to music in any situation. Just as important is the number and variety of songs that we can access, something that the informants were very aware of. When the first iPod was released in 2001, the key selling point was that it could keep "a thousand songs in your pocket" (Hormby & Knight, 2007), the idea being that you could carry around a considerable part of your personal music library. This was a step change from the Walkman and Discman (a CD-based portable player), which would provide mobile access to 10 to 20 songs. However, more recently streaming of music from a central library accessed through the Internet is a common way of exploring music for these young people, and here the choice is no longer thousands, but millions of songs (Levy, 2011).

Heather explained that she uses "YouTube a lot of the time . . . but mostly for music." Andrew's friend Barry "uses YouTube for most of his music," and Andrew himself would also share music by sending friends YouTube links. Several other informants also used YouTube in this way, either to find new music or share it with fiends. At the time of the interviews, Spotify, which is a dedicated music streaming service, was only mentioned by one informant, but this and similar services have since increased in popularity throughout the world, often through the use of dedicated apps on mobile phones (streaming requires access to the Internet to work, something regular MP3 players do not offer). It was also interesting to note that last.fm, a specialist site for interacting around music, was only mentioned by Thomas, possibly because it only lets you listen to 30 seconds of a song.

Beyond the practicalities of accessing music online, which was done in a variety of ways by the informants, there was a strong feeling that this instant access to a vast and free library of music positively broadened their tastes. Marcia felt that

> [YouTube and streaming services] has definitely changed it a lot, because it is much easier to get more music, so it doesn't costs as much to get music and listen to it, so I think that has varied [sic] people's styles quite a lot.

Andrew, although concerned about the legality of music online, explained that:

the [online music] industry has kind of, it's just broadened so many people's kind of taste in music and stuff. . . . I wouldn't have such a wide taste in music I don't think, if I could not [use YouTube, MySpace, iTunes].

This sharing of music and taste is not only about accessing music on the Internet, Iris discussed more local and intimate sharing:

If I'm going out with friends, usually one of them will have their phone on loud and put their, like, the Walkman setting on, so that they can, like, blurt music out. [Interviewer: Why do you do that do you think?] Just so that you can, like, share your music taste with everybody, and it opens up conversations, like can find out more about what music people like.

This virtual smorgasbord of music can be overwhelming as well, Heather felt that "it is kind of annoying because it's such a wide variety of, like, music choices that you don't know . . . but, ummm, they have lots of links to, like, artist which is similar, so you get to know different people."

However, overall the low cost/free access to music of many different genres, often facilitated by automatic recommendation systems, has (to some extent at least) broadened their tastes, as they explained. In terms of tuning into emotions, this means one is more likely to find music that is relevant to the person and their current context. And in situations where you listen to music with others, a wider choice (that is instantly accessible) means that there is more likelihood of reaching a consensus as to what music suits the specific situation, which in turns strengthens the cohesiveness of the group; (practically) unlimited access to music (by quantity and location) means that more people can be included in the selection, sharing and exploring of music. Wayne discussed this when he was talking about listening to music publicly in parks or other places (there is a large park next to the school the informants attended).

I mean, everyone has an iPod and everyone switches their iPods and puts it into the sound system, everyone plays their own music, it's not just one person playing the tunes they like, everyone gets to express what they are listening to at the moment, and see the reaction of their friends. And it's just something which, as I said, creates conversation, creates a . . . people have a good mood! [sic]

The technologies that facilitate choice (Internet, MP3 players with a lot of storage space) and access (portable players and portable loudspeakers) are therefore important parts of the negotiation process on a number of levels. Firstly, in simple numeric terms you are more likely to encounter a song that matches the emotion(s) you try to tune in to, whether this is a private or shared emotion. Secondly, the ability to choose gives a feeling of being involved, which (even if there will be others present who disagree) makes one feel that there is a choice available. This is in strong contrast to either going to a concert or listening to a single album/CD, where it is more about you trying to fit into the mood presented by the music than the other way around. Finally, the ability to play back the music anywhere means that emotions can be tuned into in "real time" and are not put aside for later processing, although the idea discussed earlier about pushing emotions away by using music as a distraction clearly suggests that the opposite can also be true.

This negotiation/tuning in process also plays out differently depending on time and place. When on their own, it was clear that deeper and more complex interactions with the music, and often emotions, were on the agenda, as Marcia explained with regards to listening to whole albums at home. "I like listening to albums when I'm just, like, in a place, and like to listen to the whole thing and, like, go through the stages of it. And, like, when I'm moving I cannot concentrate on it so much, so I just kind of listen to random songs that I like." This awareness of the inherent limitations of different music for different contexts in terms of suitability for different occasions enables the informants to tune in at different levels, echoing in some ways Stockfelt's (2004) suggestion that here are "adequate modes of listening" for different circumstances.

It seems that overall the informants are using these enabling technologies to build up a vast dictionary of music that references different emotions that can be deployed instantly depending on situational parameters. Thomas for instance "try to listen to some more relaxing music when I'm at home.... Like when I am reading, or if I'm trying to get to sleep, I won't listen to some, like, heavy music which I might if I am going out."

The emotions that the informants tune into can also be memory based, or what Sloboda terms "episodic associations" (2005, p. 337). Iris mentioned several examples of how music from the past triggered emotions:

> It's just one that's cropped up recently and I'm not sure why it makes you feel this way, but you know the *Scrubs* theme tune? [Interviewer: Yeah, Lazlo Bane; Superman] Yeah, the start of it. I don't know what it is about it, but, it makes me feel *really sad*, like I just don't know what it is, I'm reminiscent of a certain time, like.... [Interviewer: Really? Do you know what time it is?] I think it's probably when I was going out with [ex-boyfriend name] we watched a lot of *Scrubs*. [Interviewer and interviewee laughs. Interviewer: First boyfriend?] Yeah, first like proper boyfriend, well not really but, you know, it was a good time of my life. And I think I feel sad thinking about it now because it's like reminiscent of that and it's not there anymore. I am pleased about where I am now, but it is just kind of sad when you think about past times that aren't around anymore.

Several of the other informant discussed similar evocative memories triggered by music. Given their age, "distant" memories was often only a year or two in the past, but nevertheless felt distant to them. The ubiquity of music and our ability to preserve and access it all means that these triggers are more likely than not to occur even in young people's lives, and it may also be sought out deliberately. Andrew, for instance, connected the group Placebo with "happier times," although as he still listened a lot to them so he felt their memory effect was not as strong as "if I hear 'Naive' by the Kooks or any of the Kooks songs really, I'll instantly remember year 7 and year 8 and things like that. Just because I listened to them so much then and I don't listen that much to them now."

The finding discussed here are not new in themselves, whether from research (DeNora, 2002; Greasley, 2008; Hara, 2013) or from our own experience, we know that we will select music based on a range of contextual parameters. The key difference is that for these young informants there is always music available to match the mood they are trying to tune in to. Andrew, for example, who earlier explained how Internet access to music had broadened his taste explained that

> Because my moods are always affected by the weather, . . . like today Sid asked me if I wanted to go out with him, and Ned, to the park, and I said no. It's not just because in the park I'll get wet, that doesn't bother me much, it just because the wet weather has affected my mood now and made me feel like . . . [interviewer: cozy?] yeah, cozy, and . . . basically, so the scale kinda goes down and down, and in my mind I can always pick the right kind of music to fit for the right kind of time for me.

THE SEAMLESSNESS OF CURRENT MUSIC TECHNOLOGY

Previous research has shown the impact of technology on music listening, i.e., how they can open up new ways of experiencing music, and how such experiences affect us (Bijsterveld & Van Dijck, 2009; O'Hara & Brown, 2006; Schönhammer, 1989; Skånland, 2009; Williams, 2004). In a previous article I have, together with DeNora and Bergh (Bergh, DeNora, & Bergh 2014), enumerated the differences between current mobile music devices (iPod and other MP3 players and mobile phones) and older music playback devices, and explained how these differences represent physical, exploratory, and storage conveniences (that did not exist prior to these devices), which influence the way people interact with music.

In terms of tuning into emotions I would suggest that there are four issues that differentiate current music technology from earlier incarnations.

- There is (as discussed above) no gap between when you feel certain emotions (or feel the need to deal with them) and when you have access to music that may be used to tune in to these emotions. Skånland (2009, p. 11) has also discussed this instant access and what it means in terms of individuals' self-regulation through listening to music on MP3 players.

- Due to the broadening of taste that some of the informants felt had occurred and the larger number of individual songs one can access, the different emotions/moods that different songs represents has a greater potential for a close(r) match to one's own emotions than is possible with less music available.
- The electronic music formats are largely interchangeable and can be played on a cheap mobile phone or a large home computer, and a wide variety of other devices. Thus pretty much any young adolescent in high income countries such as the United Kingdom will be able to play back and exchange music, which lowers the threshold for members of a group when it comes to participating in tuning in to emotions.
- The differentiation between private and public music listening is more permeable than before as users can easily switch between headphones or portable speakers or mobile phone speakers when playing back the music.

The common denominator here is the seamlessness with which music can be accessed and deployed regardless of context, as Bull (2000) has discussed. This seamlessness underpins the ease with which music can now be used to tune into different emotions. For instance, several of the informants explained how listening to music on the way to school was important to them. Wayne discussed this at length, in the process highlighting the switch between the personal and social:

> I don't hear a lot of music in school, but I listen to my iPod on my way to school I listen to it occasionally during the day.... [Interviewer: Why do you listen to music on the way to school?] It prepares me for the day, it's something to do in the morning when people aren't as social as perhaps they would be later in the day.... [Interviewer: What about a nonschool day?] Well, it depends on the atmosphere, for example, you may be at a party or something, or you may just be on your own, it depends on how you feel. In the example of the party, I want to listen to exciting music, and music which is loud, but when I'm at home I generally just want to enjoy music with good lyrics, music which makes you think.

> [18 minutes later in the interview when asked if he listens to different music when home or out with friends:] Well, I'd say there's some form of difference, but I listen to the music I listen to with my friends at home as well, but I also listen to other bands which perhaps I wouldn't listen to with my friends, because it is a personal thing. It's maybe a song which isn't great for a party

or isn't great for people's moods, but it may just be something which makes me think or something, which I wouldn't necessarily play to my friends. I wouldn't say I just listen to different music on my own, I listen to the music I just want to listen to, and sometimes that may be music I wouldn't show my friends, sometimes it is, it completely depends on my mood or what I want to listen to.

Here we see how one can easily turn to solitary music use when "people aren't as social," or with the very same device and music collection, switch to a socially inclusive mode later without any preparation required. With earlier technology there was no such ease of use/access (although one or two of the points above might be available in certain devices, such as portable radios), and it is this seamlessness that not only lets people tune into emotions more easily, but also makes this process more obvious to younger people, as we saw in earlier quotes. By providing unhampered access to any music, any time, any place the links between music and emotion are easier for all to see, and the sophistication with which young adolescents slip in and out of different moods is, I would suggest, unmatched by what any previous music technology could offer.

EMOTIONAL IDENTITY GROUPS BASED AROUND MUSIC

A final, and somewhat speculative, point that I want to raise is the idea that one can have what I will term "emotional identity groups" based on music. Further research is most certainly required, but based on the data in this research project I believe this is something that can be fruitfully examined in other contexts. Earlier research into mobile music (Bull, 2000; Bull, 2007; Chen, 1998; Hosokawa, 1984; Simun, 2009), which forms the majority of the modern technologies we discuss here, has tended to focus on the isolation that these devices offered (and which their users often took up). The data from this research however, clearly show that this is not caused by the technology as such, but more probably a result of the age groups who were involved in previous research (Bergh, DeNora, & Bergh. 2014). Marcia, for example, discussed the socializing around mobile music that she and her friends engaged in:

Like, if it's a party than all the boys will put music on through some iPod speakers and people will be dancing to it, or, erm, like, if people are just relaxing in the park usually, someone will have their phone and they'll just play some music on their speakers. Or, like, if I'm with, like, a couple of friends then it might be, like, just singing along to it and, like, changing songs and, like, talking about music and stuff.

Similarly, Elisa's discussion about her home use of music highlights a sense of virtual togetherness, even if she feels alone at that particular time and place:

> Most of the time when I, like, listen to happy music . . . I will probably be on my own. [Interviewer: Any particular reason for that?] Well, I think that when you are with your friends, I don't know, you are kind of more engaged with that. Whereas, like, on your own you are more likely to kind of feel sad and think about things that, like, might depress you. [Interviewer: And music is a good way of dealing with that you think?] Yeah, music can, like, often take your mind off things, and, like, . . . and also uplift you as I was saying, so I think it is a good thing, to be able to listen to music when you are feeling sad. . . . It can make you feel, like, sort of, less alone, if you're, like, part of, like, all the people that listen to this music and stuff, and, like, the person singing is talking to you.

This is strongly reminiscent of Anderson's discussion of the nation as an imagined community: "It is imagined because the members of even the smallest nation will never know most of their fellow-members, meet them, or even hear of them, yet in the minds of each lives the image of their communion" (Anderson, 1991, p. 6). And it is important to remember that when it comes to music, emotions are not a superfluous "icing on the cake," they are an important part of the social interactions around music. As Becker (2001, p. 157) puts it when discussing music and emotions: "The emotions are private and public, interior and exterior, individual and communal." When looking at larger groups such as social/protest movements, we know that emotions can form an important part of their identity (Jasper, 1998). Furthermore, the use of music that is linked to emotions in those groups is well documented (Corte & Edwards, 2008; Eyerman 2002; Eyerman & Jamison 1998; Roscigno, Danaher, & Summers-Effler, 2002). The idea that emotions arising from music shape and promote group membership is therefore complementary to the idea of tuning into emotions through music.

However, can musical emotions provide identities for people in smaller and more intimate groups? If so, a music based emotional identity group could be perceived to provide additional feelings of belonging on top of existing group ties; all the informants in this research came from the same cohort at the same school, and they therefore had close existing ties. However, through music, and more specifically the emotions engendered by music, even stronger group feelings are created for a short period. In effect, music acts as a temporary "social movement" and the emotions that emerge around it are the cause (in both senses of the word) of this movement.

Some of the informants were aware of such groups, Wayne for example clearly identified "Emo" music as an emotional identity group based on music, albeit (in his opinion) a very negative one. He explained that

in my opinion I don't think Emo music's very good, I think it's manufactured...a lot of band [who] don't necessarily write all the music, and it's a
very contrived genre to fit in with the audience, and I don't think it's particularly good, I think it's all samey, it's all whiny, the lyrics are just clichéd and
boring and just, people listen to it to try and connect to it and feel worse,
rather than listening to music which they generally have a passion about, and
generally enjoy rather than just music which is trying to upset themselves
more and feel special, I don't know.

When asked to explain why he thought people would listen to music that
gave them negative emotions, he suggested that

if you are in sad mood, you can listen to music and just, sort of, wallow in pity,
which can be good,... [but] I don't think you should go and telling people
you listen to this sort of, you know, melancholic music, it should be a personal
thing if you are sad about it, and I think that's the difference..., bands like
My Chemical Romance for example, I don't think they have done anything
positive at all, I think they've only increased teenage depression and negativ-
ity as a whole and apathy. I don't think they're very productive at all.

However, Emo is a large musical category whose followers form "neo-
tribes" as Bennett (1999) terms groups of young people who share musical preferences. The sort of identity groups that the shared tuning in to
emotions represent is focused on and around songs that do not fit into a
particular category, but rather that which succeeds in uniting those present
around certain emotions for a short period of time.

CONCLUSION

It is clear from the data discussed in this paper that young adolescents, at
least those present in our sample, can be very aware of the opportunities
and limitations inherent in music when it comes to exploring and tuning
in to your emotions. The ubiquitous nature of current mobile music technologies open up for a continuous and tightly integrated experience when
it comes to using music in a deliberate effort to explore and tune into ones
emotions. This is in strong contrast to how music was used prior to the late
1990s: although one could use a limited amount of music in a Walkman or
on a car stereo, most of the time the emotional aspect of music use was set
aside for special occasions, either intense music listening at home, or going
out to concerts. The music-emotion links were therefore on one level more
valued, but perhaps this also led to it being taken too seriously, and reserved for special occasions, rather than being an ever present companion

and sounding board. In other words, before we had to get into the music, now the music is getting into us.

NOTES

1. All names have been changed.
2. In other parts of the interview Andrew put forward his ideas of "thick" or "thin" music, thick being music with a lot of bass and thin music being Billie Holiday for instance.
3. An earlier paper discussing different aspects of this data was written with Tia DeNora and Maia Bergh (Bergh, DeNora, & Bergh, 2014).
4. The original intent was for the author to conduct the interviews, however Ms. Bergh felt that this caused respondents to "censor" their comments (i.e., package them "for parents"). Furthermore, after Ms. Bergh agreed to work as a research assistant to collect data, we suggested the focus group format. Ms. Bergh again felt that this would be less than ideal as, in her experience, it could result in "show off" displays as opposed to discussions about what really takes place.
5. The project proposal was submitted to the University of Exeter's School of Humanities and Social Sciences Ethics Review Panel, from which it received approval to proceed. Identifying details have been anonymised.
6. Originally a Leonard Cohen song from 1984, later covered by a large number of artists. Heather knew the song from the film *Shrek* where it was sung by Rufus Wainwright.
7. iTunes is a proprietary software program from Apple that is used to manage your music collection and copy songs to iPods and other Apple products.

REFERENCES

Anderson, B. R. (1991). *Imagined communities: Reflections on the origin and spread of nationalism.* London, England: Verso.

Batt-Rawden, K., Trythall, S., & DeNora, T. (2007). Health musicking as cultural inclusion. In J. Edwards (Ed.), *Music: Promoting health and creating community in healthcare* (pp. 64–82). Newcastle, England: Cambridge Scholars.

Becker, J. (2001). Anthropological perspectives on music and emotion. In P. N. Juslin & J. A. Sloboda (Eds.), *Music and emotion: Theory and research. Series in affective science.* New York, NY: Oxford University Press.

Bennett, A. (1999). Subcultures or neo-tribes? Rethinking the relationship between youth, style and musical taste. *Sociology, 33*(3), 599–617.

Bergh, A., & DeNora, T. (2009). From wind-up to iPod: Techno-cultures of listening. In E. Clarke, N. Cook, D. Leech-Wilkinson, & J. Rink (Eds.), *The Cambridge companion to recorded music* (pp. 102–115). Cambridge, England: Cambridge University Press.

Bergh, A., DeNora, T., & Bergh, M. (2014). Forever and ever: Mobile music in the life of young teens. In J. Stanyek & S. Gopinath (Eds.), *Oxford handbook of mobile music and sound studies* (Vol. 1). New York, NY: Oxford University Press.

Bijsterveld, K., & Van Dijck, J. (2009). *Sound souvenirs: Audio technologies, memory and cultural practices.* Amsterdam, Netherlands: Amsterdam University Press.

Bonny, H. L. (1997). State of the art of music therapy. *The Arts in Psychotherapy, 24*(1), 65–73.

Bull, M. (2000). *Sounding out the city: Personal stereos and the management of everyday life.* Oxford, England: Berg.

Bull, M. (2007). *Sound moves: iPod culture and urban experience.* London, England: Routledge.

Chen, S. L. (1998). Electronic narcissism: College students' experiences of Walkman listening. *Qualitative Sociology, 21*(3), 255–276.

Corte, U., & Edwards, B. (2008). White power music and the mobilization of racist social movements. *Music and Arts in Action, 1*(1), 4–20.

Crafts, S. D., Cavicchi, D., & Keil, C. (1993). *My music.* Middletown, CT: Wesleyan University Press.

DeNora, T. (1986, Spring). How is extra-musical meaning possible? Music as a place and space for work. *Sociological Theory, 4,* 84–94.

DeNora, T. (1999). Music as a technology of the self. *Poetics, 27,* 31–56.

DeNora, T. (2000). *Music in everyday life.* Cambridge, England: Cambridge University Press.

DeNora, T. (2001). Aesthetic agency and musical practice: New directions in the sociology of music and emotion. In P. N. Juslin & J. A. Sloboda (Eds.), *Music and emotion: Theory and research. Series in Affective Science* (pp. 161–180). New York, NY: Oxford University Press.

DeNora, T. (2002). The role of music in intimate culture: A case study. *Feminism Psychology, 12*(2), 176–181.

Eyerman, R. (2002). Music in movement: Cultural politics and old and new social movements. *Qualitative Sociology, 25*(3), 443–458.

Eyerman, R., & Jamison, A. (1998). *Music and social movements: Mobilizing traditions in the twentieth century.* Cambridge, England: Cambridge University Press.

Gabrielson, A. (2001). Emotions in strong experiences with music. In P. N. Juslin & J. A. Sloboda (Eds.), *Music and emotion: Theory and research. Series in affective science* (pp. 431–449). New York, NY: Oxford University Press.

Gomart, É., & Hennion, A. (1999). A sociology of attachment: Music amateurs, drug users. In J. Law & J. Hassard (Eds.), *Actor network theory and after* (pp. 220–247). Oxford, England: Blackwell.

Greasley, A. (2008). *Musical preferences and listening behaviours* (Doctoral dissertation). Keele University, Stratfordshire, England.

Hara, M. (2011). Expanding a care network for people with dementia and their carers through musicking: Participant observation with "Singing for the Brain." *Voices: A World Forum For Music Therapy, 11*(2). doi:10.15845/voices.v11i2.570

Hara, M. (2013). *We'll meet again: Music in dementia care* (Doctoral thesis). University of Exeter, Exeter, England. Retrieved from https://ore.exeter.ac.uk/repository/handle/10871/8861

Harden, J., Backett-Milburn, K., Scott, S., & Jackson, S. (2000). Scary faces, scary places: Children's perceptions of risk and safety. *Health Education Journal, 59*(1), 12.

Harden, J., Scott, S., Backett-Milburn, K., & Jackson, S. (2000). Can't talk, won't talk? Methodological issues in researching children. *Sociological Research Online, 5.* Retrieved from http://ideas.repec.org/a/sro/srosro/2000-32-2.html

Hennion, A. (2001). Music lovers, taste as performance. *Theory, Culture & Society, 18*(5), 1–22.

Hormby, T., & Knight, D. (2007). A history of the iPod: 2000 to 2004. *LowEndMac.* Retrieved December 3, 2011, from http://lowendmac.com/orchard/05/origin-of-the-ipod.html

Hosokawa, S. (1984). The Walkman effect. *Popular Music, 4*, 165–180.

Jasper, J. M. (1998). The emotions of protest: Affective and reactive emotions in and around social movements. *Sociological Forum, 13*(3), 397–424.

Katz, J. E., Lever, K. M., & Chen, Y. F. (2008). Mobile music as environmental control and prosocial entertainment. In J. E. Katz (Ed.), *Handbook of mobile communication studies,* (p. 367). Cambridge, MA: MIT Press.

Lanza, J. (2004). *Elevator music: A surreal history of Muzak, easy-listening, and other moodsong.* Ann Arbor, MI: University of Michigan Press.

Levy, S. (2011). Steven Levy on Facebook, Spotify and the future of music. *Wired Magazine.* Retrieved December 10, 2011, from www.wired.com/magazine/2011/10/ff_music/all/1

Maslow, A. (1994). *Religions, values, and peak-experiences.* New York, NY: Atlantic Books.

Meyer, L. B. (1956). *Emotion and meaning in music.* Chicago, IL: University of Chicago Press.

O'Hara, K., & Brown, B. (2006). *Consuming music together: Social and collaborative aspects of music consumption technologies* (Vol. 35). New York, NY: Springer-Verlag.

Redpath Cole, L. (2011). Open dictionary word of the week: Sodcasting. *MacMillan dictionary.* Retrieved December 10, 2011, from http://www.macmillandictionaryblog.com/open-dictionary-word-of-the-week-sodcasting

Roscigno, V. J., Danaher, W. F., & Summers-Effler, E. (2002). Music, culture and social movements: Song and southern textile worker mobilization, 1929. *International Journal of Sociology and Social Policy, 22*(1/2/3), 141–174.

Schönhammer, R. (1989). The Walkman and the primary world of the senses. *Phenomenology+ Pedagogy, 7*, 127–144.

Simun, M. (2009). My music, my world: Using the MP3 player to shape experience in London. *New Media & Society, 11*(6), 921.

Skånland, M. (2009). Bruk av MP3-spillere som verktøy for selvregulering. *Musikkterapi,* (4), 6–14.

Sloboda, J. A. (2000). Musical performance and emotion: Issues and developments. In S. Won Yi (Ed.), *Music, mind, and science* (pp. 220–238). Seoul, Korea: Western Music Research Institute.

Sloboda, J. A. (2005). *Exploring the musical mind: Cognition, emotion, ability, function.* New York, NY: Oxford University Press.

Sloboda, J. A. (2011). Music in everyday life: The role of emotions. In P. N. Juslin & J. A. Sloboda (Eds.), *Handbook of music and emotion: Theory, research, applications* (pp. 493–514). New York, NY: Oxford University Press.

Stockfelt, O. (2004). Adequate modes of listening. In C. Cox & D. Warner (Eds.), *Audio culture: Readings in modern music* (pp. 88–93). New York, NY: Continuum Books.

Wierzbicka, A. (2003). Emotion and culture: Arguing with Martha Nussbaum. *Ethos: Berkeley, CA, 31*(4), 577–600.

Williams, A. P. (2004). *The functions of Walkman music* (Doctoral thesis). University of Adelaide, Adelaide, South Australia.

Yaksich, M. J. (2007). *Plugged in: A qualitative analysis of the ways iPod users produce and experience social connection* (Master's thesis). University of Maryland, College Park, MD.

CHAPTER 8

EVERYTHING EXCEPT DANCE BAND MUSIC

Cultural Omnivorousness, Norms, and the Formation of Taboos

Petter Dyndahl

There has been a tendency in Western high culture over the past couple of decades to expand the selection of musical genres and styles that are recognized as valuable. Music that was previously characterized as being of little value, such as popular music, has achieved higher status. This tends to happen gradually and by means of cultural psychological processes and mechanisms that lead to our internalizing and thus experiencing the renewed values as natural, inherent properties of cultural and aesthetic products and artifacts. The normative unconscious formation of the dynamic anatomy of taste is acquired, however, according to social power relations and structures. And, not all music achieves increased social and cultural standing. Rather than speaking of value relativism, one can thus argue that there are still hierarchical distinctions, yet along new dividing lines. Even now there is music being marginalized and excluded from education, research, the

Cultural Psychology of Musical Experience, pages 143–163
Copyright © 2016 by Information Age Publishing
All rights of reproduction in any form reserved.

media, and the public sphere. In the following sections, this process of exclusion will be examined from a Scandinavian perspective.

THEORETICAL APPROACHES

Pierre Bourdieu (1984) opens his main study of the social character of taste, *Distinction*, with the following sentence: "Sociology is rarely more akin to social psychoanalysis than when it confronts an object like taste, one of the most vital stakes in the struggles fought in the field of the dominant class and the field of cultural production" (p. 11). He situates one of the key concepts of his social theory, the notion of habitus, within the unconscious domain: "The schemes of the habitus, the primary forms of classification, owe their specific efficacy to the fact that they function below the level of consciousness and language, beyond the reach of introspective scrutiny or control by the will" (p. 466). Moreover, Bourdieu suggests that these schemes of perception and appreciation are grounded in unconscious relational patterns of social inequality and distinction:

> If a group's whole lifestyle can be read off from the style it adopts in furnishing or clothing, this is not only because these properties are the objectification of the economic and cultural necessity which determined their selection, but also because the social relations objectified in familiar objects, in their luxury or poverty, their "distinction" or "vulgarity," their "beauty" or "ugliness," impress themselves through bodily experiences which may be as profoundly unconscious as the quiet caress of beige carpets or the thin clamminess of tattered, garish linoleum, the harsh smell of bleach or perfumes as imperceptible as a negative scent.... Experiences of this sort would be the material of a social psychoanalysis which set out to grasp the logic whereby the social relations objectified in things and also, of course, in people are insensibly internalized, taking their place in a lasting relation to the world and to others, which manifests itself, for example, in thresholds of tolerance of the natural and social world... and of which the mode of appropriation of cultural goods is one dimension. (p. 77)

Whatever Bourdieu might mean by the term social psychoanalysis, it seems obvious that since the core sociological concepts he identifies operate largely on an unconscious level, they might be of relevance to a cultural psychological perspective on taste, distinction, and power with regard to the appropriation and approval, or disapproval, of cultural products and commodities.

Drawing on Bourdieu's work on class, taste, and distinction, psychoanalytic social theorist Lynne Layton (2006) launches the notion of a normative unconscious: "that part of the unconscious that is produced by social

hierarchies of various kinds and that, in turn, works to reproduce and se-
cure a hierarchical status quo" (p. 53). She has studied the workings of a dynamic normative unconscious in terms of how a sample of middle-class and
upper-middle-class respondents react emotionally to shopping situations in
low-end and high-end stores, respectively. The results show an overall disdain not only for the lower-class goods in low-end stores but for the lower-
class shoppers and employees as well. Layton discusses how this stance, on
the one hand, is associated with those whose origins are middle-to-upper
class, and how they maintain that position by disregarding anything related
to the lower classes. On the other hand, for others with a different background, an aversion against the lower-class taste may derive from the fear
of falling back into the class from which they have emerged through social
mobility, especially by means of education. For this group, the shopping in
low-end stores may also evoke shame, as when they recall painful experiences of having less than other children, wearing the wrong kind of clothes,
or when seeing family members working there for low pay. The humiliation
felt in relation to the better off seems to produce the disdainful reaction
toward the lower class. In line with this, Layton recounts Patricia Williams'
(1997) analysis of why members of the White lower classes are not likely to
trust middle-class liberals:

> Williams writes that while liberals may politically fight for the poor, they make
> it clear in many other ways that they don't want to be anywhere near the poor.
> They have nothing but disdain for the poor habitus, and the poor know it.
> Yet it is significant for a social psychoanalysis to recognize that the disdain
> has different emotional underpinnings for the two class fractions. (Layton,
> 2006, p. 56)

Additionally, Layton's finding that some of her respondents feel a kind
of pity for the poor quality of goods the lower classes appear to be forced
to consume may be regarded as yet an example of a top-down approach.

Among the results are also responses that show that some middle-class
people feel uncomfortable, anxious, and afraid of making social *faux pas* in
high-end stores. One aspect of this may reflect an observation that Bourdieu touches upon but does not pursue in *Distinction*, namely the way in
which age, gender, and other dimensions of identity intersect with social
class to mediate between habitus and taste. In this context, middle-class
women seem to have a greater propensity to feel that they neither have the
right age nor body, especially not for clothing boutiques and commodities,
while men of the same class often look as if they have an obvious right to get
what the high-end shops have to offer.

Clearly, Layton's results point to significant "issues that sustain class
conflict, particularly connections between emotions and the unconscious,
conflictual internalizations of class relations that sustain well-defended

identities" (2006, p. 51). She goes on to elucidate the difference between operations on both conscious and unconscious levels, in connection with the above-mentioned female experience of apprehension in upper-class stores: "What is conscious is the shame or anxiety she and I experience in the store; what is structuring the unconscious is the taboo on having a proprietary relation to culture and knowledge" (pp. 54–55).

In the light of these comments an avenue that may be worth exploring would involve combining the notion of how the normative unconscious is structured by cultural taboos at the same time as it may constitute the taboos themselves, with an attempt to see music in a similar perspective, relating to approval/disapproval of cultural products and commodities. Reflecting the complex, contingent, and always already contextual relations between the self and the social, between agency and structure, as well as between aesthetic and cultural meaning, a basic assumption is that music may constitute an arena for "the study of the culture's role in the mental life of human beings," which is Michael Cole's (1996, p. 1) description of a cultural psychology, but the present approach will be equally concerned with the cultural, sociological, and political conditions for, and consequences of, psychological concepts and mental dispositions.

When exploring how musical taste may work to uphold the social hierarchies of Scandinavian societies, various sociological approaches have been employed, from which the concept of cultural capital have proven highly relevant for the understanding of how aesthetic preferences are associated with social positions. In Bourdieu's (1986/2011) notion of cultural capital, he differentiates between three forms, which are embodied, objectified, and institutionalized cultural capital. This division forms a cultural circuit of capital that links institutions, specific cultural artifacts, and individual agents together. Bourdieu pointed out how cultural capital may be defined in terms of whatever objects and practices that are approved by the education system, and are thus able to be mobilized by privileged classes as a key strategy of inheritance to the next generation. Hence he asserts that the sociology of culture is inseparable from the sociology of education, and vice versa. The mechanisms of scholastic recognition, rewarding, and ranking create not only academic differences but also long-lasting cultural differences, which point to habitus as a system of perception and appreciation of socially situated practices: "Habitus thus implies a 'sense of one's place' but also a 'sense of the place of others.' For example, we say of a piece of clothing, a piece of furniture, or a book: 'that looks petty-bourgeois' or 'that's intellectual'" (Bourdieu, 1990, p. 131). Certainly, these terms may be used about a piece of music as well. Bourdieu further states: "All of this is exactly encapsulated in the expression 'that looks'... which serves to locate a position in social space through a stance taken in symbolic space" (p. 113).

There have been a number of important post-Bourdieuian studies that focus not only on how institutions consecrate specific cultural forms, but also if and how individuals and groups embody cultural capital. Modern education is often regarded as essentially a middle-class endeavor. It may therefore be of interest to confront this point of view, and the notion of cultural capital as well, with some studies that explore the cultural configuration of the middle classes, in which it seems as if a degree of cultural variety that apparently does not delineate any hegemonic form of cultural capital is established. For instance, in the 1990s, American sociologist Richard A. Peterson and his collaborators published a series of articles in which they argued that openness to diversity was beginning to replace exclusive preference for high culture as a means of class distinction (Peterson, 1992; Peterson & Kern, 1996; Peterson & Simkus, 1992). This idea, designated as cultural omnivorousness, suggests that middle-to-upper class taste does not necessarily take an elitist or "snob" form, but that high status, at this time in history, is associated with preference for, and participation in, a broad range of cultural genres and activities, compared with similar studies the research team had conducted in the 1980s. This is consistent with the assessment that late or post-modern cultural formations encourage the aptitude to sample, mix, and match cultural forms. Peterson argues that the distinction between omnivores and univores tends to be replacing the opposition between highbrow and lowbrow taste as a central criterion for classifying cultural practices and styles of consumption.[1] In other words, knowing about and participating in a wide repertoire of cultural practices seems now to become a badge of distinction.

Peterson's approach differs from Bourdieu's social theory in that, rather than consuming only high culture, members of the dominant classes now also consume much of what had previously been dismissed as low culture. For example, in the studies conducted by Peterson (Peterson, 1992; Peterson & Simkus, 1992), when North-American high-status groups were asked to name their favorite music, country music scored higher than opera. Peterson assumes that this need not mean that "the US is becoming a more egalitarian society," nor does it mean "that leisure activities and taste in music are losing their efficacy as status markers for the elite.... It may just mean that the image of the taste-*exclusive* highbrow, along with ranking from 'snob' to 'slob' is obsolete" (Peterson, 1992, p. 252). That way one can say that the symbolic boundaries of taste still remain, as do the social hierarchies they support and make visible, but they are increasingly no longer based on cultural exclusivity but on a special mode of cultural appropriation, which is both intellectual and intertextual (Bennett et al., 2009; Dyndahl, Karlsen, Skårberg, & Nielsen, 2014).

MUSICAL OMNIVOROUSNESS

In their study, Peterson and Kern show how country music has changed its social recognition and reputation, in line with the shift in the high status groups "from exclusionist snob to inclusionist omnivore" (1996, p. 905). In the 1960s and 1970s, country music was often associated with, on the one hand, the "tasteless" aesthetics and traditionalist, conservative values of the commercial country music industry, or, on the other hand, the "otherness" and primitivism of its folk music origin, for instance in Appalachian bluegrass music. Later, parts of country music—not least bluegrass music—earned more respect and gained quite another cultural status. As the above study brought out, new authenticity discourses, providing an almost autonomous aesthetic understanding, had in the 1990s made it possible to regard this music as distinguished and distinguishing. Peterson and Kern point out that elite magazines and journals at this point had begun to discuss country music, roots music, and Americana music with a level of seriousness once reserved only for classical music and opera; that such articles and essays "provide omnivores with the tools they need to develop an aesthetic understanding of country music" (p. 904).

This approach also seems to be applicable for developing understanding of an ongoing tendency in the Scandinavian countries from the late 1970s onwards, in which the repertoires and resources of music as an educational subject, an academic field, as well as an area for support and funding from cultural authorities, organizations, and institutions, have expanded considerably. One consequence of the institutionalizing of jazz, rock, and so-called "rhythmic music" in Scandinavian conservatoires (Christophersen, 2009; Olsson, 1993; Tønsberg, 2013), and the parallel academization of popular music within the fields of ethnomusicology and musicology has been that classical music's hegemony in higher music education has been brought to an end, a situation that also applies to the subject music in teacher education and the school system (Nielsen, 2010).

Hence, on the one hand, one might appreciate what seems to be an increasing willingness to recognize the other in music education and research, consistent with certain ethical norms and democratic educational values (Dyndahl, 2008; Dyndahl & Ellefsen, 2009). However, on the other hand, one may also argue that omnivorousness represents a more subtle form of cultural capital, since the ability to range between cultural forms requires a particular aesthetic distance habitually associated with educated cultural agents and privileged consumers, most of all when their gaze seems to be most disinterested, which would be, according to Bourdieu, when symbolic violence is exercised. In this perspective, one could look at the academization and institutionalization of other musics (Born & Hesmondhalgh, 2000) as a form of "musical gentrification" (Dyndahl et al., 2014), where what Richard Florida (2002) entitled "the creative class" takes new possession of popular cultures.

I will return to the concept musical gentrification in the final section, but at this point it may be appropriate to mention David Hesmondhalgh's (2008) critical reminder that even if music may work as an affordance for self-identity, growth, and development, as argued by Tia DeNora (2000), Ruth Finnegan (2003), and others—whom Hesmondhalgh entitles "the dominant conception"—it is also likely that:

> If music is as imbricated with social processes as the dominant conception suggests, then it is hard to see how people's engagement with music can be so consistently positive in their effects, when we live in societies that are marked by inequality, exploitation and suffering. (Hesmondhalgh, 2008, p. 334)

It thus might be argued that cultural omnivorousness can operate to distinguish social groups. From this perspective I will present some theoretical considerations relating to how music education and research can result in the construction of the "insignificant other" of society, to twist George Herbert Mead's (1934) concept of the "significant other" to instead describe individuals and groups tendentiously marginalized and given the experience of having little social and cultural significance. What, in the light of omnivorousness, could give the initial impression of representing cultural diversity and aesthetic acceptance, may, in this respect, contribute to the drawing of some relatively clear-cut boundaries, even within popular music itself. And, not surprisingly, it is the music that provokes a normative unconscious "allergic reaction" in middle-class academics and educators that is kept out, in line with the emotional reactions depicted by Layton (2006) in the previous section. Layton describes an unconscious disdain for lower-class values and practices, produced by social inequality, which simultaneously works to reproduce the same difference and distinction. She further argues that "[t]he notion of normative unconsciousness socializes that insight: once internalized class relations produce splits between what is proper to one's class identity and what is not" (p. 62). Given this background, omnivorous cultural capital can constitute cultural taboos.

THE NORMATIVE UNCONSCIOUS FORMATION OF CULTURAL TABOOS

The types of music excluded by omnivores will obviously vary between diverse academic and cultural fields in time-space, but in contemporary Scandinavian context it seems that the most popular genres—in the sense of genres enjoyed and embraced by a substantial audience—which in general are excluded from the canons of music education and research, are the music and practices that are often given the role of defining the restricted, "one-dimensional" taste of "ordinary people" in opposition to omnivorous, hegemonic forms of cultural capital. Here, Scandinavian dance band music—or *dansbandsmusik* as it is called using the original Swedish term—may serve as a good example. The labels *dansbandsmusik* and *dansband* (dance band) were assigned to a signature style in Swedish popular music that developed in the transition between the 1950s and 1960s (Eriksson, 2008). The genre first arose in Sweden, but soon became very popular in neighboring Norway as well, primarily in the regions bordering Sweden. It has, to a certain extent, also spread to Denmark and the Swedish speaking regions of Finland.

Scandinavian dance band music is characterized by its functional purpose. The music is usually performed live at venues where most people are dancing in pairs, rather than watching the performance of the bands on stage.[2] Even if the main audience might be middle-aged adults, it is noteworthy that, when performed at public dance events, dancing camps, dance classes, and dance clubs, it brings together intergenerational audiences at shared arenas to a larger extent than most other popular music cultures.

Scandinavian dance band music has been stylistically influenced by folk and traditional dance music from the region, swing jazz, country and western music, and New Orleans swamp, among others. The most common instruments are guitar, keyboard, tenor saxophone, bass, drums, and, from time to time, accordion and/or pedal steel guitar. Since the 1970s, the music can be recognized by its reverberated vocals and overall compressed sound production. Today there are varied styles within this genre, representing both the traditional and a more pop, rock, or country oriented sound.

Typical band names refer to leading members' first names: Sven-Ingvars, Ole Ivars, Lasse Stefanz etc., with the letter "z" often replacing "s" as a stylistic marker for the genre. A regular band lineup is all-male, with the possible exception of a female lead singer. The musicians usually wear uniformed outfits. Dialect or vernacular lyrics are common; dealing with the everyday concerns of ordinary people, anticipating and celebrating heteronormativity and traditional values.

Seen as a cultural practice, dance band music provides an all-white, mono-ethnic, and rural reference and scope. Still, one can say that the Scandinavian dance band cultures constitute comprehensive cultural fields for the conscious and unconscious elaboration of meaning and identity that encircle key pivot points such as gender, sexuality, ethnicity, generation, social class affiliation, and the significance of time, place, and space.[3] In that sense, what is highly valued is the right to maintain traditional values and customs concerning gender roles, sexual orientation, morality, and so on, in times where long-established institutions and conventions are being questioned.

Dance band music in general has low status and is despised by a lot of people. Nonetheless, it is an immensely popular genre among the many who enjoy dancing to this music every weekend. Also, a good number of fans follow their favorite bands from venue to venue. Swedish cultural sociologist Mats Trondman (1999) believes that few people have a neutral relationship to dance band music: either you love it or hate it. In line with this, a quick Google search for phrases meaning something like "everything except dance band music"[4] returns numerous Facebook profiles and other self-presentations in which one can find similar judgments of taste, frequently used as markers of cultural dissociation and disdain. Trondman (1990) speaks of two distinct cultural trends in taste; the first exercised by those who support the legitimate culture, and the second by those who do not identify with it. With regard to the notion of cultural omnivorousness, we can say that this dividing line runs through the popular music field as well. The popular music that the middle class embraces within its omnivorous taste regime will thereby also gain entry into the legitimate culture.

What is more, as cultural theorist Johan Fornäs (1995) points out: "It is not only status factors that determine what becomes legitimate taste for someone, but also political, social, psychological and aesthetic qualities related to other needs than the will to be recognized and to dominate" (p. 98). There are indeed various ways of expressing alternative social and political positions aesthetically, where, for example, one "is to flaunt provocative symbols and activities—and for that purpose some forms of rock have always provided a rich reservoir of possibilities," according to Keith Roe (1993, p. 54) in his article "Academic Capital and Music Tastes Among Swedish Adolescents." Rock and related kinds of popular music have undoubtedly served as countercultural fields of radical opposition against a conservative education and academic system. Furthermore, popular music has functioned as an alternative cultural trajectory for social mobility and elevated cultural status. For some time now, popular music has even operated as a valuable cultural, as well as academic, capital. In many respects, this corresponds with a description given by Frede V. Nielsen (2010) in a comprehensive report he and his colleagues have published on Danish music education and its status in historical perspective from 1970 to 2010. The report states that, on one side, a value-neutral or polyvalent tendency has spread, which means that various music cultures apparently have achieved equal status and value. On the other side, this may also prove to be consistent with middle-class postures regarding tolerance, inclusion, and openness to diversity, at the expense to some extent of other social class norms and strategies of enhancing cultural capital.

For that reason, Peterson and Kern (1996) remind us that the shift from the exclusive highbrow to the inclusive omnivore does not prevent both headings from remaining elitist positions, although based on different aesthetic stances. Thus, in spite of the apparently open-minded, all-embracing attitude of omnivorousness, music that is considered to represent a narrow-minded, low cultural discernment would hardly be approved of by academics. According to the above Danish report, an opposite tendency has also been manifested in recent music education, in which some cultural value criteria have shown to be successful on their own terms, which in turn has led to intolerance, isolation, or marginalization of other values and norms. From this perspective, it seems obvious that Scandinavian dance band music may represent such a marginalized culture. Besides, unlike many other popular music genres, this music has never been considered alternative or countercultural in any positive sense of these words, rather as simply *uncultured.* And, possibly therefore, dance band music is hardly a favored music genre among urban, globally oriented middle-class liberals or leftist academics. This must, however, be understood in the complex duality that forms the basis for Layton's interpretation of the middle class' unconscious disdain for low culture.

So, if intellectuals or the media should break the taboo and make reference to dance band music, it would most likely be in terms of irony and parody, making fun of the bigotry and prejudice of this culture,[5] for instance in the way the fictitious dance band Lennartz was portrayed in a Swedish television series (Hylander, Goessens, & Weidemann, 2007) a few years ago: 23-year-old Lennart Johansson of rural Sweden is dedicated to becoming a dance band star. He wants to sing with the band Sven Bodin, but is rejected based on the band's presumption of racial prejudice in the dance band genre, as Lennart's skin color leaves no doubt about his African ancestry. Lennart then decides to start his own band, which happens to be composed of other others of Swedish society. The idea of a Scandinavian dance band with a Black lead singer, a female guitarist, and most of the band members seemingly being immigrants from the Middle East, is so unorthodox—or heterodox—that an omnivorous spectator might easily describe it as viciously funny. How the dance band community felt about it, has not been recorded.

For many reasons, this case might be seen as equivalent to the so-called *culture war,* which in a North American context is a metaphor used to claim that political conflict is based on sets of conflicting cultural values, which, of course, from a strict Marxist perspective represents a simplification. The term, however, implies a conflict between those values considered progressive or liberal and those considered traditionalist or conservative—with the latter, lately, ostensibly represented by interest and pressure groups like the Tea Party movement. Obviously, this position points to the rhetorical, cultural psychological connection that is established between certain lifestyles, taste, and stylistic preferences on the one hand and various degrees of confidence in the government and support for different economic policies on the other hand, apparently no matter whose interests these politics may serve in real, everyday life.

Dance band music could be seen as taking part in a parallel Nordic culture war rhetoric, symbolizing endorsement of ordinary common sense, moral traditionalism, conservative gender roles, ethnocentric xenophobia, and reluctance toward governmental regulations and restrictions, paired with working-class and rural affiliation. The fact that voters for the Norwegian Progress Party—a right-wing populist party that, in coalition with the Conservative Party, formed its first ever government in 2013—prefer Scandinavian dance band music to a significantly larger degree than those who vote for other political parties (TNS Gallup, n.d.) appears in this respect as another indicator of a populist movement against the elite culture. However, the question may be asked whether this countercultural opposition allows for social mobility or immobility (see Willis, 1977). According to recent Norwegian opinion polls (TNS Gallup, n.d.) the appeal of dance band music falls heavily dependent on both education and income levels. Similarly, the polls show that education works in two interesting ways in terms of taste: on the one hand, that interest in traditional high culture, such as classical music, increases with education level, while interest in certain parts of popular culture, like a selection of rock music and movies, also increases according to the length of education. The latter is a relatively new trend. Trondman (1990) argues that different tastes in rock have marked social distance between classes and have been related to the establishment of social hierarchies from the early 1990s on. In a nutshell, and described in detail in the previous section, highly educated people may now obtain both high and low culture, or at least components of them.

On the other hand, this situation also demonstrates that the spread has only been in one direction: people with low education do not access high culture. This shows that there are still relatively clear links between cultural tastes, socioeconomic and educational background, and that we are far from living in a totally individualized and fragmented social landscape. There are quite evident social, cultural, and psychological structures and patterns embedded in the taste regimes. Indeed, as stated above, parts of popular culture still have such a low status that they may instinctively appear as cultural taboos for the dominant classes (Bennett et al., 2009), in other words, they are grounded in a normative unconscious class habitus.

WHO CAN SPEAK FOR WHOM?

I mentioned the gentrification above—a term that originates from urban geography and city planning—but I did not discuss critically some of its consequences. One can claim that some city planners have adopted the rhetoric and beliefs of politicians and public opinion-makers when asserting the blessing of gentrification. This may be because they belong to privileged classes and benefit from living in and visiting neighborhoods with qualities appropriate to their own omnivorous taste and "open-minded" lifestyle. But it also implies that they have omitted part of the original definition of the gentrification concept, which is that in the process of renewal and rebuilding accompanying the influx of affluent people into deteriorating areas, the original, poorer residents are often marginalized or displaced (Glass, 1963). With both dimensions in mind, a group of Norwegian researchers are trying to explore whether it might make sense to use the term gentrification metaphorically to describe similar tendencies in the musical field (Dyndahl et al., 2014). In this attempt, musical gentrification may be understood as parallel to what happens in urban gentrification when for instance artists, academics, and educated-class residents begin to settle in low-income and working-class areas, thus raising both the standard and the status of the properties and the neighborhood, whereas many of the original residents are forced to move out, in addition to the obvious economic reasons arising from the fact that renting or buying property becomes unaffordable, because they feel alienated from an area that once was familiar. From this, musical gentrification needs to be understood in the same way as complex processes with both inclusionary and exclusionary outcomes, by which music, music practices, and music cultures of relatively lower status are made to be objects of acquisition by subjects who inhabit higher or more powerful positions.

It is in this connection worth mentioning that, in 2011, the Norwegian government proposed that a country music festival should receive state funding, in line with several ongoing festivals within classical music, church music, contemporary music, jazz, folk, blues, rock, Sami music, and multicultural music, which were previously assigned the role as leaders in their respective musical fields (Kulturdepartementet, 2011). It was, however, a controversial decision that even a country festival, located in a small village in western Norway, should get so-called national hub status, which triggered a debate about which criteria were needed to deserve it. In that respect it was interesting to see that a few cultural journalists and connoisseurs from some of Norway's leading broadsheet newspapers led the way in the discussion, acting as gatekeepers for a rather elitist comprehension of country music. According to this, they characterized the audience of the proposed festivals as unqualified and unable to distinguish between ostensibly proper, authentic country music, and what they assumed to be "dance bands with steel guitar and cowboy hats" (Asker, 2010, October 10). "I have been there and seen how an audience well marinated in alcohol, wearing camping outfits, have ruined the experience for the seriously interested," author and critic Vidar Kvalshaug reported to the metropolitan newspaper *Aftenposten* (2011, author's translation). Moreover, he was highly critical of the booking policy conducted in these kinds of festivals, where popular bands like Norwegian Vassendgutane are often booked to ensure the financial basis for the event:

> A government-supported festival cannot book Vassendgutane as headliner or give access to more and more of the dance band community, as we have seen in recent years. There is an infinite distance between international quality country music and Norwegian dance band music. (Kvalshaug, 2011, author's translation)

It is evident that one may detect a number of differences between a country inspired dance band like Vassendgutane and bluegrass supergroup Alison Krauss & Union Station—whom Kvalshaug points to as an example of "quality country music"—just as one can distinguish between a variety of other styles within the broad genre field known as country music. It would certainly be interesting to dig deeper into the authenticity discourse that seems to regulate this issue (Dyndahl & Nielsen, 2014). However, what I see as the crucial point here is that "the seriously interested" audience in this case may represent the culturally affluent middle-to-upper-class listeners, moving into formerly underprivileged music cultures, displacing, marginalizing, or excluding the original, less culturally affluent population of the festival, in order "to gentrify elements of popular culture and incorporate them into the dominant status-group culture" (Peterson & Kern, 1996, p. 906).

The above inclusion/exclusion—or musical gentrification—processes, concerning country music as well as dance band music, arguably confront music education and research with some important challenges too. Scandinavian dance band music may in this respect serve as a major example of a cultural form that to a large extent is excluded from education and scholarship. In relation to its popularity and prevalence, remarkably little research has been done on this music and its practices in the Nordic countries. There are also no courses or programs to be found in dance band music, taught at music academies or universities. This contrasts with jazz, rock, pop, and other former low musical forms, which gradually have found their place in music education, in line with the current academic status of popular music studies. However, this situation also indicates which aesthetic objects and cultural practices are approved by the education system—including the overall state school system—and are thus worth paying attention to.

If music educators and researchers are reluctant to acknowledge the musical, aesthetic, and cultural practices that numerous individuals and groups strongly identify with, they could, perhaps, indirectly open access to movements that nurture a basic skepticism towards academics, education, and research, instead celebrating—at least apparently—ordinary people's commonsensical ability to cope with questions, challenges, and options regarding musical taste, aesthetic and cultural significance, regardless of what "so-called experts" might tell you. This opposition can thus be understood as caused by the patronizing mixture of disdain and pity that middle-class liberals habitually display to the lower classes. Populist politicians and parties have seized the opportunity and have already embraced the Norwegian dance band culture, which may be regarded as a particular kind of musical gentrification, in this case highlighting the reluctance to submit to the "political correctness" of the cultural elite, its media and institutions. As mentioned above, voters and supporters of the Progress Party prefer dance band music to a larger degree than those who vote for other political parties. For instance, in the 2009 campaign for the Norwegian parliamentary election, the Progress Party produced a compilation album, entitled *Politisk ukorrekt* (Politically Incorrect; Fremskrittspartiet, n.d.), in large part consisting of dance band music, as part of its campaign material. In addition, there are videos posted on YouTube, wherein the leader of the Progress Party, Siv Jensen, sings along with Norway's most popular dance band, Ole Ivars (Steenersen1, 2009). However, it is worth noting that the Progress Party, despite the fact that they won 22.9 % of the total votes of the 2009 election, becoming in the process the second-largest party of the country, still nourished an image as a protest party, while they, as indicated above, in the subsequent general election appeared to be a more accountable party, ready to take responsibility of government. Since 2013, Siv Jensen has been the minister of finance of Norway.

Nonetheless, the populist truism that everyone should be given what they want, since everyone has the right to define one's own needs and interests, even if they are not appreciated by authorities and the media, seems to be a common feature of populist politics as well as of the dance band culture. On these grounds, dance band music may very well be seen as one of the most distinctive politicized musics of Norway today,[6] demonstrating the political impact of music as a symbolic, social marker, in this case associated with resistance to elitist cultural and educational ideals, advanced and advocated by right-wing populists (Lykkeberg, 2008; Marsdal, 2007; Olsen, 2010).

This raises some important questions about gentrification, marginalization, and "tabooification" of music cultures. The overall issue, however, seems to be the problem of representation. In her seminal essay "Can the Subaltern Speak?" Gayatri Chakravorty Spivak (1988) discusses how Gilles Deleuze and Michel Foucault (Foucault, 1977) fail in their analysis of the international division of labor and global capitalism, because they believe that the oppressed should be given the opportunity to speak for themselves and not be represented by others. Spivak problematizes the very idea of representation. With reference to Karl Marx' *The Eighteenth Brumaire of Louis Bonaparte* (1852/1954), in which Marx differentiates the notion of representation by means of the two German words *vertreten* and *darstellen*, she explains how Deleuze and Foucault do not distinguish clearly between the two different meanings: "Two senses of representation are being run together: representation as 'speaking for,' as in politics, and representation as 're-presentation,' as in art or philosophy" (Spivak, 1988, p. 275). She further elaborates:

> There is, of course, a relationship between them, one that has received po-litical and ideological exacerbation in the European tradition at least since the poet and the sophist, the actor and the orator, have both been seen as harmful. In the guise of a post-Marxist description of the scene of power, we thus encounter a much older debate: between representation or rhetoric as tropology and as persuasion. *Darstellen* belongs to the first constellation, *ver-treten*—with stronger suggestions of substitution—to the second. Again, they are related, but running them together, especially in order to say that beyond both is where oppressed subjects speak, act, and know for *themselves*, leads to an essentialist, utopian politics. (p. 276)

Spivak criticizes the prominent French intellectuals for—unconsciously normative—reintroducing an undivided subject into the discourse of power. The consequence is a renunciation of the role of ideology in reproducing the social relations of production, which may convey an unquestioned in-terpretation of the oppressed as subject, implying that there are essentialist relations between concrete experiences, interests, and actions. The presup-position that there is a "'true correspondence to own being is as artificial or social as the patronymic" (p. 285), Spivak argues. There is obviously a huge difference between the doubly oppressed Indian women she refers to, and participants in the Nordic dance band community. The Hindu widows, who ascended the pyre of their deceased husbands, were muted—these subal-terns could not speak. Those who take part in Scandinavian low culture can certainly talk, as they can also create Facebook groups, run fan clubs, and so on. And, not least, they can vote in elections and participate fully in society. But even though one may ascribe to them a privileged, genuine articula-tion of people's interests, the point in this particular context is that neither their voices nor their utterances can escape from being situated in specific social, cultural, and psychological contexts and power structures—as with the Southern subaltern.

But Spivak also criticizes Western academics for apparently re-pre-senting the voice of the oppressed as if they themselves were "absent nonrepresenters." In this way, she argues that, at the same time as they are seemingly "representing them, the intellectuals represent themselves as transparent" (p. 275), whereas they actually represent the dominated from a normative unconscious or unreflective position that implicitly contributes to define them as the other, in part by consistently presenting them as being more homogeneous than the intellectuals' own group or class:

> Yet even this does not encompass the heterogeneous Other. Outside (though not completely so) the circuit of the international division of labor, there are people whose consciousness we cannot grasp if we close off our benevolence by constructing a homogeneous Other referring only to our own place in the seat of the Same or the Self. (p. 288)

Both aforementioned aspects of representation can be discussed critically in relation to the musical configuration of class distinctions, the construction of the insignificant other, and the constitution of cultural taboos. Cultural psychology and sociology have among their objectives to scrutinize and display the interests of traditions and positions that claim to represent political and cultural interests of ordinary people, but also of those who claim to govern good taste, aesthetic quality, and authentic culture, ostensibly on a completely different level than vernacular vulgarity. However, this becomes especially challenging when it affects the supposedly tolerant and inclusive omnivores.

Moreover, recognizing that when acting as a representative of something, one simultaneously re-presents or interprets it from a certain position—such as concepts like situated knowledge, subject position, or the deeply rooted habitus indicate—should lead to improved acknowledgement that any statement as well as any attitude conveys a positional, normative interpretation; conscious or unconscious. This applies not least to the researcher and the teacher who master the knowledge and the mediation of knowledge. Education and research, along with the academization, institutionalization, and gentrification of different music, should in this context be understood as cultivation practices relating to the power, significance, and distinctions arising from the specific values of cultural capital—including the social anatomy of taste—as well as the embodied norms of habitus.

Based on this it would be hard to understand representation without bringing in re-presentation. It is also difficult to engage the concept re-presentation without acting as a representative of any interests. This raises the question whether it is at all possible to take a position beyond both dimensions of representation, where oppressed subjects can speak, act, and know for themselves, and where one can avoid ending up in an essentialist pose? Spivak twists the problem and responds: "To confront them is not to represent (*vertreten*) them but to learn to represent (*darstellen*) ourselves. This argument would take us into a critique of a disciplinary anthropology and the relationship between elementary pedagogy and disciplinary formation" (pp. 288–289).

In other words: *we*—in this context implied as middle-to-upper class academics, educators, and researchers—should address our own position thoroughly, in order to remove the transparency cloak and thereby make some of our class habitus and culturally capitalized power evident, not least when it comes to music genres and cultural practices we may despise for various normative unconscious reasons.

NOTES

1. Several sociologists have raised critical objections to Peterson's concepts omnivore and univore (see for example Atkinson, 2011). Purhonen, Gronow, and Rahkonen (2010) claim, for instance, that the hypothetical 'univore snob' is practically non-existent, empirically considered. Bennett et al. (2009) have conducted a comprehensive, Bourdieu-inspired study on cultural practices in the United Kingdom, in which their empirical findings appear to refine also Peterson's concept of cultural omnivorousness in a number of ways. One finding is that cultural omnivorousness is not exclusively associated with well-educated people; instead it seems to be age, as much as social class that distinguishes. In music, they find that there are still genre boundaries that are not easily crossed; for instance, classical music still belongs mainly to the elite, while some popular music genres are considered to be unambiguously lowbrow, which seems applicable for Scandinavian dance band music too. For my part I still find the notion of omnivorousness fruitful, but will make no further reference to the term 'univore' (Dyndahl et al., 2014 for supplementary discussion).

2. In a recent study of Norwegian dance band culture, Stavrum (2014) finds that a group of mainly listening audience has arisen.

3. This is an assumption that of course presupposes active audiences and creative consumers as interpreted by *cultural studies* (see for example Hall, 1980; Morley, 1992), rather than the passive and paralyzed 'victims' of the *culture industry*, as described by the *Frankfurt School* (Adorno, 1941/2009; Adorno & Horkheimer, 1944/2011). See Hesmondhalgh (2008) for a further discussion on the active and reflexive agency of consumers in cultural music studies.

4. In Swedish: "allt utom dansband" or "allt utom dansbandsmusik", in Norwegian: "alt unntatt danseband."

5. There are, however, some very recent exceptions, like the television reality show *Dansbandskampen* [The dance band battle] (Settman, 2008), which has been broadcast by Sveriges Television [The Swedish publish service broadcaster] since 2008. Possibly, this type of show might signal that a certain inclusion, and perhaps in turn, gentrification of dance band music is about to take place. Another indication of the same phenomenon is that a show based on the song universe of Norway's most popular dance band, Ole Ivars, was put on stage at the Torshov Theatre in Oslo in 2014.

6. There is a difference between Norwegian and Swedish dance band music in the sense that the Norwegian has shown a certain affinity towards right-wing populism, while the Swedish may still be associated with social democratic culture and values, for instance in connection with the country's Folkpark institution and tradition.

REFERENCES

Adorno, T. W. (1941/2009). On popular music. In J. Storey (Ed.), *Cultural theory and popular culture: A reader* (pp. 63–74), Harlow, England: Pearson Education.

Adorno, T. W., & Horkheimer, M. (1944/2011). The culture industry: Enlightenment as mass deception. In I. Szeman & T. Kaposy (Eds.), *Cultural theory: An anthology* (pp. 40–52). Malden, MA: Wiley-Blackwell.

Asker, C. (2010, October 10). *Country-musikken inn i varmen* [Acceptance of country music]. Retrieved from http://www.aftenposten.no/kultur/article3848476.ece#.Tyk3Zhx0zXE

Atkinson, W. (2011). The context and genesis of musical tastes: Omnivorousness debunked, Bourdieu buttressed. *Poetics, 39*(3), 169–186.

Bennett, T., Savage, M., Silva, E., Warde, A., Gayo-Cal, M., & Wright, D. (2009). *Culture, class, distinction.* New York, NY: Routledge.

Born, G., & Hesmondhalgh, D. (2000). *Western music and its others: Difference, representation, and appropriation in music.* Berkeley, CA: University of California Press.

Bourdieu, P. (1984). *Distinction: A social critique of the judgement of taste.* London, England: Routledge & Kegan Paul.

Bourdieu, P. (1986/2011). The forms of capital. In I. Szeman & T. Kaposy (Eds.), *Cultural theory: An anthology* (pp. 81–93), Malden, MA: Wiley-Blackwell.

Bourdieu, P. (1990). *In other words: Essays towards a reflexive sociology.* Cambridge, England: Polity.

Christophersen, C. (2009). *Rytmisk musikkundervisning som estetisk praksis: En casestudie* [Rhythmic music education as aesthetic practice: A case study]. Oslo, Norway: NMH-publikasjoner.

Cole, M. (1996). *Cultural psychology. A once and future discipline.* London, England: The Belknap Press of Harvard University Press.

DeNora, T. (2000). *Music in everyday life.* Cambridge, England: Cambridge University Press.

Dyndahl, P. (2008). Music education in the sign of deconstruction. *Philosophy of music education review, 16*(2), 124–144.

Dyndahl, P., & Ellefsen, L. W. (2009). Music didactics as a multifaceted field of cultural didactic studies. In F. V. Nielsen, S-E. Holgersen & S. G. Nielsen (Eds.), *Nordic research in music education yearbook* (Vol. 11; pp. 9–32). Oslo, Norway: NMH-publikasjoner.

Dyndahl, P., Karlsen, S., Skårberg, O., & Nielsen, S. G. (2014). Cultural omnivorousness and musical gentrification: An outline of a sociological framework and its applications for music education research. *Action, Criticism, and Theory for Music Education, 13*(1), 40–69.

Dyndahl, P., & Nielsen, S. G. (2014). Shifting authenticities in Scandinavian music education. *Music Education Research 16*(1), 105–118.

Eriksson, L. (2008). *Livets band: den svenska dansbandskulturens historia* [Band of the life: The history of the Swedish dance band culture]. Stockholm, Sweden: Prisma.

Finnegan, R. (2003). Music, experience and the anthropology of emotion. In M. Clayton, T. Herbert, & R. Middleton (Eds.), *The cultural study of music* (pp. 181–192). London, England: Routledge.

Florida, R. (2002). *The rise of the creative class: And how it's transforming work, leisure, community and everyday life.* New York, NY: Basic Books.

Fornäs, J. (1995). *Cultural theory and late modernity.* London, England: Sage.

Foucault, M. (1977). Intellectuals and power. In M. Focault, *Language, counter-memory, practice: Selected essays and interviews* (pp. 206–217). Oxford, England: Basil Blackwell.

Fremskrittspartiet. (n.d.). *Politisk ukorrekt* [Politically incorrect]. Retrieved April 1, 2011, from http://www.frp.no/Kjøp+CDn+Politisk+ukorrekt.d25-ThljG2d.ips

Glass, R. (1963). *Introduction to London: Aspects of change.* London, England: Centre for Urban Studies.

Hall, S. (1980). Encoding/decoding. In S. Hall, D. Hobson, A. Lowe, & P. Willis (Eds.), *Culture, media, language* (pp. 128–138). London, England: Hutchinson.

Hesmondhalgh, D. (2008). Towards a critical understanding of music, emotion and self-identity. *Consumption, markets and culture, 11*(4), 329–343.

Hylander, A., Goessens, E., & Weidemann, A. (2007). *Leende guldbruna ögon* [Smiling golden-brown eyes]. Stockholm, Sweden: Sveriges Television.

Kulturdepartementet. (2011). *Prop. 1 S (2011–2012) Proposisjon til Stortinget* [Proposition to the Parliament]. Retrieved February 1, 2012, from http://www.regjeringen.no/nb/dep/kud/dok/regpubl/prop/2011-2012/prop-1-s-20112012.html?id=658383

Kvalshaug, V. (2011, July 11). *Gi pengene til en klubb* [Give the money to a club]. Retrieved from http://www.aftenposten.no/meninger/kommentarer/article4170712.ece#.Tyk3shx0zXE

Kvalshaug, V. (2011, September 5). *Countryfestival må snart levere kvalitet* [Country festival must deliver quality in short time]. Retrieved from http://www.aftenposten.no/meninger/kommentatorer/kvalshaug/article4217807.ece#.Tyk38hx0zXE

Layton, L. (2006). That place gives me the heebie jeebies. In L. Layton, N. C. Hollander, & S. Gutwill (Eds.), *Psychoanalysis, class and politics* (pp. 51–64). New York, NY: Routledge.

Lykkeberg, R. (2008). *Kampen om sandhederne: Om det kulturelle borgerskabs storhed og fald* [The battle of truths: On the rise and fall of the cultural bourgeoisie]. Copenhagen, Denmark: Gyldendal.

Marsdal, M. E. (2007). *Frp-koden: Hemmeligheten bak Fremskrittspartiets suksess* [The Frp code: The secret of the Progress Party's success]. Oslo, Norway: Manifest.

Marx, K. (1852/1954). *The eighteenth Brumaire of Louis Bonaparte.* Moscow, Russia: Progress Publishers.

Mead, G. H. (1934). *Mind, self, and society.* Chicago, IL: University of Chicago Press.

Morley, D. (1992). *Television, audiences and cultural studies.* New York, NY: Routledge.

Nielsen, F. V. (2010). *Musikfaget i undervisning og uddannelse: Status og perspektiv 2010* [The music subject in teaching and education: Status and perspectives 2010]. Copenhagen, Denmark: Danmarks Pædagogiske Universitetsskole, Aarhus Universitet.

Olsen, L. (2010). *Eliternes triumf: Da de uddannede klasser tog magten* [Triumph of the elites: When the educated classes seized power]. Rødovre, Denmark: Sohn.

Olsson, B. (1993). *SÄMUS: Musikutbildning i kulturpolitikens tjänst? En studie om en musikutbildning på 1970-talet* [SÄMUS: Music education in the service of cultural policies? A study on musical education in the 1970s]. Göteborg, Sweden: Avdelningen för musikvetenskap, Göteborgs Universitet.

Peterson, R. A. (1992). Understanding audience segmentation: From elite and mass to omnivore and univore. *Poetics, 21*(4), 243–258.

Peterson, R. A., & Kern, R. M. (1996). Changing highbrow taste: From snob to omnivore. *American Sociological Review, 61*(5), 900–907.

Peterson, R. A., & Simkus, A. (1992). How musical tastes mark occupational status groups. In M. Lamont & M. Fournier (Eds.), *Cultivating difference: Symbolic boundaries and the making of inequality* (pp. 152–186). Chicago, IL: University of Chicago Press.

Purhonen, S., Gronow, J., & Rahkonen, K. (2011). Nordic democracy of taste? Cultural omnivorousness in musical and literary taste preferences in Finland. *Poetics, 38*(3), 266–298.

Roe, K. (1993). Academic capital and music tastes among Swedish adolescents. *Young, 1*(3), 40–55.

Settman, P. (2008). *Dansbandskampen* [The dance band battle]. Stockholm, Sweden: Sveriges Television.

Spivak, G. C. (1988). Can the subaltern speak? In C. Nelson & L. Grossberg (Eds.), *Marxism and the interpretation of culture* (pp. 277–313). Urbana, IL: University of Illinois Press.

Stavrum, H. (2014). Hvor mange gullplater henger på veggen? Om danseband og kvalitet [How many gold record awards hanging on the wall? On dance band and quality]. *Sosiologi i dag, 44*(1), 90–116.

Steenersen1 (2009, June 27; Poster). Siv Jensen synger 'jeg trodde englane fans' [sic.] med Ole Ivars [Siv Jensen sings 'I thought there were angels' along with the band Ole Ivars] [Video]. Retrieved from http://www.youtube.com/watch?v=TLYM2zaz8a4

TNS Gallup. (n.d.). *Consumer & media.* Retrieved April 6, 2011, from www.tns-gallup.no

Trondman, M. (1990). Rock taste—On rock as symbolic capital: A study of young people's music, taste and music making. In K. Roe & U. Carlsson (Eds.), *Popular music research* (pp. 71–85). Göteborg, Sweden: NORDICOM.

Trondman, M. (1999). *Kultursociologi i praktiken* [Cultural sociology in practice]. Lund, Sweden: Studentlitteratur.

Tønsberg, K. (2013). *Akademiseringen av jazz, pop og rock: En dannelsesreise* [The academization of jazz, pop and rock: A journey of formation]. Trondheim, Norway: Akademika forlag.

Williams, P. (1997). The ethnic scarring of American whiteness. In W. Lubiano (Ed.), *The house that race built* (pp. 253–263). New York, NY: Pantheon.

Willis, P. (1977). *Learning to labour. How working class kids get working class jobs.* Farnborough, England: Saxon House.

CHAPTER 9

TIMESCALES IN MUSICAL EXPERIENCE

Rolf Inge Godøy

Performing music, and listening or moving to music, takes time, time that can be measured in milliseconds, seconds, minutes and hours. Yet in the face of this truism, we have intriguing issues of how we subjectively experience various musical features in the seemingly continuous flow of time. The topic of time in musical experience has indeed generated innumerable publications in music theory, analysis, aesthetics and philosophy, and in more recent decades in music performance and music perception research. Being aware of this vast backdrop, my aim with the present chapter is rather modest, namely to present a hopefully useful overview of perceptual features that we typically encounter at different timescales in music, an overview that can help us make good choices of focus in music-related research, and possibly also shed light on the interplay of physiological-cognitive constraints and cultural factors in music.

The term *timescales* is here used to designate chronometric duration ranges, to designate how long a given musical excerpt has to last in order to enable subjective perception of salient features such as pitch, timbre, texture, rhythmic and melodic patterns, style, affect and mood, in short, all kinds of features we think of as integral to musical experience. The main

Cultural Psychology of Musical Experience, pages 165–178
Copyright © 2016 by Information Age Publishing
All rights of reproduction in any form reserved.

idea of this chapter is that although we may have a continuum of timescales between the very small and the very large in music, there are significant qualitative distinctions between the timescales. It is suggested that we have three main timescales in musical experience, namely the *micro, meso,* and *macro* timescales, designating respectively the timescale of continuous features, of more discontinuous chunks, and of large-scale forms. These three timescales may very well (and usually do) coexist in musical experience, yet they encompass distinct perceptual features. Furthermore, these three timescales are seen as based on constraints of music-related body motion, i.e., biomechanical and motor control constraints, as well as constraints of perception, and manifest in interaction with musical culture factors.

The present chapter reflects several years of research on music-related body motion and findings on how musical experience is embodied. For this reason, we shall after a brief presentation of audio feature timescales have a look at so-called *motor theory* perspectives on musical experience, followed by considerations of body motion timescales in music. This prepares the ground for the mentioned three-timescale model of micro, meso, and macro, followed by some ideas in our current and upcoming research on exploring *intermittent chunk formation* in music, something we see as an essential element in understanding musical experience. Finally, issues of timescales are seen as important in understanding differences between musical cultures, including understanding some peculiarities of our inherited Western notions of musical experience.

AUDIO FEATURES TIMESCALES

As we know, audible sound (in the case of human hearing) is situated in the region of approximately 20 to 20,000 Hz and is the basis for perceiving continuous features such as pitch, loudness and stationary timbre (more precisely so-called *quasi stationary,* nontransient spectral components, sometimes referred to as "tone color"), as well as location of sound sources. But there are also *duration thresholds* for perceiving these features in that we have to hear some minimum duration of sound in order to judge whether it is pitched or nonpitched, perceive its stationary timbre features, loudness, location, as well as other features such as synchrony and order of sound events. These minimum duration thresholds typically vary considerably with the content and context of the sounds (Moore, 1995), but may (very approximately) be found in the sub 50-ms timescale. Perceptually salient changes in the sound, such as fluctuations in pitch (e.g., vibrato, trill), loudness (e.g., tremolo, drum roll) or timbre (e.g., open-closing of mutes, bow placement changes), more continuous evolutions, or overall dynamic, pitch and timbre related shapes (so-called *envelopes*), are typically found below the 20 Hz rate, i.e., above the approximately 50 ms duration, threshold.

Musical sound will in most cases consist of features at different timescales in parallel, typically of more or less quasi-stationary features combined with evolution and/or fluctuations in pitch, timbre and loudness. These above 50 ms duration features are essential for musical experience, apparently readily perceived, yet mostly beyond the reach of traditional Western music theory. The concept of so-called *categorical perception* of pitch, duration and timbre (meaning that deviations and/or nuances are mostly disregarded [Snyder, 2000]), has been one of the hallmarks of Western musical culture, whereas other musical cultures have more subtle notions of note level and subnote level features, e.g., the nuanced notions of pitch found in some Indian music. In practice however, Western music has needless to say had a very large repertoire of sonic nuances, but concepts of such nuances have typically been confined to the practical sphere of instrumental or vocal teaching, and until quite recently been outside the realm of more systematic music theory research. Even with present day profusion of digital audio effects in music, effects strongly affecting note level and subnote level features (e.g., *compression, distortion, flanging, autotune*, etc.), there is a deficit of conceptual tools for features at this timescale.

In the pioneering work of Pierre Schaeffer and his coworkers during the 1950s and 1960s, this domain of auditory features was studied from a subjective perspective in what Schaeffer called the *morphology of the sonic object* (Chion, 1983; Schaeffer, 1966; Schaeffer, 1967/1998 for sound examples). The method in this research was to differentiate subjectively experienced sound features by using metaphorical labels, e.g., like "grain" to denote various rapid fluctuations in sounds, and then to qualify this grain feature further by depicting is relative rate, ambit, regularity-irregularity, etc. More recent psychoacoustic research has made advances in singling out such features (Peeters, Giordano, Susini, Misdariis, & McAdams, 2011), but there are still gaps to be filled here, i.e., we have many more unnamed salient features in music at this timescale. The combined audio rate and sub-audio rate features are the content of what is rather loosely referred to as the "sound" of certain styles and/or musicians, and listeners' ability to recognize such features is evidently quite robust even for excerpts as short as 250 ms (Gjerdingen & Perrott, 2008).

Several tone and/or sound events (nonpitched sounds) in the above 50 ms duration range may fuse into what we perceive as units, into bursts of rapid tremolos, trills, ornaments, arpeggios and other figures. This means that in the very approximately 0.5 to 5 s duration range, we have all kinds of rhythmic patterns, textures, motives, melodic fragments and phrases which are in most cases perceived holistically as units, as what we shall call *chunks*. Notably, very many expressive (timing, intonation and articulation nuances) and affective features are found at this chunk timescale, and it will later be argued that this timescale has a privileged role in musical experience, in part based on constraints of human body motion and perception.

Beyond the timescale of the chunk, we also have timescales of sections, tunes, movements, whole works and prolonged events, extending from several seconds to minutes and even hours in the case of large-scale Western musical works or in cases of rituals or events in various cultures, however the perceptual effects of such large-scale musical experiences seem so far not so well studied. So also in view of getting a better understanding large-scale forms in music, it would be a good idea to make a tour of some constraints that seem to be at work in musical experience, starting with a look at body motion elements in musical experience.

MOTOR THEORY PERSPECTIVES

Since the end of the 20th century, various so-called *embodied* perspectives on human cognition in general, and on music cognition in particular, have become quite popular (Godøy, 2003; Godøy & Leman, 2010; Leman, 2008). The gist of these perspectives is that human cognition is understood not as a matter of abstract, computer-like calculations, but rather as a matter of our bodies sensing and interacting with the environment. In the case of music, this means that listening to music is not only a matter of processing sound input, but just as much a matter of reenacting or mentally simulating body motion we associate with the sound we are hearing. For instance, hearing fast and loud drumming, we tend to have mental images of energetic mallet-hand-arm motion, or hearing slow and soft string orchestra music, tend to have mental images of protracted and slow bow motion. In this mental re-enactment in listening, there may be both such *sound-producing motion*, i.e., motion we believe go into producing the sound, but also *sound-accompanying motion*, i.e., motion we believe is afforded by the sound, but more independent of the directly sound-producing motion (Godøy, 2010b).

The idea of mental reenactment in perception was presented as the so-called motor theory of perception in linguistics in the 1960s, and the gist of this theory was that perceiving and understanding spoken language also includes a constant process of mental simulation of the articulatory motion believed to be at the source of what we are hearing (Galantucci, Fowler, & Turvey, 2006; Liberman & Mattingly, 1985). With the ensuing spreading of the embodied perspective in the cognitive sciences, the idea of motor involvement in perception and cognition has been extended to most areas of human experience (Berthoz, 1997; Gallese & Lakoff, 2005).

In view of timescales in musical experience, motor theory suggests that all sound is included in some action trajectory: a single drum sound is the result of the hand and mallet moving from an initial position to the impact point with the drum and bouncing back again to the initial position; a violin tone is the result of the bow being lifted, placed on a string, pulled downwards, and lifted off the string at the end of the downstroke. Notably, such action trajectory inclusion also concerns quasistationary postures in the case of sustained tones such as in singing, and even repeated tones such as in a prolonged tremolo on a keyboard.

In a motor theory perspective, sound features are hypothesized to be spontaneously correlated with body motion features, both in mentally simulated motion, and in some cases, visibly reenacted motion. For this reason, we have in our previous research tried to study how listeners with different backgrounds and levels of musical expertise would be able to spontaneously render sound-producing actions by so-called *air instrument performance*. As expected, there was considerable variation in the results, but most listeners seemed to have some knowledge of basic sound-producing actions (Godøy, Haga, & Jensenius, 2006). In a similar vein, we also studied other spontaneous body motion to music, so-called *free dance* (Haga, 2008), as well as more extensive studies of so-called *sound tracing*, meaning spontaneous hand/arm rendering motion of perceived salient features (Nymoen, Godøy, Jensenius, & Tørresen, 2013). The results here were again quite clear when it came to the perception of pitch and dynamic envelopes, and more varied for composite features like timbre.

Although much remains to be explored further here, we have good reason to believe that the motor theory perspective can be extended to most sound features, ranging from more or less stationary sounds and minute inflections to all kinds of rhythmical patterns, textures, grooves, expressive features, etc., and also affective features like tension-relaxation, calmness-agitation, etc. In summary, the motor theory perspective is another way of saying that whatever we hear is fitted into some kind of body motion schema.

BODY MOTION TIMESCALES

The range of timescales of body motion is more restricted than that of sound: there are clearly limits to speed in human motion (usually well below the auditory threshold rate of 20 Hz) as well as restrictions on duration because of the need for rests and/or change in postures to avoid fatigue or strain injury. As for getting around restrictions on maximal speed, there is the possibility of some clever exploitation of rebound as in drumrolls, and there is also the washboard or maracas type of very rapid sound onsets due to a single stroking motion across a dented surface, similar to fast glissandi on a harp or a keyboard instrument. Related to this is the reaction of the instrument or the voice to sound-producing actions, reactions that may produce motion in the sound faster than possible to make as singular motions, e.g., the "growling" quality of a deep trombone tone, the "shimmer" of a trumpet, or "the grain of the voice," to use Roland Barthes's expression. (Barthes, 1977).

Obviously, we can see music-related body motion everywhere, and it is useful to have some classification scheme here. Following long-lasting discussions in the international research community that culminated in Godøy and Leman 2010, it seemed convenient to classify music-related body motion according to functions as briefly mentioned above:

- *Sound-producing motion* primarily includes *excitatory motion*, motion that transfers energy from the body to the instrument by stroking, bowing, hitting, kicking, blowing, etc. but also *modulatory motion*, e.g., changing the pitch with the left hand on a string instrument or the valves on a wind instrument. Additionally, there is so-called *ancillary motion*, motion that is not directly excitatory or modulatory, but apparently still indispensable for ergonomic, expressive and/or communicative reasons.
- *Sound-accompanying motion* includes all kinds of motion that listeners may make to music, prominently in dance, but also in various everyday listening situations, in walking, gesticulating, nodding head, swaying torso, etc., often displaying so-called *entrainment* with the music, i.e., synchronizing the body motion with the perceived beat of the music. In this category, motion may also be more independent of detail features of the music (e.g., of the beat), yet reflect overall features such as level of activity, mode of motion (e.g., calm, agitated, jerky), and affect.

All through these categories, it is important to recognize that any particular music-related motion might have multiple functions, e.g., an upward hand/arm/shoulder motion may at the same time be a preparation for the coming accented chord on a keyboard, an upbeat communicative gesture to fellow musicians in an ensemble, as well as a theatrical gesture to convey a sense of energy to the audience.

As for more biomechanical and motor control perspectives, we have the following basic categories of music-related body motion:

- *Sustained,* meaning continuous motion such as in protracted bowing or blowing.
- *Impulsive,* with a short burst of effort followed by relaxation, typical of percussion (including the piano).

- *Iterative,* meaning a rapid back and forth motion such as in tremolo motion on string instruments and keyboards, or continuous motion over a bumpy surface, e.g., maracas or washboard, creating a series of impulses as mentioned previously.

Between these basic categories, we can often see so-called *phase transitions*, meaning transitions from one mode of motion to another (Haken, Kelso, & Bunz, 1985), as in the transition from walking to running, depending on variables such as duration, speed, and rate: if a sustained motion is becoming very short, it will flip over to become an impulsive motion, and conversely, if an impulsive motion becomes elongated, it will become a sustained motion. Likewise, if we have an accelerating series of impulsive motions, these will fuse and become a continuous iterative motion. Such and similar changes in duration, speed, rate, and also ambit, will variably result in fused chunks, or what Schaeffer called *sonic objects* (Chion, 1983; Godøy, 2006; Schaeffer, 1966), such as tremolos, trills, glissandi (also on keyboards and plucked instruments), and various rhythmical and textural patterns.

Finally, chunks can be combined into more complex and extended action scripts, often also with different simultaneous strata and motion types, e.g., sustained background motion and sound combined with faster foreground motion and sound.

MICRO, MESO, AND MACRO TIMESCALES

Combining the auditory and motion feature perspectives, the different timescales at work in musical experience can be grouped into the following three main categories:

- Micro timescale, meaning continuous features mentioned in section 2 above, i.e., stationary pitch, dynamics, timbre, as well as various fluctuations and transients, corresponding to stationary body postures and/or continuous motion such as continuous bowing or blowing. This is typically the timescale of what Schaeffer called the *morphology of the sonic object,* and the timescale sufficient for a recognition of the "sound" of various kinds of music (Gjerdingen & Perrott, 2008)
- Meso timescale, typically in the very approximate 0.5 to 5 seconds range (often in the shorter end of this range), including the mentioned micro timescale continuous features, but additionally having new emergent features not found on the micro timescale. At this meso timescale we find chunks of sound and motion, chunks perceived and conceived holistically as somehow meaningful units

in the sense of enabling identification of salient musical features such as overall pitch-related, dynamic and timbral profiles, rhythmic and textural patterns, melodic fragments, sense of motion, affect, and stylistic features. The meso timescale is also where we find what Schaeffer called the *typology of the sonic object*, meaning the overall dynamic, pitch-related and timbre-related shapes, different from the mentioned *morphology of the sonic object*, which was primarily concerned with micro timescale features.

- Macro timescale, based on the concatenation of several chunks in succession, as found in sections, whole tunes, movements, and whole works, in duration extending from that of the upper limits of the chunk to minutes and even hours. Although we do not seem to have much research on the perceptual workings of such large-scale forms, we may reasonably assume that long-term memory and ability to recall various chunks and sections in the work play an important role at this timescale (Snyder, 2000).

These three timescales often coexist and interact. However, in terms of carrier of salient musical features, the most important is no doubt the meso timescale of the chunk.

EXPLORING INTERMITTENT CHUNK FORMATION IN MUSIC

What are then the factors that lead to the emergence of holistically perceived meso timescale chunks? One obvious factor is that of meaning, meaning in the sense of identifying perceptually salient features such as rhythmical, textural, melodic, modal, harmonic, etc. patterns, in short, stylistic and affective features, something that is usually achieved at the very approximately 0.5 to 5 s timescale, simply because such durations are sufficient for recognition of various patterns. As pointed out by Pöppel, very many human "meaning phenomena" are found at this timescale, in his view because of a convergence of typical human body motion duration and attention span durations (Pöppel, 1989, 1997). Applied to music, Pöppel's line of reasoning would suggest that the production and perception of music has been adapted to a more basic and general constraint of meaning-formation at the meso timescale of the chunk.

Taking this meaning reasoning one step further, many events in our environment, like a pebble hitting a quiet pond, a bell struck with a hammer, a sustained trumpet tone, or a car crash, tend to be perceived as coherent chunks in the approximately 0.5 to 5 s duration range because the motion generating the sound and the sounds themselves have envelopes (overall shape) and various gestalt features that create fusion and a sense of coherence (Bregman, 1990). Factors that make chunks stand out from their context can be collectively called *qualitative discontinuities*. Qualitative discontinuities, like shifts between silence and sound, stillness and motion, one timbre and another timbre, low pitch and high pitch, etc., are salient indications of change, of borders between events in our perception of the world.

But additionally, we could create chunks of sound and motion by more arbitrary cuttings, e.g., by sound or video editing software make a cut of one second of a car sound or one second of a head nodding. With repeated perceptions of such arbitrary cuttings, e.g., as with so-called *samples* in DJ scratching, they tend to be transformed into holistically perceived chunks. This kind of artificial origin of chunks by cutting was in fact one of the experiences of the *musique concrète* with the use of looped sound fragments, the so-called *sillon fermé* (Chion, 1983, Schaeffer, 1966), hence actually a precursor to present-day use of "samples" in DJ scratching.

Qualitative discontinuities in sound and motion, regardless of whether they are natural (environmental events) or artificial (made by arbitrary cutting) clearly contribute to chunk formation. However, qualitative discontinuities in signals of sound and/or motion are often not enough for chunking because there may be competing discontinuities (as in a series of identical sound or motion impulses) or there may be no qualitative discontinuities (as in a sustained steady sound or motion). In such cases we need to chunk continuous sensations using mental schemas, schemas that in a motor theory perspective are derived from embodied knowledge of production constraints. The elements listed here all converge in suggesting that there is a basic discontinuity, or intermittency, at work in motor control of body motion:

- Classical theories of continuous feedback and adjustment in motor control, so-called *closed loop* control, have been challenged by the idea of intermittent, meaning discontinuous, point-by-point, control (Loram, Gollee, Lakie, & Gawthrop, 2011). It can be shown that continuous feedback control is too slow to be feasible at short timescales, and also that intermittent control and more predictive control, sometimes referred to as *open loop* control, can be more efficient in many cases.
- Although we do not have so much information about the distribution of effort in music-related body motion, it seems rather unlikely that effort is uniformly distributed in performance because of biomechanical and efficiency (energy conservation) constraints, meaning that effort may be intermittent as well. Our own studies of sound-producing motion indicate acceleration peaks suggesting force peaks, in connection with downbeat points and other accented points in the

music. Intermittent energy infusion is particularly clear in so-called *ballistic motion* (e.g., hitting, kicking, fast stroking), typical of the mentioned impulsive body motion, but probably also present in the initial phases of more sustained kinds of body motion.

- The phenomenon of *coarticulation*, meaning that otherwise singular actions and sounds fuse into higher-level chunks of action and sound, effectively results in a contextual smearing of singular events and has to be conceived and perceived holistically, as a chunk of motion and sound. Coarticulation includes *anticipatory motion*, meaning that the effectors (fingers, hands, arms, etc.) have to be in place before the actual task is to be performed, otherwise the task would be carried out too late, as well as *carryover effects* from just performed actions, meaning present position of effectors are dependent also on just performed tasks (Godøy, 2014; Godøy, Jensenius, & Nymoen, 2010; Hardcastle & Hewlett, 1999; Rosenbaum, 2009)
- There is also increasing evidence for the hierarchical and goal-directed nature of body motion (Grafton & Hamilton, 2007). This means that anticipatory cognition in motor control makes the whole meso timescale chunk present as a mental action gestalt before the actual starting of the motion (Klapp & Jagacinski, 2011).
- An aspect of this goal-directed nature of human body motion is that it is oriented around certain postures at salient stages of the motion (Rosenbaum, Cohen, Jax, Weiss, & van der Wel, 2007). In music-related body motion, we find these postures at salient moments in time such as downbeats and other accents, creating what we have called *goal points* in music (Godøy, 2008). Trying to single out such goal points seems to make sense compared with trying to find the boundaries between motion chunks based on qualitative discontinuities alone, because human motion tends to be continuous (we are usually never still) and boundaries would have to be based on some kind of threshold value for motion, i.e., determine a boundaries between chunks as points with relative minima in quantity of motion (Hogan & Sternad, 2007).

What emerges from these constraints is that at the meso timescale of the chunk, we have a fusion or "lumping" of continuous motion into holistically conceived units. Recognizing this timescale-based constraint on chunk formation in music is important for advancing our understanding of embodied music cognition as this also applies to perception: perception of chunks in a motor theory perspective means projections of production schemas onto perception, hence, *production intermittency* contributes to perceptual chunking. This production-related intermittency is also interesting in view of discontinuity in mental processes in general: in a rereading of Husserl's thoughts on intermittency in time perception by a series of "now-points" (Husserl, 1991), the existence of such now-points seem to make good sense in relation to the previously mentioned motor theory constraints (Godøy, 2010a).

In summary, we see evidence of intermittency resulting in what could be called "quantal elements" in musical experience (Godøy, 2013):

- Temporal coherence in sound and motion below the meso timescale duration of the chunk is due to production constraints of motion, principally that of intermittent motor control and resultant coarticulation in motion and sound.
- We have new emergent features in the chunk not present at the micro timescale due to coarticulatory contextual smearing and the corresponding holistic perception of the chunk as a whole.
- Given the sequential nature of sound and motion, it seems that our perceptual apparatus is attuned to the meso timescale with some kind of "buffer" that keeps the whole chunk present as it unfolds.
- With the goal-directed nature of body motion, the goal points are often more important than the boundaries between the chunks, boundaries that in many cases may be difficult to determine from signal features alone.

If we hypothesize intermittency as integral to musical experience, as a reconciliation of discontinuity and continuity, how should we proceed in exploring chunk formation and intermittency in musical experience? There are some avenues of research that we are presently pursuing and will continue to do so in the future:

- Collecting and analyzing data through behavior studies of sound-producing and sound-accompanying body motion by motion capture technologies, revealing continuity and coarticulation at work in the chunks. Notably, this also means collecting behavior data from different musical cultures, in view of exploring differences in chunk features.
- Focus on postures and short-term, meso timescale motion trajectories, i.e., vocal tract, fingers/hands on instrument, torso/whole body in relation to instrument or in dance (in the case of sound-accompanying motion).
- Simulating the goal point model of intermittency in chunk formation by animations of music-related body motion, applying an analysis-by-synthesis approach.

TIMESCALES IN A CULTURE PERSPECTIVE

It is always useful to remind ourselves that all perceptual features of music are related to time, in particular so when we with present technology have the means to explore musical experience with very different perspectives, ranging from micro to macro timescale features. Also, given the multitude of music of different cultures and styles presently available to us at a mouse click, the need for more universal and comparative methods is obvious. As pointed out by Pierre Schaeffer several decades ago (Schaeffer, 1966), the confrontation with the music of other cultures challenges us to think music theory differently, and in particular, to make more systematic overviews of salient perceptual features at different timescales.

When studying various musical cultures, one question should then be: what timescale(s) is(are) the most essential for musical experience? With our Western musical culture's predominant categorical perception of pitch, duration, and instrument timbre, other micro timescale features such as nuances of pitch, duration (and "timing"), dynamics and timbre have been recognized as belonging to the sphere of musical expression, yet until quite recently largely excluded from music theory. And at the other end of timescales, we have in our Western "classical" tradition been told that the large-scale musical forms in the Western canon are essential for musical experience with their dramaturgical or narrative architecture and large-scale tonal-harmonic and thematic development schemes. Other musical cultures seem not have such large-scale schemes, and seem to have musical utterances basically quite short in duration, or to have music that is more a collection of fragments that can be permutated in order of occurrence. Yet other musical cultures may have long-lasting musical events, e.g., in connection with various rituals or as in the case of Western so-called *electronic dance music*, however without the dramaturgical spans of e.g., 19th century Western music. The few perception studies we have of large-scale musical forms suggests that we should be suspicious of the inherited Western *Formenlehre* notions of the efficacy of such forms in music (Eitan & Granot, 2008), and that the focus to a large extent may very well be on smaller timescales, e.g., on meso timescale chunks. As suggested by Schaeffer (Schaeffer, 1966) and as confirmed more recently by Gjerdingen and Perrott (2008), the meso timescale is indeed quite robust for recognizing very many salient musical features.

It seems that the Western fixation (for good and bad) on notation, has had as one consequence the blocking of access to significant tone and subtone features, and as a more general consequence, lead to an at times abstract, disembodied approach to musical knowledge. In a more embodied perspective on musical cultures, modes of motion and affect at the meso timescale are essential to look at. With available methods and technologies, this has become possible, and we can already now see close correspondences between body motion data such as speed and amplitude of motion and derivatives such as acceleration, jerk, regularity, irregularity, etc., with salient aesthetic and affective features of musical experience.

REFERENCES

Barthes, R. (1977). *Image-music-text*. Glasgow, Scotland: Fontana/Collins.

Berthoz, A. (1997). *Le sens du mouvement*. Paris, France: Odile Jacob.

Bregman, A. (1990) *Auditory scene analysis*. Cambridge, MA: The MIT Press.

Chion, M. (1983). *Guide des objets sonores*. Paris, France: INA/GRM Buchet/Chastel.

Eitan, Z., & Granot, R. Y. (2008). Growing oranges on Mozart's apple tree: "Inner form" and aesthetic judgment. *Music Perception 25*(5), 397–417.

Galantucci, B., Fowler, C. A., & Turvey, M. T. (2006). The motor theory of speech perception reviewed. *Psychonomic Bulletin & Review, 1*(3), 361–377.

Gallese, V., & Lakoff, G. (2005). The brain's concepts: The role of the sensory-motor system in conceptual knowledge. *Cognitive Neuropsychology, 22*(3/4), 455–79.

Gjerdingen, R., & Perrott, D. (2008). Scanning the dial: The rapid recognition of music genres. *Journal of New Music Research, 37*(2), 93–100.

Godøy, R. I. (2003). Motor-mimetic music cognition. *Leonardo, 36*(4), 317–319.

Godøy, R. I. (2006). Gestural-sonorous objects: Embodied extensions of Schaeffer's conceptual apparatus. *Organised Sound, 11*(2), 149–157.

Godøy, R. I. (2008). Reflections on chunking in music. In A. Schneider (Ed.), *Systematic and comparative musicology: Concepts, methods, findings* (pp. 117–132). Frankfurt, Germany: Peter Lang.

Godøy, R. I. (2010a). Thinking now-points in music-related movement. In R. Bader, C. Neuhaus, & U. Morgenstern (Eds.), *Concepts, experiments, and fieldwork: Studies in systematic musicology and ethnomusicology* (pp. 245–260). Frankfurt, Germany: Peter Lang.

Godøy, R. I. (2010b). Gestural affordances of musical sound. In R. I. Godøy, & M. Leman (Eds.), *Musical gestures: Sound, movement, and meaning* (pp. 103–125). New York, NY: Routledge.

Godøy, R. I. (2013). Quantal elements in musical experience. In. R Bader (Ed.), *Sound – perception – performance: Current research in systematic musicology* (Vol. 1; pp. 113–128). Heidelberg, Germany: Springer.

Godøy, R. I. (2014). Understanding coarticulation in musical experience. In M. Aramaki, M. Derrien, R. Kronland-Martinet, & S. Ystad (Eds.), *Sound, music, and motion: Lecture notes in computer science* (pp. 535–547). Berlin: Springer.

Godøy, R. I., Haga, E., & Jensenius, A. (2006). Playing 'air instruments': Mimicry of sound-producing gestures by novices and experts. In S. Gibet, N. Courty, & J.-F. Kamp (Eds.), *GW2005, LNAI 3881* (pp. 256–267). Heidelberg, Germany: Springer-Verlag,

Godøy, R. I., Jensenius, A. R., & Nymoen, K. (2010). Chunking in music by coarticulation. *Acta Acustica United With Acustica, 96*(4), 690–700.

Godøy, R. I., & Leman, M. (2010). *Musical gestures: Sound, movement, and meaning*. New York, NY: Routledge.

Grafton, S. T., & Hamilton, A. F. (2007). Evidence for a distributed hierarchy of action representation in the brain. *Human Movement Science, 26*, 590–616.

Haga, E. (2008). *Correspondences between music and body movement* (Doctoral thesis). University of Oslo, Oslo, Norway.

Haken, H., Kelso, J., & Bunz, H. (1985). A theoretical model of phase transitions in human hand movements. *Biological Cybernetics, 51*(5), 347–356.

Hardcastle, W. J., & Hewlett, N. (1999). *Coarticulation: Theory, data and techniques.* Cambridge, England: Cambridge University Press.

Hogan, N., & Sternad, D. (2007). On rhythmic and discrete movements: Reflections, definitions and implications for motor control. *Experimental Brain Research, 181,* 13–30.

Husserl, E. (1991) *On the phenomenology of the consciousness of internal time, 1893–1917.* (J. B. Brough, Trans.). London, England: Kluwer Academic.

Klapp, S. T., & Jagacinski, R. J. (2011). Gestalt principles in the control of motor action. *Psychological Bulletin, 137*(3), 443–462.

Leman, M. (2008). *Embodied music cognition and mediation technology.* Cambridge, MA: MIT Press.

Liberman, A. M., & Mattingly, I. G. (1985). The motor theory of speech perception revised. *Cognition, 21,* 1–36.

Loram, I. D., Gollee, H., Lakie, M., & Gawthrop, P. J. (2011). Human control of an inverted pendulum: Is continuous control necessary? Is intermittent control effective? Is intermittent control physiological? *The Journal of Physiology, 589*(2), 307–324.

Moore, B. C. J. (Ed.). (1995). *Hearing.* San Diego, CA: Academic Press.

Nymoen, K., Godøy, R. I., Jensenius, A. R., & Tørresen, J. (2013). Analyzing correspondence between sound objects and body motion. *ACM Transactions on Applied Perception 10*(2). doi:http://dx.doi.org/10.1145/2465780.2465783

Peeters, G., Giordano, B. L., Susini, P., Misdariis, N., & McAdams, S. (2011). The timbre toolbox: Extracting audio descriptors from musical signals. *Journal of the Acoustical Society of America, 130*(5), 2902–2916.

Pöppel, E. (1989). The measurement of music and the cerebral clock: A new theory. *Leonardo, 22*(1), 83–89.

Pöppel, E. (1997). A hierarchical model of time perception. *Trends in Cognitive Science, 1*(2), 56–61.

Rosenbaum, D. (2009). *Human motor control* (2nd ed.). Amsterdam, the Netherlands: Elsevier.

Rosenbaum, D., Cohen, R. G., Jax, S. A., Weiss, D. J., & van der Wel, R. (2007). The problem of serial order in behavior: Lashley's legacy. *Human Movement Science, 26*(4), 525–554.

Schaeffer, P. (1966). *Traité des objets musicaux.* Paris, France: Éditions du Seuil.

Schaeffer, P. (1998). Solfège de l'objet sonore (with sound examples by G. Reibel, & B. Ferreyra). First published in 1967. Paris, France: INA/GRM.

Snyder, B. (2000). *Music and memory: An introduction.* London, England: The MIT Press.

PART IV
MUSICAL TRANSFORMATIONS

CHAPTER 10

MUSIC, MEDICINE, AND PSYCHIATRY IN LATE 18TH AND FIRST HALF 19TH CENTURY VIENNA

Andrea Korenjak

In the Viennese lunatic asylums ... the attempt is currently being undertaken to heal mentally ill persons through music and dance. In the near future a series of concerts will begin and the physicians are expecting much from the effect of the music on the patients.
—*Neue Zeitschrift für Musik*, 1847, p. 112

With these words the *Neue Zeitschrift für Musik*, published in Leipzig in 1847, calls attention to the use of music in Viennese psychiatric institutions. However the idea that music can be of benefit to mental and physical health is not new in the middle of the 19th century. In every epoch, music has been ascribed the ability to relieve or heal suffering of the body, mind, and spirit in different ways.

Since the mid 20th century, various concepts and methods of "active" and "receptive music therapy" have been reformulated and further developed. Today, music therapy is an established, autonomous scientific discipline. Of modern schools, the so-called *Viennese Music Therapy* ranks internationally among the most traditional.

Cultural Psychology of Musical Experience, pages 181–205
Copyright © 2016 by Information Age Publishing

While we face an almost unlimited abundance of modern music therapy concepts today, the historical background of this field—particularly the beginnings of the use of music in asylums—has been almost entirely neglected. Today's increasing interest in music-related treatments, however, calls for a consideration of their historical beginnings and ensuing developments. These are not only of profound importance for the understanding of modern therapy concepts, but can also open new perspectives on music, medicine, and psychology, as well as psychiatry and therapeutics.[1]

Up to now, the cultural-historical background of the practice of healing through music has lacked a detailed analysis. In pertinent music therapy literature, "the history of music therapy" appears merely as the history of the development of a specific *moden* music therapy school from its beginnings around 1950. With few exceptions, introductions to the history of music therapy limit themselves to the reference that "David healed King Saul through his music" and strikingly often lack a study of historical source material. In this context, with few exceptions (e.g., Gouk, 2000; Horden, 2001; Kennaway, 2010; Kramer, 2000, 2001; Kümmel, 1977; Möller, 1971a, 1971b, 1974; Schumacher, 1982; Schwartz, 2012; Steffen, 1966; Völkel, 1979; Ziemann, 1970) the lack of publications on the cultural history of musical healing experiences is remarkable.

In this article I focus on the interrelation of music, medicine, and psychiatry in Vienna from c. 1780 (Maria Theresia's death and Joseph's II accession to the throne, opening of the Viennese General Hospital and *k. k. Irren-Anstalt*[2] in 1784) to c. 1850 (closure of the Viennese *k. k. Irren-Anstalt* due to a lack of room and opening of the *Niederösterreichische Landesirrenanstalt* "am Brünnlfeld" in 1853).

MUSIC-RELATED CURES IN VIENNESE HISTORY

Let me now outline some of the multifaceted medical approaches to music in Viennese history. As early as 1665 the Turkish traveller Evliyā Çelebi (c. 1611–1684, called also Derviş Mehmed Zilli) visited the Viennese court hospitals, where, according to Çelebi, music was played for patients: "If the patient's state of health allows it, musicians are sent to play on their instruments." (Çelebi, 1665/1963, p. 139, [trans. AK]). In 1783 a close friend of Ludwig van Beethoven, Johann Peter Frank (1745–1821), founder of the "public healthcare" and modernizer of the institute at the Viennese *Allgemeine Krankenhaus*[3] advises medical authorities to employ "encouraging music" as the "most effective remedy to raise the low spirits of the people" (Frank, 1783, pp. 807–808, [trans. AK]). Maximilian Stoll (1742–1787), head of the Wiener Klinik,[4] mentions "chastisement and music" to relieve "mad ideas" (Stoll, 1791 [Vol. 2], p. 12).[5]

In the 19th century, for instance, Peter Lichtenthal's (1780–1853) book *Der musikalische Arzt*[6] (1807), Johann Josef Denk's medical dissertation *De musices vi medicatrice* (1822), Carl Franz Hofgartner's *Dissertatio inauguralis medica exponens effectum musices in hominem sanum et aegrotum* (1847) as well as Hugo T. C. Kramoling's *Die Musik als Heilmittel*[7] (1847; dedicated to Franz Liszt)[8] can be seen as evidence of physicians' broad considerations regarding the use of music in a medico-therapeutic way in Vienna.

In his *Lehrsätze aus der Physiologie des Menschen*[9] (1802), the Czech-Austrian anatomist, physiologist, and ophthalmologist Georg Prochaska (1749–1820) is convinced that music can achieve a change of "mood" (literally "tune"—*Stimmung*) if it corresponds to the "tuning of the nerves" (*Nervenstimmung*) (Prochaska, 1802 [Vol. 1], p. 319) and can thereby induce "the wellbeing of body and soul" (Prochaska, 1802 [Vol. 1], p. 176). In 1814 the Viennese physician Joseph von Quarin (1733–1814), chosen by Joseph II to head the *Allgemeine Krankenhaus*, reports of a young girl suffering from epilepsy who (amongst other things) was healed through music she enjoyed (Quarin, 1814, p. 32f). In his *Lehrbuch der ärztlichen Seelenkunde*[10] the Viennese physician and well-known poet, Ernst von Feuchtersleben (1806–1849), points out that music "has been rightfully praised as a means of psychic healing, was used in antiquity, and has been unfairly neglected in recent times" (Feuchtersleben, 1845, pp. 251–352 [trans. AK]).[11]

This overview gives insight into the broad range of historical approaches. At this point I want to emphasize one fact that is crucial for a better understanding of the theme: Even though each epoch since antiquity has created its own idea of a medical, "therapeutic," and "psychological" function of music, it is important to realize that music therapy did not develop in a unified, target-oriented way. In the history of music as an "art of healing," there have been different interpretative approaches to explaining the effects of music on the human body and soul rather than a homogenous history or concept of music therapy. In European history, these approaches are strongly connected to the state of medical knowledge and to (music) philosophical ideas within the specific sociocultural contexts of that time.[12]

The history of music therapy for the mentally ill can be seen in the light of Richard Shweder's modern definition of cultural psychology as "the study of the way cultural traditions and social practices regulate, express, and transform the human psyche" (Shweder, 1991, p. 73). In the 18th century, for instance, the questionable idea emerged that "lunatics" could be brought to "reason," if need be, by force. Furthermore, in the cross-cultural context, ideas and "performances" of musical healing reveal "ethnic divergences" regarding the concepts of "mind, self, and emotion," as well as "mental illness and health" (Kleinman, 1980; Shweder, 1991). In this regard, the German terms used widely in the 18th and 19th century of *Gemüth* and *Gemüthskrankheit* (illness of the *Gemüth*) can be seen as "historical- and culture-bound" notions and expressions of the "soul," or a specific "state of the soul" respectively. (These concepts will be discussed in detail later.)

This article will show that even "music therapeutic" ideas and practices in the specific Viennese context and within a relative short period of time (c. 1780–c. 1850) were multifaceted. The interface between music, medicine, and psychiatry in late 18th and 19th century Vienna was particularly diversified. On the one hand, Viennese physicians were sometimes brilliant musicians as well as composers—amongst the most famous the surgeon, violinist and professor at the *Allgemeine Krankenhaus*[13] Franz Schuh (1804–1865); Leopold Auenbrugger (1722–1809), inventor of "(medical) percussion" (Auenbrugger, 1761), who was not only acquainted with the Mozart family but also the librettist of Antonio Salieris's "Lustspiel" *Der Rauchfangkehrer*[14] (premiere in 1781); as well as Theodor Billroth (1829–1894), who was a close friend of Johannes Brahms (1833–1897) and of Eduard Hanslick (1825–1904),[15] and consulted by Clara Schumann (concerning the drug abuse of her son, Ferdinand). However, musically gifted physicians did not necessarily consider music in medical treatment.

Although many physicians mention music and its benefit for medicine, they do not provide a "therapeutic concept," not even rudimentally. Furthermore, the spectrum of "music in medicine" ranges from Franz Anton Mesmer's (1734–1815) spectacular "music-magnetic cures," for instance in the case of the young Viennese musician Maria Theresia von Paradis (1759–1824), to Franz Joseph Gall's (1758–1828) phrenological reflections on an intact "musical sense" (*Musiksinn, Tonsinn*) of "maniacs" and "idiots" (Gall, 1829, p. 349ff).

Viennese history of music in psychiatric institutions from the late 18th century onwards conveys a similar nonhomogenous picture (I will detail later). Moreover, medical, psychological, and in particular music aesthetic and philosophical explanations of the effects of music of this period are vast and range from wild speculations on the dangerous effect of the glass harmonica on the nerves (see the letter of the Viennese Court Librarian, Carl Leopold Röllig to Elector Friedrich August III of Saxony in 1785, in Drechsel, 1927/1928, p. 261) to the use of music as distraction, entertainment, and enjoyment, particularly for *Gemüthskranke* ("patients suffering from an illness of the *Gemüth*/soul") in Viennese private mental homes (e.g., *Privat-Heilanstalt für Gemüthskranke*[16] Dr. Goergen).

Before I illustrate the use of music in two Viennese psychiatric institutions, I would like to address its sociocultural context.

CULTURAL-HISTORICAL CONTEXT

In the course of the 18th century, psychiatry—the "cure of the mad"—evolves into a distinct medical discipline.[17] The ideals of neohumanism (humanity, moral education, *Bildung* in the sense of *studia humanitatis*)[18] and the Enlightenment (respect for the individual, freedom, equality) lead in general to a paradigm shift concerning the treatment of the mentally ill and resulted in an emerging philanthropic mission. The thoughts of the Enlightenment, which dismiss superstition and the belief in demons, lead to the tendency to regard lunatics more and more as human beings, affected by illness.

Under the rule of Emperor Joseph II, himself a dedicated follower of the ideas of the Enlightenment and an excellent musician, the *k. k. Irren-Anstalt*—the later ill-famed *Narrenthurm* (*Fool's Tower*) or *Tollhaus* (*bedlam*)— was erected as part of the Viennese *Allgemeine Krankenhaus* (Figure 10.1), which opened in 1784. Joseph von Quarin commissioned the plan of the asylum which is considered Europe's first institution exclusively for the mentally ill.

Figure 10.1 *Allgemeine Krankenhaus* (General Hospital) and *Narrenthurm* (Fool's Tower; 1781). Picture text, *recto*: View of the Fool's Tower and back of the General- and Military-Hospital. Picture text, *verso*: North view with accessories. Drawn and engraved drawn from nature by Josef and Peter Schaffer. *Source:* Austrian National Library, Austrian Picture Library, item number: BDA 1.226–C

The new *k. k. Irren-Anstalt*en superseded the early modern *Arbeits-, Zucht-* and *Tollhäuser* (workhouses, bedlams), which were oriented towards labor and discipline.[19] The emergence of the *k. k. Irren-Anstalten*, however, must be seen in the broader international context, particularly with regard to the emergence of "modern" psychiatry and its reform movements in France (e.g., Philippe Pinel)[20] and Germany (e.g., Johann Christian Reil). (Both Pinel and Reil argued in favor of the use of music in the treatment of the mentally ill.)

The idea that the mentally ill could benefit from moral-psychological care characterizes the psychiatry of the Enlightenment and is reflected in terms such as *cura morale* (Chiarugi, 1793/1794), *traitement moral* (Pinel, 1798), *psychische Curmethode* (Reil, 1803), or *moral management* (Willis, 1823). In the course of the Enlightenment, the "alienist" regards himself increasingly as a "moral guide" and "educator." In some cases, music too is explicitly recommended in the treatment of "moral disorders" (see e.g., Pohl, 1818, p. 25). (In spite of this, coercive measures continue to exist for a long time.)

In this sense, the Viennese chief physician at the General Hospital, Carl Haller (1809–1887) refers to Philippe Pinel, Étienne Pariset, Étienne Esquirol, Benjamin Appert, and others (all of them pleaded for music in psychiatry or in prison) in his speech at the general assembly of the *k. k. Gesellschaft für Ärzte*[21] in Vienna on April 15, 1851:

> If the majority of criminals, which are . . . in the end also a kind of enraged and dangerous lunatics . . . , were employed with field/outdoor work, were read moral books, were left to moral/ethical recreation in company on feast and rest days, were engaged in singing and music, certainly, one would for the most part rehabilitate their moral and physical capabilities. (Haller, 1851, p. 514, [trans. AK]; see also Appert, 1851, p. 19)

The idea of a "moral influence "through music (in the sense of the so-called "ethos-doctrine" of Greek antiquity, see Korenjak, 2003b) had been passed on for centuries. In the course of neohumanism and Enlightenment, music's "ethical influence" is discussed preferably together with "reason" (see e.g., Aldung, 1758; André, 1740; Avison, 1753; Sulzer, 1798). "Madness" becomes more commonly explained as a "dysfunction" of an originally sane, "naturally inherent faculty of reason" (Groos, 1828, p. 16). In this sense, Friedrich Groos (1768–1852) assumes in his *Psychiatrischen Fragmenten*[22] that reason is innate in human beings and need not be learned later in life (Groos, 1828, p. 16). In the context of psychiatry, the key idea is oriented towards a "correction" of "unreasonable behavior." Thus, music is often not regarded as an "artistic medium," but far more as a "pedagogical activity." Consequently, even the copying of (sheet) music by hand was considered a suitable means of teaching "concentration, calmness," and "occupational engagement" to the mentally ill.

In this context, many physicians regarded music far more as an "occupation" or "useful entertainment" rather than a "therapeutic agent" (see e.g., Bird, 1835; de Boismont, 1860; Esquirol, 1838; Guislain, 1854; Haslam, 1819; Heinroth, 1818; Laehr, 1854; Leuret, 1835; Mahir, 1846; Nostitz & Jänkendorf, 1829; Pilcz, 1905; Riedel, 1830; Griesinger, 1845; Rush, 1825; Schilling & Kaulbach, 1863; Tschallener, 1842; Wallaschek, 1905). In addition to this, physicians sometimes assumed that physical activity—such as outdoor work—was "more effective" than music. These concepts point to the tension between music as an "aesthetic experience" on the one hand and music as an instrument of pedagogical and moral purpose on the other.[23]

MUSIC IN VIENNESE PSYCHIATRY: *K. K. IRREN-ANSTALT, DÖBLINGER PRIVATANSTALT*

In 1847 Hugo Kramoling outlines his high optimism concerning music in psychiatry as follows: "In Parisian, London, Praguer, Viennese, Berlin, and other madhouses the patients are educated in music and, with very happy success, music is applied as an auxiliary means in the healing intention/schedule" (Kramoling, 1847, p. 30). Indeed, many success stories of the use of music in asylums were recorded.[24] Nevertheless, this quotation should not obscure the fact that music found its way into the so-called madhouses in Vienna at a relatively late date.[25] Whereas the fourth volume of the *Medicinische Jahrbücher des k. k. österreichischen Staates*[26] (Medicinische, Vol. IV, 1817, p. 45) reports that in the Viennese *Irrenthurme* (*Fool's Tower*, i.e., *k. k. Irren-Anstalt* erected by Joseph II) "all those who are able to pursue an activity, which does not require tools that could be harmful to themselves or others, are occupied diversely, depending on their condition, with writing, drawing, painting, music, and such," travel reports from later times tell an entirely different story. In his travel report *Ueber die Medicinischen Anstalten*,[27] published on June 1, 1844, Heinrich Walber remarks that the "Viennese asylum" is "far behind the times" in comparison with Prague's: In the Viennese *k. k. Irren-Anstalt*, Walber found "raving madmen in the most miserable conditions." The inmates were lying "fettered in heavy chains on the stone floor, where some straw had been scattered...sometimes also entirely naked, divested even of their shirts" (Walber, 1844, p. 267 [trans. AK]).

In contrast, according to Walber, the inmates of the Prague Asylum were accommodated in rooms, where "cleanliness and tidiness" prevailed. Additionally, the "curable" inmates in particular were encouraged to pursue an activity such as music. The inhuman conditions in the Viennese "Fool's Tower" were confirmed by the Munich physician Oscar Mahir (1814–1895), who, shocked, described the impressions of his visit to the *Narrenturm* as "the unhappiest time" of his life, something he wishes he had never experienced. Mahir expresses his disbelief in finding these conditions in Vienna of all places "which has always excelled above all other countries through the most significant progress in science and arts, especially through its splendid medical school" (Mahir, 1846, p. 129, [trans. AK]).

One of the most important proponents for the use of music was Bruno Goergen (1777–1842), native of Trier, who also headed the *k. k. Irren-Anstalt* in Vienna from 1806 to 1814 and may also have been responsible for the previously mentioned attempts to integrate music in treatment.

In 1819 Goergen founded the first private *Irren-Heilanstalt*[28] in Gumpendorf, Vienna, (Palais Windisch-Graetz), which he relocated to Upper-Döbling in 1831 (*Döblinger Privatanstalt*). Goergen (Figure 10.2) pointed out that he had chosen "a big, beautiful, vaulted salon in his house especially for gatherings, carefully-directed conversations, games and in particular for music and literature appropriate" for *Gemüthskranke* (Goergen, 1820, p. 13).

Figure 10.2 Bruno Goergen (1777–1842). *Source:* Austrian National Library, Portrait Collection, item number: PORT_00004311_01.

Nikolaus Lenau (1802–1850), for instance, was one of Goergen's most prominent patients. He died in the Döblinger Privatanstalt in 1850. The "illness of the *Gemüth*" is mirrored in Lenau's poem *Der Urwald* (*The Jungle*):

So sind vielleicht gar bald auch mir verblüht	(Thus, perhaps soon they will fade
Die schönen Ahnungsblumen im Gemüth;	The beautiful inkling flowers of my soul;
Und ist der Wuchs des Lebens mir verdorrt,	And when the growth of life has withered,
Sind auch die Vögel, meine Lieder, fort.	Gone too are the birds, my songs.)

(Lenau 1855, p. 219, [trans. AK])

Goergen promised that he was able to offer every patient, whose upbringing and education had been interrupted by their *Gemüthskrankheit* lessons in languages, music and other subjects. With regard to music as a means of healing, Goergen argued that patients should not only be regarded as "passive" listeners but should also be encouraged to make music together. In support of this argument Goergen pointed to his previous position as director of the Viennese *k. k. Irren-Anstalt* where he had already got lunatics to perform the "most difficult musical productions", admired too by music connoisseurs (Goergen, 1820, p. 26).

It is important to remember that the Private Sanatorium Döbling, as well as private mental homes in general, were accessible only to wealthy clientele and the nobility respectively. (Likewise, the music salon of the *Niederösterreichischen Landes-Heil- und Pflegeanstalt für Geistes- und Nervenkranke 'am Steinhof,'*[29] established between 1904–1907 in the XIII district of Vienna—today's *Otto-Wagner-Spital*—was in the wing reserved for private patients.)

The use of music in Viennese mental homes is linked primarily to the neohumanist educational ideal and to the idea of music's beneficial effect on the illnesses of the *Gemüth*.

MUSIC AND THE *GEMÜTH*

Whereas today the term *Gemüth* is almost arbitrarily translated as mind, temper, disposition, or soul, in the historical context this term is clearly circumscribed and strongly determined by the "spirit of the time."

Basically, it is historically accepted that the "ideal state" (of the "soul," the "affects," and the "mind") is "calmness of the *Gemüth*" (Walch, 1740, column 1173 ff). According to Johann Georg Walch's (1693–1775) *Philosophisches Lexikon*[30] (1740, 2nd ed.), the essence of the *Gemüth's* serenity and peace is truth and goodness when seeking reason. Conversely, the restlessness and disturbance of the *Gemüth* is the state of the soul in which one allows oneself to follow corrupt tendencies and affects whereby the craving cannot be satisfied as it pursues unreason (Walch, 1740, column 1173–1175). This definition of an ideal state of the soul/*Gemüth* reveals moral implications. (Unsurprisingly, Walch was a Lutheran theologian.) Since the calmness of the *Gemüth* is seen as one's own responsibility, the conviction emerged (not only in religious contexts) that "mad people" must be brought "to reason," if necessary, by employing coercive measures.

In the first half of the 19th century, Michael von Lenhossék's (1773–1840) often-quoted two-volume *Darstellung des menschlichen Gemüths in seinen Beziehungen zum geistigen und leiblichen Leben*[31] (1824/1825) is an important source text when considering the (Biedermeier/Vormärz) notion of music's effect on the *Gemüth*. Lenhossék defines the term *Gemüth* as the "individual state of the soul," which allows both the soul to be touched through the body, and the body to be affected through the soul (Lenhossék [Vol. 1], 1824, p. 282). In Lenhossék's definition, the *Gemüth* links the soul to the body and vice versa. Moral implications do not prevail in Lenhosséks discourse, quite the contrary: "Appropriate distractions and merriments are the essential antidote against moral poisoning." (Lenhossék [Vol. 2], 1825, p. 115, [trans. AK]). Although the *perfect* calmness of the *Gemüth* (*tranquillitas animi*) is unachievable for the "conscious man," there is a "s e e m i n g calmness of the *Gemüth*" which manifests itself through the "absence of the more vivid feelings and desires" and which quite often occurs in mental and *gemütlich[en]* entertainments [*Zerstreuungen*] (Lenhossék [Vol. 2], 1825, p. 5). For this reason Lenhossék (as well as Goergen) is convinced that *appropriate* amusement (*unterhaltungslust*)—such as music—is "one of the best psychic r e m e d i e s" (Lenhossék [Vol. 2], 1825, p. 115; spacing in the original). In this sense, also the Swiss physician Simon-André Tissot (1728–1797) regards music as a remedy particularly effective for "sad passions" as it can restore calmness and mirth to the *Gemüth* (Tissot, 1781, p. 720).

Furthermore, in the 19th century context, music is recommended specifically for "nervous diseases." Whereas the term *Gemüthskrankheit* implies more a "psychic state" (such as "melancholy"), the term "nervous disease" points to the "fibres" of the body. Consequently, Lenhossék summarizes the twofold force of music and singing as the "physical stimulus" of the nerves and the "psychic incitement" (Lenhossék [Vol. 1], 1824, p. 493). In his book *Die Musik als Heilmittel*,[32] published in Vienna in 1847, Hugo Kramoling combines both of the above concepts of music's influence on the human body and soul: "We call music the heavenly language of our otherwise silent heart and our *Gemüth*, whereby music, after having touched the nervous system (this touch occurs through sound waves reaching the auditory nerve, which are then conveyed to the brain and to other nerves), induces manifold feelings and movements in the *Gemüth*." (Kramoling, 1848, p. 8, [trans. AK]).

In general, in the 18th and in the first half 19th century two main approaches towards music as a "remedy" can be identified: music and its connection to the "heart," "soul," and *Gemüth* (e.g., Friedreich, 1842; Hegel, 1835–1838; Reil, 1803; Sulzer, 1793, etc.) and music and its influence on the "body," "nerves," and subsequently, on the brain (e.g., Camus & Eicken, 1798; Feuchtersleben, 1846; Prochaska, 1810; Rochlitz, 1830, etc.).

MUSIC, "MENTAL DISTURBANCES," AND THE BRAIN

An increasing use of music is noticeable at the beginning of the 19th century in European psychiatric institutions in general, and in France, Germany, and England in particular. Remarkably, also in the international context the application of music as a means of healing is confined primarily to the area of "mental diseases" or "mental disturbances" (*Geisteszerrüttungen*). Correspondingly, the German physician and music specialist, Friedrich August Weber (1753–1806), indicated that "only on the evil inherent in the category of nervous diseases can the application of music be expected to produce something beneficial." (Weber, 1801/1802, column 567, [trans. AK]).

The medical orientation towards a nervous system which transmits impulses to the brain lead increasingly to the awareness that mental illnesses may be caused by a functional disorder of the nervous system and the brain: "To which organ does the phenomenon of madness belong?", the German neurologist and psychiatrist, Wilhelm Griesinger (1817–1868), raises the question on the first page of his famous book *Die Pathologie und Therapie der psychischen Krankheiten*:[33]

> Which organ must invariably and necessarily be diseased where madness exists? The answer to this question is the starting point of psychiatry. Physiological and pathological facts show us that this organ can only be the brain, so we must primarily, and in every case of mental disease, recognize an i l l n e s s o f t h e b r a i n." (Griesinger, 1845, p. 1; spacing in the original, [trans. AK])

Accordingly, in the second volume of his *Vollständigen Geisteskunde*[34] (1829) Franz Josef Gall (1758–1828) points out that "mental illnesses, which cause mania or idiocy, are merely a disturbance in the activities of the brain, just as all other diseases are merely disturbances in the activities of other parts of the body" (Gall, 1829, p. 76, [trans. AK]).[35] The idea of a "disturbed organization of the brain" is also reflected in Philipp Carl Hartmann's (1773–1830) *Der Geist des Menschen in seinen Verhältnissen zum physischen Leben, oder Grundzüge einer Physiologie des Denkens*[36] (1820): "as H a y d n and M o z a r t would have been unable to create harmonies on untuned instruments, the higher entity of the human spirit cannot manifest itself in a disturbed organization." (Hartmann, 1832, p. 358; spacing in the original, [trans. AK].) The exploration of this "disturbed organization" became the declared target of the emerging

Viennese "anatomical school," founded by Carl von Rokitansky (1804–1878) and Josef von Škoda (1805–1881). Even though Roktiansky and his wife, Marie Anna (neé Weis, 1806–1888), a singer educated by A. Salieri, hosted a private music salon,[37] Viennese anatomists were generally focused on the "freedom of natural sciences" and on debunking the *physica speculativa* rather than on "medical music."

Nevertheless, results from experimental physics and acoustics inspired new ideas on the effects of music in a science-oriented manner. Whereas the humoral doctrine had correlated the "movement of music" (in the sense of the medival idea *musica movet affectus*) with the "movement of the humors" and the "movement of the *spiritus*" (Korenjak, 2006), solidism attempted to explain the influence of music on nerve/tissue fibres in particular through its "vibrations" and "reverberations."[38] Furthermore, John Brown's (1735–1788) concept of the *excitability* of the nervous system (Brown, 1784, 1795) was mirrored in considerations of music's influence on *sthenia* and *asthenia.*[39]

Basically, the general scientific idea that prevails in the late 18th and the 19th century is that the "vibrations" of the sound can evoke "vibrations" of the nerves (in the sense of "physical/musical resonance").

CONCEPTS OF *STIMMUNG*, RESONANCE, AND *SYMPATHIE*

The comparison of the human body with the "body of the lyre" can be traced back to antiquity. Already Plato symbolized the relation of soul and body as a lyre: While the invisible and immaterial harmony (tune) symbolizes the divine realm or the soul, the material lyre symbolizes the mundane realm or the body. Through the strings, the mundane realm is merged with the divine (Platon, 1991, p. 85). This idea was passed on for centuries. Francis Bacon (1561–1626), for instance, associated the human body with the "sensitivity of a lyre." According to Bacon the physician's task is to "tune and play" on the "lyre of the human body," so that "the slightest discordance can be heard" (Bacon, 1783/1966, p. 378). From the 17th century onwards, the medical idea of a "taut fibre" had increased in significance. Thus, the metaphor of the "strings of the body" seemed a "realistic counterpart." These concepts are also reflected in German music aesthetic terms such as *Resonanz,* meaning both "acoustic resonance" and "response" ("inner movement"), *Stimmung,* meaning both "tune" and "mood," and *Sympathie,* meaning both "resonance"[40] and "affection." Plato's allegory became also a source for metaphysical and mystical notions of the Romantic period: "Nature is an aeolian harp, a musical instrument, whose tones are again keys of higher strings in ourself," Novalis writes in his *Aphorisms* (Novalis, 1992, p. 126, [trans. AK]).

The concepts of *Stimmung, Resonanz,* and *Sympathie* in the context of the *Gemüth* is mirrored also in Eduard Mörike's (1804–1875) poem *An eine Aeolsharfe* (To an Aeolian Harp):

"*Angelehnt an die Epheuwand*	[Leaning against the ivy wall
Dieser alten Terrasse,	Of this old terrace,
Du, einer luftgebornen Muse	Thou, a mysterious lute melody
Geheimnißvolles Saitenspiel,	Of an air-borne muse,
Fang' an,	Strike up,
Fange wieder an	Strike up again,
Deine melodische Klage!	Your melodious lament!
. . .	. . .
Wie süß bedrängt ihr dies Herz!	How sweet you besiege this heart!
Und säuselt her in die Saiten,	And whisper in the strings,
Angezogen von wohllautender Wehmuth,	Drawn by harmonious wistfulness,
Wachsend im Zug meiner Sehnsucht,	Growing, drawn by my longing,
Und hinsterbend wieder.	And then dying down again.
Aber auf einmal,	But all at once,
Wie der Wind heftiger herstößt,	When the wind blows harder,
Ein holder Schrei der Harfe	A lovely cry of the harp
Wiederholt, mir zu süßem Erschrecken	Echoes to my sweet fright
Meiner Seele plötzliche Regung;	The sudden stirring of my soul;
Und hier—die volle Rose streut,	And here—the ample rose strews,
geschüttelt	shaken
All' ihre Blätter vor meine Füße!"	All its petals at my feet!]
	(Mörike, 1838, p. 52–53, [trans. AK])

This poem was not only set to music by Johannes Brahms (1833–1897) but also by Hugo Wolf (1860–1903). Hugo Wolf was brought to the *Privat-Heilanstalt für Gemüthskranke auf dem Erdberge zu Wien,*[41] where he was treated by the Viennese neurologist Wilhelm Svetlin (1849–1914).[42] Although Svetlin was aware of Hugo Wolf's severe psychic disease, he released him from psychiatric care on January 24, 1898. After trying to commit suicide in 1899, Hugo Wolf was taken to the *Niederösterreichische Landesirrenanstalt 'am Brünnlfeld'*[43] on his own request, where he died on February 22, 1903.

In general, two approaches toward music and its benefit for soul and body can be identified: a more "iatro-medical" or "mechanical" one, and a more "psychic" or "romantic" one. While in scientifically oriented writings music's vibrations and the triggered "tremor" of the nerves appear as a *physical* principle, romanticists interpreted *Resonanz, Stimmung,* and *Sympathie* as the "acoustics of the *soul*."[44] In addition, romantic-religious and romantic-mystical ideas are based on these terms,[45] sometimes also with recourse on the antique concept of the harmony of the spheres (Korenjak, 2003c; Korenjak, 2011).

Likewise the concepts of *vitalism* and *animism*[46] inspired new considerations regarding the relationship between the "emotional activity of the soul" and mental illness.[47] Franz Anton Mesmer, for instance, was affected by vitalist ideas. Influenced by romantic-metaphysical ideas in medicine, speculative attempts also persisted (Coló, 1815; Kluge, 1818; Kerner, 1829; Mesmer, 1766). W. A. Mozart, whose family were close friends of Mesmer, became acquainted with the glass harmonica in Mesmer's home.[48] Later, Mozart caricatured Mesmer's curative approach in his opera *Così fan Tutte.* Despina, dressed up as the physician Ferrando (sic),[49] places a big magnet on Guglielmo to bring him back to life after an alleged arsenic poisoning.

With university medicine's orientation towards the standards of experimental science around 1840, medicine increasingly loses its interest in music, the effects of which defied scientific prediction and control at that time. This paradigm shift is particularly relevant to Viennese medicine. Notwithstanding, considerations of music's influence on the body and soul is continuously discussed in philosophical and aesthetic writings.

VIENNESE WRITINGS ON MUSIC'S INFLUENCE ON BODY AND SOUL (A SELECTION)

In addition to Lenhossék and Kramoling, other writings published between 1807 and 1847 in Vienna address music explicitly as a "therapeutic agent": e.g., Peter Lichtenthal's *Der Musikalische Arzt* (1807), Johann Joseph Denk's *De musices vi medicatrice* (1822), W. A. Bauer's *Ueber den Einfluß der Musik auf den Menschen im gesunden und im kranken Zustande*[50] (1837), and Franz Carl Hofgartner's *Dissertatio inauguralis medica exponens effectum musices in hominem sanum et aegrotum* (1847). All these writings promote music's *concrete* application in medicine and psychiatry (referring, amongst others, to the previously mentioned Goergen, Stoll, Frank, and Quarin). Although eclectic, Lichtenthal, Denk, Bauer, Hofgartner, and Kramoling offer insight into historical, medical, and aesthetic aspects of the theme and, to a certain extent, summarize the "state of knowledge" in the first half of 19th century Vienna.

While their historical references align themselves mainly with the discourse popular since antiquity (such as the story of David and Saul, older theories on music's influence on the four *humores* or the impact of specific musical modes on the mood),[51] some new aspects, however, are noteworthy:

considerations on patients' preferences and receptiveness (*Empfänglichkeit, Empfindlichkeit*), for instance, folk and "simple" music for musically uneducated patients, national music for different ethnic groups, art music for music connoisseurs as well as gender specific aspects,[52] etc. Despite the authors' remarks on music's effect on the human body, their obvious interest in its influence on the *Gemüth* prevails: music does not only affect the *Gemüth*, music *is* the "language of the *Gemüth*." (Lenhossék 1824 [Vol. 1], p. 495).[53] Furthermore, all authors endeavor to describe the influence of music on the nerves scientifically. Remarkably, also aesthetic reflections are integrated in medical dissertations.

Confronting clinical evidence of the time, however, aesthetic concepts and philosophical ideas were "on trial." The belief in the marvelous healing powers of music in stories harking back to antiquity, could not be maintained when compared with the *empirical clinical experience* of that time. Empirical evidence gained in psychiatry did away with the idea of the compelling (mechanistic-physical or affective) healing impact of music. This situation induced new considerations on music and the patient's individuality.

Rudolf Leubuscher (1822–1861) emphasizes for instance the "(mental) state" of patients as well as their music-educational background in his *Handbuch der Medicinischen Klinik*[54] (1861): "The poetic stories..., however, which relate to the healing of mental disease through music alone, do not prove to be true in practice; these are only fleeting impressions which are stirred by music, and require an educated appreciation of music and a particularly sensitive mind (*Gemüth*)" (Leubuscher, 1861, p. 315 [trans. AK]).[55] Likewise, Wilhelm Christian Müller (1752–1831) comes to the following conclusion: " T r u e   m u s i c   r e q u i r e s   e d u c a t i o n   i n   a e s t h e t i c s. . . . Where this aesthetic sense is missing, no healing effect or cure of an illness can be expected." (Müller, 1830, p. 335; spacing in the original, [trans. AK]).

In his famous writing *Vom Musikalisch-Schönen*[56] (1854), the Austrian music aesthetic and critic Eduard Hanslick points to the manifold literature on the physical effects of music as well as on its curative application. Hanslick summarizes the prevailing tendencies of his time as follows: Music effects the body physically through sound waves, which are transferred to the auditory nerve. Through its "general vibrations" music has a healing impact on the disturbed organism. Hence, affects are seen as a result of a "nervous tremor." Following Johann Georg Sulzer's (1720–1779) parable, according to which not only thin windows but also thick walls can be shattered by the power of sound, Hanslick raises the question of whether there are no differences between windows, walls, and humans. Hanslick himself is convinced that "the art of music (*Tonkunst*) begins right there where these isolated sound effects" (Hanslick, 1854/1991, p. 62 [trans. AK]; see also Sulzer, 1793, p. 433). Interestingly, this tension between a purely "scientific" approach (in terms of a linear S-R scheme) on the one hand and an "aesthetic" approach on the other can be observed to this day (Korenjak & Allesch, 2014).

CONCLUSION AND OUTLOOK

The significance of music in medicine and psychiatry, as well as the concepts of mental health, illness, and healing, is to a high degree culture specific and has to be interpreted within the particular sociocultural and historical context. Although it is not possible to know how patients might have experienced musical treatments in psychiatric institutions of the late 18th and the 19th century, Viennese reports turn out to be remarkably positive (a fact, which was not always mentioned in the broader international context). The positive effects seem to be generally linked to a new understanding and humanitarian attitude regarding the mentally ill, factors which affected patients "systemically." In general, music in the first half of 19th-century Viennese psychiatry was seen as a "moral-pedagogical" and "educational activity" and as a means of distraction and amusement, particularly for *Gemüthskranke* in private mental homes. To some extent, music was also regarded as an "artistic medium," for instance, when encouraging patients to play music together.

The beginnings of modern Viennese music therapy around 1958, however, are characterized by the idea that the music-therapeutic *process* between the patient/client *and* the therapist is crucial. Since the emergence of modern music therapy in the middle of the 20th century, the idea has prevailed that it is not the listening to music that is primarily "healing" but rather the *interaction with* music. According to Alfred Schmölz (1921–1995), one of the most prominent originators of the modern training in music therapy in Vienna, the main form of active music therapy is (free) improvisation within a patient-therapist activity. Furthermore, the first decades of modern Viennese music therapy were also considerably influenced by psychoanalytical theories. Consequently, music has often been seen as a conflict-centered and analytical medium, which is supposed to offer the patient an initial nonverbal access to the unconscious.

The (psychological) idea of music's influence on the *Gemüth* faded out in the 19th century but remained alive in the traditional *Wiener Lied* and in the broader notion of a "Viennese *Gemüthlichkeit*" (Viennese sociability).

ACKNOWLEDGMENTS

As part of the project "Music, Medicine, and Psychiatry in Vienna (c. 1780–1850)" at the Institute for the History of Art and Musicology, Austrian Academy of Sciences, this article was written with generous support from the Austrian Science Fund (FWF), project number P 27287-G21.

NOTES

1. At this point, in particular with regard to the well-established modern music therapy school in Vienna, there is a striking lack of historical research. It is missing almost completely on the period dealing with the first attempts to integrate music in medical and psychiatric institutions in Vienna up until the beginning of the institutionalization of modern *Viennese Music Therapy* in the second half of the 20th century.
2. "Imperial-Royal Lunatic Asylum"
3. "General Hospital"
4. "Viennese Clinic"
5. Stoll's pupils were Carl von Rokitansky (1804–1878), Josef von Škoda (1805–1881), and Franz Josef Gall (1758–1828).
6. "The Musical Physician"
7. "Music as a Remedy"
8. Franz Liszt himself was invited to play at the *Salpêtrière* for an sixty-year-old woman who had been there since childhood. See Kramer, 2001, p. 343
9. "Doctrines on the Physiology of Man"
10. "Coursebook of Medical Psychics"
11. Feuchtersleben was a disciple of Philipp Karl Hartmann (1773–1830).
12. These approaches can be summarized as follows: ritual, mythical, religious, ethical, cathartic, sphere-harmonious, astrologically-speculative, humoral-medical, dietetic, affectious, iatro-medical, moral-educational, scientific, and music therapeutic in modern sense. See Korenjak, 2003a.
13. "General Hospital"
14. "The Chimney Sweep"
15. Theodor Billroth's book *Wer ist musikalisch?* was published posthumously by Eduard Hanslick in 1895.
16. "Private sanatorium for those suffering from illness of the *Gemüth*"
17. Johann Christian Reil (1759–1813) implemented the term "Psychiaterie" in 1808. Reil/Hoffbauer, 1808, p. 237 [§. 7] and *passim*. In addition, Reil postulates a differentiation between "curable" and "incurable" mental illnesses.
18. Friedrich August Wolf (1759–1824) characterizes the neohumanist educational ideal as follows: "*Humanitatis studia*...comprise everything that furthers the education of human beings and the enhancement of all powers of the mind and the Gemüth to form a beautiful harmony of the inner and outer being." Wolf, 1833, p. 45 [see endnote]; italics in the original [tran. AK]
19. Nonetheless, humanist and therapeutic considerations emerged no earlier than in the course of the 19th century, when the so-called *Irren-Anstalten* [lunatic asylums] came to be regarded as *Heil-Anstalten* [institutions for curative purposes].
20. Even though the beginning of a new era in the history of "psychiatry" has commonly been associated with Philippe Pinel (1745–1826), others too—

such as the English physician William Battie (1703–1776) and the Italian physician Vincenzo Chiarugi (1759–1820)—had advanced the treatment of the mentally ill before Pinel.

21. "Imperial-Royal Society for Physicians"
22. "Psychiatric Fragments"
23. While François Leuret (1797–1851) in his discourse *Du traitment moral de la folie* (1840) argues in favor of enforcing musical activities if necessary also against the inmates' will and with force, Joseph Mason Cox (1763–1818) considers a "withdrawal of music" as a punishment for disobedient inmates. See Leuret, 1840, 295–296, p. 304 and Cox, 1811, p. 91
24. These include success stories about the specific use of music involving the active participation of psychiatric patients, for instance through the establishment and institutionalization of asylum choirs and aesthetic considerations, e.g., in the letter of Marquis de Louvais to Hector Berlioz 1848 (see Louvais, 1848), Guislain 1854, de Boismont 1860, Laurent 1860, Güntz 1861.
25. The discussion about the necessity and dubiousness of inhuman coercive measures in psychiatric asylums had already started at the turn of the 18th to the 19th century in France, England, Germany, and Italy, see e.g., Pinel, 1798; Esquirol, 1827, 1838; Battie, 1758; Tuke, 1813; Haslam, 1819; Hill, 1839; Conolly, 1856; Reil, 1803; Groos, 1828; Griesinger, 1845; Neumann, 1822; Chiarugi, 1793–94. However, the abolition of these coercive means was not always reliably carried out, see e.g., Horn, 1818.
26. "Medical Annuals of the Imperial-Royal Austrian State"
27. "On Medical Institutions"
28. "lunatic sanatorium"
29. "Lower Austrian Provincial Institution for the Cure and Care of the Mentally and Nervously Ill 'at Steinhof'"
30. "Philosophical Lexicon"
31. "Description of the Human *Gemüth* and its Relations to the Mental and Physical Life"
32. "Music as a Remedy"
33. "The Pathology and Treatment of Mental Illnesses"
34. "Complete Science of the Mind"
35. The *Josephinum* hosts the skull of a man who died in the Viennese *Allgemeine Krankenhaus* in 1797, which was phronologically examined by Gall himself.
36. "The Human Spirit and its Relation to the Physical Life, or Principles of a Physiology of Mind"
37. Marie Anna von Rokitansky gave the first performance of Franz Schubert's *Erlkönig* in their private home.
38. These medical theories are reflected for instance in Krause, 1752; Sulzer, 1793; Pargeter, 1893.
39. In his *Tractatus de ventriculo et intestinis* Francis Glisson (1597–1677) disseminated the doctrine of the irritability (*irritabilitas*) of the vitalized fibre (*fibra*), which was further developed inter alia by Albrecht von Haller (1708–1777), Friedrich Hoffmann (1660–1742), and John Brown (1735–1788). The concept of music's influence on *sthenia* and *asthenia* is reflected i.a. by Tissot,

1781b; Weber, 1801/02; Lichtenthal, 1807; Erdmann, 1809; Reil, 1796; Esquirol, 1827; Luzinsky, 1882a, 1882b.

40. The iatro-mechanical and -medical idea of a musical impact on the nerves/ nerve fibres was supported by the strong interest in the phenomenon of "resonance" in the 18th and 19th century in the 18th and 19th century.

41. "Private Sanatorium for *Gemüthskranke* at Erdberg in Vienna"

42. According to Svetlin's description of the *Privatheilanstalt für Gemüthskranke auf dem Erdberge zu Wien*, social games—such as billiards, chess, domino and cards—as well as music were offered to the patients. Also physical exercises and reading matter (library) were part of the treatment. Nevertheless, Svetlin regarded work and occupation as the most effective remedy. See Svetlin, 1884, p. 46–47

43. "Lower Austrian Provincial Lunatic Asylum 'at Brünnlfeld'"

44. "The term *stimmung* indicates musical states/relations of the soul. The acoustics of the soul is yet a dark, perhaps important field. Harmonious and disharmonious vibrations." Novalis, 1992, p. 116; italics added [tran. AK].

45. "An inexplicable *Sympathie* between particular mathematical tone relationships and particular fibres of the human heart has unfolded through which the art of music has become a rich and illustrative work for the depiction of human feelings." Wackenroder/Tieck 1799, p. 78; italics added [tran. AK]

46. developed by Georg Ernst Stahl (1659–1734)

47. While the "Psychiker" [*psychicists*]—such as Johann Christian Heinroth (1773–1843), Johann Gottfried Langermann (1768–1832), and Karl Wilhelm Ideler (1795–1860)—described mental illnesses (in a sometimes moralizing fashion) as purely diseases of the soul, the "Somatiker" [*somaticists*]—such as Friedrich Nasse (1778–1851) and Johann Baptist Friedrich (1796–1862)— regarded them primarily as expressions of physical disturbances with (attending) symptoms in the soul.

48. In the year of his death, W. A. Mozart wrote the *Adagio* and *Rondo* for glass harmonica, flute, oboe, viola and cello KV 617.

49. Mesmer experimented with iron filings.

50. "On the Influence of Music on the Human's State of Health and Illness"

51. With the further development of science-orientated- and experimental medicine the significance of humoral pathology recedes generally in importance. However, e.g., Lichtenthal, Denk, Hofgartner, and Kramoling dwell also on the concept of music's influence on different temperaments.

52. The idea that a woman's nervous system is "more excitable/irritable and sensitive" must be seen in the context of gender ideologies of that time.

53. Ideler states that the "ear is preferably the sense of the *Gemüth.*" Ideler, 1838, p. 439

54. "Handbook of the Medical Clinic"

55. Early considerations on a connection between a "successful healing" and musical education or knowledge, as well as the influence of "musical preferences", gender and age are mentioned e.g., by Cox, 1806 [1811]; Heinroth, 1818; Müller, 1830; Schmolznop, 1836; Mahir, 1846; Vering, 1817; Guislain, 1826; Rochlitz, 1830.

56. "On the Musically Beautiful"

REFERENCES

Aldung, J. M. (1758). *Anleitung zu der musikalischen Gelahrtheit.* Erfurt, Germany: J. D. Jungnicol.

André, Y.-M. (1740). *Essai sur le beau, où l'on examine en quoi consiste précisément le beau dans le physique, dans le moral, dans les ouvrages d'esprit et dans la musique.* Paris, France: H.-L. Guérin et J. Guérin.

Appert, B. N. M. (1851). *Die Gefängnisse, Spitäler, Schülen, Civil- und Militär-Anstalten in Oesterreich, Baiern, Preussen, Sachsen, Belgien* (Vol. 1). Wien, Austria: L. Sommer.

Auenbrugger, L. (1761). *Inventum novum ex percussione thoracis humani ut signo abstrusos interni pectoris morbos detegendi.* Vindobonae: J. T. Trattner.

Avison, C. (1753). *An essay on musical expression.* London, England: C. Davis.

Bacon, F. (1783/1966). *Über die Würde und den Fortgang der Wissenschaften.* Darmstadt, Germany: Wissenschaftliche Buchgesellschaft.

Battie, W. (1758). *A treatise on madness.* London, England: J. Whiston & B. White.

Billroth, T. (1895). *Wer ist musikalisch?* Berlin, Germany: Paetel.

Bird, F. (1835). *Ueber Einrichtung und Zweck der Krankenhäuser für Geisteskranke.* Berlin, Germany: Hirschwald.

Boismont, B. de (1860). De la musique dans les asiles d'aliénés et des concerts de la senavra et de quatre-mars. *L'Union Medicale, 7*(100), 337–345.

Brown, J. (1784). *Elementa medicinae.* Edinburgi, Scotland: Excudit C. Denovan.

Brown, J., P., & Beddoes, T. (1795). *The elements of medicine.* London, England: J. Johnson.

Camus, A. de, & Eicken, G. W. v. (1798). *Grundsätze der praktischen Seelenheilkunde.* Elberfeld, Germany: Comptoir für Litteratur.

Çelebi, E. (1665/1963). *Im Reiche des goldenen Apfels: Des türkischen Weltenbummlers Evliyā Celebis denkwürdige Reise in das Giaurenland und in die Stadt und Festung Wien anno 1665* (2nd ed.) Graz, Austria: Styria.

Chiarugi, V. (1793/1794). *Trattato della pazzia in genere e in specie con una centuria di osservazioni.* Firenze, Italy: L. Carlieri.

Coló, A. (1815). *Prodromo sull'azione salutare del magnetismo animale e della musica.* Bologna, Italy: G. Lucchesini.

Conolly, J. (1856). *The treatment of the insane without mechanical restraints.* London, England: Smith, Elder & Co.

Cox, J. M. (1806). *Practical observations on insanity.* London, England: Baldwin and Murray.

Cox, J. M. (1811). *Praktische Bemerkungen über Geisteszerrüttung.* Halle, Germany: Gengersche Buchhandlung.

Denk, J. J. (1822). *De musices vi medicatrice.* Vindobonae, Austria: Sollinger.

Drechsel, F. A. (1927/1928). Carl Leopold Röllig und die Glas-Harmonika. *Zeitschrift für Instrumentenbau, 48*, 260–261.

Erdmann, J. F. (1809). Ueber den Einfluss der Musik auf Kranke. *Archiv für Medizinische Erfahrung, 2*, 121–134.

Esquirol, J. E. (1838). *Des maladies mentales considérées sous les rapports medical, hygiénique et médico-légal* (Vol. 2). Paris, France: J.-B. Baillière.

Esquirol, J. E. D., & Hille, K. C. (1827). *Esquirols allgemeine und specielle Pathologie und Therapie der Seelenstörungen.* Leipzig, Germany: Hartmann.

Feuchtersleben, E. F. (1845). *Lehrbuch der ärztlichen Seelenkunde.* Wien, Austria: C. Gerold.

Feuchtersleben, E. F. (1846). *Zur Diätetik der Seele.* Wien, Austria: C. Gerold.

Frank, J. P. (1783). *System einer vollständigen medicinischen Polizey* (Vol 3). Mannheim, Germany: C. F. Schwan.

Friedreich, J. B. (1842). *Zur psychiatrischen Literatur des neunzehnten Jahrhunderts.* Regensburg, Germany: Manz.

Gall, F. J. (1829). *Vollständige Geisteskunde* (Vol. 2). Nürnberg, Germany: C. Leuchs.

Glisson, F. (1677). *Tractatus de ventriculo et intestinis cui praemittitur alius de partibus continentibus in genere et in specie de iis abdominis.* Amstelodami, Netherlands: Jacobus Jun.

Goergen, B. (1820). *Privat-heilanstalt für Gemüthskranke in Wien eröffnet von Dr. B. Goergen.* Wien, Austria: F. Wimmer.

Gouk, P. (Ed.). (2000a). *Musical healing in cultural contexts.* Brookfield, England: Ashgate.

Griesinger, W. (1845). *Die Pathologie und Therapie der psychischen Krankheiten.* Stuttgart, Germany: A. Krabbe.

Groos, F. (1828). *Psychiatrische Fragmente* (Vol. 1). Leipzig, Germany: Buchhandlung K. Groos.

Güntz, E. W. (1861). *Die Irren-Heil- und Pflege-Anstalt Thonberg.* Leipzig, Germany: Reclam Jun.

Guislain, J. (1826). *Traité sur l'aliéntation mental et sur les hospices des aliénés.* Amsterdam, the Netherlands: J. v. d. Hey & fils.

Guislain, J. (1854). *Joseph Guislain's klinische Vorträge über Geistes-Krankheiten.* Berlin, Germany: August Hirschwald.

Haller, C. (1851). Die Gefängnisse, Spitäler, Schulen, Civil- und Militäranstalten in Oesterreich, Baiern, Preussen, Sachsen und Belgien . . . kritisch beleuchtet, und in der allgemeinen Versammlung der k. k. Gesellschaft der Ärzte am 15. April 1851 vorgetragen. *Zeitschrift der k. k. Gesellschaft der Aerzte zu Wien, 7*(2), 509–526.

Hanslick, E. (1854/1991). *Vom Musikalisch-Schönen.* Darmstadt, Germany: Wissenschaftliche Buchgesellschaft.

Hartmann, P. C. (1832). *Der Geist des Menschen in seinen Verhältnissen zum physischen Leben, oder Grundzüge einer Physiologie des Denkens.* Wien, Austria: C. Gerold.

Haslam, J. (1819). Ueber die psychische behandlung der wahnsinnigen. *Zeitschrischt für Psychische* Ärzte, *2,* 105–156.

Hegel, G. W. F., & Hotho, H. G. (1835–1838). *Georg Wilhelm Friedrich Hegel's Vorlesungen über die Aesthetik.* Berlin, Germany: Duncker & Humblot.

Heinroth, J. C. A. (1818). *Lehrbuch der Störungen des Seelenlebens.* Leipzig, Germany: Vogel.

Hill, R. G. (1839). *Total abolition of personal restraint in the treatment of the insane.* London, England: Simpkin.

Hofgartner, F. C. (1847). *Dissertatio inauguralis medica exponens effectum musices in hominem sanum et aegrotum.* Vindobonae, Austria: Typis Congregationis Mechitharisticae.

Horden, P. (Ed.). (2001). *Music as medicine: The history of music therapy since antiquity.* Aldershot, England: Ashgate.

Horn, E. (1818). *Oeffentliche Rechenschaft über meine zwölfjährige Dienstführung als zweiter Arzt des königl. Charité-Krankenhauses zu Berlin.* Berlin, Germany: Realschulbuchhandlung.

Ideler, K. W. (1838). *Grundriss der Seelenheilkunde* (Vol. 2). Berlin, Germany: Enslin.

Kennaway, J. (2010). From sensibility to pathology: The origins of the idea of nervous music around 1800. *Journal of the History of Medicine and Allied Sciences, 65*(3), 396–426.

Kerner, J. (1829). *Die Seherin von Prevorst: Part 1 & 2.* Stuttgart, Germany: J.G. Cotta'sche Buchhandlung.

Kluge, K. (1818). *Versuch einer Darstellung des animalischen Magnetismus als Heilmittel.* Berlin, Germany: Realschulbuchhandlung.

Korenjak, A. (2003a). *Musik als Heilkunst. Eine vergleichende Kulturgeschichte musikalischen Heilens, reflektiert an Therapiekonzepten der Gegenwart.* Doctoral dissertation, University Mozarteum, Salzburg, Austria.

Korenjak, A. (2003b). Ethos und katharsis: Zur pädagogischen und therapeutischen bedeutung der musik in der griechischen antike. *Studien zur Deutschkunde, XXVI,* 191–218.

Korenjak, A. (2003c). Sphärenharmonie und seelenstimmung. In M. Schwarzbauer (Ed.), *Harmonie und konflikt* (pp. 48–64). Frankfurt, Germany: Peter Lang.

Korenjak, A. (2006). Musica movet affectus: Zum barocken Affektverständnis im Spiegel der galenischen Spirituslehre. *Studien zur Deutschkunde, 32,* 69–102.

Korenjak, A. (2011). „Wer wird die Harmonie des Himmels zum Schweigen bringen?" Zur vorstellung einer Harmonie der Sphären in Antike und Mittelalter. In E. Hamberger et al. (Eds.), (2011). *Natürlich Kunst...* (pp. 75–100). Wien, Austria: LIT.

Korenjak, A., & Allesch, C. (2014). Kunst als Therapie: Über die Schwierigkeiten, die Ursachen heilender Wirkungen ästhetischer Erfahrungen einzugrenzen. *Person: Internationale Zeitschrift für Personenzentrierte und Experienzielle Psychotherapie und Beratung, 18*(1), 44–53.

Kramer, C. (2000). Soul music as exemplified in nineteenth-century German psychiatry. In P. Gouk (Ed.), *Musical healing in cultural contexts* (pp. 137–148). Brookfield, England: Ashgate.

Kramer, C. (2001). Music as cause and cure of illness in nineteenth-century Europe. In P. Horden (Ed.), *Music as medicine* (pp. 338–352). Hampshire, England: Ashgate.

Kramoling, H. S. [Dr. H. S. K.] (1847). *Die Musik als Heilmittel.* Wien, Austria: Verlag von Anton Doll's Enkel.

Krause, C. G. (1752). *Von der musikalischen poesie.* Berlin, Germany: J. F. Voß.

Kümmel, W. F. (1977). *Musik als Medizin: Ihre Wechselbeziehungen in Theorie und Praxis von 800 bis 1800.* München, Germany: K. Alber.

Laehr, H. (1854). *Bericht über die Leistungen in der Psychiatrik. Canstatt's Jahresbericht über die Fortschritte der gesammten Medicin* (Vol. 3). (pp. 9–46). Würzburg, Germany: Stahle'sche Buchhandlung.

Lenau, N. (1855). *Sämmtliche Werke* (Vol. 1; A. Grün, Ed.). Stuttgart, Germany: Cotta'scher Verlag.

Lenhossék, M. v. (1824/25). *Darstellung des menschlichen Gemüths in seinen Beziehungen zum geistigen und leiblichen Leben* (Vol. 1 & 2). Wien, Austria: Carl Gerold.

Leubuscher, R. (1861). *Handbuch der medicinischen Klinik* (Vol. 2). Leipzig, Germany: W. Engelmann.

Leuret, F. (1835). *Observation d'un cas de sentiment musical très-développé chez une idiote.* Paris, France: [sine nomine].

Leuret, F. (1840). *Du traitement moral de la folie.* Paris, France: J.-B. Baillière.

Lichtenthal, P. (1807). *Der musikalische Arzt, oder: Abhandlung von dem Einflusse der Musik auf den Körper, und von ihrer Anwendung in gewissen Krankheiten.* Wien, Austria: Christian Friedrich Wappler & Beck.

Louvais, M. de (1848). Brief an Hector Berlioz über die Irrenanstalt zu Auxerre. *Allgemeine Zeitschrift für Psychiatrie und Psychisch-Gerichtliche Medicin 5*(4), 495–496.

Luzinsky, A. M. (1882a). Die musik in der medizin. *Allgemeine Wiener Medizinische Zeitung, 27*(25), 271–273.

Luzinsky, A. M. (1882b). Die Musik in der Medizin. *Allgemeine Wiener Medizinische Zeitung 27* (26), 283–285.

Mahir, O. (1846). *Ueber Irrenheilanstalten, Pflege und Behandlung der Geisteskranken, nach den Principien der bewährtesten Irren—Aerzte Belgiens, Englands, Frankreichs und Deutschlands.* Stuttgart, Germany: J.G. Cotta.

Medicinische Jahrbücher des kaiserl. königl. österreichischen Staates IV. (1817). Wien, Austria: Hupffer & Wimmer.

Mesmer, F. A. (1766). *Dissertatio physico-medica de planetarum influxu.* Wien, Austria: Typis Ghelenianis.

Möller, H.-J. (1971a). *Geschichte und Gegenwart musiktherapeutischer Vorstellungen.* Stuttgart, Germany: Fink.

Möller, H.-J. (1917b). Aufklärische Traktate über die „heilenden Wirkungen" der Musik. Eine Untersuchung über die Beziehungen zwischen Musiktheorie und medizinischen Vorstellungen zur Zeit det Aufklärung. *Neue Zeitschrift der Musik, 132*(9), 472–477.

Möller, H.-J. (1974). Psychotherapeutische Aspekte in der Musikanschauung der Jahrtausende. In W. J. Revers et al. (Eds.), *Neue Wege der Musiktherapie* (pp. 53–160). Wien, Austria: Econ.

Mörike, E. (1838). *Gedichte.* Stuttgart, Germany: J. G. Cotta'sche Buchhandlung

Müller, W. C. (1830). *Aesthetisch-historische Einleitung in die Wissenschaft der Tonkunst, Part 1.* Leipzig, Germany: Breitkopf & Härtel.

Neue Zeitschrift für Musik (1847). Kleine Zeitung, p. 112 [No. 26, March 29, 1847].

Neumann, K. G. (1822). *Die krankheiten des vorstellungsvermögens.* Leipzig, Germany: C. Cnobloch.

Nostitz und Jänkendorf, Gottlob A. E. v. (1829). *Beschreibung der königlich sächsischen heil- und verpflegungsanstalt sonnenstein, Part 2, 2nd treatise.* Dresden, Germany: Walthersche Buchhandlung.

Novalis (1992). *Aphorismen* (1st ed.; M. Brucker, Ed.). Leipzig, Germany: Insel.

Pargeter, W. (1793). *Abhandlung über den Wahnsinn.* Leipzig, Germany: Johann Friedrich Junius.

Pilcz, A. (1905). *Psychiatrie und Musik.* Wien, Austria: Verlag des Verfassers.

Pinel, P. (1798). *Recherches et observations sur le traitement moral des aliénés.* Paris, France [sine nomine].

Platon (1991). *Phaidon*. Hamburg, Germany: Felix Meiner.

Pohl, J. F. B. (1818). *De artis musicae in sanos et aegrotantes effectu*. Doctoral dissertation. Berolini, Germany: Petsch.

Prochaska, G. (1802). *Lehrsätze aus der Physiologie des Menschen* (Vol. 1 & 2; 2nd ed.). Wien, Austria: C. F. Wappler.

Prochaska, G. (1810). *Bemerkungen über den Organismus des menschlichen Körpers*. Wien, Austria: C. F. Wappler.

Quarin, J. v. (1814). *Animadversiones practicae in diversos morbos: Tomus secundus*. Viennae, Austria: Schaumburg et Soc.

Reil, J. C. (1796). Von der Lebenskraft. In *Archiv für die Physiologie 1* (pp. 8–162).

Reil, J. C. (1803). *Rhapsodieen über die Anwendung der psychischen Curmethode auf Geisteszerrüttungen*. Halle, Germany: Curtsche Buchhandlung.

Reil, J. C., & Hoffbauer, J. C. (1808). *Beyträge zur Beförderung einer Kurmethode auf psychischem Wege* (Vol. 1). Halle, Germany: Curtsche Buchhandlung.

Riedel, J. G. (1830). *Prags Irrenanstalt und ihre Leistungen*. Prag, Czechia: Sommersche Buchdruckerei.

Rochlitz, F. (1830). *Für Freunde der Tonkunst* (Vol. 3). Leipzig, Germany: Carl Ensbloch.

Rush, B. (1825). *Medizinische Untersuchungen und Beobachtungen über die Seelenkrankheiten*. Leipzig, Germany: C. Cnobloch.

Schilling, J. A., & Kaulbach, W. v. (1863). *Psychiatrische Briefe oder die Irren, das Irresein und das Irrenhaus*. Augsburg, Germany: J. A. Schlosser's Buch und Kunsthandlung.

Schumacher, R. (1982*). Die Musik in der Psychiatrie des 19. Jahrhunderts*. Bern, Switzerland: Peter Lang.

Schwartz, M. (2012). Und es geht doch um die Musik: Zur musikalischen Heilkunde im 19 und 20. Jahrhundert, Parts 1 & 2. *Musiktherapeutische Umschau, 33*(2/3), 113–125, 333–348.

Shweder, R. A. (1991). *Thinking through cultures. Expeditions in cultura psychology*. Cambridge, MA, Harvard University Press.

Steffen, H. (1966). *Zur Theorie und Praxis der Iatromusik zwischen 1770 und 1830*. Doctoral dissertation. Ruprecht-Karl-University, Heidelberg, Germany.

Stoll, M. (1791). *Vorlesungen über einige langwierige Krankheiten* (Vol. 2). Wien, Austria: C. F. Wappler.

Sulzer, J. G. (1793). *Allgemeine Theorie der schönen Künste, Part 3* (2nd ed.). Leipzig, Germany: Weidmannische Buchhandlung.

Sulzer, J. G. (1798). *Allgemeine Theorie der schönen Künste. Part 2* (3rd ed.). Leipzig, Germany: Weidmannisch Buchhandlung.

Svetlin, W. (1884). *Die Privatheilanstalt für Gemüthskranke auf dem Erdberge zu Wien II, Leonhardgasse 3 und 5*. Wien, Austria: Wilhelm Braumüller.

Tissot, S.-A. (1781). *Sämtliche zur Arztneykunst gehörige Schriften, Part 4*. Leipzig, Germany: F. G. Jacobäer & Sohn.

Tschallener, J. (1842). *Beschreibung der k. k. Provinzial=Irren=Heilanstalt zu Hall in Tirol*. Innsbruck, Austria: Wagner'sche Buchhandlung.

Tuke, S. (1813). *Description of the retreat, an institution near York*. London, England: W. Alexander.

Vering, A. M. (1817). *Psychische Heilkunde*. Leipzig, Germany: J. A. Barth.

Völkel, E. (1979). *Die spekulative Musiktherapie zur Zeit der Romantik.* Düsseldorf, Germany: Triltsch.

Wackenroder, W., & Tieck, H. (1799). *Phantasien über die Kunst, für Freunde der Kunst.* Hamburg, Germany: [sine nomine].

Walber, H. (1844, June 1). Ueber die medicinischen Anstalten. *Allgemeine Zeitung für Chirurgie, innere Heilkunde und ihre Hülfswissenschaften,, 22,* 169–173, 266–269.

Walch, J. G. (Ed.). (1740). *Philosophisches Lexikon* (2nd ed.). Leipzig, Germany: J. F. Gleditsch.

Wallaschek, R. (1905). *Psychologie und Pathologie der Vorstellung.* Leipzig, Germany: J. A. Barth.

Weber, F. A. (1801/1802). Abhandlung von dem Einflusse der Musik auf den menschlichen Körper und ihrer medicinischen Anwendung. *Allgemeine Musikalische Zeitung, 4,* col. 561–569, col. 577–589, col. 593–599, col. 609–617.

Willis, F. (1823). *A treatise on mental derangement.* London, England: Longman.

Wolf, F. A. (1833). *Fr. Aug. Wolfs darstellung der alterthumswissenschaft* (S. F. W. Hoffmann, Ed.). Leipzig, Germany: Lehnhold.

Ziemann, J. (1970). *Die musik in der medizinischen theorie und praxis des* 19. Jahrhunderts. Doctoral dissertation. J. W. Goethe University, Frankfurt, Germany.

CHAPTER 11

MUSIC LISTENING AND THE EXPERIENCE OF SURRENDER

An Exploration of Imagery Experiences Evoked by Selected Classical Music From the Western Tradition

Lars Ole Bonde and Katarina Mårtenson Blom

*The five strings play. I walk home through tepid forests with the
ground springing under me
crawl up like an unborn, fall asleep, roll weightless into the future,
suddenly feel that the plants have thoughts.*

—Tomas Tranströmer, "Schubertiana, III" (1978, trans. K. Räisänen)

In the last decade, "strong music experiences," especially as a result of listening to music, have become a hot topic in music psychology research
(Gabrielsson, 2011; Bossius & Lilliestam, 2011). A closely related topic is
music listening as a medium for entering altered states of consciousness,
e.g., trance states (Aldridge & Fachner, 2006; Becker, 2004; Herbert, 2011).
In music therapy, many different receptive methods have been developed
for different clinical purposes, e.g., for relaxation and reduction of anxiety,
for visualization and imagery, for reminiscence, life review, or for perceptual

Cultural Psychology of Musical Experience, pages 207–234
Copyright © 2016 by Information Age Publishing
All rights of reproduction in any form reserved.

listening (for an overview of methods and clinical populations see Grocke & Wigram, 2007). In this article, the focus will be on a specific receptive model developed to promote strong imagery experiences during music listening. This clinical method is called the Bonny method of guided imagery and music (GIM) (Bonny, 1878/2002; Bruscia & Grocke, 2002). It was developed by music therapist Helen Bonny in the 1970s, originally within the framework of experimental, drug-based psychotherapy. Bonny worked at the Maryland Psychiatric Research Center together with pioneers such as Walter Pahnke and Stanislav Grof. Her job was to select music to support the various phases of the experimental LSD sessions, and she identified some of the dynamics involved in this process, which seemed to be of a universal nature (Bonny & Pahnke, 1972/2002). When LSD was prohibited in the United States, also for research purposes (around 1972), Bonny used her experiences to develop a drug-free psychotherapy model where relaxation and deep music listening was sufficient to enter and sustain an altered state of consciousness in a one-to-one relationship. Other advantages of the new model were that clients would remember their experiences clearly, and that a session would last 90–120 min instead of 8–12 hrs.

According to Bonny, "GIM is a process, where imagery is evoked during music listening" (Bonny, 2002), and from a neuropsychological point of view Bonny compared the altered states of consciousness (ASC) in GIM with dream states (Bonny & Panhke, 1972/2002; for an update, see Hunt, 2011). A more in depth definition is offered by Frances Goldberg (1995):

> GIM is a depth approach to music psychotherapy in which specifically programmed classical music is used to generate a dynamic unfolding of inner experiences... (it is) holistic, humanistic and transpersonal, allowing for the emergence of all aspects of the human experience: psychological, emotional, physical, social, spiritual, and the collective unconscious. (p. 114)

Even if GIM has worked well with many different populations and with people of different cultural backgrounds, it was never intended or thought to be a clinical method relevant for all people irrespective of cultural or social background. As GIM trainer and researcher Ken Bruscia once said in a training course: "GIM is primarily for Western, white, middle-class people!" (Bruscia, personal communication).

Nevertheless, GIM and the GIM music programs with selected classical music is used in many countries and continents. The 2016 list of fellows, trainers, and training programs (Association for Music and Imagery, 2016) documents that GIM is practiced and taught in 27 American states and 25 countries in four continents. However, it remains an open question whether imagery responses to Western classical music are deeply culturally specific, or only culturally specific at a surface level of image appearances, and universal at a deeper level of patterns, modalities, and structures.

The present chapter begins with a review of studies addressing this question. It continues with a presentation of an empirical study of how GIM may support deeper processes of transformation, called processes of "surrender." It is hypothesized that surrender is a universal, deeply human inclination and attitude towards the numinous or noetic aspects of life, be it beauty in nature and art, religious or transpersonal realms, or intrapersonal and interpersonal experiences of a transformative nature.

LITERATURE REVIEW

The "monopoly" of Western classical music in GIM has been questioned and broken several times. New music programs with nonclassical or ethnic music have been created. Two examples can be given here: Ian Leslie's program Awakenings with jazz and ethnic selections, and Wai Man's two programs with selections of Chinese music, Harvest and Springs. In this context, however, we will only include papers discussing issues of culture versus universality in GIM.

In a phenomenological cross-cultural study, Hanks (1992) compared responses of imagery and affect to Western classical music and music from China. Chinese subjects from Taiwan and Western subjects in the United States listened to selected classical music from the two cultures in a relaxed state (ad modum GIM) and reported their imagery. Based on phenomenological analysis, Hanks found that (a) all subjects produced imagery on three levels: personal, cultural and archetypal "with less personal and more archetypal imagery than might have been expected"; and (b) there were "striking patterns of cross-cultural response" to one of the Chinese and two of the Western pieces: similar archetypal figures occurred in the imagery of many subjects. Hanks concluded that "the psyche has a propensity to respond in patterns, including archetypal content, to the widely disparate music of two very different cultures."

Kim (2010) questioned the transcultural nature of GIM. Being a Korean woman working as a music therapist in Germany, she explored how GIM would work with five Korean women living in Germany. Based on an analysis of case material from three of these cases, Kim concluded that "GIM cannot be carried over 1:1 between cultures, but must be interpreted within the context of the client's particular social and cultural distinctions." Kim suggests that GIM can be understood as a "transdifferent therapy model." This means that culturally specific factors influence processes as well as experiences in GIM therapy, be it at the phenomenological level of concrete imagery or at the structural level of expectations, attitudes and responses to the imagery. Nevertheless, women with a Korean background are able to use their imagery experiences to become aware of relationship dynamics, psychological scripts and conflicts, and to develop new ways of coping with these problems and with their lives as migrants.

Maack (2006) expands this discussion at a more general level. For instance, she presents the following list of "areas of cultural difference" (Maack, 2006, based on Spering, 2001):

Individualism versus collectivism

Confrontational versus modest and tender

Strong future orientation (planning, investing in the future) versus weak future orientation (shorter thinking, instant gratification)

Little gender differentiation (women have equal status as men) versus high degree of gender differentiation (men have higher social status)

Safety (order, structure) versus uncertainty (strong tolerance of ambiguity)

Equal power (egalitarian) versus high power distance (obedience towards superiors is expected)

Altruism, caring, and support versus self-enhancement, assertiveness and importance of material possessions.

It is obvious that such differences in outlook, self-understanding, and psychological make-up will influence how a client experiences and interprets music and imagery, and the guide must never ignore this deeply cultural aspect of the process. Maack provides a systematic exploration of the influence of culture within four areas:

1. *The therapeutic relationship:* In GIM the relationship between client and therapist, and between client and music, can be characterized with the concepts of transference and countertransference. Both can be intercultural and intracultural, e.g., over compliance and friendliness (intercultural transference) or over-identification (intracultural counter transference). Also language and modes of thinking are important aspects of culture that may influence the GIM process, e.g., Western analytical thinking versus Asian synthetic thinking.

2. *Imagery and symbols:* Signs, symbols and metaphors are culturally different, while archetypal symbolism can be understood as transcending time and culture. In some cultures, symbols, dream work, and visions are more valued than in others. The therapist must reflect on such differences in order to facilitate the imagery work in a nonethnocentric way.

3. *Music:* Even if music can be said to have many common features and functions in all cultures (Merriam 1964), there are just as

many differences in all musical parameters (modes and scales, timbres, rhythms, texture etc.), and Western classical music may also appear alien to some people for socioeconomic reasons. The therapist must reflect on cultural aspects of the music listening experience, e.g., (omitted) lyrics and symbolism in specific music selections of the GIM repertoire.

4. *Altered states of consciousness:* As with dreams and imagery, different cultures have different attitudes toward nonordinary states of consciousness. Since ASC experiences are at the core of GIM, the therapist must not only be well-trained, but also be reflective toward the client's possible cultural bias towards ASC. Western clients, for example, may have reservations toward letting go of ego defenses and delving into ASC (for example, into what we in this context call "surrender").

In a heuristic study of cultural dimensions of music and imagery, Short (2005) identified five cultural or ethnic areas of concern in GIM therapy:

Language and expression: Especially with clients (or the therapist) talking in their second language there may be mistakes and idiosyncrasies in the verbal expression.

Relationship and context: Patterns of relationship (not least between therapist and client) and hidden contexts (events, festivals, etc.) are culturally influenced.

Cultural connotations and icons: Imagery leans heavily on culture-related icons and locations of which the therapist should inform herself by clarification

Cultural values and spirituality: There are many specific cultural belief systems, core values of family and society and ideas about spirituality and its expressions.

The role of music and culture: In many cultures music is not a specific or independent area, but integrated in social and religious practices; in others music is one of many independent cultural practices.

Short's study is based on a review of client experiences and reflections on her own work during 16 years of practice. The study underlines the importance of the GIM therapist's cultural awareness and sensitivity toward the client's cultural background, but also his or her need to consider one's own cultural boundedness that inevitably influences interpretations of imagery as well as choice and understanding of the music.

Even if GIM is practiced and has been found to be effective across cultures, the literature presented here points to the need for awareness of the therapist toward a number of culturally influenced factors in the therapy process. At the surface level, imagery and language are inevitably culturally bound, and the music is experienced within a certain framework of preferences and habits. At a deeper level the responses of the client is related to culturally specific values and psychological orientations and attitudes towards relationships, self, conflict solution, and the spiritual/transpersonal realm. This leads us to the specific theme of the article: The process of surrender, and the questions: (a) how is this process culturally influenced and (b) how can music and imagery facilitate the process?

In summary, Maack and Short have identified the main areas of cultural influence on the GIM process and both point to the importance of the therapist's awareness of all these issues. Based on such an awareness, they still maintain that GIM can be used across cultures as an effective form of psychotherapy.

THE PROCESS OF SURRENDER AND MENTAL HEALTH

The concept of surrender is historically rooted in religion and psychology of religion, frequently occurring in all religious traditions, and characterizing a crucial state or step on paths towards transcendence and spiritual development (Geels & Wikström, 2005). In that sense, surrender as phenomenon can be found universally in religious traditions of most cultures (Eliade, 1957/1987).

Within psychology and psychotherapy, surrender as a psychological concept has been illuminated by relational psychoanalysts and psychotherapists (Amadei & Bianci, 2008; Benjamin, 1995, 1998; Ghent, 1990; Mitchell & Aron, 1999). There is a growing awareness of how people searching psychotherapy often carry a deep longing for transcendence, embedded in their problems and sufferings. The intersubjective turn in psychotherapy has brought forth how intersubjectivity and subjectivity challenges a more traditional Western concept of individuality and autonomy. Ghent and Benjamin have contributed through stating how genuine subjectivity rests on the relational mode of receiving or giving in to "the third," something transcending the self. The capacity to do so enhances mental health (Ghent, 1990). Emanuel Ghent writes:

> In many people in our culture the wish for surrender remains buried; in some it is expressed in creative and productive ways, and in others its derivatives appear in pathological form, deflected away from normal channels by that most unwelcome price tag: dread. (Ghent, 1990, p. 219)

Within the field of relational psychotherapy (Aron, 1999; Benjamin, 1998; Mitchell, & Aron, 1999; Mitchell, 2000), the central issue concerns how therapists and researchers can explore and understand more deeply the interaction and collaboration between therapist and client. The reason for this importance is the developed knowledge about how human interaction is ruled by factors mostly outside or beyond consciousness and control—within the implicit and unconscious domain—and it is of great importance to understand how the therapeutic alliance is developed and maintained, since its qualities are correlated to positive outcomes in psychotherapy (Norcross & Lambert, 2006). Research on parent-child interaction shows that children and their parents are only affectively attuned about 40% of their interactive time (Stern, 2004). During the rest of their time together, they are unsynchronized, in the sense that they are in different incongruent affective states and are in the process of reconnecting or restoring states of match and attunement. This work is usually described as "ruptures and repairs" (Beebe & Lachmann, 2005).

Jeremy Safran and Christopher Muran (2000) have researched this part in the process of developing alliance and collaboration, and state that the frequency and balancing of ruptures and repairs in the therapeutic relationship is crucial to a good outcome of psychotherapy. The therapeutic relationship contains continuous negotiation both explicitly and implicitly about differences between therapist and client, and the ruptures and repairs are strengthening the alliance.

The relational turn in psychotherapy emphasizes process versus content. Beebe & Lachmann, in their parent-infant research (2005) have explored relational patterns that generate change. They describe three principles in this process: ongoing regulations, disruptions and repairs, and heightened affective moments.

Experiencing nonconfirmation and difference on the one hand, and confirmation and recognition on the other, can be seen as analogous to disruption and repair.

The process of surrender is also connected to altered states of consciousness (ASC), or rather to the movement between and into ASC. The phenomenon is deeply human and connects humanities across cultural boundaries (Maslow, 1968/1999; Smith, 1991). When we open up and connect with deeper levels of consciousness, we inevitably also connect to that which connects us all as human beings. Surrender helps us to discover identity and self beyond psychodynamic and cultural levels, senses of wholeness and unity with all living beings. In Western cultures, as Ghent states, we suffer from the Cartesian duality, and still overvalue individuality, often with a strong sense of being lost and alone. We might even characterize this as an existential "depression of abandonment" (Masterson, 2000), where dread takes many forms.

Almost like a hidden intention, our Western culture has also produced the overwhelming richness in classical music, which may assist in healing depressions of abandonment. Granted that this healing takes place within a psychotherapeutic framework, ASC and a surrendering process, may generate transpersonal or spiritual experiences.

STUDYING THE PROCESS OF SURRENDER
IN GIM THERAPY

With the purpose of further understanding the change power of transpersonal and spiritual experiences in GIM therapy where Western classical music is used, a small study of GIM transcripts was conducted (Mårtenson Blom, 2011). The intention was also to develop the theoretical understanding of the general psychotherapeutic change process in GIM with the help of a new developmental and relational theory. The categories were constructed in a theory-based analysis of a number of GIM session transcripts. The first three categories are basic ways of sharing attention, intention and affectivity in the client-therapist dialogue. The last three categories are truly interpersonal, shared experiences of confirmation, nonconfirmation, and transcendence/surrender. Table 11.1 is a brief presentation of the developed categories of analysis.

When analyzing the transcripts, it became clear how transpersonal and spiritual experiences were connected to "the traveler's *ways of relating/being in relation;* to courses of events in her inner world, to the music and to the therapist's presence."(Mårtenson Blom, 2011, p. 198). The surrendering process described in the transcripts moved the traveler through ways of sharing focus of attention, directions of intentionality, and affect attunement in relation to the music and the therapist. The altered states of consciousness were regulated (with music and therapist's presence) through fields of tension between experiences of deep recognition (category 4) on one hand, and deep nonconfirmation or differentiation (category 5) on the other. This field of tension was found to be a crucial ingredient in the surrendering process eventually leading into experiences of transpersonal and/or spiritual character, transcending duality.

Surrender, as a concept from psychological and spiritual development, was in Mårtenson Blom's study further developed into the concept of the relational mode of surrender, emerging from a process of surrender (category 6), and defined as follows:

> A deepened capacity to share and regulate experiences of coherence and difference in attention, intentions and affectivity, in different interactive meetings; being able to find a surrendering mode in relation to something "third," something beyond the self and/or the other, or to something greater. (p. 11)

TABLE 11.1   Six Categories of Analysis, With Definitions and Examples From GIM Sessions

	Category of analysis	Definition	Examples from GIM sessions
1	Focus of attention— sharing attention	1st person descriptions and expressions of where in the experiential field the attentional focus of the traveler is, establishing a starting point for movement and direction.	*I see myself,* *I can sense water.*
2	Movement and direction— sharing intention	Descriptions and expressions of intention, directions, movements, experienced as more or less deliberate.	*Warm air is coming towards me.* *Perhaps I will fall.*
3	Affectivity—shared and conveyed in words and expression— attunement	Descriptions and expressions of the affective qualities surrounding and colouring the relational sequence, (vitality affects and/or categorial affects)	*Sad and melancholic, Pleasant and powerful*
4	Share and regulate coherence/ correspondence in attention, intention and/or affectivity.	Expressions of experiencing qualities of recognition and/or confirmation and belonging. Often also strong activating affects.	*The air is balancing my body, me.* *I can feel the mountain under my feet.*
5	Share and regulate difference/ nonconfirmation in attention, intention and/or affectivity.	Expressions of experiencing tensions, differences, ruptures and/or nonconfirmation. Often also anxiety, shame or other inhibiting affects.	*I need to work in order not to fall. Feel fear, and dizziness.*
6	Surrender [Swedish: överlåtelse] in relation to something "third, " something "greater" and/or "beyond."	Expressions of effortless containing fields of tensions, letting go and transcending duality, and qualities of core affects, core states.	*I am connected to, one with nature.* *I am light, it is inside and around me.*

A surrendering process defined in terms of relational modes may be cross-culturally crucial to mental health. Cultural differences with reference to the culture sensitive areas identified by Maack (2006), can be managed in the therapeutic relationship. Music as relational partner in the therapeutic relational field can contribute, if the surrendering process is allowed to mediate between

Individualism and collectivism
Confrontation and tenderness

Postponed and instant satisfaction
Gender equality and inequality
High and low tolerance of insecurity/ambiguity
Authoritarian and democratic
Self assertiveness and caring compassion

STUDY DESIGN

"Strong music experiences" (Gabrielsson, 2011), "peak experiences" (Maslow, 1968; Bonny & Savary, 1973), or "transpersonal/spiritual experiences" (Bonny, 1978/2002; Abrams, 2002) related to an individual's appropriations of music are quite well documented, but rarely discussed in the research literature as a potential health strategy. Few music therapy models have these experiences as a primary goal, however (as described previously), the Bonny method of guided imagery and music (GIM) was developed with this potential in mind, and therefore GIM therapy may be the starting point of research in the health potential of music-related peak or transpersonal experiences. One important question is whether these experiences can be induced, evoked, or stimulated by carefully selected music and listening procedures (including guiding). The research reported in this chapter brings together findings from two connected studies: (a) Katarina Mårtenson Blom's doctoral study at Aalborg University, Faculty of the Humanities, Department of Communication and Psychology, with the title *Transpersonal & Spiritual GIM Experiences and the Process of Surrender: Development of New Understanding Through Theories of Intersubjectivity and Change Factors in Psychotherapy,* and (b) Lars Ole Bonde's explorative study of nonclinical participants' experiences of selected GIM music programs, all constructed with the specific purpose of facilitating and supporting peak or transpersonal experiences. The two studies have the same data material, and therefore they are reported together in the following.

Research Questions

Based on (a) client experiences related to GIM music programs aimed at facilitating psychological transformation and transpersonal experiences, and (b) Mårtenson Blom's (2010) theory on transpersonal experiences as "outcomes of the relational mode of surrender" (as explained previously), the study addressed the following questions:

Is it possible that GIM music programs with transformative aims ("Peak Experience," "Positive Affect," "Faith," "Gaia," "Sublime I+II,") can evoke and support strong/spiritual/peak/transpersonal/relational mode of surrender experiences?

If yes, how can these experiences be described and documented?

Can such experiences be described and understood within the theoretical framework of interpersonal/relational theory?

Method

Based on theoretical discussion and heuristic music analysis six GIM music programs (four from the 1990s—Faith, Gaia, and Sublime I+II; and two from the 1970s—Peak Experience and Positive Affect) were selected for the study.

Experienced GIM clients ($n = 6$) were offered three sessions (minimum two with a new program), while inexperienced/"GIM-naïve" participants ($n = 4$) were offered five sessions. The first session was a trial/assessment session to decide whether the participant met the inclusion criteria (see list). Participants were not informed about the specific goal of the project, they were informed that they were participating in an investigation of the image potential of selected music programs.

The following questionnaires were filled out before the first and after the last session: SOC 29, WHOQoL-Bref, FACIT-4. After the last session, the participants also scored on a scale from 0 to 3 how much they agreed with four statements about the music therapy: (a) Music therapy helps me get on with my life, (b) the music experiences are meaningful, (c) the music is meaningful, and (d) the music therapy is useful. Participants could also freely address qualitative questions about the music, the imagery, the guiding, and what had been most important for them personally.

Session transcripts were analyzed (a) in categories and themes, and (b) based on Mårtenson Blom's categorization of interactive and implicit relational modes (Table 11.1).

Four participants and the GIM therapist (Ellen Thomasen, FAMI and primary trainer) participated in collaborative interviews on selected aspects of their experience.

Recruitment Procedure

GIM clients, trainees or facilitators with a minimum experience equal to completed level 2 of GIM training (2 years) were invited through the national GIM societies of Denmark and Norway. GIM-naïve participants were recruited through announcements in selected institutions or media.

Inclusion Criteria

Participants should have personal development and exploration of consciousness as a life goal, existential and musical openness and curiosity, ability of mental imagery, and readiness to report imagery experiences.

Exclusion Criteria

Participants should have no psychiatric diagnoses or issues, acute personal crisis or deep, active psychodynamic conflicts, and use antipsychotic medicine or drug abuse.

Data

The questionnaires mentioned were filled out by all 10 participants; 6 GIM music programs; transcripts of recorded GIM sessions ($n = 38$); transcripts of focus group interviews with GIM therapists ($n = 2 \times 3$ and 4); and transcripts of collaborative interviews with therapist and participants together ($n = 4$).

RESULTS FROM THE QUESTIONNAIRES

A statistical analysis of pretherapy and posttherapy scores of all 10 participants revealed no significant differences between pre and post scores in any of the three questionnaires. Even if there had been significance, the difference could not be attributed to the music therapy, since there was no control group. The four music therapy questions were only scored post therapy. Statistically significant results could not be expected with such a small sample, however, there were some interesting tendencies in the material. The scores of the four music therapy questions revealed that all participants found their experiences meaningful and helpful, independent of an increase or decrease in the other scores. The mean of the SOC scores was high as compared to the reference values or normative data given by Antonovsky (1987). Some of the participants had remarkably high scores at pretest, but in three cases even very high prescores increased at posttest.

Three participants' scores were markedly different from the rest: they were the only ones with decreasing scores in all three questionnaires. During the therapy process (2–3 months) it became clear that these participants had personal problems that were not observed at the screening. They should actually have been excluded. If the three were taken out of the statistics, the result would be much more homogenous and approaching significance. A closer look at the three participants that should have been excluded reveals that they reported a very positive outcome of the therapy process even if their scores decreased, reflecting that the work with difficult personal conflict material. In other words, a lower score does not

TABLE 11.2   The Most Important Aspect of the GIM Therapy as Reported by All GIM-Experienced and Inexperienced Participants.

"What was the most important for you?" (Answers from all 10 participants)

A. Inexperienced participants

Participant 6: It did me so well. The frame is well defined and safe. The process amplified what I am already working on.

Participant 7: Being able to surrender, trusting that the music would be benevolent and that I would be "sounded" by it. Experiencing myself in a different way.

Participant 8: The most important was the span between the physical and the nonphysical world. That I could exist in both worlds at the same time.

Participant 9: It was the experience of a process. I think there is a long-term effect, and that the outcome will have a lasting influence.

B. Experienced participants

Participant 1: The chance to engage in my inner life through the music.

Participant 2: The experience of serenity and at the same time feeling alive in body and mind was very strong—including the experience of being a small part of a great community with everyone, feeling good.

Participant 3: Admiration of the therapist's professionalism (I have always been a rather critical person)—plus enjoyment of my focused mandalas.

Participant 4: Deep existential themes were worked through.

Participant 5: Re-experiencing the strong growth potential of GIM.

Participant 10: The music travels: experiences of struggle, grief, inner support and transformational powers.

necessarily indicate decreased coping or quality of life. It can be seen as the numerical expression of a more realistic attitude toward life and self facilitated by a therapy enabling also a surrender to personal problem issues—to be explored in the music imagery.

There was no difference between GIM-experienced and unexperienced participants in the experience of meaningful imagery and music. Table 11.2 lists what experienced and unexperienced participants indicated as "the most important" in their process.

The GIM-inexperienced participants used one or two sessions to get used to the format. From then on no major differences could be observed between the two groups in their report of important issues. The major outcome themes were psychological growth, mind-body integration, and transformation.

RESULTS FROM ANALYSIS OF MUSIC AND IMAGERY

It is not possible to give a comprehensive analysis of the relationship between music and imagery in all 36 sessions (this will be reported in

Mårtenson Blom's doctoral dissertation). We have chosen to present one example of how specific music was experienced by the participants in their sessions: An analysis of music and imagery to the music program Gaia. The program was created by Professor Ken Bruscia in 1995 as a sequence of five independent and otherwise unrelated movements plus a possible extender: Frederic Delius, "North Country Sketches (Autumn)" (8:20); Arvo Pärt, "Fratres" (version VI; 9:57); Edward Elgar, "Sospiri" (5:17); J. S. Bach (arr. O. Respighi), "Chorale Prelude" BWV 62 (Come Redeemer) (5:33); Richard Strauss: "Four Last Songs (At Sunset)" (9:54); and G. F. Händel, "Pastorale" (4:04). Bruscia provides the following description of the program sequence. He refers to stages in "The Great Round of the Mandala," a model used to interpret mandala drawings, developed by the art therapist Joan Kellogg during the 1970s. It consists of 12 prototypical mandala forms, which according to Kellogg reflect a spiraling path of psychological development. Personal growth is seen as a dynamic relationship between ego and self, from the open, dark space of stage 1 (the void) through maturation and training (stage 2–7) to completion and perfection (stage 9), through crisis and fragmentation (10 and 11), to transcendence (12), and a new beginning (1). (Fincher, 1991. See examples in Table 11.3).

In "Autumn," Delius uses scalar melodies to depict leaves gently falling to the ground in soft winds. In terms of the Great Round, Delius moves the listener from stage 3, to stage 2, to stage 1. The next piece by Arvo Pärt is stark and empty, and takes the listener into the darkness of stage 1, the

TABLE 11.3 The Relationship of Music, Participants' Imagery, and Participants' Basic Attitude in the Imagery Experience, to the First Three Music Selections of the Program Gaia

	Delius	Pärt	Elgar
Music: Salient features	Unstable tonality—impressonist style. Unclear form. Drifting. Everchanging	Stable yet "exotic" tonality. Clear form: 10 sections. Dynamic intensity <slow crescendo—climax—slow decrecendo> Melody moving down	Stable minor tonality. Clear form. Strong melodic-harmonic tension. Ends in major
Imagery: Predominant modalities (other modalities)	From Visual to Bodily-kinaesthetic	Bodily-kinaesthetic Auditive Visual	Emotional Bodily-Kinaesthetic Noetic Auditive
What the Music Did	Opening Waiting	Welcoming Rooting Embodying Coherence	Folding and unfolding

void. The Elgar continues the upward struggle toward aliveness, and perhaps even the awakening of the psyche. If a shorter version of this program is needed, the Elgar may be omitted, moving from the Pärt directly to the Bach. The Bach begins in the lower depths where the Pärt ended, and immediately one hears the upwardness and directionality of its melody, and the connectedness of each tone. This is what the listener has been waiting for—it is the hope of life. After a lush orchestral introduction (in Strauss), the voice of "Gaia" enters: "Through joy and sorrow we have walked hand in hand; we are resting from our wandering now above the quiet country side." The program ends with a return to the beauty of stage 1, the secret of the void—hope. (The Handel "Pastorale" is short, repetitive, and dance-like, providing a close to the program when necessary.)"

The imagery of one participant to Gaia will be closely examined later, as related to the process of surrender. Here is a synthesis of six participants' experiences of listening to the first three pieces, as related to a short phenomenological description of the music.

In the Delius there is no tonal center, and the music is ever changing in mood, timbre, melody, and rhythm. The tendency in the imagery is that predominantly visual images are replaced by bodily awareness and kinesthetic experiences. This continues and deepens in the Pärt, which has a mysterious atmosphere, marked by the drums introducing/ending each of the 10 sections. With three layers of texture: a drone, drums, and claves, and the melody in strings, it has the character of a ritual procession, approaching, coming close, and moving away again. A sense of grounding is apparent in what the music brought the participant. With Elgar the emotions surface. "Sospiri" (tears) is sad and solemn, like a short Mahler adagio including comforting harp arpeggios.

The whole program engages the participants deeply and takes them through many moods, facilitating emotional release and strong bodily processes, as witnessed in Table 11.4, which presents the mandala drawings of each participant, made right after the music travel, together with the "essence" of what the session brought the participant, often identical with the title given to the mandala.

RESULTS BASED ON TRANSCRIPT ANALYSIS

Written transcripts from GIM sessions reflect two levels of the therapeutic process: *contents* in imagery and emotions, and *process* of how the participant relates to music, imagery, emotions, and therapist/guide (Mårtenson Blom, 2010). Transcripts were thematically analyzed focusing on relational modes of the participant, contents of imagery, and choice of music, through the use of the categories of analysis presented in Table 11.1.

TABLE 11.4   Mandalas and Essences of Six Participants Music Travels to the Gaia Program

Title/Essence	Mandala
P10: New beginning, warm and alive. Rest.	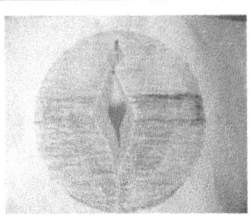
P3: Hold on to waiting. Hold on!	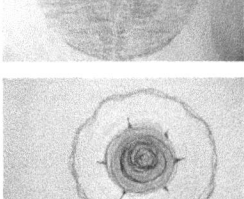
P1: Peace in my inner space	
P8: Peace—Containment—Balance	
P7: ”Dwelling in my tree”—Grounding + Overview	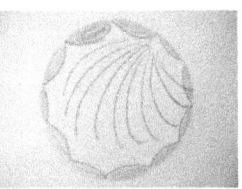
P2: ”Life is Being”—Sharing the same pulse	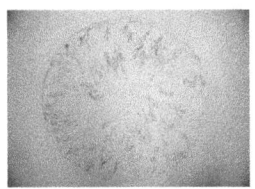

The collaborative interview analysis focused on interaction with music, and the interplay of therapist and participant, including readiness and willingness of the participant, and mutual trust and agreement between therapist and participant. In the following, examples of analyzed transcripts and collaborative interviews are presented to illustrate the emergence of the process of surrender.

Excerpts of Analyzed Transcripts: Tracking the Process of Surrender in One Participant

The experiences of one participant (Participant 7) will illustrate the explorative process of the sessions. She was a woman of 60, working as psychotherapist with no previous experience of GIM. She lost her mother when she was 11-years-old: I was supposed to take care of myself." She is now married, has three children from a former marriage, two boys in their 40s, one of them with severe brain damage due to early meningitis. The other son has a 4-year-old daughter. The third child is a daughter. She has several years of experience from personal psychotherapy, and volunteered as a participant in the research project because of a curiosity in music. She received five sessions.

The excerpts in Table 11.5 illustrate how examples of categories 4, 5, and 6 emerged in each session. In the next step of the analysis, the music connected to the dynamics between categories 4, 5, and 6 is highlighted.

The participant, with no former GIM experience, developed an experiential field in an ASC, with a surrendering process, in interaction with

---

TABLE 11.5 Excerpts of One Participant's (Participant 7) Imagery in Three Different Sessions

A. Excerpts From Session 1: Music Explorations		
Music	**Transcript notes (translated and edited)**	**Category of analysis**
Ravel	Happiness to be in life! Grateful, warmth in chest and stomach.	4
Respighi Debussy	Music is moving around in my body. Really nice!	4
	Grand Canyon – on the edge, deep down, amazing!	4
		5
	Heavier in my left side of body..can fall	4
Chesnokov	down..lonely..	6
Pachelbel	Hold myself like a small child..feel all is ok.. ..(no words)..(Ther:"noetic") dancing with grandchild..fully connected	4
		(continued)

TABLE 11.5 Excerpts of One Participant's (Participant 7) Imagery in Three Different Sessions (continued)

B. Excerpts From Session 2: Music Gaia		
Music	**Transcript notes (translated and edited)**	**Category of analysis**
Delius	I am under the earth in a dark tunnel . . . a door..am high up..as if throw myself out.. a deer says "you can"..	5
Pärt	..winds come..have control..now I do it..like the eagle..all free	4
	..I AM the Eagle, large wings, notice my bird body..FREEDOM	6
Elgar	Enormous wings..I am the wind..no body, only wind, like my breath...can see everything..	6
Bach/ Respighi	no limits..want people to notice me..difficult..different frequences..takes a lot of energy	5
Strauss	see the sea . . . the wind says..be patient . . . darkness . . . fall asleep . . .	5?
Handel	..climb a tree . . . the tree and me!..follow the seasons . . . humbling..tree likes my presence..can	4
Handel	come inside the tree . . . great to be a tree!! Amazing! Can reach far, see far..	6

C. Excerpts From Session 5: Music Sublime 2		
Music	**Transcript notes**	**Category of analysis**
Finzi	(. . .. . ..cresc) I am all the notes, when I'm struck I leave the paper.	6!(from the start..)
Bach	Weightless . . . birds..so nice to be a "note-bird"and be strucked!..body weightless, moves like water	
Mozart	Sit on the water..waves lap.. A wedge at my right side..don't know..(eyelids vibrate)..	5
Vaughan Williams	..like a mountain . . . sad to be a mountain..needs to cry..knows that . . . (sensations in body)..in legs..heart . . . (is rowing a boat)..strenuous,	4
	hard . . . tired..(wind helps)..My body is large and flat like a pancake! Remarkable!	5
Rachmaninov	Cannot turn..(cries)..	5
##	Huge landscape! Need that since I'm so big..sad and happy now..	4+5
	can unfold now..no more a pancake..(smiles	6?
###	through tears)..New sensation to be me. I know what its like to be different! Great! Unlock/open up towards the world. Good to know.	6?

the music and therapist that generated a transpersonal and/or spiritual experience in three out of five sessions. These experiences, and their specific experiential qualities in relation to the music were later verified by the participant in the collaborative interview:

> What stands out as the strongest to me is that music becomes part of me and I become part of the music...and we become colors...and the strongest...are the images/experience I got of becoming an eagle (shows with arms stretched out)...yes.

Music Used in Connection to Categories 4, 5, and 6

According to the analysis, shifts between experiences of deep recognition and confirmation (category 4) on one hand, and deep nonconfirmation, relational rupture and differentiation (category 5) on the other, and eventually transfer into a relational mode of surrender (category 6), as developed through the process of surrender, are clearly found in sessions 1, 2, and 5. The music during these processes is presented here in more detail.

Session 1: A shift emerged between the end of Debussy and the start of Chesnokov. Before Debussy, the pieces were Ravel and Respighi, during which the participant had several experiences categorized as 4. The Debussy also provided energy, coded as category 4. Eventually it changed into a category 5, and this mode continued, until during Chesnokov there was a shift into a category 6.

Session 2: The session started with a piece by Delius, and the participant rather immediately had and experience categorized as 5. This continued into Pärt where the experience changed into a category 4, even more confirmed in Elgar, with the development of a category 6.

Session 5: Already within the first piece by Finzi, the participant experienced a process categorized as 6. During the rest of the program, several examples of moving between categories 4, 5 and 6 were found, with emphasis on the pieces by Vaughan Williams, Rachmaninov and Kedrov which sustained the experience categorized as 6.

Table 11.6 shows these variations in experiences during each piece of music. (Numbers in parenthesis show how many times out of the total number of sessions (38), each music program was used.)

Music provides, at one end of a continuum, predictability in rhythm, intensity, and melody, balance between harmony and disharmony, continuous texture in instrumentation and voices.

At the other end, unpredictability (surprises) in rhythm, intensity and melody, unbalance between harmony and disharmony favoring unresolved disharmony, and discontinuity and contrasts in texture. This corresponds

TABLE 11.6   Three Examples of Variations in Experiences to Three Different Music Programs

Explorations (used 3/38)					
Session	Ravel	Brahms	Respighi	Debussy	Chesnokov	Pachelb.
Part. 7–1	4	—	4	4–5–4	6	4
Gaia (used 6/38)					
Session	Delius	Pärt	Elgar	Bach	Strauss	Handel
Part. 7–2	5–4	4–6	6	5	5–4	6
Sublime 2 (used 9/38)					
Session	Finzi	Bach	Mozart	V. Williams	Rachmon.	Kedrov
Part. 7–5	6	5–4	5	5–6	5–6	6

to the field of tension in the experienced ASC, between deep recognition and confirmation and deep nonconfirmation and relational rupture.

When the traveler experienced a process of surrender from the very start, for example during the first piece in session 5 (Finzi), this piece seemed to encompass the whole process in a very balanced way, and during that experience moved through 4, 5, and 6.

Most of the time though, travelers/participants needed pieces in a row—more or less a whole program—to move through the process of surrender. It is also worth noting that session 5 in this case was the last session and the participant was deeper into her own process.

The movement between the two poles described above may also be frequent when music is shifting from one piece to the next, or within a piece.

The inherent structure of a GIM program was from the beginning intended to provide a "wholeness," or a "narrative form," for the musical experience (Bonny, 1978/2002).

In terms of relational theory and a relational mode of surrender, this characteristic of the GIM music experience becomes connected to contemporary theories of intersubjectivity and change mechanisms in the therapeutic relationship, in psychotherapy. Western classical music's potential in providing or supporting this dynamic will be discussed later.

The Collaborative Interview With Therapist and Participant

The second question in the beginning of this article (Can imagery evoked by classical music from the Western tradition faciltate modes of surrender in listeners from Western cultures?) can, so far, be positively answered. In the process of compiling results, this will hopefully be even more confirmed. However, it is not a complete and trustworthy answer to what seems to happen. The process, illuminated through analysis of the collaborative interviews (Mårtenson Blom, 2006), is more complex. Two themes are in focus here:

Experiences of specific moments from the perspective of the participant
Experiences of the "fit" of the music from the perspective of the participant

Specific Moments?

Participant 7: What stands out as the strongest to me is that music becomes part of me and I become part of the music...and we become colors...and the strongest...are the images/experience I got of becoming an eagle... (shows with arms)...yes.

T: Yes!!

I: That was the strongest...

Participant 7: I am a huge bird, and I have wings with 2–3 meters in width... and I have an overview and I have freedom and I can fly, and I!!

T & I: Ahhhh!!

Participant 7: (deep exhale)...It's so strong....I think it might be the trust I had in T...and in the project we were into...it...there comes a freedom...I am set free by the music.

I: You were set free...and what is T's contribution to that?

Participant 7: It's that I have trust in T, that this is something she knows something about...how its supposed to be...she knows the framework.

Experience of Music's "Fit"?

Participant 7: Music has given me much joy...after, the months after. I listen to it often...it has become a part of my life...something I don't want to miss...each time...I have received it...not even paid for it...it is big for me...to receive...not easy for me...it's much easier for me to give than to receive....It was a big thing to get these sessions with T.

I: Something about having an experience of receiving?

Participant 7: Yes, both receive something outside myself and from myself.

I: Is it possible to say something about what in the music making that possible?

Participant 7: Even if I have heard it many times...it is as if I become the music...and it becomes me.

Participant 7 acknowledges the sequence in session 2 when she experienced becoming an eagle. This started in a challenging mode (category 5), leading into an experience of confirming and a recognizing quality (category 4), and then into a transpersonal experience, becoming the eagle. The last sequence can be characterized as a process of surrender (category 6).

Later on in the interview, therapist and participant 7 compare the "eagle experience" with a strong body experience, characterized as a deep nonconfirming experience. During the interview, the participant acknowledges the importance of the wedge. In the conversation, the therapist and participant 7 reconnect and continue processing. Participant 7 concludes that the opening eagle experience and the narrowing/closing wedge are two poles on a continuum, where she often moves, and that she sometimes needs more openness in life and less reluctance.

The therapist's experience of music's fit is that her choices went easily with no hang-ups or questions, and that the music she chose to use fit very well. The participant conveyed a deep attachment to the music, developing through the series of sessions. She also connects that trust to her confidence in the therapist and her skills.

In the collaborative interview, the overarching focus is the collaborative qualities in the relationship between therapist and client. However, since one transforming power is to be found in the experiences of the process of surrender and transpersonal and/or spiritual experiences, the connections between the collaborative qualities and these experiences are of special interest.

Another Example:

Participant 7: I know I had trust ... and you experienced me as trustful ... but I could just as well have shut down and ... yes, it was important ... and I remember it said, ... "now, you don't need to be that much on the guard" ... that's when the wedge comes ... it was strong.

T: Something that wedged ... that image of something wedging (T making a gesture with hands).

I: So it was a shape of something very important?

Participant 7: Indeed ... you could almost see its polarity to the eagle with the freedom to open up (gestures) ... then comes the other and closes (new gesture) ... it's really about my personal work, my whole process in finding ... a place to be here (shows the open gesture) where it's ok ... where I don't shut myself up ... where I can stay open.

The collaborative qualities illuminate the importance of the therapeutic relationship, and in GIM this also includes the relationship with the music. In the interview, the transforming process and its oscillation between correspondence/recognition (category 4) and more relationally rupturing or disconfirming modes (category 5) is confirmed through the dialogue between therapist and participant. They both acknowledge two key sequences, though from different perspectives. Both lead into a surrendering process, the first into a clear transpersonal experience, the second more into an experience of a "core state" (Fosha, 2000). The experiential qualities are confirmed by the participant's subjective experience stated in the collaborative interview.

In summary, the results from transcript analysis and collaborative interview from one case allow us to answer yes to the initially posed question—Can imagery evoked by classical music from the Western tradition faciltate modes of surrender in listeners from Western cultures?—given that the following prerequisites or ingredients interact and contribute in the process:

GIM music's characteristics (mentioned previously)
GIM-specific therapeutic setting; ASC, how music is chosen and presented
Readiness and willingness of the participant
Therapist's skills, experienced and described by the participant
Mutual trust and agreement between therapist and participant

DISCUSSION

The GIM literature suggests that there are personal, cultural, and universal aspects of music listening experiences. Maack and Short identified the main areas of cultural influence on the GIM process and pointed to the importance of the therapist's/facilitator's awareness of all these issues. Given this awareness, they maintain that GIM can be used across cultures as an effective form of psychotherapy and for self development or personal growth.

Our empirical study was not designed to confirm this hypothesis, however, short-term GIM (three to five sessions) proved effective in evoking both personal imagery, transpersonal/peak experiences, and what we call relational modes of surrender: category 6 experiences were identified in 21 of 38 sessions. The contribution form the collaborative qualities between therapist, participant, and music to this process was strongly illuminated in the collaborative interviews. The potential of Western classical music is strengthened through readiness and willingness of the participant, therapist's skills experienced and described by the participant, and mutual trust and agreement between therapist and participant. Western classical music's cultural bias can also be balanced through these qualities in a collaborative therapeutic alliance.

Collaborative qualities are on a meta level synchronous to the relational mode of surrender. Perhaps Western classical music's ingredients, matched to collaborative "ingredients" in the T-P relationship and experienced in an ASC, carry the potential to move a person "beyond" both self- and cultural boundaries. Perhaps self-boundaries and cultural boundaries are often synchronized or at least overlapping? Perhaps development into a process of surrender goes beyond culture, and more into the domain of what is universally human, and perhaps collaboration also is such a universally human need (Feher, 1984).

Our study makes it clear that a peak experience is not necessarily an experience of surrender. The difference between category 4 (deep recognition and confirmation, which is often characteristic of a peak experience) and category 6 (the relational mode of surrender) was documented, and the path toward category 6 experiences in the transcripts suggest that the listener's readiness to experience deep nonconfirmation, relational rupture, and differentiation (category 5) is an indispensable part of the process of surrender. Such transformational processes have a strong health potential for people of all cultures. They may be challenging and difficult, but the study documents that such challenges can be overcome or contained in a trust-based therapeutic relationship.

The structure of a GIM session and of a music program was from the beginning intended to provide a "wholeness," or a double "narrative form," for the music/imagery experience (Bonny, 1978/2002). The listening experience in GIM takes place in an altered state of consciousness (ASC), and the traveler moves into her or his deeper implicit relational knowing (Stern et al., 1998). Even though the music in GIM is not a living interactional being or partner, its characteristics serve as interactive components for the traveler. The music is also chosen by the therapist to meet the client's needs, and the music is "accompanied" by the therapist's interactive skills and implicit relational knowing.

The characteristics of the GIM music provides a spectrum with predictability in all or most musical parameters at one end, unpredictability at the other end. Predictable music offers the traveler an embodied, interactive field with possible support, attunement, reparation, and recognition. Unpredictable music gives the traveler opportunities to be challenged, experience relational ruptures, and disconfirmation. In this field of tensions and resolutions, the traveler can develop an implicit relational knowing, confirm and deepen one's self-experience with a possibility to transcend the very boundaries of this self-experience. This surrendering and transcending process is fundamental to the development of mental, existential, and spiritual health (Eliade, 1957/1987; Geels & Wikström, 2005; Koenig, McCullough, & Larson, 2001; Lines, 2006), irrespective of cultural affiliation or ethnicity.

After the relational turn in psychotherapy, process has been emphasized versus content. It is not relational contents but relational patterns that generate change. Beebe & Lachman's (1994/2005) three principles of "ongoing regulations," "disruptions and repairs," and "heightened affective moments" exemplify such health-promoting patterns. Using the terminology of the present study, we can say that experiencing nonconfirmation and difference on the one hand, and confirmation and recognition on the other, can be seen as analogous to disruption and repair.

From the point of view of relational and systems theory, psychological movement between experiential poles or contrasts must be contained in a fundamental sense of recognition, in order for the developing process to move into a new level of complexity (Amadei & Bianci, 2008). We propose that the process of surrender constitutes such a shift of developmental level.

> We can view the progress of the developmental process as one of integration, one that brings together apparently contrasting poles on levels of new and increasing complexity. Ultimately it is this process that constructs the wide spectrum of pathways that, at the same time, preserve the uniqueness of the individual. (Amadei & Bianci, 2008, p. 174)

CONCLUSION

The main results of the empirical study were that

- All participants were able to use music and imagery in deep existential work
- All participants had strong musical experiences of beauty and affirmation
- All participants found music and imagery meaningful and personally relevant
- The relational mode of surrender and transformational processes was identified in many sessions (category 6 was identified in 21 of 38 sessions).

Relational surrender seems to be based on deeply embodied imagery, supported by music, guiding, enabling nonthreatening shifts between experiences of coherence and difference.

Both research questions can therefore be answered with a "yes."

A method was developed to identify and categorize experiences connected to the "mode of surrender." Interpersonal/relational theory can serve as a relevant theoretical framework, even if other theoretical approaches may also be appropriate and useful. At a surface level, images evoked in GIM are often culturally specific, and cultural differences influence both experience and interpretation of imagery. However, we believe that the mode of surrender is a common human need, and that such health-promoting experiences can be facilitated by Western classical music.

We began with a quote from Nobel laureate Tomas Tranströmer, and we would like to end with another quote from the same poem ("Schubertiana, IV"). Tranströmer writes about trust—the need for connecting ourselves to basic trust in order to surrender, the paradox in trust—to feel it is to lose it.

The five strings say we can trust something else.

Trust what? Something else, and they follow us part of the way there.

As when the lights turn off in the stair-well and the hand follows—with confidence—the blind handrail that finds its way in the dark.

REFERENCES

Abrams, B. (2001). Defining transpersonal experiences of guided imagery & music (GIM). *Dissertation Abstracts International: Section A, 61(10), 3817.*

Abrams, B. (2002). Definitions of transpersonal GIM experience. *Nordic Journal of Music Therapy, 11*(2), 103–26.

Aldridge, D., & Fachner, J. (Eds.). (2006). *Music and altered states: Consciousness, transcendence, therapy and addictions.* London, England: Jessica Kingsley.

Amadei, G., & Bianci, I. (Eds.) (2008). *Living systems, evolving consciousness and the emerging person. A selection of papers from the life work of Louis Sanders.* New York, NY: The Analytic Press.

Antonovsky, A. (1987). *Unraveling the mystery of health: How people manage stress and stay well.* San Francisco, CA: Jossey-Bass.

Association of Music and Imagery (2016). *Interactive directory of GIM practitioners.* http://ami-bonnymethod.org/resources/directory/

Becker, J. O. (2004). *Deep listeners: Music, emotion, and trancing.* Bloomington, IN: Indiana University Press.

Beebe, B., & Lachmann, F. M. (2005). Representation and internalization in infancy: Three principles of salience. In L. Aron & A. Harris (Eds.), *Relational psychoanalysis: Innovation and expansion* (Vol. 2). Mahwah, NJ: Analytic Press.

Benjamin, J. (1995). *Like subjects, love objects.* New Haven, CT: Yale University Press.

Benjamin, J. (1998). *Shadow of the other. Intersubjectivity and gender in psychoanalysis.* New York, NY. Routledge.

Bonny, H. L. (1878/2002). *Music & consciousness: The evolution of guided imagery and music* (L. Summer, Ed.). Gilsum, NH: Barcelona.

Bonny, H. L., & Pahnke, W. (1972/2002). The use of music in psychedelic (LSD) psychotherapy. In L. Summer (Ed.), *Music & consciousness: The evolution of guided imagery and music* (pp. 19–42). Gilsum, NH: Barcelona.

Bonny, H. L., & Savary, L. M. (1973/ 1990). *Music and your mind: Listening with a new consciousness* (1st ed.). New York, NY: Station Hill Press.

Bossius, T., & Lilliestam, L. (2011). *Musiken och jag. Rapport från forskningsprojektet Musik I Människors Liv.* [The music and me. Report from the research study Music in the life of people]. Göteborg: Bo Ejeby Förlag.

Bruscia, K. E., & Grocke, D. E. (Eds.). (2002). *Guided imagery and music: The Bonny method and beyond.* Gilsum, NH: Barcelona.

Eliade, M. (1957/1987). *The sacred and the profane.* Boston, MA: Harcourt.

Feher, J. (1984). On surrender, death, and the sociology of knowledge. *Human Studies 7,* 211–226.

Fincher, S. (1991). *Creating mandalas: For insight, healing, and self-expression.* Boston, MA: Shambhala.

Fosha, D. (2000). *The transforming power of affect.* New York, NY: Basic Books.

Gabrielsson, A. (2011). *Strong experiences with music: Music is much more than just music.* Oxford, England: Oxford University Press.

Geels, A., & Wikström, O. (2005). *Den religiösa människan.* Stockholm, Sweden: Natur & Kultur.

Ghent, E. (1990). Masochism, submission, surrender: Masochism as a perversion of surrender. In A. Michell & L. Aron (Eds.), *Relational psychoanalysis: The emergence of a tradition.* London, England: Analytic Press.

Goldberg, F. (1995). The Bonny method of guided imagery and music. In T. Wigram, B. Saperston, & R. West (Eds.), *The art and science of music therapy: A handbook* (pp. 112–128). Chur, Switzerland: Harwood Academic.

Grocke, D. E., & Wigram, T. (2007). *Receptive methods in music therapy: Techniques and clinical applications for music therapy clinicians, educators and students.* London, England: Jessica Kingsley.

Hanks, K. (1992). Music, affect and imagery: A cross-cultural exploration. *Journal of the Association for Music and Imagery, 1,* 19–32.

Herbert, R. (2010): *Everyday music listening: Absorption, dissociation and trancing.* Farnham, England: Ashgate.

Hunt, A.M. (2011). *A neurophenomenological description of the guided imagery and music experience.* (Unpublished doctoral dissertation). Temple University, Philadelphia, PA.

Kim, J.H. (2010).Imagination und symbolbildung in der methode guided imagery and music (GIM): Interkulturelle aspekte in der musiktherapie mit koreanischen frauen in Deutschland. In *Jahrbuch Musiktherapie* (Vol. 6; pp. 119–150). Wiesbaden, Germany: Reichert Verlag.

Koenig, H., McCullough, M., & Larson, D. (2001). *Handbook of religion and health.* Oxford England: Oxford University Press.

Lines, D. (2006). *Spirituality in counselling and psychotherapy.* Thousand Oaks, CA: Sage.

Maack, C. (2006). Cultural aspects of the Bonny method of guided imagery and music (BMGIM). In I. Frohne-Hagemann (Ed.), *Receptive music therapy: Theory and practice* Wiesbaden, Germany: Ludwig Reichert Verlag.

Mårtenson Blom, K. (2006): Samspela, samtala, samforska – om ömsesidiga processer i terapi och forskning. *Fokus på Familien, 34,* 256–275.

Mårtenson Blom, K. (2011). Transpersonal-spiritual BMGIM experiences and the process of surrender. *Nordic Journal of Music Therapy, 20*(2), 185–203.

Maslow, A. (1968/1999). *Towards a new psychology of being.* New York, NY: Wiley & Sons.

Masterson, J. F. (2000). *The personality disorders: A new look at the developmental self and object relations approach.* New York, NY: Zeig, Tucker.

Merriam, A. (1964). *The anthropology of music.* Evanston, IL: Northwestern University Press.

Mitchell, S. (2000). *Relationality: From attachment to intersubjectivity.* London, England: Analytic Press.

Mitchell, S., & Aron, L. (Eds.). (1999). *Relational psychoanalysis: The emergence of a tradition.* London, England: Analytic Press.

Norcross, J. C., & Lambert, M. J. (2006). *The therapy relationship.* Washington, DC: American Psychological Association.

Safran, J. D., & Muran, J. C. (2000). *Negotiating the therapeutic alliance: A relational treatment guide.* New York, NY: Guilford Press.

Short, A. (2005). Cultural dimensions of music and imagery: Archetype and ethnicity in GIM practice. *Journal of the Association for Music and Imagery, 10,* 75–90.

Smith, H. (1991). *The world's religions.* San Francisco, CA: Harper.

Spering, M. (2001). *Current issues in cross-cultural psychology: Research topics, applications, and perspectives.* Heidelberg, Germany: Institute of Psychology, University of Heidelberg.

Stern, D. (2004). *The present moment. In psychotherapy and everyday life.* New York, NY: Norton.

Stern, D., Sander, L. W., Nahum, J. P., Harrison, A. M., Lyons-Ruth, K., Morgan, A. C., . . . Tronick, E.Z. (1998). Non-interpretive mechanisms in psychoanalytic therapy: The 'something more' than interpretation. *Journal of Psychoanalysis, 79,* 903–931.

Tranströmer, T. (1978). *Schubertiana,* translated by I. Räisänen. Schubertiana III and IV Downloaded 210316 from https://middleschoolpoetry180.wordpress.com/2011/10/07/159-schubertiana-tomas-transtromer/

CHAPTER 12

MUSICAL AGENCY

A Perspective From Community Music Therapy

Viggo Krüger and Brynjulf Stige

As a discipline and practice music therapy explores how music can be a resource for change in individual, group, and society. The range of music therapy practices is broad and there are many ways of defining and understanding the roles, relationships, and rituals that characterize practice. In the present chapter we will focus on community music therapy, which is an emerging area of practice that challenges some of the more conventional notions of music therapy. One basic idea in community music therapy is that resources for change can be mobilized in and through communities of practice (Wenger, 1998). In other words, community music therapy involves a decentering of practice so that resources beyond those that typically reside within a therapeutic relationship are acknowledged and explored. This implies a practice that is participatory and performative. The possibilities and limitations of music as a vehicle for human agency comes into focus (Stige & Aarø, 2012).

In the present chapter we will explore this theme through an elaboration of music as a *structuring resource* that constrains and enables human action.

Cultural Psychology of Musical Experience, pages 235–251
Copyright © 2016 by Information Age Publishing
All rights of reproduction in any form reserved.

An understanding borrowed from cultural psychology and other relevant social theory will be used in order to elucidate how human beings' inner and outer activities are mutually constitutive. This suggests that relations in humans, between humans, and between humans and their surroundings are established through active participation in activities. Our needs, motives, skills, competencies, and social roles are created and modified as we take part—or refuse to take part—in practices. From this angle we may examine the question of how and when music can be a resource that we use and produce in order to develop, transform, and change individually or communally.

COMMUNITY MUSIC THERAPY

Community music therapy is a nonmedical tradition of music therapy focusing on health promotion and social change in and through musical participation. In many ways this is a rich tradition of music therapy, but the documentation of this tradition in the literature has been variable. Since 2000 the international interest and debate has increased rapidly. During the last decade there has also been an increased interest in the music field, more generally for exploration of how music can be a resource for benefits such as health, quality of life, and social change (Batt-Rawden, 2005; Batt-Rawden & Tellnes, 2011; DeNora, 2000; Mattern, 1998; Rolvsjord, 2007; Ruud, 1997, 1998; Small, 1998; Stige, 2002). This literature examines relationships between music and identity, relationships, values, and community. Music is considered a tool people use in order to achieve valued benefits in various settings. In light of this way of looking at music, benefits such as health and quality of life are performed.

Community music therapy practices employ social and ecological perspectives on music and health, which implies that health-promoting connections between individuals and various communities are explored (Ansdell, 2002; Kenny & Stige, 2002; Pavlicevic & Ansdell, 2004; Stige, 2002, 2003/2012; Stige, Ansdell, Elefant, & Pavlicevic, 2010; Stige & Aarø, 2012). Community music therapy is contextualized practice and therefore too complex and varied for straightforward definition. Community music therapy is developed in relation to a range of local contexts, cultures, and social situations and there are limits to how clarifying general definitions can be. The term has also been controversial:

> For some, community music therapy is a contradiction in terms, since the term therapy quite often is used as a synonym to treatment or curative intervention at the individual level. We find it relevant to retain the term, both because we consider the relationships to the larger discipline of music therapy important and because therapy might be understood in broader terms, including mean-

ings such as care and service. This also links to popular language use, where music is often described as therapeutic, since many people find music helpful in various ways in their everyday life activities. Community music therapy goes beyond this to also embrace practices of health promotion and social change. (Stige & Aarø, 2012, p. 14)

Community music therapy might grow out of the health care services, but is often not, and it is usually not linked to the medical logic. There is not so much focus on "fixing people's problems," then, but more of a focus on mobilizing resources that might help people to grow and build relationships in the context of improved practices and policies. Since people's problems sometimes are linked to processes such as marginalization and health inequities, activism and social change might be on the community music therapy agenda (Stige & Aarø, 2012).

RELATIONSHIPS BETWEEN CULTURAL PSYCHOLOGY AND COMMUNITY MUSIC THERAPY

A cultural psychology perspective suggests that the individual is constituted by what he or she does with others, with the tools that are either available or being developed as a consequence of the current practice. Based on what we do, we can draw conclusions about what we feel, think, and believe. This means that feelings, competences, and ideas occur when people carry out actions in the contexts they take part in (Bruner, 1990; Vygotsky, 1930/1978; Wertsch, 1998). The perspective of cultural psychology tells us that it is through the various practices we participate in that we are able to format, attain, and alter our personal, cultural and social identities. The view implies that an understanding of interpersonal relationships is dependent on an understanding of the practices that have created these relationships. Thus, concepts like learning and participation have to be seen in relation to situated practices where the use of tools is crucial in order to understand the situation.

From a philosophical point of view, cultural psychology builds on a tradition that can be traced back to Hegel (1807/1977) and Marx (1845/1970). Hegel argued for the developmental perspective that human knowledge is related to historical and sociocultural change, a dialectical view that was elaborated by Marx who believed that people create and are created by the conditions around them. Therefore, subjective meanings are determined by the use of objects. Marx based his view on a perspective that human activity is directed toward objects and that the objects have repercussions on human practice. There is a duality or "dialogue" involved.

The legacy of Hegel and Marx has led to a number of cultural psychological traditions that have different geographic locations. The first generation of theorists includes Russian psychologists working in the 1920s and 1930s, such as Vygotsky (1930/1978), Leont'ev (1978), and Luria (1930/1979). These theorists launched what would become an influential approach to psychology, particularly in relation to learning and socialization. The first Russian pioneers have had their followers in American scholars such as Rogoff (1990, 2003), Lave and Wenger (1991), Cole (1996), and many others. This second generation of theorists in the field further emphasizes concepts such as community, roles, and communication. The newer generation of cultural psychologists thus builds on and develops the view that knowledge is constructed through interaction with others in different social practices.

Stige (2002) has previously argued that cultural psychology is a useful theoretical approach to the study of how music therapy can afford community and reflexivity:

> Humans are born with a strong need for experience of community, with motives for cultural learning and with communicative skills that enable them to engage in the interactive learning processes necessary to achieve this. The path to individualization thus goes through the experience of *community* and intersubjectivity, through social and cultural learning, and through internalization of cultural values, knowledge, and skills. An indispensable element in this process is *reflexivity*, the ability to think of oneself in relation to others. While the experience of community is framed by social organization, reflexivity is made possible by the operation of signs belonging to cultural systems. (Stige, 2002, p. 33)

In community music therapy, as described previously, community and reflexivity are central elements and cultural psychology might be one theoretical tool allowing for participatory practice with negotiated understandings of situations and directions of involvement.

THE CONCEPT OF STRUCTURING RESOURCES

As human beings are we creatures of society or creators of society? The theoretical tradition of cultural psychology suggests that we move beyond the polarization implied in such a question. We need to understand how structure enables agency and how human action has the potential both to reproduce and to transform structure. Of course, the contributions of Hegel and Marx have inspired not only cultural psychologists but also scholars from a range of other disciplines, including sociology. We will approach the topic of musical agency by taking a detour to the theory of structuration that was first introduced by sociologist Anthony Giddens (1979, 1984) and later appropriated by social anthropologist Jean Lave and educational theorist Etienne Wenger (Lave, 1988; Lave & Wenger, 1991; Wenger, 1998).

Giddens argues that our opportunities for action are linked to each individual's power to employ and transform structure (Giddens, 1984, 1991). As such, human resources such as knowledge, language, art, and music (authoritative resources in the terminology of Giddens) can be used for reproduction of structure but also for creativity and change. Through use of communicative media and cultural artifacts people can produce resources that exceed the individual's limitations and the hindrances of established social systems. Agency is always within constraints, of course. Appropriation of resources requires access and capacity, but in his theory of structuration Giddens argues that such constraints can also be changed in the process of use.

Sewell (1992) criticizes some of the conceptual distinctions and lack of distinctions in his theory. For instance, Sewell argues that both of the terms that Giddens uses when defining structure (rules and resources) are undertheorized. Criticism has also been directed toward Giddens in relation to his lack of focus on aspects such as feelings, everyday life, habits, and traditional ritual community experiences. The work of Giddens has been characterized as a rationalist social theory, which disregards human life and participation in local contexts (Møen, 2009, p. 155). Although this criticism is relevant and interesting, we still consider the theory of structuration as one important attempt to resolve the dichotomy between structure and action. In the context of this chapter, we will focus on the notion of *structuring resources,* as developed by Lave (1988). Related discussion by DeNora (2000) and Säljö (2001) and others will also be taken into consideration.

Lave (1988) uses the concept of structuring resources to describe how individuals create continuity and meaning in the transitions between different everyday life situations and contexts. Structuring resources restrain and enable activity and are produced and reproduced through use. Lave's understanding of structuring resources is complex and she presents different explanations of the term in relation to various contexts. Play is an example of a set of social practices where structuring resources at different levels come into play simultaneously. A specific example is chess. To play chess offers opportunities to learn the rules of the game and the names of objects, while there is simultaneously a social interaction between players who can experience humor, frustration, or joy together. By taking part in the activity of playing chess, the participants also take part in the activities of thinking and feeling. The game is not just about moving pieces according to certain rules, but also about observing body language and facial movements, listening to the other's breath, and so on (Sæljö, 2001).

Each situation offers resources that the individual can use to solve advanced problems. Lave's point, as we see it, is that one type of activity can trigger a different type of activity and that they influence each other reciprocally. The activity of shopping gives form to the activity of doing math. In other words, human activity, as situated activity, can use and develop structuring resources in an almost infinite number of ways (Lave, 1988).

The notion of structuring resources provides an opportunity to look at how actions are nested together and work as mutually constitutive (Giddens, 1979; Lave, 1988; Säljö, 2001; Wenger, 1998). By taking part in a particular activity, we also take part in a wide variety of other constitutive activities, which affect a set of relationships that are developed through the participation. By the relations that develop through activities that emerge, there is more or less continuity between the various events. According to Lave, the continuity is dependent on whether we experience the relationship between activities as meaningful and thus are able to articulate and appropriate a set of structuring resources. The structuring resources we use in order to make sense of a situation depend on knowledge and experience. A concept that illuminates this is *transparency*: "The way in which using artifacts and understanding their significance interact to become one learning process" (Lave & Wenger, 1991, p. 102).

Transparency, regarded this way, characterize processes where artifacts and objects are transformed tools for change and learning. The articulation and appropriation of structuring resources therefore is related to how artifacts and activities in a situation come together, shape each other, and generate qualitative differences. Expressed in the words of Lave, structuring resources are "to be found not only in the memory of the person acting but in activity, in relation with the setting, taking shape at the intersection of multiple realities, produced in conflict, and creating value" (Lave, 1988, pp. 97–98).

Structuring resources is thus a concept that suggests that things, activities, and participants should be seen in relation to each other. Artifacts, activities, situations, settings, and participants are regarded as dialectically constituted in more or less shared practices. As we see it, the concept of structuring resources implies attention to how experiences from well-known situations can be used to make sense of new and novel situations, and what implications it will have for the activities going on. Therefore, to examine how people make use of structuring resources is necessary for an understanding of the quality of participatory processes of change and learning.

In sum, the concept of structuring resource can be used in order to reflect on how the use of tools is a multifaceted process, mutually constitutive between individual and collective factors. Participation in social practices gives influence of individual skills and insights. Simultaneously we are affected by the structures in our environment that prevent or facilitate participation. Taken together, structuring resources are about the double constitutive influences that prepare the individual for participation in future social situations. This notion is in our appraisal highly relevant in relation to community music therapy, where people's identities are often influenced by the self-narratives that are created in the interaction with other people and with environments and technologies. How do we facilitate and participate in people's "reality production"? In which ways do we consider knowledge, skills, and values as potential resources when people try to create meaning and negotiate their identity in relation to a community?

MUSIC AS STRUCTURING RESOURCE

In music sociology, Tia DeNora (2000, 2003) has developed a perspective that is similar yet slightly different to the one that we have outlined here. DeNora takes the perspective that music can be a resource used when linking activities, people, communities, and social practices. She writes about how music is a resource people use to shape their environment to make it easier to achieve advantages and avoid disadvantages. According to DeNora, music initiates actions within and between people; music gets into the action in ways that create ripple effects in individuals and between groups and communities. DeNora uses the concept of *affordance* to communicate that the effect and meaning of music is not given, but relative to appropriation in a given context. In other words, music's potential is realized through use.

DeNora borrows the notion of affordance from Gibson's (1979) ecological theory of animal perception. The original articulation of the notion focuses on the relationships between animal and physical environment. DeNora uses the notion as a metaphor for the relationship between the human subject and the musical object. She does transcend this by stressing the process of appropriation and the situated character of this process, and therefore her discussion is close to how we use the notion of structuring resources in and through musicking. However, we do think that the theory of structuration and the notion of structuring resources do offer some specific advantages, especially if we take the critique referred to above into consideration also. The tradition of social theory that we here relate to clarifies how the use of resources is multifaceted and complex and how it is woven into a range of activities.

A notion of human agency can be developed in relation to a multiple, fractured, and contingent conception of society and structure (Sewell, 1992). In this way, we have a language for understanding how ordinary operations of structures (such as use of resources) can generate change. The notion of structuring resources implies that there is a wide variety of levels that can be taken into consideration when analyzing the individual's relation to society, not solely the physical or cultural environment. The individual is part of an ongoing meaning making processes where cultural and social factors transform and are transformed by individual and communal identities. Put another way, our identities become a meeting place. As music therapists we can use this notion of identity and facilitate musical participation that enables processes where different sets of structuring resources can be used and produced.

THREE EXAMPLES FROM COMMUNITY MUSIC THERAPY

In the following we will describe three different case examples, which give content to this discussion about music as a structuring resource. The stories are based on experiences done by the authors in relation to community music therapy projects. We will illuminate how music can be a structuring resource for three different but related processes. The first case example focuses on bonding, the second on identity building, and the third on bridging. All examples illuminate how the "power of musicking" emerges from situated use of a range of resources (Stige, 2002). The first example illuminates how human *protomusicality* is a resource in the process of developing a sense of individuality and community in a group. The second example illuminates how specific *musics* (genres, traditions, repertoires) can be used as resources for personal identity development, if used in appropriate activities and arenas. The third example illuminates how the activity of musicking is multifaceted, where one partial activity can enable several others.

Bonding: Human Protomusicality Gives Structure to a "Practice of Belonging"

The first case example is based on a study of a cultural festival for people with intellectual disabilities (Stige, 2010), focusing on the importance of everyday rituals that can structure and animate such festive events.

The greeting ritual that we will examine is a song used by the group "Singing and Playing," in a session in the second day of the festival. While one music therapist accompanies on guitar or piano, the other walks around in the open space created by the semicircle of participants. She looks at each person with anticipation. As she starts to sing, her eyes wander around, sometimes focusing upon one participant, sometimes upon another seated somewhere else in the room. As an observer I cannot help but be pulled into the situation: Who is going to have the next verse? It's Maria. The music therapist approaches her and addresses her with words, sounds, and movements. The therapist slows down her singing to adjust to the singing of Maria, who knows the words and the tune well, but joins in with a somewhat different pace. Both persons stretch out their hands and they touch each other delicately. In this position, with the music therapist kneeling and Maria sitting with her hands planted in the open hands of the therapist, they sing a slow and sensitive version of the verse that the conventions of this greeting ritual have assigned for this moment. As they sing, the surrounding participants turn their heads and bodies toward Maria and the music therapist. They watch closely, they seem to listen carefully, and they smile. (Stige, 2010, pp. 134–135)

This simple ritual of a greeting song—as performed here—seems to be able to establish bodily copresence, a shared focus, and a shared mood. The fact that a preproduced song is used, perhaps suggests that we can describe this as a partially scripted ritual. According to the theories Erving Goffman (1955/1967) developed on face-to-face communication, this process could equally well be conceptualized as an *interaction ritual*. According to Randall Collins (2004, pp. 47–101), the central ingredients of an interaction ritual are bodily copresence, mutual focus of attention, and shared mood, framed by a "barrier" to outsiders (in this case exemplified by the semicircle of chairs that the participants used).

The structure of the song is arranged so that each verse gives attention to one participant at the time. The music therapist then intensifies the bodily copresence by approaching the person in question, kneeling down in front of her. A rationale for kneeling down could be that this establishes eye contact at the same horizontal level and thus could promote interaction at an equal level. But the therapist at times puts herself in a lower position than that of the other person. This could be arbitrary, but it could also be interpreted as an act communicating deference. This would suggest that part of the process involves what we could call "sanctification" of the other participant's face. As mentioned earlier, Goffman (1955/1967) argued that one's face is a sacred thing in ordinary face-to-face interaction. By exaggerating everyday procedures in greeting the other, the music therapist could be interpreted as attempting to approve the other's face (Stige, 2010, pp. 135–136).

The greeting song is obviously a structuring resource in this case. It is worth noting that the evolving and flexible use of this resource depends on the use of several other resources, ranging from the nonhuman (material) resources of chairs and instruments to the human resource of protomusicality, or communicative musicality as Malloch and Trevarthen (2009) will have it. Protomusicality is the shared human capacity (evolved in the phylogeny of the species) that enables us to relate to each other, with anticipation of rhythmic sensory consequences and varied emotional evaluations. Through use of our protomusicality, humans interact with one another at great speed, synchronizing in subtle and nonconscious rhythms of exchange.

According to Collins (2004), two of the outcomes of such an interaction ritual are group solidarity (a feeling of membership) and emotional energy (feelings of confidence, elation, strength, enthusiasm, and initiative in taking action). To think of participation as a mutually empowering process in this way has implications for our understanding of various ways of taking part in a musical situation. For instance, if there is silent participation (being there but not joining in), the question is not just whether or not the participant is passive or watching and listening, but whether or not his or her presence is witnessed by other people in the situation. Taking part, then, might involve more than following the conventions of joining in. Musical interactions allow for flexible use of human protomusicality, within and without the boundaries of a given musical structure. In the particular case example discussed here, several of the participants responded to the greeting song in adventurous or eccentric ways, stretching expectations or going across and changing the activity altogether. These interaction rituals, then, not only used and produced community but also individuality (Stige, 2010).

Identity Building: Music Gives Structure to Adolescents' Identity Negotiation

The second case example is from a community music therapy project in a secondary school (Krüger, 2004). A group of adolescents with various learning problems or social challenges participated in a rock band as part of their special education program. Throughout the project, which lasted for approximately three years, the members of the group learned how to play instruments, they took part in creative music-making processes such as recording, and they performed music within and outside the school arena. Several members of the band had severe behavioral problems and were often labeled as troubled kids by the other pupils as well as the staff. Through active music-making processes, the members in the rock group were given the chance to renegotiate the slightly stigmatizing identity as troubled kids and problem seekers. An important part of this renegotiation of identity had to do with giving the young people a chance to perform positive aspects of their behavior as restless and active children. In other words, the rock band constellation structured and transformed potentially negative behavior into positive and meaningful action. One concrete example illuminates this.

The drummer in the band, a boy diagnosed and given medication for his AD/HD condition, was reported in the school journals for his increasingly positive school attendance, mastery, and social participation as a result of the project. The possibility the drummer was given in the rock band setting improved his potentials for succeeding in various school situations. Even his own family, represented by his mother and father, gave feedback to the school that their son's behavior at home improved during the project. Another way to put this is to say that music helped the drummer in the band to negotiate his identity as a child that fails in school. Peers, school teachers, and family members became not only witnesses to but also participants in his attempts of making a better situation for himself and for others.

The story of this rock band shows how participatory projects can lead to inclusion and mastery in the context of a school setting. The young people's participation in the band can be described as development from the status of being novice to that of full membership, cf. Lave and Wenger's (1991) discussion of what they call *legitimate peripheral participation.* The process of learning can be described as movement toward better skills and as identity formation as musicians becoming more and more integrated as members in the band. Being a full member of a rock band involves to be seen as a competent member of a community of practice and to make their new identities visible to others, for example teachers or family members. A membership in a band like this can be connected with a sense of meaning and it can provide the members possibilities for identity formation and negotiation. Being a drummer or a singer in a band thus has the potential of building self-confidence and agency. In turn the musical agency that evolves provides new possibilities for the production of structuring resources (Krüger, 2004, p. 94).

For example we could say that participation in the rock band provides the young people with identity markers and social roles and codes. In that way, music gives cues to follow and frames for the participants to tell their stories within. This example, focusing on the use of music in the context of the rock band, suggests that we take a closer look at the role of popular music for adolescents (McFerran, 2010). Interest in the role of popular music in the lives of young people is shared by musicologists such as Willis (1978), Frith (1996), and Rojek (2011). These theorists have shown that pop music is an essential medium for adolescents, allowing them to form their own identity protest attitudes and sense of belonging. In many ways pop music offers the individual the possibility to articulate and perform opinions and attitudes in such a way that the basis for identity development is strengthened. The use of pop music, whether it is by listening to it, performing it, talking about it, or reflecting on it, becomes part of the young people's everyday life situations. As music therapists, we can take seriously young people's opinions about pop music, and take part in situations where meanings about pop music are being created and negotiated.

Bridging: The Activity of Songwriting Gives Structure to the Activities of Storytelling and Performance

The third example focuses on bridging (the linking of heterogeneous groups) based on work with songwriting in the context of a music therapy workshop in child welfare practice (Krüger, 2009, 2012; Krüger & Stige, 2014). In the workshop, it is possible to receive instruction on instruments, write songs, play together in rock bands, or perform in concerts. It is also possible to invite family members, social workers, or teachers from school. Work with music consists of many different tasks, with possibilities for the development of many associate social roles and social identities. As a concrete example of how songwriting can be done, we will present a vignette from the workshop called Unglyd. In the following case story, an adolescent hereby called Anne learned how to use aspects of her own life story in order to express feelings and thoughts, join the peer community, and to communicate important messages to a listening audience of significant adults such as social workers, family members, or teachers (Krüger, 2009).

Anne joined Unglyd during four years. Through these years Anne went from being a silent and neglected child living in a child protection institution to becoming confident in performing her own views and attitudes in front of others. The process of developing confidence can partly by explained by the use of songwriting and performing. By the use of songwriting, Anne identified and expressed her views of how she felt living under care. The activity of songwriting helped her develop a language for her problems and to find names for future solutions. The songs she wrote, partly in collaboration with the music therapist, became tools for managing hard feelings and difficulties in her life situation. As an example, Anne wrote a song called "Moving." This particularly song became a tag for naming what was challenging in her life, namely the fact that she had been forced to move around as a child. In the age of 16, she had been moving already 11 times as a consequence of her situation as living under the care of the child welfare system. In the song, she tells a story that informs the listeners of the difficulties of moving around from place to place, never to be given the opportunity to settle down and find peace for herself and her needs. The following lyrics are excerpts from the song.

> Where do I go?
>
> Where am I coming from?
>
> How long shall I stay?
>
> I'll stay for awhile
>
> Then I must go
>
> That is why I always keep my jacket on.

Based on the case story of Anne, we could say that the use of music helped Anne to articulate a set of resources that helped her to organize and to make meanings in everyday life situations. Music became part of the way she processed thoughts, feelings, and experiences of social participation. Her music making can be understood as a way of creating space for personal reflection and to engage in social participation. The use of music provided her with continuity of autobiographical stories including narratives about places, people, and events. As such, music gave structure to help and support situations from adults and peer relations. Moreover, music gave Anne opportunities to challenge established positions of power, namely the positions of adults in the child welfare system. By giving Anne a voice to be heard through her music, acceptable protest actions such as creating an alternative child welfare identity could be attained.

The use of music in order to create autobiographical stories and social participation is supported by DeNora (2000), who writes about how music is part of the way we as individuals edit and pave in the autobiographical self-narrative. Music as a key resource for the autobiography and the narrative thread of self (DeNora, 2000, p. 158).

DeNora's view supports the assumption that the young people's songwriting and music use provides resources for the construction of the self. The music therapy workshop offers possibilities for choosing different strategies related to different focuses. The songwriting process may also be performed in a collective setting, whereas peer relations or grown-ups may take part in the young people's storytelling. Music becomes a medium for stories that communicate important aspects of how life may be experienced for the individual adolescent. Through the active use of songwriting, the young people are given the possibility to demonstrate, share, and give voice to protests that are important to listen to in context of the child protection institution. In other words, songwriting facilitates visibility of young people's meanings, culture, and attitudes. Through stories shaped into song lyrics, the voice of the adolescents can be heard and thus they can be given power in relation to the child protection system.

CONCLUSION

In his appropriation and critique of Giddens and his theory of structuration, Sewell argues that humans have an evolved and evolving capacity for agency:

> I would argue that a capacity for agency—for desiring, for forming intentions, and for acting creatively—is inherent in all humans. But I would also argue that humans are born with only a highly generalized capacity for agency, analogous to their capacity to use language. Just as linguistic capacity takes the form of becoming a competent speaker of some particular language-French, or Arabic, or Swahili, or Urdu-agency is formed by a specific range of cultural schemas and resources available in a person's particular social milieu. The specific forms that agency will take consequently vary enormously and are culturally and historically determined. (Sewell, 1992, p. 20)

In other words, agency and structure are not opposed but presuppose each other. As we have seen in the theory of structuration, resources are considered one important dimension of social structure. Schemas (or rules in Giddens's original formulation) constitute the other dimension. While resources are actual (whether human or material), schemas are usually considered virtual. Schemas are "generalizable procedures applied in the enactment/reproduction of social life" (Giddens as quoted by Sewell, 1992, p. 7). Examples include aesthetic norms, rules of etiquette, and guidelines for group action (for instance when standing in line). Sewell argues convincingly that schemas are the effects of resources and vice versa: "Sets of schemas and resources may properly be said to constitute structures only when they mutually imply and sustain each other over time" (Sewell, 1992, p. 13).

Throughout this chapter we have explored musical agency by examining different aspects of music as a structuring resource. For example, we have focused on how the use of music can aid the individual in giving structure to acts, thoughts, and feelings in social practices. Mostly we have focused upon health promoting and positive aspects of musical participation. It is important to remember that music as a structuring resource also can be linked to negative aspects of human behavior. Music can, for instance, give structure to massive conflicts (see Bergh & Sloboda, 2010). All resources can be used and misused, depending not only on our values and intentions, but on actual conditions and situations as well. And, of course, we can never fully plan the outcome of our actions. We can use music to prepare for future actions, but there are always unpredictable elements and implications. In this sense we will never be able to master music fully.

In conclusion we will try to clarify aspects of how music allows for agency. To be an agent means to be able to exercise some control over the relations that you are part of. This also involves the capacity to contribute to change in those relations. We have seen that music as a structuring resource is extraordinarily fluid and multifaceted and woven into a range of different practices, from the most basic interaction ritual (where contributions to change are often spontaneous) to the more advanced activities of writing songs and performing them (with the expressed goal of inducing change in society).

In conclusion, community music therapy cannot develop a notion of agency and change that solely relies on the qualities of music as a flexible and multifaceted resource. Our capacity to induce change and to experience efficacy of action also relies on our ability to employ schemas in new and creative ways. Our knowledge of schemas is to a large degree due to the situated learning of culture in everyday life. In this process there is often an inbuilt bias in the direction of reproduction of schemas (and thus resources), rather than change and transformation. But agency can arise when the individual and community collaborate in reinterpreting resources and thus mobilizing them in new ways. This is what community music therapy is about.

Because music is a part of our social environment, it can be used to shape aspects of our personal and communal lives. Music in itself does not have a positive effect for the person or persons concerned. Whether or not it could be considered as a positive resource, depends on who uses it where and how it is used.

REFERENCES

Ansdell, G. (2002). Community music therapy and the winds of change—A discussion paper. *Voices: A World Forum for Music Therapy, 2*(2). Retrieved February 23, 2011 from https://normt.uib.no/index.php/voices/article/view/83/65

Batt-Rawden, K. B. (2005). Music listening and empowerment in health promotion: A study of the role and significance of music in everyday life of the long-term ill. *Nordic Journal of Music Therapy, 14*(2), 120–136.

Batt-Rawden, K., & Tellnes, G. (2011). How music may promote healthy behavior, *Scandinavian Journal of Public Health, 39*(2), 113–120.

Bergh, A., & Sloboda, J. (2010). Music and art in conflict transformation: A review. *Music and Arts in Action, 2*(2).

Bruner, J. (1990). *Acts of meaning*. Cambridge, MA: Harvard University Press.

Bruscia, K. (1998). *Defining music therapy*. Gilsum, NH: Barcelona.

Cole, M. (1996). *Cultural psychology. A once and future discipline*. Cambridge, MA: The Belknap Press of Harvard University Press.

Collins, R. (2004). *Interaction ritual chains*. Princeton, NJ: Princeton University Press.

DeNora, T. (2000). *Music in everyday life*, Cambridge, MA: University Press.

DeNora, T. (2003). *After Adorno, rethinking music sociology*. Cambridge, MA: University Press.

Frith, S. (1996). *Performing rites, evaluating popular music*. Oxford, England: Oxford University Press.

Giddens, A. (1979). *Central problems in social theory: Action, structure and contradiction in social analysis*. Oakland, CA: University of California Press.

Giddens, A. (1984). *The constitution of society: Outline of the theory of structuration*. Cambridge, MA: Cambridge University Press.

Giddens, A. (1991). *Modernity and self-identity, self and society in the late modern age*. Cambridge, England: Polity Press.

Goffman, E. (1955/1967). *Interaction ritual. Essays on face-to-face behavior*. New York, NY: Anchor Books.

Hegel, G. W. F. (1807/1977). *Phenomenology of spirit* (A.V. Miller, Trans.). Oxford, England: Oxford University Press.

Krüger, V. (2004). *Hovedoppgave, Læring gjennom deltagelse i et rockeband*. Oslo, Norway: Norges Musikkhøgskole.

Krüger, V. (2009). Musikkterapi som hjelp til selvhjelp. In E. Ruud, E. (Ed.), *Musikk i psykisk helsearbeid med barn og unge* (pp. 171–186). Oslo, Norway: Norges musikkhøgskole.

Krüger, V. (2012). Musikk—fortelling—fellesskap, en kvalitativ undersøkelse av ungdommers perspektiver på deltagelse i samfunnsmusikkterapeutisk praksis i barnevernsarbeid, doktorgradsavhandling, Griegakademiet, Universitetet i Bergen.

Krüger, V., & Stige, B. (2014). Between rights and realities—Music as a structuring resource in the context of child welfare aftercare. A qualitative study. *Nordic Journal of Music Therapy.* DOI: 10.1080/08098131.2014.890242

Lave, J. (1988). *Cognition in practice.* Cambridge, England: Cambridge University Press.

Lave, J., & Wenger, E. (1991). *Situated learning: Legitimate peripheral participation.* Cambridge, MA: University Press.

Leon`tev, A. N. (1978). *Activity, consciousness and personality.* Englewood Cliffs, NJ: Prentice Hall.

Luria, A. R. (1930/1979). *Cognitive development, its cultural and social foundation.* Cambridge, MA: Harvard University Press.

Malloch, S., & Trevarthen, C. (Eds.). (2009). *Communicative musicality, exploring the basis of human companionship.* Oxford, England: Oxford University Press.

Marx, K. (1845/1970). Teser om Feuerbach [Theses on Feuerbach]. In J. Elster, J. & E. Lorenz, *Verker i Utvalg* (Vol. 2). Oslo, Norway: Pax Forlag AS.

Mattern, M. (1998). *Acting in concert: Music, community, and political action.* New Brunswick, NJ: Rutgers University Press.

McFerran, K. (2010). *Adolescents, music and music therapy: Methods and technique for clinicians, educators and students.* London, England: Jessica Kingsley.

Møen, A. (2009). Langs den tredje vegen–Eit gjensyn med Anthony Giddens sitt sosiologiske politiske manifest. *Sosiologisk Tidsskrift, 17*(2), 143–157.

Pavlicevic, M., & Ansdell, G. (Eds.) (2004). *Community music therapy.* London, England: Jessica Kingsley.

Rogoff, B. (1990). *Apprenticeship in thinking, cognitive development in social context.* Oxford, England: Oxford University Press.

Rogoff, B. (2003). *The cultural nature of child development.* New York, NY: Oxford University Press.

Rojek, C. (2011). *Pop music, pop culture.* Cambridge, England: Polity.

Rolvsjord, R. (2007). *Blackbirds singing: Explorations of resource-oriented music therapy in mental health care* (Doctoral dissertation). University of Aalborg, Aalborg, Denmark.

Ruud, E. (1997). *Musikk og identitet.* Oslo, Norway: University Publishing House.

Ruud, E. (1998). *Music therapy, improvisation, communication, and culture.* Gilsum, NH: Barcelona.

Säljö, R. (2001). *Læring i praksis–et sosiokulturelt perspektiv.* Oslo, Norway: Cappelen Akademisk.

Sewell, W. H., Jr. (1992). A theory of structure: Duality, agency, and transformation. *American Journal of Sociology, 98*(1), 1–29.

Small, C. (1998). *Musicking: The meanings of performing and listening.* Hanover, NH: Wesleyan University Press.

Stige, B. (2002). *Culture-centered music therapy.* Gilsum, NH: Barcelona Publishers.

Stige, B. (2003). *Elaborations toward a notion of community music therapy.* Gilsum, NH: Barcelona.

Stige, B., & Aarø, L. E. (2012). *Invitation to community music therapy.* New York, NY: Routledge.

Stige, B., Ansdell, G., Elefant, C., & Pavlicevic, M. (2010). *Where music helps: Community music therapy in action and reflection.* Farnham, England: Routledge.

Vygotsky, L. (1930/1978). *Mind in society, the development of higher psychological processes,* Cambridge, MA: Harvard University Press.

Wenger, E. (1998). *Communities of practice, learning, meaning, and identity.* New York, NY: Cambridge University Press.

Wertsch, J. V. (1998). *Mind as action.* Oxford, England: Oxford University Press.

Willis, P. (1978). *Profane culture.* London, England: Routledge.

CHAPTER 13

MUSIC, A BEDROCK IN THE RIVER OF LIFE

Exploring Health Assets in Rhythm Sound Movement and Community Musicking

Lise Jaastad

Music sets up a certain vibration which unquestionably results in a physical reaction.
Eventually the proper vibration for every person will be found and utilized.
—George Gershwin (Gershwin A–Z Quotes, n.d.)

This chapter is written with a notion that multidisciplinary studies on music practices as part of culture heritage may provide valuable knowledge on the complexity of potentials and impacts of culture activities like community musicking (Friedson, 1996; Hall & Diallo, 1989; Nzewi, 2002). Fieldwork was carried out in the Kenya coastal region in villages near Mombasa, Kilifi, and Malindi between 2001 and 2003, and in July and August of 2004 (Jaastad, 2005). Supplementary field observations near Malindi took place in July and August of 2007 and July 2012. Informants were professional musicians and lecturers at Kenyatta University, local musicians, and sermon leaders. Fieldwork observations and interviews were accomplished

Cultural Psychology of Musical Experience, pages 253–278
Copyright © 2016 by Information Age Publishing
All rights of reproduction in any form reserved.

in cooperation with multilingual field assistants (English, Kiswahili, and Kigiriama). The Permanent Presidential Music Commission, Nairobi, also offered great support. Some demographic information is included as contextual background and reference. All notations and translations from Kigiriama and Kiswahili to English were supervised by field assistants. Field note quotations are marked in brackets.

THEORY

The musicological foundation of this paper is in line with Timothy Rice's theoretic framework on how to conceptualize music as part of the social activity in everyday life, music as *formative processes:* historically constructed, socially maintained, and individually practiced (Rice, 1987). Rice's model and conceptual framework for doing ethnomusicology aims to move away from Merriam's process to the product model from 1964 (Nettl, 1983, pp. 22–23, 131–146). Rice chooses an interpretative perspective on how to study music along with other human action (Harwood, 1987). Cultural praxis is a conglomerate of ongoing processes (Barth, 1987). Every aspect of culture contributes in a continuous making of complex dynamic patterns, a thick description of meaning loaded codes (Geertz, 1973). Musicking, a conceptualization introduced by Christopher Small (Small, 1998), embraces music as formative processes in the making: historical construction, social maintenance, individual and colloquial performance as it comes to play in community settings. Though not in main focus, tacit knowledge dimensions (Polanyi, 1966/2009) and how to verbalize nonverbal forms of communication are embedded, as all intra- and and inter-personal communication hold dynamic complexities of various communicative forms. In line with many other African music styles, Giriama music holds multilayered rhythmic cycles and timelines rather than single beats and bars like a two- or four-beat structure, the most common in Western music (Nketia, 1974; Stone, 1998). Another significant characteristic is heeding the unity of all musical elements rather than the individual voices. Giriama music share basic common features of Bantu music traditions and practices (Guthrie, 1962) known as *drums of affliction* (Turner, 1981) or *doing Ngoma* (Janzen, 1992). (For a short bibliography on Ngoma tradition, see Merolla (ed). 2013). Among earlier East Africa studies with similar observations concerning the role and function of local music traditions are Cory (1936), a study from the then colonized (and partly Islamized) coast of Tanganyika and Clyde (1956) from (then) northern Rhodesia (Zambia).

As significant in identity building and formation, music exists in dynamic complexities of various intra- and interpersonal aspects and processes linked to national and international political and social change factors like migration, diaspora, HIV, etc. (Akrofi, Smit, & Thorsén, 2007; Barz 2006; Earl 2004; Post 2006). In the 21st century, the diversity of ethnic identity and local culture practices on all continents seem increasingly threatened with extirpation due to rapid changes and more or less forced adaptation to late modern and economically driven values and processes, in the last couple of decades known as globalization (Appadurai, 1990, 1996; Heywood, 2000, 2012). For centuries indigenous music practices have suffered ridicule and ignorance by political and socioeconomic elites. A condescending attitude towards cultural inheritance from a precolonial past may be seen as long term damaging repercussions of colonization of the mind (Dascal, 2007; Hotep, 2003). To some extent ethno-musicological studies from Africa in the 1950s and 1960s focused on music traditions and practice as political tools against foreign colonization and social inequality. Later studies include a health promotional, by most (foreign) researchers referred to as a "healing" perspective (Janzen, 1992; Ngubane, 1981; van Dijk, Reis, & Spierenburg, 2000).

Rhythm is a core element in daily activities, in communication and movement, the arts, in nature and cosmos. All life, even at micro cellular levels, is and is affected by rhythm (Campbell, 1997; Capra & Luisi, 2014; Husebø, 1992; Lefebvre, 1992). Distinctly founded in rhythm, music activities hold a unique and dynamic complexity of intra- and interpersonal forms of communication. In spite of growing interdisciplinary academic consensus regarding music as an effective health promotional strategy, we are far from knowing its full potential (Aldridge, 1992; Levitin, 2006, 2008; MacDonald, Kreutz, & Michell, 2012; Myskja, 1999, 2012; Ruud, 1986; Sacks, 2007; Thaut, Leins, & Rice, 1996; Thaut, McIntosh, & Rice, 2007; Willems et al., 2006).To some extent medical research literature on the clinical potentials in music is included for supplementary reference.

A salutogenic approach combining the Canadian QOL-model (Raphael, 2010) and Ubuntu, a Bantu philosophical concept (Eze, 1998; Mbiti, 1969/2002), each with particular focus on individual and communal, material and spiritual being, becoming and belonging, is included as foundational platform of this work. Salutogenesis, salus (Latin, health) and genesis (Greek, origin), is a theory within positive psychology focusing on the origin of health (Antonovsky, 1979, 1983, 1984a, 1984b, 1987, 1993, 1996; Lindström & Eriksson, 2010). Quality of life (QOL) is a core theoretic concept within the theory of Salutogenesis.

BEING, BECOMING, AND BELONGING IN ENVIRONMENTS UNDERGOING SEVERE AND RAPID CHANGE

The Giriama (alternative spelling Giryama) claim indigenous African origin as opposed to Arab or Swahili (Horton & Middleton, 2001; Spear 2000).

Current home-place follows the coastline from northern Mombasa district, Kilifi and Kwale district to Malindi. Giriama settlements continue across the Galana River toward Tsavo National Park and northeast of Garissa. The population according to the 2009 census is 750,000 (Lewis, Simons, & Fennig, 2013). The Giriama is one of nine Mijikenda tribes. According to living mythology, nine sites along the northern coast known as *kaya* are considered ancestral homes of the Mijikenda peoples. Though strong indications point toward a prehistoric origin somewhere between current Somalia and the northern coast of Kenya, the actual place of origin provides more questions than answers (Spear, 1978; Walsh, 1992). Mijikenda languages sort under Bantu languages and use Latin script. (For more about the Kigiriama language see Lewis et al., 2013). The nine Mijikenda clans are Karuma, Giriama, Chonyi, Jibana, Kambe, Ribe (northern), Rabai, Duruma (central), and Digo (southern). Additionally there are numerous subclans, each with distinct dialects.

Driven by an urge for economic growth and modernization, Giriama villages currently undergo severe and rapid changes. A seasonal rise in tourism provides new job opportunities in nearby towns. On the negative side is a rise in prostitution and drug trafficking. Village plots are divided and sold to private local or other investors as the young increasingly are attracted to "city life." Among the consequences are demolished cultural sites like old shrines and curing sites, commonly situated near old and huge indigenous trees now being removed on a large scale. Due to decades of exporting of hardwood and foreign sport hunting for wild animals, local populations are currently deprived of traditional small scale wild hunting or wood cutting. Cultural practices, one example being maintaining and pursuing inherited knowledge on sound making in musical instruments for health promotional purposes, is deteriorating as orally transferred cultural practices are restricted by national laws implemented as to protect indigenous flora and fauna.

Traditional Giriama longhouses, grass huts dimensioned to house several polygamous families of several generations, have become rare. Smaller mud or brick houses are preferred homes of one husband with one or several wives with children. As with earlier generations, polygamy is the norm though not an absolute rule. In the past, marriages were alliances made to enhance reciprocity based security and the prosperity of large extended families and villages. Smaller and more individualistic oriented family alliances seem to depreciate the status of women as well as reduce the level of unity and security between families and villages, as wives tend to be considered property of one individual man rather than being vital actors in complex patterns for socioeconomic reciprocity and growth. Nevertheless, a complexity of traditional, interconnected, patriarchal, matrilineal, and unilateral systems for heritage seem to coexist. On the village level, men and women seem to operate on rather equal terms, and in line with what is considered local tradition.

Both men and women hold positions like musician, seer, or healer. Several informants made comments indicating a long-term pressure from Christian missionaries to "suppress women." According to several senior male informants this idea is quite unpopular among elders.

Centrally in every village are the *khoma* sites. Khoma means "forefathers/dreams from forefathers." These sites are marked by nicely carved wooden poles stuck in the ground in remembrance of dead family members who are considered present in the form of ancestral spirits. Burial sites are situated near the houses or at the outskirts of a village. Big trees, and quite commonly those upon a near hill, may serve as "meeting places" (*muzimu*). These are "harmonizing sites" where people gather to strengthen or restore contact and good relations between humans (the dead, the living, and the unborn), all other life (animals, plants, water, winds, fire, stones, and soil) and cosmos (the earth, the atmosphere, and other planets). Whereas sermon leaders must have the ability to "communicate with spirits," some members of a community claim never to have been in touch with "the spirit world." Still there seems to be broad consensus about the actual existence of spirit characters and a general need for "spiritual guidance." Common features, well documented in African Bantu philosophy and religious thinking concerning life as being vulnerable to, and dependent of harmony between man ancestors nature and cosmos, was seem to come fore in everyday village life. Giriama mythology holds a wide range of commonly known nature-, human-, or animal-like spiritual characters. According to traditional belief, spirits reside in persons, animals, trees, stones, in the elements and all other natural environments. Ancestral spirits and shadows of the body are considered aspects of a person's identity.

Whereas some interviews and conversations seemed to echo early literal descriptions of indigenous culture activity as presented by European missionaries and scholars (Okot, 1970), others depicted cultural pride. Among well-educated Kenyans many carry memories of having been forced by their own parents to flag distance to African cultural identity marks from early childhood. To consider indigenous traditions and health strategies "savage customs from an uncivilized past" or something associated with "evil spirit possession" seemed to correspond with the urge for a "modern," Christian or Muslim rather than African, culturally rooted personal identity.

Ubuntu, a core concept in African (Bantu) philosophy defining individual and colloquial being, becoming and belonging (Eze, 1998) seemed recognizable in everyday life in various villages. Ubuntu: "I am because we are, and since we are, therefore I am" (Mbiti, 1969/1992), p. 109). Fascinating similarities occur comparing the Ubuntu concept to the theory of salutogenesis. In Ubuntu, as in a salutogenic health perspective, individual and colloquial opportunities and access to resources are conceptualized with reference to physical mental and spiritual being becoming and belonging

(Raphael 2010, pp. 30–33). However, social reciprocal links according to the Ubuntu concept include past, present, and future generations (van Beek, 2012; Okot in Eze, 1998, pp. 73–74). In African philosophy, material and spiritual dimensions are to be understood as equally real and interweaving dimensions of life. Any activity in everyday life is believed to bring spiritual repercussions and vice versa. "The physical and the spiritual are but two dimensions of one and the same universe. These dimensions dovetail each other to the extent that at times and in places one is apparently more real than, but not exclusive of, the other" (Mbiti, 1969, p. 57).

To a European, a local (Giriama) concept known as *peho* may be considered linkage between spiritual and material matters. In Kigiriama the lexical meaning of peho varies according to context. Common translations are spirit, air and wind. This has connotations to Western frameworks on how to understand soul, from the Latin *anima* and *animus*, and from the Greek *anemos* wind. According to local informants "peho travels through air." Questions like "do you have peho" was explained equivalent to "are you feeling cold." Water was on some occasions referred to as peho. Could hydrogen and oxygen be included as possible translations? "We are all peho" was translated by both field assistants and others as "we are all spirit." Other translations of peho are herb, sound, rhythm, and universal spirits. In Kigiriama, peho and *pepo* also serve as lexical prefixes used to indicate spiritual origin. These prefixes are applied with reference to a wide range of subjects or phenomena. Names of spirit, health conditions (diseases), and curing ingredients may have an identical prefix as well as other names. *Pepo mulungu* is one example where health condition, specific rhythms songs and dances, herbs, clothes, colors, and a variety of other requisites used at healing sermons, all share the name and reference to a very strong spirit character, pepo Mulungu (the sky).

Curing and healing processes seem to belong in psycho-social complexities including man and nature in a material and spiritual sphere of existence. No individual can be held fully responsible for the outcome of a cure as nobody will claim to be personally capable of curing. (Local informants tended to prefer "cure" rather than "healing," the latter a label introduced by foreign ethnographers). Every action or ingredient of a curing strategy is made in cooperation involving several village members and according to "traditional" and "spiritual" frameworks for understanding. On "spirit demand," pregnant women are told to eat certain minerals and herbs. During the rainy season, children will be told to eat a certain "bitter grass" (*muzhumaa/mutzunga*) or else scary spirit characters will come to bring harm. Tested in a laboratory, this plant proved to contain high concentrations of quinine, known as a rather effective malaria prophylaxis and cure. At one time I was given a combination of "spirit chosen" herbs to cure a running stomach. Within one hour the problem was gone. These are but a few examples where inherited knowledge is carried on within oral and cultural specific frameworks for understanding.

In historical context, The Ottawa Charter reinforces The Declaration of Human Rights (UN 1948) from a health perspective (Lindström & Eriksson 2010:26-29). The definition of health as presented in The Ottawa Charter (WHO 1986) provides a turn of focus towards health- rather than risk- factors and a shift from a biomedical- to public health- perspective. Its definition of health promotion goes beyond individual behavior and includes a wide range of contextual, social and environmental interventions. In line with the Ottawa Charter, the theory of Salutogenes defines health as process and movement towards the health end of a health/disease continuum (Antonovsky, 1993). A salutogenic approach implies how to develop and to improve opportunities, assets, methods, and tools needed to increase health resources in order to manage life challenges (Eriksson & Lindström, 2008). This is a vertical move towards meaning, predictability, and manageability, core health factors in the theory of Salutogenesis. Central concepts are Sense of Coherence (SOC; Eriksson & Lindström, 2007a, 2007b) and Life Quality (QoL; Raphael, 2010). A current salutogenic understanding of health promotion is "the process enabling people to gain control over their health determinants, thereby improving their health in order to be able to lead an active and productive life" (Lindström & Eriksson ibid: 26, "the "genetic code" of health promotion). Comparing the concepts of Sense of Coherence (SOC) and Quality of Life (QoL) to the the Giriama concept Mafiga, "the perfect balance," significant similarities appear. In Giriama thinking, sickness "the feeling of not being happy" (*mukongo*) or "not to feel the sweetness of life" (*katsamirwa kutsama*) is considered a natural part of everyday living. Individual and common opportunities and access to common resources is regarded fundamental for well-being and life quality. However *mafiga* as a health concept (my suggestion) holds additional translations: three stones, woman, life, and harmony. The first with reference to a "Giriama kitchen," which is a kettle balanced on top of three stones. To consider newborns replacement of lives removed from the material sphere and population balance dependent on "the grace of women's ability to give birth" seem motivated by an overall strive for balance. The experience of meaning, purpose, and predictability as central health factors seems common ground when comparing salutogenesis to the mafiga concept. As widely recognized in African philosophy (Eze, 1998), and to my understanding of Giriama thinking and health strategies, good life and good health are considered dependent on the level of harmony between humans as part of local environments, nature, and the cosmos. Living becomes a matter of coexistence with all creations in one material and spiritual sphere, embracing the past, the present, and the future.

AWARENESS

Observation, coordination, and mental and bodily awareness are all considered skills of great importance and something that needs to be trained at all life stages. About once a month people gather for community song, dance, and play. The music goes on from sunset to dawn. Regular community musicking have a high priority, especially among elders. These are opportunities to discuss news and other important matters. It is a time to share sorrow and happiness and to consult elders, local "specialists" and ancestral spirits for advice and guidance. On certain occasions, like funerals, people may travel long distances to participate. Regular community gatherings serve as arenas where social disturbance and health problems can be discovered, and dealt with, at an early stage. Sickness, misfortune, or other challenges are considered community tasks. One sick or unfortunate village member is a potential threat to the whole village. When illness is discovered, disturbed social relations are among the first suspected causes. Physical and psychological imbalance is seen as a symptom of disharmony between villagers, members of neighboring villages, distant relatives, and ancestral and nature related spirits. Jealousy and bitterness are conditions believed to cause illness, be it somatic, psychosomatic, mental, or emotional.

Local specialists titled "mganga" (pl. *waganga*) or (the English) "seer/s": "those who are able to see the truth of matters" are in command at community gatherings. These are village members known to excel in the inherited knowledge on how to cure. Aspiring candidates spend months, or even years of training for the mganga title. Well-experienced elders take responsibility as local tutors, who in turn legitimate their tutorship subjected to guidance from ancestral and nature spirits. Oath taking is mandatory at the initiation sermon of a new mganga. The purpose is to assure good intentions, never to harm anyone. Candidates who refuse to take this oath, or if suspected of using their knowledge to harm others, are called *mutsai*, a label indicating "poison" and "witchcraft." The work of a local specialist (mganga) seem to hold many similarities with what in Western scholarship is known as psychotherapy or therapy enhancing mindfulness. "Mindfulness is a state of consciousness in which one's awareness is directed toward here-and-now internal experience, with the intention of simply observing rather than changing the experience" (Ogden & Minton, 2000, in Mace, 2008, p. 101).

Analyses of internal processes like breathing, movement, and other body sensations along with verbal, vocal, facial and bodily expressions are closely observed by local "specialists" (waganga) at "diagnostic settings." A mganga cannot afford to be judgmental or communicate exclusion. Much effort is made in order to ensure that what has been explained is "a full understanding of the matter." A consultation may take hours. Several sessions may be needed. Whereas some (*mganga wa umburugu*) have a reputation for "seeing the truth of matters," others (*mganga wa kombo*) are known for their knowledge to cure. Some hold both titles. A mganga initially consulted to *see* the matter (set a diagnosis) may recommend another to treat specific matters. When more than one local specialist is engaged in a sermon, both share responsibility and leading roles.

SOUND IS LIFE IS RHYTHM

Sound, be it from animals, nature, the human voice, or any other instruments, initiate from an invisible sphere. As described in physics textbooks, sound waves let into free air move in a lineal direction from its source and somehow disturb and penetrate its environment. The physical phenomenon called "sound" may be defined as a time-varying disturbance of the density of a fluid medium, which is associated with every small vibrational movements of the fluid particles" (Fahy, 1989/1995, p. 1). Sonic speed varies with material density and temperature and is four times faster in water than in dry air. According to the French philosopher Michael Serres, sound may be understood as any vibration perceptible by any living organism, a sum total: a "global tympanum" (Sterne, 2003, in Roosth, 2009), "a soundscape" of "waves rather than spaces" that "moulds and indents" listening organisms (Serres, 1998, in Roosth, 2009).

Though sound sourced healing strategies have ancient and global roots, the healing mechanism or its potential is far from understood. In modern Western medicine, new interest of a possible healing potential in sound began in the 1930s with the discovery of ultrasound. To some extent ultrasound is used to crunch kidney stones and in treatment of certain types of cancer. Sonocytology, a technique within nanotechnology research using a scanning probe microscope to record and amplify vibrations in cell walls, is a recent approach to study cellular activity and function (Gimzewski, 2006; Roosth, 2009). Among recent discoveries is a mechanism that the brain uses to filter out distracting thoughts in order to focus on a single bit of information. Gamma waves in particular seem to be involved in communication across cell groups in the hippocampus in a radio-like system inside the brain (Colgin et al., 2009). To be "on the same wavelength" may then actually make sense, as brain cells wanting to connect with each other synchronize their activity by tuning into each other's wavelength. According to this study, lower frequencies seem transmitters of memories of past experiences and higher frequencies convey recent happenings. Healthy brains seem able to tune into the right (wanted) frequencies and filter out unwanted disturbances (noise). Given thousands of inputs continuously rapidly changing, brain cells seem able to select which signals to choose and which to ignore. This indicates superfast routing of information handling in the brain, a "gamma switch," as suggested by Colgin, as a general principle employed throughout the brain to enhance interregional communication. Could this discovery imply new clinical potentials on how to correct malfunctioning brain signals and thereby enhance cognitive, emotional, and motor skills by the use of sound, rhythm, and body movement?

Giriama musical leaders (sound specialists) and local curing specialists (waganga) tend to work together on a permanent basis. As with mganga, to serve as musician is a position of great responsibility. When new instruments and songs are introduced, senior musicians and waganga are always at hand ensuring that every action is conducted according to traditional procedures. Musical innovation is encouraged and highly appreciated. Rusty and empty spray box rattles (*checkmeko*), glass pieces in a tray (*ndema*), metal rattles and sticks hitting metal rings (*lungu*), and plastic-tube flutes in various seize and lengths may serve as examples of instrumental newcomers. As drums also serve as tables in everyday life, they are easily accessed by children. Young talents willing to learn are easily discovered and taken in by well-experienced and highly respected musical tutors of the ancestral knowledge. Their teaching must be carried out in line with traditional procedures which implies guidance from ancestral and nature spirits. To become a good musician takes years of training. To excel in instrument making and masterly perform a large repertoire of old and new songs is a goal for any aspiring musician. An excellent instrument maker is known as a "sound expert" (*fundi wa maira* or *mupizi*). Detailed explanations revealed a complexity of procedures and knowledge concerning where and when to cut specific trees and which metals bones or skins to use in order to achieve optimal sound. As always every action is subjected to "spiritual guidance" by ancestor spirits and spirits connected to nature. Perfect timbre and rhythm is essential as it is believed to affect a wide range of individual and communal factors, hence the level of harmony between man nature and cosmos. Every instrument maker (and musician) is expected to perfect the art craft in line with his (or her) "inherited knowledge." To play at community gatherings is an honor. During sermons, that I have observed, musicians were eager to take turns and replace each other at the slightest sign of fatigue or rhythmic instability. Excellent playing skills is required at all times. Poor performance is considered harmful.

According to local informants, all sounds in nature are considered essential in the upkeeping and continuous creation of the universe. In the villages, morning is defined by the very first cracking sounds from a certain type of light grass-like branches: "*vigongo vina banda*, the beginning of the first morning hour." *Gomeira ganende gakazikihei?* is a common greeting when meeting someone carrying drums. The initial translation was: "Hello, how are you, where are you heading?" Somehow this is also correct. However (and with reference to local musicians) the lexical meaning is: "Where will those drums heal tonight"? In cases of a lunar eclipse, people gather "to sing the moon back" and thereby "save the earth from destruction." What initially was translated "full moon" (*kutsan gira mwezi*) also means "to welcome the moon with song." Nobody will tell another person to shut up or to be quiet, as that would be wishing him/her dead. On the contrary people are urged to "follow" at conversations.

Though there seem to be no official rules concerning accurate standards of design, size etc., the different categories of musical instruments in various villages seemed to share an overall similarity in shape and sound. A male solo drum *(mshondo)* in Gede looked and sounded very similar to a mshondo in Madungoni, and this (at least to a foreign ear) was the case with all other instruments. In various villages from upper Galana River, in and in the outskirts of Kilifi Malindi and Mombasa, there seemed to be an overall agreement among village musicians and others on how to define good or bad music and sound quality. However, purchasing the right type of wood or animal skins in order to make the best drums has become very risky. To be caught by Kenya National Wild Life Officers and charged with an illegal hunt is no joke. At one time in Griokokole, a village far away from other towns (in the outback of Malindi, upper Galana River bordering Tsavo National Park), we observed that traditional drums had been replaced by plastic cans. This incident had a dramatic impact on the musician and "sound specialist" Kahinde Tsanje, who took a day off as a field assistant as he needed to be alone and mourn.

When music is used for the sake of healing (curing) it is considered a core ingredient. "To present spiritual play, dance, and song for the sake of healing" *(kuzaziga maira ga peho)* refers to the music activity at healing sermons. *Kuzikia* means "to treat/cure." The word *maira* was explained as "a unity of dance play and song." General music activity (*mshindo wa maira)* embraces sound quality (timbre) rhythm and movement. Just listening, dancing, or playing wouldn't make sense according to local informants. Yet Kigiriama holds separate words for song (*kuimba),* dance (*kuvina),* and play *(upisi).* All musical instruments are tuned over a bonfire before use. Membrane drums are tuned individually and with special care. The (male) solo drum *(mshonsoh)* and the small (female, *kita mbele)* are tuned several times: at the beginning of a sermon and several times during a night-long session. Common combinations of intervals heard between the different drums are: major and/or minor 3rds, 5ths, major and/or minor 6ths, and octaves. The two-membrane drum *(chapuo)* holds a minor 6th. Flat rattles made from two layers of dried, thick grasses with seeds inside are called *kayambas.* One by one drums and rattles are heated "until the sound is right." After heating, kayambas are turned toward the same side to ensure "identical material and spiritual conditions" at the beginning. Kayamba means "swaying." Its sound is associated with "swaying grass or movements of a snake." Kayamba is also known as "the voice of the bush spirits." According to local mythology, the kayamba was brought from Tanzania and used by the Giriama since the 1850s as a result of Christian missionaries' prohibition of drums. The church named after the first missionary in this region Dr. Ludwig Krapf (Sudkler & Steed, 2001) still exists. In 2002 both kayamba and local drums were forbidden instruments in this church.

The most "effective" sound in a good kayamba is believed to be achieved right before dawn. Locally this is explained as a result of "bush spirits being most active at this time." The very first morning hour is also the time when the air is most humid, causing the seeds inside to become heavier, and the sound to be deeper and more intense. It seems natural to assume that "curing programs" may hold practical inherited knowledge of natural science including circadian rhythms. Daily living seem to hold many examples of culturally transferred understanding and awareness of nature and the cosmos as sources of influence on human internal and external processes, and of sound, rhythm, and musicking as health assets for people in given environments.

Synchronization and coherence, are organizing principles in biology, as in music, and in social interaction. "Life is unity" (*maisha ni omwenga*), is a Giriama saying (Kahindi Tsanje, Giriama musician; Jaastad, 2005, p. 36).

In a broad sense synchronization implies interaction and coordination of rhythmic oscillators. When two people are walking together, their footsteps tend to synchronize, even if their foot lengths or their intrinsic cycles are different (Bernieri & Rosenthal, 1991; Butgoon, Stern, & Dillman, 1995; Judee, Burgoon, Stern, & Dillman, 2006). Synchronized finger tapping and change in unconscious mimicry are other examples where people's behavior may change in order to match with other's (Chartand & Bargh, 1999; Kendon, 1970). Positive experiences and positive feelings seem to produce cardiac coherence, whereas incoherence in electrocardiographic patterns seem to correlate with negative feelings (McCraty, Atkinson, Tomasino, & Bradley, 2006; Tiller, McCraty, & Atkinson, 1996). More or less unconscious change towards increased synchronic body movements during interpersonal interaction may indicate significant correlations and a possible measurable basis for social interaction. As a pioneer in transdisciplinary and transcultural perspective on holistic medicine, Marco Bischof (2008) presents a wide range of examples from previous and current international research on synchronization in neurobiology, human interactional synchrony and coherence, psycho-physiological coherence and consciousness, health and well-being. Bischof suggests a biophysical correspondence to Antonovsky's concept of sense of coherence, a "complete integration of all systems of body and mind, of holistic and optional functioning, optimal sensitivity, optimal regularity capability, and immune resistance of the organism, the electromagnetic field of the body may be in a state of high coherence" (Bischof, 2008, pp. 440–451).

Rhythm seems a core element in constant brain—as part of body—continual internal and external interaction with social and material environments. At giriama community musicking gatherings dancers and musicians appear to become one. A core skill for musicians is the ability to precisely follow and lead the specific body parts of the dancers in perfect movements and tempi. Some music repertoire is generation or gender specific. Nevertheless, everybody is welcome to join in any dancing circle. Children's repertoires contain a variety of songs. Some have complex clapping patterns. As with other song repertoires, nursery rhymes follow a call-response pattern (Nketia, 1974). Children join and leave a musicking circle without breaking the flow of activity. Clapping, song, dance, and play may include polyrhythmic catch-bounce and pause games involving dynamic groups of participants. Sticks, ropes, or stones are commonly used to perform a variety of rhythmic tasks. Some songs encourage the young to show their talents. Women's dances emphasize femininity, flexibility, and strength. Men's dances, and particularly solo performances, can be quite acrobatic. Even what is considered "old people's music" may hold spectacular dance. Solid body control, strength and balance, free breathing, and natural posture are basic skills to be emphasized and trained at every stage in life. So are social awareness, self-esteem, communication, interaction, and attachment to others. Interacting crowds of dancing men and women, some of them great, even great-grand-parents. People of all ages radiating strength and energy, fantastic body posture and amazing body coordination. To me, quite a sight. "Just normal" according to my informants.

If any participant falls out of rhythm during music activity, it is regarded as a clear sign of disturbance or sickness that needs curing. Community musicking seems to bring people "back in tune." As with all other activities a solo performance can only excel in full harmony with other musicians and dancers. Sermon stages of high intensity could be described as moments of perfect flow, of intra- and interpersonal synchronization and coherence. Individual expressions interweave and create harmony. The dance holds all kinds of life experiences. Synchronized stamping feet and flexible springy jumps end in joint restoration with mother earth. Calm phases are followed by increasing intensity in movement, sound level, and tempi. Social or other health related problems discovered at regular community gatherings may result in future "healing sermons," gatherings arranged with a purpose to cure specific conditions, be it illness or misfortune. All preparations are instructed by local specialists (waganga) who act on demand from ancestral and nature spirit. For each healing sermon, specific music programs, songs, and rhythms are carefully prepared along with other ingredients like herbs, minerals, animal blood or intestines, fire, smoke, water, oils, and perfumes (usually almond or rose water). All necessary ingredients are provided through community fund-raising. In case of funerals or other healing sermons lasting from 2–6 days, considerable fund-raising *(harambee)* is needed as food must be provided for all participants. Such gatherings seem to enhance essential meaning and purpose, social affiliation, culture identity and growth.

On several occasions I observed leading musicians and dancers wearing spectacular costumes. Feathers on the head, shawls decorated with tiny glass beads (pearls) wrapped around shoulders, several clothes *(kanga)* or even padded skirts enlarging the size of hips and bells attached to waist and/or ankles are ways to exaggerate body movements and thereby assist the communication between musicians and dancers, particularly useful perhaps after dark. Whereas big and deep sounding drums like *mshondo* or *bumbumbu* are expected to lead legs and waist, rattles and smaller lighter sounding drums initiate specific moves of the chest, shoulders, and head. The flow of multilayered and polyphone rhythmic dance song and play provide effective training of physical fitness as well as demanding exercise of attention, communication, coordination, and collaboration skills. As in all other movements, a solo performance can only excel in full harmony with other musicians and dancers. Interlocking symmetric and asymmetric rhythms develop enhancing full body-movement flows. Each region of the body is recognized in specific patterns, communicated in culture specific music codes. My questions concerning specific bodily response to specific rhythms and instruments caused small laughter and comments like, "Don't you know your body?" To my experience all activity bore proof of a holistic understanding of body and mind as one organic whole, of embodied meaning expressed through community dance song and play. What I observed seems to be in line with Mark Johnson's philosophical implications of the body-mind and body-based meaning (Johnson, 2007).

Expected health promotional effect from community musicking seems considered proportional to the number of participating villagers. At sermons, leading musicians and specialists (waganga) pay careful attention to natural body coordination and flow. One example is gait movements. On one occasion I watched a whole community spending the first couple of hours of a healing sermon walking together to the beat of drums and rattles. I was told this had been done because "it is important to be well co-ordinated." During healing sermons, patients are urged to take active part and to move the body as much as possible. One may argue that *mafiga* (the perfect balance) as health concept, (my suggestion) indicate movement and processes rather than static conditions. Every approach to restore mental, physical, and psycho-social well-being involves intra- and interpersonal communication, social fellowship, and a physical (musical) workout. The overall challenge at every regular community gathering or specific healing sermon is to provide the right music program and other ingredients in order to uphold and restore good life. Community musicking implies joint efforts, common focus and goal. Here I sense a musical Ubuntu. Singing moments enhancing individual and communal (material and spiritual) being becoming and belonging in reciprocal chains (including nature and cosmos), embracing the past, the present and the future.

Funerals are arenas for innovation and life celebration as well as being recognized as healing sermons. A funeral normally lasts for 5–7 days and nights. During the first 2–3 days family members and others sit, cry, talk, and sing by the deathbed. Some ask forgiveness. Some continue an argument or even a dispute, most likely over land or other property issues. Some cry out in grief over the loss of a loved one. Others bring forward their worries about the future. People comfort each other, show support and love. Good memories are shared. The only loud noises during the first couple of days are songs of sorrow and people crying out in grief. Some stay sober, others get drunk. Nobody seems bothered by either behavior. These are times of solidarity, comfort, and support.

On burial day, all guests line up in procession to follow the diseased to a prepared grave site. The music played at funerals is named *maira ga kuziga*. A song known as "Zombe" is sung at every funeral parade as the dead body is carried (in an open or closed coffin) from the earthly- to the spiritual home-site. Zombe means power. The song is performed very loud in order to attract as many helpers as possible. Help to carry the dead, to dig the grave, and to chase "the spirit of death" away from this village. Other songs urge ancestor spirits to be good to the newcomer, to notice, and to be pleased with all efforts made by the living in order to promote harmony. After the body is laid to rest, people gather around the grave to bid farewell. Songs are sung as the grave is covered with soil. When a musicians dies, his or her compositions are performed as guest of honor.

Shortly after the grave is covered, a small group of elders begin to dance from the top of the grave. The deep sounding three-legged membrane drum (*bumbumbu*) initiate *ndimba,* a funeral dance. The bumbumbu is made from a hardwood known as *m'bamba* (currently illegal to cut) with a membrane skin made from a type of antelope known as *m'bala* (currently illegal to hunt). The sound resembles the majestic rolling sea of the shores of Malindi. Other joining instruments are the tall (male) mshundoh, the two-membrane chapuo, the smaller three-legged drums *kapita mbele,* the metal plate debe, and the antelope horn gunda along with all other traditional instruments including calabash rattles and military signal flutes. The repertoire may include traditional funeral songs and any popular songs, songs particularly favored by the diseased including song rhymes in memory of childhood or love stories.

At funerals a primary obligation is to help the diseased over to a new form of existence among the ancestor spirits. Poor performance on this matter is believed to cause future obstacles or even disaster to family members and to the entire community. As always the matter of inclusion is important. As with the living, all ancestors of a village must be recognized with respect and remembered during burial rituals and sermons. Ancestors are mentioned in songs of honor and praise. Great thanks are given for their braveness, strength, wisdom, or any other good contribution made to the community during their days among the living. Humbly the diseased is introduced among ancestors and other spirits along with gentle demands to conduce to peace and harmony among the living, the dead, nature, and the cosmos.

The music activity increases during the funeral week. More participants and groups of musicians arrive. More instruments are heard like a variety of membranophones, flutes, rattles, and drums. Music groups take turns to play and lead the crowd in song and dance throughout the remaining days and nights. People sleep a little and rejoin. Toward the last days the atmosphere changes from grief to celebration. This is a time to celebrate life, and to replace the life that has been lost. I was told the purpose of the music at this stage is to seduce. Preferred instruments are *ndema*, an iron ring played with a metal stick, and *lungu*, which is rattling pieces of glass in a sisal tray. *Lungu* means "bat" and the sound it produces resembles the morning sounds of bats. This combination of instruments is considered tempting and lust giving. For young adults a funeral is a potential courting arena. During the last 2 days the young become more visible on the musicking arena. As the young women dance the men are watching and vice versa. Every dancing circle is led by a group of musicians. Young people's dances hold lots of individual solo performances. Men's solo dances can be quite acrobatic. In the midst of a solo performance, young men run into the crowd of ululating and giggling women. This is his chance to seek a response from a woman of his choice by grabbing her wrist between his fore and middle finger. It is a man's task to propose and a woman's privilege to accept or turn down an offer. If she answers his grip by grabbing his hand in the same way, this could be the beginning of a relationship. In the case of no interest all she needs to do is not to respond. The whole thing happens incredibly fast. Whatever outcome, it may be kept a secret between the two, at least for a while.

At the end of a funeral, the grave is danced to flat ground. Family and community bonds are strengthened. As many travel far to participate, these are opportunities to keep in touch with distant relatives and for new alliances to be made (Jaastad, 2005). Close relatives of the diseased have received mental, practical, and economic support. Quite often, and particularly in cases of women being widowed, arrangements may have been made to provide her household with any support needed for the first coming year. Funerals clearly illustrate the importance of human relations as health resource. The scope of action for each family and village member, bound in reciprocal relations with past, present, and future generations. To be is to belong.

At healing sermons musicians line up in a half circle, and if possible in front of a wall. Every musician and instrument has its place and specific role to play. Based on information received at diagnostic settings, some music herbs or other ingredients are selected and prepared in advance. However the total program and development of a sermon is an interactive process, a unity of joint efforts where mganga (waganga), musicians, the patient, and all other participants have specific roles to play. Patients are under close observation by mganga and musicians all times of a sermon. Whereas the sound of some instruments is considered "penetrative," others are referred to as "harmonizing." A common setting at healing sermons is as follows: The large, tall leading drum mshondo, also referred to as "male" and "solo-drum," and the smaller three-legged "female" drum *kapita mbele* ('those who stand in front") are placed a few meters in straight line behind the patient. These drums are both played by the leading musician. A metal board named debe and an antelope horn *(gunda)* are placed on either side of the mshondo. The sound of these instruments are classified as "penetrative." On both sides, now forming a half circle is the *chapuo*, an oblong cylindrical drum with two membranes (in both ends). Its purpose is to be "harmonizing." Metal bells, *nzugu*, (small bells to be carried around ankle or waist) and *maasai* (a cow bell, adopted from the herding Maasai) have no fixed place and may move freely among all participants. The purpose of these instruments as well as the song is "to promote harmony." Singers and dancers occupy the other circle half. The mganga and a few assistants will be tending the patient, usually placed sitting or lying a few meters in front of the musicians as the sermon begins. At times the mganga mingle freely among the crowd of participants. This gives an opportunity for close observation and communication with every participant and to receive information that otherwise could have been missed out. It also gives the opportunity to be in close contact with the musicians at all times and to regulate the intensity of soundly exposure.

FREEZE SHIVERS AND SHAKES

At diagnostic settings, as well as during healing sermons, rhythm is used to seek a better understanding of the matter. Problematic health conditions are identified and dealt with according to standard (traditional) procedures subjected to spiritual guidance. Health disturbing conditions are discovered, diagnosed and treated by the use of specific sound sources (instruments), rhythmic patterns and combinations. To set diagnose is referred to as to shake the *kititi* seeds *(kutsuha mburugu)*. *Kititi* is a small shaker made from a dried kalebass filled with seeds. These rattles are commonly used by mganga during introductory and investigational consultations. Intense rattle shaking take place at conversational pauses. The sound is quite intense in the long run. A mganga at work is believed to communicate with a wide range of spirits. I was told the kititi enhances the ability to communicate with the *Mbengu* spirits, known for their "curing wisdom." During kititi-shaking sessions the specialist (mganga) undergoes significant changes of appearance. Rolling eyes, significant changes in body moves and color of voice, as if he or she has become a different person, seems quite common. According to local informants the rhythmic stimulation and sound from the kititi shaker is used to reach a deeper level of consciousness, which is considered necessary in order to "see" the truth of the matter. The severe change of appearance observed during diagnostic sessions (and other sermon climaxes) seems beyond rational comprehension. Nevertheless it fits well with classical descriptions of trance conditions, state of transcendence (Rouget, 1985). This altered level of consciousness is locally known as *kuhaiuka*, "to be mad, out of control," and "able to see things that otherwise are hidden." Mrs. Dama Shutu, daughter of a famous musician and healer (the late Mr. Charo Shutu, Malindi) and holder of both mganga titles, gave the following explanation:

> Kuhaiuka means communication with several, even many spirits who are all talking at the same time. My task is to find the right voices and listen carefully. Usually I keep special attention to those who speak last. These spirit voices may have been there all the time, though not easily heard in the midst of more noisy spirits. (Jaastad, 2005, p. 78)

The the intensity of activities during healing sermons (as well as other musical gatherings) rise and fall in wave-like cycles. Quiet sessions aiming to search for problematic areas are followed by periods of rising activity before declining to further searches. Eventually all sermons rise to at least one full climax. These are stages of intense activity where patients also become increasingly active as the body now clearly responds to the music. *Kuthukusa* is a Giriama expression used to describe "musical effectiveness." Kuthukusa means "to shake." The body is compared to the harvest of a mango tree. Trees must be shaken carefully enough for unripe fruits to hang on, but enough for the ripe fruits to come off the branches. Music doses must shake the patient just right. When the two-membrane drum (chapuo) is balancing the "male" solodrum (mshondoh) and the "female" small three-legged (kaptita mbele) and the metal plate (debe) are suitably penetrative, and in case of the debe also energizing, then the music is effective according to musician and sound specialist Kahindi Tsanje, a well-known musician living in Madunguni (near Malindi). Giriama ways to describe *good* music is *kidzakola*, "when the fish is rightly salted." Other expressions are "it's in the blood/it's in the cultural droplets" (*indani ya milatso*) or "his/her father is coming back" (*ni babaye adzauya*). Music that is considered too much or too soft may be considered harmful or non effective. Poor rhythmic performance is always considered harmful (Jaastad, 2005).

Climaxes are moments marked by highly complex hocked and interlocking rhythms and solo performances (Stone, 1998, pp. 15–16, 298) in perfect harmony with all musicians, leading dancers and the crowd of all other participants. Such moments clearly illustrate how and when to make brilliant musical turns and breaks. At musical peaks several participants may go into trance. The explanation given by informants was that these are moments where mganga is "fighting with the spirits, forcing them to leave the patient." The transcendent condition is called *kubwananyama,* "to wrestle the spirits." On one occasion the local mganga, Lady Mwendenge (operating near Mombasa), explained that a young lady patient suffered due to "unhappy ancestors." On arrival she was "paralyzed and unable to walk." We were told she had been sick for a long time. Relatives had carried her several miles for treatment. At the beginning of the sermon she was placed sitting under cover of a black blanket. (Colors hold meaning loaded codes). Herbs were given to be inhaled over damping water. (Other common ways to take herbs or minerals are by swallowing, inhaling through the nose, or placed in skin cuts). Towards the sermon climax, Mrs. Mwendenge had to "wrestle, negotiate, and comfort the spirits." This happened as the patient strongly "responded" to songs and rhythm associated with *Pepo Mdigo,* a spirit character described as being "constantly on the move as it has nowhere to live." Basic line in the Pepo Mdigo rhythm is: two eighth notes over triplets. The lyrics of Pepo Mdigo's song was translated as follows: "Mdigo Mdigo let me go. I am so disturbed, so unhappy. I am in so much pain." The first visible responding signs from the patient were shaking hands and head. At some point she began to roll over from one side to the other. Eventually feet, legs, and thighs began to move. Gradually the body entered into tremendous shakes and shivers. Her legs, gently tied at the beginning of the sermon, were gradually loosened. The patient appeared to be in trance. All of a sudden she came up to her feet. Wild gesticulations followed and a tremendous flow of speech recognized as "spirit language," incomprehensive to others and phonetically quite similar to what in Christian tradition is known as speaking in tongues. A wrestling scene developed between the patient and her helpers, who at this point all appeared to be in trance. Several musicians had their rounds of transcendental "fights with spirits." As helpers regained normal behavior they managed to calm the patient who now willingly sat down on a straw mat. The music calmed. Rose water was pored over the patient's hair. Her face and hands were gently washed. Again the lady rose to her feet. Led by helpers she walked to a nearby hut. All participants followed behind. A short ritual followed "thanking Pepo Mulungu, the spirit of the sky." After weeks in misery, the young married woman and mother of a small daughter seemed well and ready to walk home.

To "shake off" unpleasant experiences is a well-known metaphor in English as in many other languages. Immobility, freeze, dissociation, and denial are inborn mechanisms. A person exposed to some kind of trauma may experience protection from emotional reaction or even from a clear memory of the incident. Trauma may be described as a condition of extreme discomfort. Trauma includes the experience of "serious threat to one's life or physical integrity beyond the range of usual human experience" (Butler, 2004). As an accurate definition of trauma is a discourse of its own and beyond the aim of this paper, my intention is only to point to the important impact from the felt sense, a response system connecting body and soul. What really matters is an experienced sense of how it feels to be in that particular situation. The stem of trauma may be described as frozen fight or flight energy trapped, unable to discharge, immobility and helplessness with a wide range of negative potentials to cause symptoms like depression, anxiety, psychosomatic, or behavioral problems (Levine, 1997).

Whereas rhythm and body movement seem recognized and appreciated on the African continent, one may argue that both may seem neglected, even suppressed in the West (Bjørkvold, 1995). Nevertheless rhythm is everywhere as a core factor in life. Our brains are rhythmic in architecture and function (Thaut, 2005). Though our bodies may scream with tension and discomfort, modern therapeutic strategies tend to take a verbal and mentally focused approach, more or less ignoring a bodily connection to thoughts and emotions. Yet we live our lives through our bodies, and our bodies are not from neutral ground. Embodied is individual and common shared social and environmental and culture related contexts. Encountered with danger our ways of reaction resemble those of other mammals. Freeze and release is a natural rhythm of life. One may argue that people belonging to Western and urban cultural adaptations seem to have lost touch with natural rhythmic flows including rapid changes between freeze and release (Levine, 1997, 2010). There seems to be good reasons to suspect considerable mismatch between the modern information-based world and the ancient, innate physical stress designed reaction mechanisms of the body. To recognize repercussions of discomfort, even after dramatic and traumatizing experiences, may be quite challenging. Could it be that culturally enhanced conscious and unconscious suppression of rhythm may affect our primitive response to trauma and could this enhance freeze rather than release resulting in stiff necks, painful shoulders, fatigue, and various other common conditions causing unwellness and sick leave in Western urban society?

Uncontrollable cold shivering is rather common in patients awaking from anesthesia. Deep spontaneous breaths, rapid shakes, and shivers are instinct reactions in animals when out of a dangerous situation (Levine,

1997). Involuntary shakes and shivers, seemingly trigged during giriama rhythm and music based healing sessions, are universal innate capacities and mechanisms to help restore equilibrium and resilience after exposure to trauma (Levine, 2010). Just how significant is the freeze-release mechanism, and what is the full health promotional potential in voluntary shake, rattle and roll, and involuntary quivers and quakes? During fieldwork I videorecorded a number of other healing sermons held to cure conditions explained as "paralysis" or "blocked body functions," conditions also explained in terms of "erectile dysfunction and infertility." According to informants these were normal health problems to be solved by the use of traditional healing sermons involving sound, rhythm, and movement in community settings.

CLOSING COMMENTS

With particular focus on sound, rhythm movement, and musical fellowship, I have attempted to take one small step into dynamic complexities on the role of musicking and of culture in a health promotional perspective. Giriama music praxis seem to hold culturally inherited recognition of rhythm (sound and movement) as essential and significant health resource. In the villages a mindful body and social awareness seems to be emphasised and trained on a daily basis at all life stages. Unity stands out as basic premise for a good life and even survival. Rhythm is clearly recognized and celebrated in everyday life. Sermons involving community musicking bare proof of a deep recognition of rhythm as a tool to enhance mental and bodily, individual and communal, synchronization and bonding. In Giriama community musicking, I sense a holistic health promotional approach, a continuous lifelong practice enhancing individual and community-focused awareness, synchronization, and bonding. To my experience community gathering where music is involved invigorate Giriama identity, well-being, and pride. However, elder informants expressed concern that their inherited knowledge is vanishing. Lack of interest among the young, laws posing restrictions making it increasingly difficult to get hold of the best materials for instrument making and other culture related practices. Hence the increasing demand for money from local musicians and "specialists" (waganga). These were mentioned by many as destructive factors corrupting local values and standards. Rhythm is a core element in life and in everyday activities, in music and in all other forms of communication. Rhythm is a key issue in unconscious and autonomous sensory-motor patterns as well as in conscious more complex and intentional patterns of movement (Thaut, 2005). In this text I attempt to suggest that community musicking, illustrated with examples from giriama music practices, music traditions strongly founded in rhythm, may hold unique potentials providing channels to combine innate and culture based, biologic, contextual, social, and relational living dimensions as health resources. Could it be that rhythm and music hold a unique potentials to trigger and to utilize these gyrations and undulations as inborn strategies for physical and mental self-regulation and resilience? Could the same tremendous energy causing disease be captured and released in rhythm-, music-, and culture-based music activities? As technology and medical science provide increasing knowledge about phenomena and processes previously unobservable or simply unknown, it also provides new perspectives and opportunities for interdisciplinary research, including culture dimensions in health and health promotion potentials in culture activities.

REFERENCES

Akrofi, E., Smit, M., & Thorsén (Eds.). (2007). *Music and identity: Transformation and negotiation.* Stellenbosch, South Africa: African Sun Media.

Aldridge, D. (1992). *Music therapy research and practice in medicine: Out of the silence.* London, England: Jessica Kingsley.

Antonovsky, A. (1979). *Health, stress and coping: New perspectives on mental and physical health and well-being.* San Fransisco, CA: Jossey-Bass.

Antonovsky, A. (1983). The sense of coherence: Determinant of a research instrument. W. S. Schwartz research center for behavioral medicine. *Tel Aviv University, Newsletter and Research Reports, 1,* 1–11.

Antonovsky, A. (1984a). The sense of coherence as a determinant of health. In J. D. Matarazzo, S. M. Weiss, J. A. Herd, M. E. Miller, & S. M. Weiss (Eds.), *Behavioral health: A handbook of health enhancement and disease prevention* (pp. 114–129). New York, NY: Wiley-Interscience.

Antonovsky, A. (1984b). A call for a new question – salutogenesis – and a proposed answer: The sense of coherence. *Journal of Preventive Psychiatry, 2,* 1–13.

Antonovsky, A. (1987). *Unraveling the mystery of health: How people manage stress and stay well.* San Francisco, CA: Jossey-Bass.

Antonovsky, A. (1993, January 21). *The salutogenic approach to aging* [Lecture]. Retrieved from http://www.angelfire.com/ok/soc/a-berkeley.html

Antonovsky, A. (1996). The salutogenic model as a theory to guide health promotion. *Health Promotion International, 11*(1), 11–18.

Appadurai, A. (1990). Disjuncture and difference in the global cultural economy. *Theory Culture and Society, 7,* 295.

Appadurai, A. (1996). *Modernity at large.* Minneapolis: University of Minnesota Press.

Barth F. (1987). *Cosmologies in the making: A generative approach to cultural variation in inner New Guinea.* Cambridge, England: Cambridge University Press.

Barz, G. (2006). *Singing for life: HIV/AIDS and music in Uganda.* New York, NY: Routledge Chapman & Hall.

Bernieri, F. J., & Rosenthal, R. (1991). Interpersonal coordination: Behavior matching and interactional synchrony. In R. S. Feldman & B. Rimé (Eds.), *Fundamentals of nonverbal behavior.* New York, NY: Cambridge University Press.

Bischof, M. (2008). Synchronization and coherence as an organizing principle in the organism, social interaction, and consciousness. *Neuroquantology, 6*(4).

Bjørkvold, J. M. (1995). *When the moment sings* [Når øyeblikket synger]. Oslo, Norway Norwegian Film Institute.

Butgoon, J. K., Stern, L. A., & Dillman, L. (1995). *Interpersonal adaptation: Dyadic interaction patterns.* Cambridge, England: Cambridge University Press.

Butler, D. (2004). *Damages for psychiatric injuries: Australian legal monographs.* Sydney, Australia: The Federation Press.

Campbell, D. (1997). *The Mozart effect.* New York, NY: Harper & Collins.

Capra, F., & Luisi, L. P. (2014). *The systems view of life. A unifying vision.* Cambridge, England: Cambridge University Press.

Chartrand, T. L., & Bargh, J. A. (1999). The chameleon effect: The perception-behavior link and social interaction. *Journal of Personality and Social Psychology, 76,* 893–910.

Clyde, M. (1956).The kalela dance: Aspects of social relationships among urban Africans in Northern Rhodesia. *Rhodes-Livingstone Journal, 27.*

Colgin, L., Denninger T., Fyhn, M., Hafting, T., Bonnevie, T., Jensen, O., Moser, M. B., & Moser, E. I. (2009). Frequency of gamma oscillations routes flow of information in the hippocampus. *Nature, 462*(7271), 353.

Cory, H. (1936). Ngoma ya Sheitani. *Journal of the Royal Anthropological Society, 66,* 209–217.

Dascal, M. (2007, May 22). Colonizing and decolonizing minds. *The New York Times.*

Earl, J. (2004). The cultural consequences of social movements. In D. Snow, S. Soule, & H. P. Kriesi, (Eds.), *The Blackwell companion to social movements* (pp. 508–527). Oxford, England: Blackwell.

Eriksson, M., & Lindström, B. (2007a). Antonovsky's sense of coherence scale and its relation with quality of life: A systematic review. *Journal of Epidemiology and Community Health, 61,* 938–944.

Eriksson, M., & Lindström, B. (2007b). A sense of coherence and health: Salutogenesis in a social context, Åland— a special case? *Journal of Epidemiology and Community Health, 61,* 689–694.

Eriksson, M., & Lindström, B. (2008). A salutogenic interpretation of the Ottawa Charter. *Health Promotion International, 23*(2), 190–199.

Eze, E. C. (Ed.). (1998). *African philosophy, an anthology.* Oxford, England: Blackwell.

Fahy, F. J. (1989/1995). *Sound intensity.* London, England: E & FN Spon.

Friedson, S. (1996). *Dancing prophets: Musical experience in Tumbuka healing.* Chicago, IL: University of Chicago Press.

Geertz, C. (1973). *Toward an interpretive theory of culture,* New York, NY: Basic.

Gershwin A–Z Quotes (n.d.) Retrieved from http://www.azquotes.com/author/5450-George_Gershwin

Gimzewski J. (2006). *Sonocytology.* Los Angeles, CA: The Mindful Awareness Research Center, University of California.

Guthrie, M. (1962). A tentative new hypothesis. *Journal of African languages, 1,* 9–21.

Hall, M., & Diallo, Y. (1989). *The healing drum, African wisdom teachings.* Rochester, VT: Destiny Books.

Harwood, D. L. (1987). Interpretive activity: A Response to Tim Rice's "toward the remodeling of ethnomusicology." *Ethnomusicology, 31*(3), 503–510.

Heywood, A. (2000). *Key concepts in politics* (pp. 243–260). New York, NY: MacMillan Press.

Heywood, A. (2012). *Political ideologies: An introduction* (5th ed.). New York, NY: Palgrave MacMillan.

Horton, M., & Middleton, J. (2001). *The social landscape of a mercantile society.* Oxford, England: Wiley-Blackwell.

Hotep, U. (2003). *Decolonizing the African mind: Further analysis and strategy.* Pittsburgh, PA: Kwame Ture Youth Leadership Institute.

Husebø, S. (1992). *Medisin kunst eller vitenskap?* Oslo, Norway: Ad Notam Gyldendal.

Jaastad, L. (2005). *Mafiga:"Tre steiner, kvinne, liv." Terapeutiske musikktradisjoner blant Giriama- og Kamba-folkene i Kenya* (Master's thesis). Norwegian University of Science and Technology, Trondheim, Norway.

Janzen, J. (1992). *Ngoma: Discourses of healing in central and southern Africa.* Berkeley, CA: University of California Press.

Johnson, M. (2007). *The meaning of the body.* Chicago, IL: Chicago University Press.

Judee, K., Burgoon, L. A., Stern, L. A., & Dillman, L. (2006). *Interpersonal adaptation dydadic interaction patterns.* Cambridge, England: Cambridge University Press.

Kendon, A. (1970). Movement coordination in social interaction: Some examples described. *Acta Psychologia, 32,* 101–125.

Lefebvre, H. (1992). *Rhythmanalysis. Space, time, and everyday life.* New York, NY: Bloomesbury.

Levine, P.A. (1997). *Waking the tiger, healing trauma: The innate capacity to transform overwhelming experiences.* Berkeley, CA: North Atlantic Books.

Levine, P. A. (2010). *In an unspoken voice: How the body releases trauma and restores goodness.* Berkley, CA: North Atlantic Books.

Levitin, D. (2006). *This is your brain on music.* New York, NY: Penguin Group.

Levitin, D. (2008). *The world in six songs: How the musical brain created human nature.* Ontario, Canada: Dutton.

Lewis, M., Paul, G., Simons, F., & Fennig, C. D. (Eds.). (2013). *Ethnologue: Languages of the world* (17th ed.). Dallas, TX: SIL International. Retrieved from http://www.ethnologue.com/country/KE/languages

Lindström, B., & Eriksson, M. (2010). The hitchhiker's guide to salutogenesis: Salutogenic pathways to health promotion. *Folkhälsan Research Center Health Promotion Research Report, 2.*

Mace, C. (2008). *Mindfulness and mental health: Therapy, theory and science.* New York, NY: Routledge.

MacDonald ,R., Kreutz, G., & Michell, L. (2012). *Music, health and wellbeing.* Oxford, England: Oxford University Press.

Mbiti, J. (1969/2002). *African religions and philosophy.* Nairobi, Kenya: East African Educational.

McCraty, R., Atkinson, M., Tomasino, D., & Bradley, R. T. (2006). *The coherent heart: Heart-brain interactions, psychophysiological coherence, and the emergence of system-wide order.* Boulder Creek, CA: Institute of Heart Math.

Merolla, D. (2013). *Zanzibar: Taraab and Ngoma performances. Verba Africana digital materials.* Leiden University, The Netherlands. Department of Studies and researches on African and Arab Countries, IUO. University of Naples, Italy. http://www.hum2.leidenuniv.nl/verba-africana/swahili/

Myskja, A. (1999). *Den musiske medisin.* Oslo, Norway: Grøndahl & Dreyer.

Myskja, A. (2012). *Integrated music in nursing homes: An approach in dementia care* (Doctoral dissertation). Bergen University (UIB) Norway.

Nettl, B. (1983). *The study of ethnomusicology: Twenty-nine issues and concepts.* Chicago, IL: Illini Books.

Ngubane, H. (1981). Aspects of clinical practice and traditional organization of indigenous healers in South Africa. In P. J. M. McEwan (Ed.), *Social science and medicine 15B.* Leicester, England: Elsevier.

Nketia, J. H. K. (1974). *The music of Africa.* New York, NY: W. W. Norton.

Nzewi, M. (2002). Backcloth to music and healing in traditional African society. *Voices: A World Forum for Music Therapy, 2*(2).

Okot, p'B. (1970). *African religions in western scholarship.* Nairobi, Kenya: Kenya Literature Bureau.

Polanyi, M. (1967/2009). *The tacit dimension.* Chicago, IL: University of Chicago Press.

Post, J. C. (2006). *Ethnomusicology: A contemporary reader.* New York, NY: Routledge.

Raphael, D. (2010). *Health promotion and quality of life.* Toronto, Ontario: Canadian Scholars Press.

Rice, T. (1987). Toward the remodeling of ethnomusicology. *Ethnomusicology, 31*(3), 469–488. Retrieved from http://www.jstor.org/stable/851667

Roosth, S. (2009). Screaming yeast: Sonocytology, cytoplasmic mileus, and cellular subjectivities. *Critical Inquiry, 35*(2), 332–350.

Rouget, G. (1985). *Music and trance, a theory of the relations between music and possession.* Chicago, IL: University of Chicago Press.

Ruud, E. (Ed.). (1986). *Music and health.* Oslo, Norway: Norsk Musikkforlag.

Sacks, O. (2007). *Musicophilia: Tales of music and the brain.* New York, NY: Alfred H. Knopf.

Small, C. (1998). *Musicking: The meanings of performing and listening.* New York, NY: Wesleyan University Press.

Spear, T. (1978): *The kaya complex: A history of the Mijilkenda peoples of the Kenya Coast to 1900.* Nairobi, Kenya: Kenya Literature Bureau.

Spear, T. (2000). Swahili history and society to 1900: A classified bibliography. *History in Africa, 27,* 339–373.

Stone, R. M. (1998). *The garland handbook of African music.* New York, NY: Taylor & Francis.

Sudkler, B., & Steed, C. (2001). *A history of the church in Africa.* New York, NY: Cambridge University Press.

Thaut, M. H. (2005). *Rhythm, music and the brain: Scientific foundations and clinical applications.* New York, NY: Routledge.

Thaut, M. H., Leins, A. K., Rice, R. R. et al. (2007). Rhythmic auditory stimulation improves gait more than NDT/Bobath training in near-ambulatory patients early post stroke: A single blind randomized control trial. *Neurorehabilitation and Neural Repair, 21,* 455–459.

Thaut, M. H., McIntosh, G. C., Rice, R. R. et al. (1996). Rhythmic auditory stimulation in gait training for Parkinson's disease patients. *Movement Disorders 11*, 193–200.

Tiller, W. A., McCraty, R., & Atkinson, M. (1996). Cardiac coherence: A new, innovative measure of autonomic nervous system order. *Altern Ther, 2,* 52–65.

Turner, V. (1969/1995). *The ritual process, structure and antistructure.* New York, NY: Aldine de Gruyter.

United Nations. (1948). *The Universal Declaration of Human Rights* (UDHR). http://www.un.org/en/universal-declaration-human-rights/

Van Beek, W. E. A. (2012). *The dancing dead: Ritual and religion among Kapsiki/Higi of north Cameroon and northeastern Nigeria.* New York, NY: Oxford University Press.

Van Dijk, R., & Spierenberg, M. (Eds.). (2000). *The quest for fruition through ngoma. The political aspects of healing in southern Africa.* Oxford, England: James Currey.

Walsh, M. (1992). Mijikenda origin: A review of the evidence of history. *Transafrican Journal of History,* (21), 1–18.

Willems, A. M., Nieuwboer, A., Chavret, F. et al. (2006). The use of rhythmic auditory cues to influence gait in patients with Parkinson's disease: Differential effect for freezers and nonfreezers. *Disability and Rehabilitation, 28,* 721–728.

WHO. (1986). *The Ottawa Charter for Health Promotion.* http://www.who.int/healthpromotion/conferences/previous/ottawa/en/

PART V

MUSICAL FUNDAMENTALS

CHAPTER 14

SILENCE AND SENSE-MAKING

The Musicality of Affect Restored to Wissenschaft in Everyday Life

Olga V. Lehmann

Everyday life is a dance between language and silence within the melodies of emotional life. Yet language is the most used and prominent source, perhaps due to our boundaries for comprehending the polysemy and polyphony of silence.

For instance, think of the peace dialogues between the government of Colombia and the FARC[1] that took place in Oslo in 2012. These sociopolitical circumstances resonate in the everyday life narrations of a woman who was growing up in a small town in southwestern Colombia, a region where there are daily bombardments between the military forces and the militias.

In 1996, when Ana was 6-years-old, her grandmother disappeared. Adults used to speak about this event, but no explanations where given to the children. One day her family organized a trip to the mountains, in the region of Patía, in order to see the glasses-bear habitat. On the road, some green

Cultural Psychology of Musical Experience, pages 281–298
Copyright © 2016 by Information Age Publishing
All rights of reproduction in any form reserved.

dressed men stopped the car and asked Ana's father to get out. Ana was eating some candies, and as long as it was Christmas Eve, she offered some of them to one of the men and he, surprised with this naïve gesture, allowed her father to get into the car again and continue the trip. Some weeks after, Grandma went back home with no Christmas presents: many people with cameras, tape recorders, and notebooks came also with her.

The kidnapping occurred in their farm, a place the family could never come back to. The travel to Patía did not have the purpose of watching the glasses bear, but of meeting in secret some members of the guerilla, in order to give them around $600,000 as the payment for the freedom of her grandmother, who was 69 and had a diagnosis of diabetes at the time she spent 4 months in the Andes. She was lucky during this journey, I guess, because she well survived and perhaps this was possible because she established a great rapport with some of the bushwhackers, teaching them how to read and write, even getting farewell letters from them on the day of the liberation.

Now Ana lives and studies political sciences in Bogotá, with a government loan to pay the stipends. Her grandmother is 85 and is very sick; the family is facing economic problems to pay for her health care treatments. Each time Ana goes home to visit her family, she lays in a hammock in the garden and reads while having the impressive landscape of the Andes in front of her. She loves to see the Puracé Volcano when there is a cloudless sky.

Here, there is a universe of meanings involving phenomena of silence within different systems of experience. For instance, from a personal perspective Ana's grandmother experienced a change in the sounds of the jungle instead of the sounds of the city, and when she heard nothing but nature, she felt a silent hope because they were no bombardments nearby. From another perspective, some Colombians could feel disappointed by the manipulation of information during the peace dialogues, being silence an arm of power there. Furthermore, think of the months without survival proves that the families of kidnapped people face, and the prisoners themselves not having anyone to speak with in the cages. How could we understand the dynamics of emotions that arise here?

The said, the silent, and the silenced dialectics of the ineffable and the inaudible constitute a tension in the process of sense-making of experiences. Life is primarily an affective process, the reflective side of mental functions being semiotic tools to organize emotional experiences (Valsiner, 2007). Although, even if our mind follows a kind of sequential order, which can be studied by linguistics, the complexity and multidimensionality of the mind recalls also considering other systems for a theoretical and empirical comprehension, where music is an integrative path (Klempe, 2015a).

Questions about human feelings go beyond the organization of our mind, where phenomenology is a bridge for the reconciliation with the central role of *sentire*,[2] foregrounding the need of theories about affective-emotive world (De Monticelli, 2012). It is not enough to gather a conceptual discrimination of the emotional, scholars need to put in order the complex painting of personal life (De Monticelli, 2012).

In this order of ideas, I wonder about the role of silence in sense-making and its relation with language, music, and other arts. Furthermore, I am particularly interested in the phenomena of silence, which process of functioning in affective fields is still a question, highlighting the necessity to pay much more attention to the multiple silences that inhabit conversations, as well as the role of emotions and feelings on them (Mazzei, 2003). Rather than an answer, this chapter is a trial of reconciliation with interdisciplinary studies that take in to account the affective resonances of language and the arts in order to gather a deep comprehension of the multiple significances of silence in the intersubjective process of making sense of experience and existence in everyday life.

SILENCE, SILENCES, AND SILENCING: SILENCE PHENOMENA AND THE SENSE OF IN BETWEENNESS

Given the polysemy of silence, I follow the distinctions aroused by Bruneau and Ishii (1988) and Orlandi (1995).[3] *Silence* is assumed as a solitary, mystical, and unconscious (involuntary) experience; *silences* are social, secular, and conscious; and *silencing* acts are rhetorical strategies of manifesting power by means of restricting someone else's expression. Ana's grandmother, a very Catholic person, encountered in the sound of the jungle the silence of God and the reassurance needed to cope with the uncertainty about her life during the months she was kidnapped. Here, silences were also present, for instance in the long walks in the Andes while moving from one encampment to another, where some turns and rules for conversations were established. All this makes also evident that the kidnap itself is an act of silencing in many senses, such as the imposed distance with her beloved ones and the impossibility to communicate with them or the avoidance of talking for long with other prisoners and with members of the guerilla.

The silence phenomena are not mere absence, but precisely what is in-between words, in-between musical notes, in-between lines, in-between beings: it is an interval (Bourbon Busset, 1984, in Orlandi, 1995). The melody in a musical piece has intervals as a basis, not specific notes (Levitin, 2006), so that these "spaces" are meaningful, rather than meaningless also in the melodies of our emotions. Of course, it is not my intention to overrate the functions of silence, silences, and silencing, but to acknowledge that, as well as language, they have a crucial role in the social demand settings where affect takes place, and in the theoretical models of affective phenomena.

Everyday life is a dance of silence, silences, and silencing signs within the fields of language and, from the smallest act until the utmost crossing of boundaries, when language faces the abyss of its possibilities, we still feel far beyond words. Furthermore, I do not pretend to stand the musicality of emotions as innovative, because there is a strong field of theories and research within multiple disciplines of psychology and the arts (Levitin, 2006; Neubauer, 1986; Sorgner & Fürbeth, 2010). Although, I am keen to highlight the role of silence in the musical scores of affective phenomena in order to develop alternative ways of comprehending sense-making process in daily life. Thus, the silence phenomena are in-between phenomena, and share an inclusive separation with arts, semiotics, and diverse voices of the self.

TOWARDS A COMPREHENSION OF SILENCE PHENOMENA WITHIN THE MUSICALITY OF AFFECT

When giving a speech to the New England Conservatory of Music in 1968, Marcuse (2007) said that even if he was not a musician, he felt more at home in the field of arts than in the fields of philosophers, sociologists, or political scientists. That's because he believed forward that the arts develop a crucial role in changing human experience. Even highlighting the changes and crisis of music, sometimes becoming a negation of art itself, he recognizes its ability to reconciliate apparent contraries and restore the forgotten truth in images, words, and sounds, by means of, for example, creating harmony from suffering or eternal joy from transitory pleasures. From this perspective, it is precisely this feeling of separation, negation, and contradiction from the "intellectual" world, what deals with the boundaries of language to explore the emotional.

Aesthetics, the science of the beautiful, is a strong field for comprehending affective life and music leads the significance of arts as a source of experiencing (Langer, 1977). A great attempt to include music as a metaphor is the work of Zittoun, Valsiner, Vedeler, Salgado, Goncalves, and Ferring (2013), who uses the term "melody" when describing contributions for the study of development, referring to human life course. In fact, musical meanings and linguistic meanings have divergences on structure and functioning (Klempe, 1996) not always mutually exclusive, even if they often become isolated in the development of methodological, empirical and theoretical fields. Furthermore, it is worth it to say that music has still unexplored metaphors in everyday life, which can be used for the comprehension of the rhythm of emotions including silence as a source. In fact:

> The tonal structures we call music bear a close logical similarity to the forms of human feelings—forms of growth and of attenuation flowing and stowing,

conflict and resolution, speed, arrest, terrific excitement, calm, or subtle activation and dreamy lapses—not joy and sorrow perhaps, but the poignancy of
either and both—the greatness and brevity and eternal passing of everything
vitally felt. Such is the pattern, or logical form, of sentience; and the pattern
of music is that same form worked out in pure, measured sound and silence.
Music is a tonal analogue of emotive life. (Langer, 1977, p. 27)

Just taking into account the logical structure of music as an analogy for
human feelings, the silence phenomena appear as they do musical notes in
the scores. They are a valuable learning source, a building space for feelings, as well as the promoter of different emotions (Cooper, 2011). From the
point of view of Cage (1961), music, and more precisely, experimental music, is nothing but sounds, being those not-notated sounds named silences
and their role, that of allowing the listener to be aware of the sounds of the
environment. In this sense, silence phenomena become crucial when studying the part-whole relationships of affective phenomena. Yet, this noninten-
tionality becomes an intention when assumed as a search, such as his "4'33"'"
piece, where sounds of silence were meant to be music (Kahn, 1997).

In fact, the coexistence of emotions has a crucial function in the relationship established between different voices of the self. Self and culture
involve the multiplicity of positions that interact and come up in dialogue
through personal and/or social voices (Hermans, 2001). In fact, dialogical
self theory, acknowledges the function of the phenomena of silence in the
processing of emotional charge involved in different I-positions (Hermans
& Hermans-Konopka, 2010). Here, both the discursive and acoustic property of voice should be addressed. By one hand, in its discursive function,
the voice guides a psychotherapeutic process that seeks to uncover the "unconscious score," as well as it serves to analyze the imperatives of political
power and ideologies (Garrofe, 2007). By the other hand, the acoustics of
voice work also as a link between music and language during human development; it has been proved that some of the very first signs of inborn subjectivity are related with the children's preference for melodies they were
exposed to prenatally, related to the intensity and rhythm of the mother's
language (Bertau, 2011).

Many writers, social scientists, and thinkers from different ideologies and
aesthetics highlight the musicality of language as a property of expression
beyond words, arguing that music can be an act of communication, but also
an act of communion, having a ritual effect (Garrofe, 2007). The silence
phenomena functions in different levels of musical expression: it belongs
to the microgenetic structure of melodies, corresponds to the search of
communion and catalyzes cultural rituals (Lehmann, 2014).

The phenomena of silence work in some microgenetic levels of music,
such as its role in the harmony of sounds, appearing in the musical scores
and having written signs. They can be also present in instrumental music

without singers or in the silent attitude when one hears a song, or the one of musicians playing an instrument. For instance, it has been documented that baroque music[4] has an interwoven link with rethorics in order to transport the listener to a particular emotional state (Neubauer, 1986). Some baroque musical figures of silence involve an ensuing purpose, as in the case of *suspiratio,* pauses used to express affections of longing (Bartel, 1997, p. 392). Another example of this is the music of Beethoven—influenced by the Enlightenment's theories of affect in music—who gave a special importance to silences, often producing unexpected or prolonged rests, which purpose was that of intensifying a great variety of emotions (Cooper, 2011). Furthermore, "Such intensive use of silence is highly unusual, and its powerful evocation of a sense of ineffable stillness and contemplation provides a good illustration of how inadequate the phrase 'absence of sound' can be as a description of silence" (Cooper 2011, p. 27). We still need further contributions concerning the comprehension of the influence of music in affect because the arousal of emotional responses depends on the listener perception of an affective meaning as present in the music they listen, and on the emotional predisposition of the person given by a certain context, which is very complex to calculate and analyze (Huss, 2008).

One aspect that helps to understand the significance of music in emotional life and its convergence and divergence with semiotics is that of polyphony. Polyphony refers to the vertical quality of a musical system, that is, the different pitches that can be simultaneously present in music, while language in this sense is linear (Klempe, 1996). This is a metaphor of the coexistence of emotions in human experience, rather than the presence of an exclusive one. Think for instance in the anticipatory grief elaboration of a tired caregiver who deals with the happiness of having his/her beloved parent with a terminal state illness still alive, the sorrow for the pain related to the illness, the desperation of an apparent infinite experience, and guilt for the sudden desires of the arrival of the death of the beloved person in order to continue with life and make up for lost time (Kübler Ross, 1993). In fact, this coexistence of emotions I recall to be understood with the musical concept of polyphony were already acknowledged by Pierre Janet (1928) as the *inversion of desires,* when there is an apparent absurd of, for instants, loving what one loathes. Furthermore, cultural developmental psychology is increasing the interest in studying processes of interdependence of "opposites" and the process of sense-making (Valsiner, 2014).

There is also documentation about the role of polyphony by semiotics and literary analysis, still being a fact of sequential order that cannot explain the coexistence of emotions. Think for instance in Eco's (2009) analysis of the fact that people can get moved by the death of Anna Karenina, even knowing she does not exist and her death had never happened, or the "Wherter effect" on suicide rates provoked by Goethe's novels. In order to explain this, Eco compares a written text, such as *Anna Karenina*, with a musical score, saying that, in semiotic terms: "It is true that Anna Karenina commits suicide by throwing herself in the path of a train in the same way in which it is true that Beethoven's 'Fifth Symphony' is in C minor (and not in F major like his sixth) and begins with G, G, G, E flat (Eco, 2009, p. 5). But there are two issues Eco did not take into account. First of all, he appeals just to the sequential order of written signs in musical scores, arguing that semiotic objects (such as musical ones) maintain a Gestalt that makes them recognizable from the melodic point of view, even if from the aesthetic one, it could vary from interpreters and instruments that can influence the identification with the piece (or the novel character) and their related emotions. Second, he does not explore the creative process of novel characters and musical pieces, ignoring the fact that signs (such as musical notes or silences, or adjectives describing a character) are not given, but constructed for communicating something and in this order of ideas, there cannot be any interpretation of a semiotic object without interpreter or a semiotic subject (Valsiner, 2009).

Another example of the contributions of music for the comprehension of the affective world is the German word *stimmungen*, usually translated into English as "moods" but referring in specific to an "emotional tone" due to their connotation about the musicality of emotions and the acoustics of the soul (Bruzzone, 2010). The course of human development is a constantly interrupted process where new persons and tasks ask us to restart again with our plans; emotional tones involve a shared atmosphere that determines our position in the world, being the color that goes through the mood giving emotions a particular and uniform character (Bollnow, 2009). That is, they are bodily and psychical states that are not yet objectified toward something, as feelings do thanks to their intentional quality; they are a common color between the I and the world, like the original unity between man and world (Bollnow, 2009). Each emotional tone contributes in a different manner to the entire knowledge of reality, and some examples of them are: existential angst, desperateness, melancholy, beatitude, calmness, foolishness, and melancholy (Bollnow, 2009; Bruzzone, 2010).

THE SENSE OF SILENCE PHENOMENA IN PSYCHOLOGY: WHY TO GO BEYOND

The words of poems are the tuft and final applause of science.
—Walt Whitman (1871)

Both music and poetry include an issue cultural studies should consider as a crucial part of the everyday experience of silence-phenomena in their many and diverse meanings. Poetry is the field where language, music, and silence phenomena are interwoven (Paz, 1994). Poems are chants, windows, doors, bridges, balconies where we feel the ineffable through a combination of words that find themselves an affective resonance. The importance of a poem rises in its music, the way of saying and not in its meaning; if there is no music, one could feel it or invent it (Borges, 2001, p. 144). After listening to the utmost verses of poets, one realizes that language can be music and passion, and precisely in this moment, poetry was revealed to humans (Borges, 2001).

Any attempt to study various forms of affective regulation in everyday life, the mechanisms that generate their extraordinary significance, and their structural and functional organization, may capture the metaphors that emerge from silence phenomena to make sense of uncertainty. When gathering and analyzing data, we as scholars often come up with linguistic and mathematical perspectives, excluding other qualities of the phenomena, and perhaps arriving to the same questions. We can conclude, for instance, that the role of emotions is important and associated with different cognitive and neurobiological basis, but still wondering how do we come up with emotions making sense of life and taking decisions that affect our future and the relationships we establish with objects and persons, and the relation with ourselves. There is still a boundary between science and mystery: How does the human brain give "rise to thoughts and feelings, hopes and desires, love, and the experience of beauty, not to mention dance, visual art, literature, and music" (Levitin, 2006, p. 4)? Yet, the question is not just empirical, but epistemological, being the distinction between theoretical and empirical statements not as clear as it seems, involving a complicated dichotomy because empirical evidence is an as-if situation, rather than a term (Klempe, 2010).

It seems clear—even obvious—for psychologists and other "scientists" that psychology's primarily intention is to comprehend the phenomena of the psyche, the anima (Valsiner & Rosa, 2007), but:

> Psychology in the 21st century is at a crossroads. Globalization acts as the extrascientific force to bring it as a science—be it considered as that of the mind, or of behavior—to new social contexts, and makes it confront new problems.... In the middle of such rapid social changes it is not surprising that psychology is losing its focus. (Valsiner, 2010, p. 2)

Everyday life is a fertile ground where sociocultural psychology is rooted, altogether with medical sciences, sociology, history, anthropology, and philosophy (Valsiner & Rosa, 2007). Now, one could say that instead of taking pictures of the leaves, flowers, or branches of science-arts forest, where the tree of psychology's sceneries are planted, one needs to arrive at a cinematographic view of the landscape. But, the risk when dealing with metaphors is to stay in the ethereal realm, thus one wonders how to develop science—better conceived as *wissenschaft*—that not just speaks about real qualities of the phenomenon in transition, but also addresses the question of how to induce changes that promote the qualities that emerge in such transition.

We humans are always coping with uncertainty. We are always making decisions within the ambivalence of future, being precisely this "capture" of ambivalence and uncertainty, the core dilemma of psychology as a science (Abbey & Valsiner, 2005). In fact, persons use to be uncertain about the reason of their acts and even if scientists should not reduce the narrations of their experiences translating them into understandable sources, it often happens that dynamic processes become into data, losing their quality (Beckstead, 2009). Furthermore, as well as uncertainty, ambiguity of human phenomena is a question that psychology itself cannot solve. For instance, in Barthes' (1972) literary critic ambiguity is not about freedom or censure of interpretations, but about coding and the plurality of symbols, the multiple senses of an oeuvre and their irony: the questions that language put to itself. This fact has also been explored by the psychology of feelings and emotions, which faces the ambiguity irreconcilable with language that emerges from its study (Klempe, 2015b). Besides, it is ironic far from the beginning because one knows that there is a rift between affective phenomena and language, but language becomes the primary path and valid tool for their study. During interviews, silences are often understood as a failure of the researcher's skills to promote talking, is confused with a problem one needs to overcome with a better technique (Poland & Pederson, 1998).

Of course talks, conversations, and linguistic contents of interviews are crucial for the description and interpretations of human phenomena, the question that arises is if our job as cultural psychologists ends in the traditional transcription of such signs. For instance, Schleiermarcher's view of semiotics represents half the truth of the comprehension of culture, as long as they face the boundary to comprehend the balance with the individual experience (Scholtz, 2010). To develop an integrative theory of emotional life, semiotics could extend its arms into the borders of arts, so that theories and methods of affective phenomena can be faithful to their qualities. Indeed, Antonio Damasio highlights the need of both contributions from neurobiology and culture, concluding that science is to be conducted toward the labor of philosophers in ways what provide faithful descriptions and existential analysis of phenomena beyond conceptual elaborations (De Monticelli, 2012). In this order of ideas, why not use everyday life cultural sources such as music and poetry to study feelings and emotions, too? Of course, as long as science has plunged into a means of production logic, arts themselves cannot escape of suffering a technicalization, being a reflection of social crisis, yet conserving its transcendent content (Adorno, 2006;

Barthes, 1972; Marcuse, 2007). In fact, if one assumes the core obligation of science that of being faithful to the phenomena (Freeman, 2011):

> Rather than the acontextual, objective, and universalist discourse that populates canonical social science, our disciplines would require an inherently self-critical and concretely contextualized discourse, one that reflects the ambiguity, serendipity, idiosyncrasy, and fundamentally moral, relational, and interested quality of all knowledge production. (Clegg, 2010, p. 250)

How can one be faithful to the phenomena when doing science? When pointing out the necessity to practice fidelity to the phenomena, Freeman (2011) recalls precisely the field of feelings as a necessary inclusion, which is also the field of poets, and poets themselves were not excluded as valuable sources of truth when psychology was assumed as wissenschaft within the early 19th century (Valsiner, 2010). In the late 18th century, there was no significant opposition between unification and separation of knowledge from poetry, literature, theology, and other emerging disciplines (for instance, the case of psychology). While in the early 20th century, the pursuit of objectivity moved away any poetic nuance of scientific inquiry (Valsiner & Cabell, 2012). This fact certainly involves the recognition of the crisis of science, because the more it belongs to the means of production of social values, the more has a role of a mean of production. In this sense, we need to recognize the historical influences of the orientation of certain methods and/or theories in science, in order to comprehend that the roots of these failures occur the positions assumed by the persons who develop them within social conditions with rational concerns in conflict (Horkheimer, 2003). Anyways, psychology itself cannot solve human questions; neither develop a general theory for the comprehension of human phenomena, being the path back wissenschaft just a step further. To comprehend the social, historical, and cultural quality of experience, we researchers need to move toward a "borderland," a fuzzy zone where the rapprochement to the in betweenness of phenomena allows the comprehension of the parts-whole relations and their gestalt qualities (Marsico, Cabell, Valsiner, & Kharlamov, 2013).

As long as the complex dynamics of affective phenomena and the inaccessibility of feelings are both the core of human condition and the basic interest of cultural psychology (Valsiner, 2007), to concentrate on "how an emotion comes into being" (Tantam, 2003, p. 26) is on the basis of sense-making, as well as sense-making process is on the basis of the intersubjective nature of human phenomena (Venuleo, 2008). For instance, Branco and Valsiner (2010) present a theoretical system to comprehend the semiotic process of affective regulation, yet realizing its boundaries in accessing immediate feelings as well as hyper-generalized—overwhelming fields. Such experiences are known as oceanic feelings,[5] emotional states that imply a subversion of time and space that are usually related to religious experiences, but not limited to them (Klempe, 1996).

In each level of affective regulation and within their untellable and speakable qualities, the silence phenomena involved in the musicality of emotions constitutes a field of research, where poetry becomes a bridge. Poems are words thats voice is a lullaby for the heart, evoking these feelings we cannot express alone, but in the rhythmical chant of boundaries. Poetry is present in every culture and time as a reference of "truth." Even if we are not poets, we have experienced something poetic at least once, read or listened to a poem from a sacred text, or an artist, and many of us have taken the challenge of writing our longings in a melody that transforms our feelings, making us aware of the dilemmatic tension of finitude and eternity. Furthermore, often, people describe their lived experiences with works of art, such as poems, as a revelation, an encounter, where the meaning appears into consciousness and was not constructed, but given.

Concerning poetry, Octavio Paz (1999) argues, language is poetic in its nature because the origin of language and the origin of the myth are straight related, being both metaphorical principles and function of symbolization (Lehmann, 2015). Moreover, Levi-Strauss (1987) points out that we all recognize words as signs, but poets are the last who remember that words have been also values. In the same line of ideas, Marcuse (2007) argues that silence is a state of tranquility where senses can see, hear, and feel what things are, what we are, what is suppressed by daily issues of life: terror and beauty, as inclusive categories. An integrative theory is to contribute for a widened comprehension of our process of grasping values from experience and existence in order to make sense of our thoughts, feelings, actions, and life itself (Lehmann, 2015). In this sense, poetry could be a path for the comprehension of affective regulation as long as its dance in between silence and language evokes the affective vibration of experience (Lehmann, 2012).

For instance, this is the case of Thomas Merton's antipoetry, a manifestation confronting violence regarding the United States of America's actions in both the Vietnam War and the Cold War (Bilbro, 2009). In this sense, it was Merton's desire to promote silence in his readers so that they become aware of the "sickness" of language in political discourses, and to realize deepen truth that cannot be said by language, validated by his nearness with Zen thought and the Christian monastic tradition (Bilbro, 2009). Also in relation with Zen thought, John Cage contributions on silence phenomena are to be highlighted. In his autobiographical statement (Cage, 1990), he said that the purpose of music is not communication, but to promote silence even if silence itself is not acoustic, but a change of mind. Even if at first impression it seems paradoxical, silence for Cage is a nonintended sound, and in fact in the foreword of his book *Silence* (Cage, 1961), he points out that a need and seeking for poetry is always present in his lectures, compositions, and performances, highlighting that precisely poetry allows musical elements, such as time or sound (included silence) to enter in the world of words. From another side, Lyotard (1972), following the ideas of Cage and relating them to psychoanalysis, considers silences/silencing as a dispositive of control both in personal and societal levels, such as the expected silence of a public during a concert, or the repression of the body dynamics of fluids, being silence displaced to involuntary noises and sounds. At this point, it is worth to describe very first theoretical steps about how to comprehend silence phenomena when studying sense-making processes.

SCORES FOR SILENCE: SOURCES TO APPROACH THE MUSICALITY OF EMOTIONS

> It seems that art as cognition and recollection depends to a great extent on the aesthetic power of silence: the silence of the picture and statue; the silence that permeates the tragedy; the silence in which the music is heard. Silence as medium of communication, the break with the familiar; silence not only at some place or time reserved for contemplation, but as a whole dimension which is there without being used. (Marcuse, 2007, p. 117)

Dennis Kurzon (1997) proposed a grammar for silence, considering it as a sign that, belonging to everyday conversations, should be analyzed in terms of their natural performance. In further papers, the author extends his model proposal for the interpretation of silence in different types of conversations, specially focused on legal contexts (Kurzon, 2007, 2011). For instance, other authors have proposed the silent nature of interview transcripts, as losing qualities of conversations when putting them into texts, but also ignoring the interstices of silence (Poland & Pederson, 1998); typologies for silence in psychotherapy processes (Levitt, 2001), mnemonic processes (Stone, Coman, Brown, Koppel, & Hirst, 2012). In contrast to some evidence-based data on phenomena of silence, it is important to consider that literature related to the topic uses to lay on theoretical speculations of its role in human relationships, rather than suggesting empirical ways for its study (Oduro-Frimpong, 2007). That is, theoretical contributions for the study of the silence phenomena in human everyday life should be legitimized by research that focuses on not just environments or sets for the development of silences/silencing, but also the process of its function on human interactions. Besides, as long as arts and life do not exist in separate forms and its frame is to be called silence (Charles, n.d.), their relationship constitutes a field of research. Furthermore:

silences are an enduring feature of human interaction and, therefore, of our work... silence is an ongoing feature of social interaction. As such, it is forever present in qualitative research. Although silences may remain unnoticed or may be seen as problems requiring corrective action, we have argued that their meanings are varied, contingent, and open to (re)interpretation. (Poland & Pederson, 1998, p. 308)

In Table 14.1 I propose three fields for the study of the phenomena of silence: as a source of saying, a source of listening, and a source of encountering. In accordance with the definitions of Bruneau and Ishii (1988) and Orlandi (1995), while saying and listening can be understood as ways of silences and silencing, encountering is meant to be the experience of silence. That way, experiencing silences could be comprehended by means of silencing inner/outer voices of the self in order to: (a) wanting to say/listen and not saying/listening, (b) wanting to say/listen and saying/listening

---

TABLE 14.1   The Scores of Silence Phenomena: Sources to Understand the Polyphony of Sensemaking

Silence as a source of saying

Wanting to say and not saying	Voluntary/involuntary silencing of inner/external voices, sounds, noises and movements
Wanting to say and saying something (in consonance or disonance with the intention)	
Not wanting to say and saying something (in consonance or disonance with the intention)	
Not wanting to say and not saying.	

Silence as a source of listening (metaphorically sensing in general)

Wanting to listen and listening	Voluntary/involuntary silencing of inner/external voices, sounds, noises and movements
Wanting to listen and not listening	
Not wanting to listen and listening	
Not wanting to listen and not listening	

Silence as a source for not-saying and not-listening

Poetic instants	Voluntary/involuntary perception of communion, fusion of borders within the person and the object of experience

something (while conserving some possible things in silence), (c) not wanting to say/listen and saying/listening something (while conserving some possible things in silence), and (d) not wanting to say/listen and not saying/listening. From another side, the experience of silence is to be studied by the experience of poetic instants. At this point, a great question for research is about the conscious and unconscious intentionality in terms of wanting, not wanting, and encountering given certain social and cultural settings, as well as "unintentional" or "surprising" encounters with life. Stone, Coman, Brown, Koppel, and Hirst (2012) have provided an inspiring platform in this regards, expanding on the over or covert expression of memories.

Of course, it would become a useless strategy to do research putting the silence phenomena into the categories presented in this table without trying to comprehend the trajectories of their development and how do they act in the sense-making process, which, as has been said here, is still an open field of research.

CONCLUSION

The study of the phenomena of silence needs to move within borders. That is, the polysemy and polyphony of silence, silences, and silencing in human everyday life function together with language, music, and other arts in the dynamics of the emotional world. Although the recognition of these phenomena is present within western and eastern cultures in different manners, it is worth it to comprehend the implications of changes in the perception and needs of ordinary life and its extraordinary significance. Even more, the implications of this fact in the comprehension that psychology is to accomplish about sense-making, decision-making, and value-grasping processes might vary from person to person, and research could attempt to gather both divergences and convergences of different trajectories from persons of different contexts and positions of the self. Yet, starting paths for the comprehension of the phenomena of silence transcend mere research proposals, and need to pursue the development of integrative theories about affective life, highlighting the contributions of poetry and music as a path back to wissenschaft?

NOTES

1. The FARC is the Spanish abbreviation of Fuerzas Armadas Revolucionarias de Colombia, which translates Colombian Revolutionary Army Forces. This army group is associated in Colombia with drug trafficking, genocide, kidnapping, and other crimes.

2. In Italian, the verb "sentire" signifies "feeling," "hear," "smell," "sense," and this polysemy is very important for the comprehension of the scopes of phenomenology (De Monticelli, 2012).
3. For an analysis in depth of this, see Lehmann (2014).
4. Luther made constant reference of the metaphysical and didactic power of music, which is also evident in baroque music: there is an underlying intention to connect individuals with God and, that way, music become a theological tool both to incorporate the affective resonance of sacred texts, and to overcome dark states such as melancholy or depression (Bartel, 1997).
5. Other similar terms are poetic instants, exhilaration, or I–Thou encounter. For an analysis in depth of their implications in sense-making of experience and existence, see Lehmann (2015).

REFERENCES

Abbey, E., & Valsiner, J. (2005). Emergence of meanings through ambivalence. *Forum: Qualitative Social Research, 6*(1), Art. 23. Retrieved from http://www.qualitative-research.net/fqs-texte/1-05/05-1-23-e.htm

Adorno, T. (2006). *Philosophy of new music.* Minneapolis, MN: University of Minnesota Press.

Bartel, D. (1997). *Música poética: Musical-rhetorical figures in German baroque music.* Lincoln, NE: University of Nebraska Press.

Barthes, R. (1972). *Crítica y verdad.* Buenos Aires, Argentina: Siglo XXI.

Beckstead, Z. (2009). Commentary: Shifting loyalties: Reconsidering psychology's subject matter. *Integrative Psychological and Behavioral Science, 43,* 221–227. doi 10.1007/s12124-009-9100-4

Bertau, M-C. (2011). Developmental origins of the dialogical self: Early childhood years. In H. M. Hermans & T. Gieser (Eds.), *Handbook of dialogical self theory* (pp. 64–81). Cambridge, England: Cambridge University Press.

Bilbro, J. (2009). From violence to silence: The rhetorical means and ends of Thomas Merton's antipoetry. *Merton Annual, 22,* 120–149.

Bollnow, O. F. (2009). *Le tonalità emotive.* Milano, Italy: Vita e Pensiero.

Borges, J. L. (2001). *Arte poética: Seis Conferencias.* Barcelona: Critica.

Branco, A., & Valsiner, J. (2010). Towards cultural psychology of affective processes: Semiotic regulation of dynamic fields. *Estudios de Psicología, 31*(3), 243–325

Bruneau, T. J., & Ishii, S. (1988). Communicative silences: East and west. *Word Communication, 17*(1), 1–33.

Bruzzone, D. (2010). *Fenomenologia dell'affettività e significato della formazione.* In V. Iori *A cura di: Quando I sentimenti interrogano l'esistenzia. orientamenti fenomenologici nel lavoro educativo e di cura.* Milano, Italy: Guerini.

Cage, J. (1961). *Silence. Lectures and writings by John Cage.* Middletown, CT: Wesleyan University Press.

Cage, J. (1990). *An autobiographical statement.* Retrieved from http://johncage.org/autobiographical_statement.html

Charles, D. (n.d.). *Aesthetics of silence: About John Cage's existential semiotics of "silence."* Retrieved from http://home.att.ne.jp/grape/charles/dc/dc_texts/dc-madrid-aesthetics_beyond_silence.pdf

Clegg, J. (2010). Commentary: Uncertainty as a fundamental scientific value. *Integrative Psychological and Behavioral Science, 44,* 245–251. doi 10.1007/s12124-010-9135-6

Cooper, B. (2011). Beethoven's uses of silence. *The Musical Times, 152*(1914), 25–43.

De Monticelli, R. (2012). *L'ordine del cuore.* Milano, Italy: Graznati.

Eco, U. (2009). On the ontology of fictional characters: A semiotic approach. *Sign System Studies, 37*(1/2), 82–97.

Freeman, M. (2011). Toward poetic science. *Integrative Psychological and Behavioral Science, 45,* 389–396. doi 10.1007/s12124-011-9171-x

Garrofe, P. (2007). *Lacan, letra, música, voz: Entre el arte y la ideología.* Buenos Aires, Argentina:Montressor.

Hermans, H. (2001). The dialogical self: Toward a theory of personal and cultural positioning. *Culture and Psychology, 7(3),* 243–281. doi:10.1177/1354067X0173001

Hermans, H., & Hermans-Konopka, A. (2010). Positioning theory and dialogue. In H. Hermans & A. Hermans-Konopka (Eds.), *Dialogical self theory: Positioning and counter-positioning in a globalizing society* (pp. 120–199). Cambridge, England: Cambridge University Press.

Horkheimer, M. (2003). *Teoría crítica.* Buenos Aires, Argentina: Amorrortu.

Huss, F. (2008). On the beautiful in music, or the emotional fly in the musical ointment. *The Musical Times, 149*(1902), 39–46. Retrieved from http://www.Jstor.Org/Stable/25434516

Janet, P. (1928). Fear of action as an essential element in the sentiment of melancholia. In M. L. Reymert (Ed.), *Feelings and emotions, The Wittenberg Symposium* (pp. 297–309). Worcester, MA: Clark University Press.

Kahn, D. (1997). John Cage: Silence and silencing. *The Musical Quarterly, 81,* 556—598. Retrieved from http://www.kim-cohen.com/Assets/CourseAssets/Texts/Kahn_Cage-Silence%20and%20Silencing%20(1997).pdf

Klempe, H. (1996). Musicalisation of metaphor and metaphorical in music. In C. Grund & A. Engström (Eds.), *Danish yearbook of philosophy* (pp. 125-136). Copenhagen, Denmark: Museum Tusculanum Press.

Klempe, H. (2010). Theoretical and empirical statements in psychology. In J. Valsiner, S. Salvatore, J. Travers Simon., & A. Gennaro (Eds.), *Year Book for idiographic science* (pp. 29–48). Roma, Italy: Firera & Liuzzo Group.

Klempe, H. (2015a). The language fallacy in psychology. In S. H. Klempe (Ed.), *Cultural psychology and musical experience.* Charlotte, NC: Information Age.

Klempe, H. (2015b). Music, language and ambiguity. In S. H. Klempe (Ed.), *Cultural psychology and musical experience.* Charlotte, NC: Information Age.

Kübler Ross, E. (1993). *De la muerte y los moribundos.* Barcelona, Spain: Grijalbo-Mondadori.

Kurzon, D. (1997). *Discourse of silence.* Amsterdam, the Netherlands: John Benjamins.

Kurzon, D. (2007). Towards a typology of silence. *Journal of Pragmatics 39,* 1673–1688. doi:10.1016/j.pragma.2007.07.003

Kurzon, D. (2011). Editorial: On silence. *Journal of Pragmatics 43,* 2275–2277. doi:10.1016/j.pragma.2010.11.011

Langer, S. (1977). *Feeling and form: A theory of arte developed from philosophy in a new key.* New York, NY: Macmillan.

Lehmann, O. (2012). Silence in the musical scores of human phenomena. *Culture & Psychology, 18*(4), 465–471. doi:10.1177/1354067X12456717

Lehmann, O. (2014). Man's search for extra-ordinary answers in life: Silence as a catalyst for crisis-solving. In K. Cabell & J. Valsiner (Eds.), *The catalyzing mind: Beyond models of causality* (Vol. 11): *Advances in theoretical psychology* (pp. 239–250). New York, NY: Springer.

Lehmann, O-V. (2015). Poetic instants in daily life: Towards the inclusion of vertical time in cultural psychology. In B. Wagoner, N. Chaudhary, & P. Hviid (Eds.), *Integrating experiences: Body and mind moving between contexts, Niels Bohr professorship lectures in cultural psychology* (Vol. 2, pp. 165–177). Charlotte, NC: Information Age.

Lehmann, O-V. (in press). The poetic resonance of an instant: Making sense of experience and existence through the emotional value of encounters. In P. Marsico & L. Tateo (Eds.), *Ordinary things and their extraordinary meanings.* Charlotte, NC: Information Age.

Levi-Strauss, C. (1987). *Antropología estructural.* Barcelona, Spain: Paidós Ibérica.

Levitin, D. J. (2006). *This is your brain on music: The science of a human obsession.* New York, NY: Dutton.

Levitt, H. (2001). Sounds Of silence in psychotherapy: The categorization of clients' pauses. *Psychotherapy Research 11*(3), 295–309.

Lyotard, J-F. (1972). Plusieurs silences. *Musique en jeu, 9,* 64–76.

Marcuse, H. (2007). *Collected papers of Herbert Marcuse* (D. Kellnerm, Ed.). New York, NY: Routledge.

Marsico G., Cabell K. R., Valsiner J., & Kharlamov N.A., (2013). Interobjectivity as a border: The fluid dynamics of betweenness. In G. Sammut, P. Daanen, & F. Moghaddam (Eds.), *Understanding the self and others: Explorations in intersubjectivity and interobjectivity* (pp. 51–65). London, England: Routledge.

Mazzei, L. (2003). Inhabited silences: In pursuit of a muffled subtext. *Qualitative Inquiry, 9*(3), 355–368. doi:10.1177/1077800403009003002

Neubauer, J. (1986). *The emancipation of music from language.* Ann Arbor, MI: Yale University Press.

Oduro-Frimpong, J. (2007). Semiotic silence: Its use as a conflict-management strategy in intimate relationships. *Semiotica, 167*(1/4), 283–308. doi:10.1515/SEM.2007.080

Orlandi, E.P. (1995). *As formas do silêncio: No movimento dos sentidos.* Campinas, Brazil: Unicamp.

Paz, O. (1994). *El arco y la lira.* Bogotá, Colombia: Fondo de Cultura Económica.

Paz, O. (1999). *La casa de la presencia.* Barcelona, Spain: Galaxia-Gutemberg.

Poland, B., & Pederson, A. (1998). Reading between the lines: Interpreting silences in qualitative research. *Qualitative Inquiry, 4*(2), 293–312. doi:10.1177/107780049800400209

Scholtz, G. (2010). Schleiermarcher. In S. L. Sorgner & O. Fürbeth (Eds.), *Music in German philosophy: An introduction.* Chicago, IL: University of Chicago Press.

Sorgner, S. L. & Fürbeth, O. (2010). *Music in German philosophy: An introduction.* Chicago, IL: University of Chicago Press.

Stone, C., Coman, A., Brown, A., Koppel, J., & Hirst, W. (2012). Toward a science of silence: The consequences of leaving a memory unsaid. *Perspectives on Psychological Science* 7(1) 39–53. doi:10.1177/1745691611427303

Tantam, D. (2003). The flavor of emotions: Psychology and psychotherapy. *Theory, Research and Practice, 76,* 23–45.

Valsiner, J. (2007). *Culture in minds and societies.* New Delhi, India: Sage

Valsiner, J. (2009). Between fiction and reality: Transforming the semiotic object. *Sign System Studies, 37*(1/2), 99–113.

Valsiner, J. (2010, April). Climbing the sacred mountain of knowledge: Psychology at its eternal crossroads. XIV Colombian Congress of Psychology, Ibagué.

Valsiner, J. (2014). Cultural psychology and its future: Complementarity in a new key. In B. Wagoner, N. Chaudhary, & P. Hviid (Eds.), *Cultural psychology and its future: Complementarity in a new key* (Vol. 1): *Niels Bohr professorship lectures in cultural psychology.* Charlotte, NC: Information Age.

Valsiner, J., & Cabell, K. (2012). Self-making through synthesis: Extending dialogical self theory. In H. Hermans & T. Gieser (Eds.), *Handbook of dialogical self theory* (pp. 82–97). New York, NY: Cambridge University Press.

Valsiner, J., & Rosa, A. (2007). The myth, and beyond: Ontology of psyche and epistemology of psychology. In J. Valsiner & A. Rosa (Eds.), *The Cambridge handbook of sociocultural psychology* (pp. 23–49). New York, NY: Cambridge University Press.

Venuleo, C. (2008). What is the nature of idiographic data? In S. Salvatore, J. Valsiner, S. Strout-Yagodzynski, & J. Clegg (Eds.), *Year book of idiographic science* (pp. 273–286). Rome, Italy: Firera & Liuzzo.

Whitman, W. (1871). Indications. In W. Whitman, *Leaves of grass.* Retrieved from http://www.whitmanarchive.org/published/LG/1871/poems/95

Zittoun, T., Valsiner, J., Vedeler, D., Salgado, J., Gonçalves, M., & Ferring, D. (2013). *Melodies of living: Developmental science of human life course.* New York, NY: Cambridge University Press.

CHAPTER 15

MUSIC BY NUMBERS

Martin Knakkergaard

Numbers, figures, and systems play central roles in the understanding of musical matters in the Western world. The kind of preorder—and also the systemic thinking—that numbers automatically bring with them seems to facilitate the access to and dealings with what is understood as fundamental musical conditions.

The number stands out as a constituent of our understanding of frequencies and their interrelations. The number as such becomes the lifeless agent of movement that without further notice is allowed to include—and systematize—the "slow" frequencies, we arithmetically acknowledge as rhythms. However, the complex systematization that hereby emerges, in which different or alternating regularities and irregularities are organized in ostensible homogeneities, appears to define the objects it claims to reflect.

With modern digital music technology the number as a describer—and constituent—of music's internal ordering seems to stand out even more prominently than before in the history of Western music and musical thinking. However, the number's inability to grasp the inner workings of the musical utterance is unveiled in correspondence with the use of new forms of transcription that technology has brought forward, as well as with the musical practices of the present.

Cultural Psychology of Musical Experience, pages 299–318
Copyright © 2016 by Information Age Publishing
299

This article takes its point of departure in the recapitulation of some analytic observations that the author did uncovering rhythmic implications in a Michael Jackson song from the 1990s by approximation.

It carries on to discuss numbers per se and by focusing on the ontology of the number 1 and its genetic status, the discussion evaluates numbers' significance as agents in organizing processes of any kind questioning their objectivity and neutrality.

The discussion takes up the importance of the number in relation to the traditional organization of musical material and sound, into pitch, metres, and duration, sporadically touching upon its impact on musical form and practice and thus reflecting upon and questioning arithmetic's influences and relevance for the understanding and creation of music. Heidegger's notion of *gestell* is integrated in the discussion as a frame of understanding leading to a consideration of the extensive long-lasting impact of the structural premises that were laid out by the ancient Greeks, to whom the numbers held mythical status.

The numbers capacity for the constituting and forming of systems, which tend to dominate the various ways in which art and science approach musical phenomena, is further investigated in the last part of the article paving the way for an evaluation of, on the one side, the role and power of the "old" systems toward the music of the present and, on the other side, the insufficiency of the number as a means for analysis in light of music's "semiotic turn."

A DIGITAL MATRIX

Modern musical artifacts are not only produced but also typically composed, designed, and performed by means of modern digital equipment. It is well-known that digital technology fundamentally is based on calculation of enormous arrays of numbers and that these arrays comprise only two different numbers, 0 and 1. Simple numbers have in this way gained a decisive position not just in relation to music but also *in* music.

It is, however, quite interesting that this development seems to cause an almost self-contradictory polarization, where on the one side, the number's central position for the creation and organization of music has become prominent, but its role as a historically dominant premise setter is paradoxically weakened, on the other.

During studies of relatively low-level rhythmical implications in modern popular music of the 1990s, I was surprised to find some intriguing rhythmical implications in Michael Jackson's "Give In to Me" from the 1991 album *Dangerous* (Knakkergaard, 1998, p. 4). Although taken from the face value of the piece it is clearly just a straightforward hard rock ballad, there is a peculiar subdivision of the eighth notes into 16th notes, today often referred to as 16th swing. The subdivision was most likely inspired by what had been going on within electronica and hip-hop in the late 1980s, and it was certainly not something that at the time was associated with rock or rock ballads. Listening to the subdivision it is obvious that it is neither straight, even eighths, nor swing, in the triplet based sense, and, lacking a better term, I decided to refer to it as shuffle, albeit that this is not a very specific term. The subdivision is actually somewhere in between straight and swing. To be exact it is 62.5%, which is certainly not at all close to straight, which is 50% or 1:1, but rather close to swing, whose mathematical approximation can be expressed as 66.6% or 2:1.[1]

Analyzing and modeling the piece by means of the computer, I was able to not just approximate but actually define the contained proportions. Working with a quantisation of 480 tics per eighth note the resolution or quantisation a straight subdivision of the eighth note equals the tics (numbers) 1 and 241, and an "ideal" swing subdivision equals 1 and 321. The subdivision heard in "Give In to Me" does not fit into these slots but instead into 1 and 301. Where the straight subdivision can be expressed as 240:240 or 1:1 and the standard swing division as 320:160 or 2:1, the division in question can be expressed as 300:180 or 5:3 a proportion that is equivalent to the simplest numerical expression of the elements—a and b—in the golden section: $a/b = b/(a + b)$.[2]

In itself this is of course highly interesting, but it is another—almost hidden—aspect of the division that I would like to bring forward. It turned out that a lot of people, when asked to evaluate and describe the division, claimed that they heard or experienced this rhythm as the particular kind of stumbling shuffle—also known as skiffle—we get when the subdivision corresponds to 3:1 (see Figure 15.1).

This apparent misperception puzzled me a great deal. At first there seems to be a great difference between what we hear and the stumbling shuffle rhythm shown. And in terms of the proportions there certainly is that difference: 3:1 has absolutely nothing in common with 5:3 (except the fact that the first element of every proportion is higher than the second). But when taking the relationship between straight and swing into consideration, it

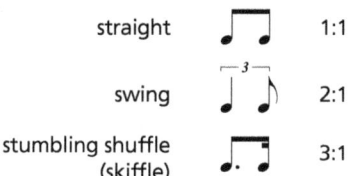

Figure 15.1 Standard two-part divisions of a quarter note.

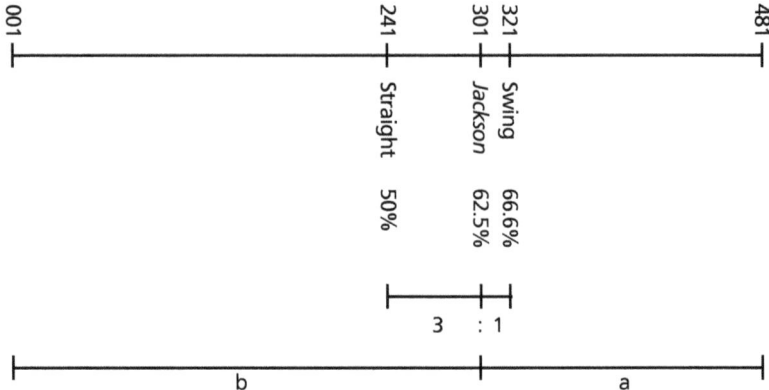

Figure 15.2 Diagram showing the relations between the discussed divisions.

turns out that the particular "Jackson" swing feel actually corresponds to a stumbling shuffle subdivision of the relation between straight and swing divisions. Within a quantization of 480 tics per eight note the difference between straight and swing is 80 (320 – 240), the difference between straight and the Jackson subdivision (or just Jackson) is 60 (300 – 240), and finally the difference between Jackson and swing of course is 20 (320 – 300). Now given the possible 80 positions between straight and swing (within the resolution of 480), Jackson describes the proportion 60:20, equalling exactly 3:1, a "stumbling shuffle" on the micro level. Figure 15.2 will possibly do better in describing the discussed implications.

At this point, the reader might be forgiven for supposing that I am creating the case that "Give In to Me" is a modern exemplar of the golden mean as musical aesthetics. However, whether the Jackson proportion is the result of a logical mathematical approach toward the aesthetics of the piece, or if it is the result of a trial and error process guided by the ear, in short: Whether this is a case of formalism or intuition is not the point here.

What is interesting is the fact that this subdivision, which was very popular at the time (it still is), and certainly was not invented by Jackson, in my understanding is closely tied to developments within music technology. With the introduction of the computer-based sequencer, divisions like this became just as "natural" as any other. This was—and is—certainly not the case within standard notation (Figure 15.3).

I will not comment on the significance of the approximation to the golden section. However, we should notice, that in contrast to standard notation the division looks very well proportioned within the realm of numbers. Actually in the context of the sequencer's event list, the number 300 is just as handy a number as 320 or 240 are. It is just a number and maybe that is all it is. What we are facing is simply a difference between the inner workings

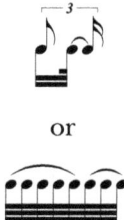

or

Figure 15.3 Approximation of the "Jackson" swing in standard notation.

of two numerically based representational systems applied to music, providing different tools and approaches to the making of music. This, however, does not imply that there is a conflict between the two systems. There is not. It does, however, suggest that numbers are playing a "new" and different role in the age of the digital protocols; a role that implies both altered and new approaches to the distribution and division of rhythm. A new matrix.[3]

THE ARMS OF THE NUMBER

It is no surprise that a notational system is based upon numeric proportions and given algebraic operations, such as division and addition. Generally numbers take an absolutely fundamental position within Western culture in terms of how we are able to think about the world, how we approach it, and how we understand elements of what we consider to be real.

Whether numbers are considered merely a special subset within language that deals with proportions (a subset that is not given much thought, just as little as letters and single words are considered when speaking), or whether they stand out as an expression of elevated beauty and truth, it does not alter the fact that numbers are tools made by man, that number is a social construction.[4] Maybe the number is often considered a neutral part of the tools we make use of for cognition, systematization, and communication, as they themselves do not represent any specific quality, characteristic, or value before they are combined with elements from—primarily —language, but for a number of reasons that I shall go into, it is not advisable to maintain a notion of fundamental neutrality regarding numbers.

As a social construction numbers are axiomatic. They bring about the basic conditions for the development of arithmetic and algebraic systems. In this sense it does not matter what kind of numbers we investigate. Whether we are talking about rational numbers, natural numbers, cardinal, or ordinal numbers, etc. the number as principle describes an axiom that in turn forms the basis for apparently inexhaustible axiomatic ramifications.

By accepting the number 2 as a multitude of 1—two 1's so to speak—the way is paved for the construction of all other possible numbers, and it becomes obvious that when we ask for the principle of numbers we are actually questioning the number 1, its validity, and its ontology. Does the number 1 exist? And if so is it possible to find more 1s?

As for the latter question the immediate answer is no. There are no genuine multitudes of 1 no matter what 1 is declared to be. It is only as a nonreferential, self-contained abstract number as well as in the digital domain that there can be more identical units or entities. And in neither of the two domains are such specifications of units more than a temporary determination that is related to a specific product or result that occurs by means of numerical processes. In other words, they are neither digital nor mere numbers.

This does not preclude the existence of 1. Quite the contrary: that 1 exists or can be delimited is already integrated in the preceding clarification as a precondition. It is in every aspect of human cognition meaningful to refer to the number 1. And it is the very fact that there are no more 1's that makes it possible for us to refer to 1. Thus, the number 1 is a carrier of contextually determined information by itself. But 1 can only become 2 by multiplication when we ignore and generalize what determines 1 as 1, the individual, the uniqueness, and focuses on common factors between two or more 1's instead. By focusing on the common factors, we are concentrating on identity excluding difference. The number 1 gains its general validity—its viability—the very moment we leave out what distinguishes 1 from every other 1, which is at exactly the point where it looses its validity by principle, its identity. By doing so, the number 1 escapes into the abstract and one can say that every number other than 1 depends on abstraction and generalization. For two 1's to become 2, we have to neglect any difference and plead for identity.

However, numbers in general can also act as differentiators between different 1's. And a number other than 1 is in this respect capable of gaining individuality or uniqueness. This is what happens in a series, an order, or a system. Sorting out different items by numbers is very common, and numbering seems in many ways to penetrate the notion and the systems of order our culture depends upon.[5] This is generally true for the occurrence of numbers in music, too.

It is one of the privileges of numbering that the number can endow both the one who designates by means of numbers as well as whom or what is designated by the number with a certain dignity and importance: I count therefore I am, or I am counted therefore I am.

The importance of the number, of numbering, and counting is thus already incorporated into the language in various forms and practices that in themselves have nothing to do with numbers: It doesn't count, I would not count on her if I were you, etc. In this way, the numbers occur in language as types of empty metaphors, apparently indicating something that has to do with simple judgments of for instance relevance. The very minute the principle of counting shifts from shear descriptive metaphors to regular analogies, the understanding of the number, however, transforms from simple ordering and identification to valuating, ranking, etc.

This understanding of numbers indicates that the use of numbers can generate proportions and value systems that actually redefine the subjects they are applied toward. In this respect it can be claimed that the numbers imply a fatal programming, formatting, or coding of the phenomena they are applied toward. That what we are left with when we think we understand something by means of or through numbers is the impact of the structure of numbers in the material we are investigating.

THE 1 IN THE MIDDLE

Generally it is remarkable that the number is central to the development of music theory, hence also in the construction of musical structures. The dimensioning of musical instruments as well as the fixation of scales and tone systems all increasingly become depended upon the number and its arithmetical potential throughout the history of Western music. The development of analytical notation such as figured bass and Roman chord indication rest upon the number and its implicit hierarchy, just as the rules for voicing—that are traceable at least to the early medieval ages—legitimizes the idea that "in music everything stems from the numbers." (Hansen, 1999, p. 22 [author trans.]). The number plays a significant role in the basic foundation of Western European music—first and foremost with respect to the construction and utilization of pitch systems, scales and instruments and somewhat later also regarding the registration of pitch and rhythm.

In a Heidegger-inspired model of understanding, inside which the nature of technology is seen as a specific uncovering of the being, the construction of pitch systems is the "scaffolding" (*gestell*)—the technical operative structure—that emerges from the read-out of pitches and their intervals from the total audible frequency spectrum as stock (*bestand*). The technique that is implied in the reading-out is in this thinking "the way the being is revealed to us." (Zahavi, 1999, p. 27, [author trans.]) In practice, the reading is to a certain degree arbitrary and in the case of the Western pitch system its 12 tones per octave is merely a choice, a decision, which the actual organization—or rationalization—of frequencies is depended upon. In oriental cultures the octave, if present at all, is divided in ways that differ drastically from that of the Western cultures. In Siamese music, the octave is, for instance, divided into seven intervals and in Javanese music into only five (Weber, 1958, p. 97).

Heidegger's understanding of phenomena as stock whose concrete manifestations are read out—out *seen*—of the order that stands out through the use of the technique (the scaffolding) toward the stock (the structure that emerges through the uncovering of the stock by the technique) appears to correspond to observations that can be made with respect to the—apparently fatal—"trick" of understanding or cognition, which has been made toward music's basic conditions. These tricks or methodical systematizations appear fatal because to the person and to the definite culture they seem to be irreversible: Once the conditions (the stock) are uncovered from within—or by utilizing—a specific system, the units of the system remain part of the constitution of the conditions. These units may be questioned, as is the case here, but they only rarely are challenged by the introduction of an alternative system or "reading."[6]

As the number at least since the Pythagoreans[7] has played a dominant part in the development of theories regarding the structuring of the "stock of pitches," what can be expressed by means of numbers as relations of proportions has gained a crucial position for both the understanding and the construction of a stock of pitches, its intervals, and design.

The ancient Greeks use of simple numbers, where the octave is defined by the relation 2:1, the fifth as 3:2, the fourth as 4:3, etc., is derived from their reading of the relations between the length of strings and the pitch from the monochord's proportions. However, this point of departure—this "benchmark"—should be seen alongside the ancient Greeks' general favoring of the small simple numbers, 1-2-3-4, as they assumed that these numbers were present in all proportions, natural as well as mystical, and that these numbers guaranteed correspondence, balance, and coherence. The scientific character that is connected to this particular use of numbers is in other words rooted in a sort of mythical understanding of unity and balance as a ruling principle.[8]

Both the design and reading of the monochord's mensural implications, when divided in decisive ways, and the ancient Greek's favoring of the small numbers function as scaffolding leading to a specific uncovering. The stock of pitches that emerges is the result of the particular uncovering the scaffolding puts forward. So what can possibly emerge is already limited by what is available and the ancient Greek's conception of music was limited by their assumptions about simple numbers and proportions and their quasimystical thinking.

In itself, it is interesting that numbers are thought to be able to express musical and acoustical matters and implications meaningfully; that numbers are expected to be better informers of pitch relations than pitch relations are by themselves. This consideration of course is not new. Galileo for instance questioned the relevance of relying on numbers as definite descriptors of musical intervals, as they were put forward by his master,

Giosoffo Zarlino, in *Le istitutioni harmoniche* (1558), just as Aristoxenus "rejected the idea of rationalization by instruments" suggesting that "the ear alone should decide upon the worth or worthlessness of melodic intervals" (Weber, 1958, p. 98).

There is hardly any doubt that one has to distinguish between striving for cognition and understanding in a scientific and also metaphysical sense on the one side and musical practice on the other, a kind of dialectic the ancient Greeks were well aware of. Nevertheless, their procedure, however metaphysical in its origin, their methods for mapping relations between pitches and for the construction of stocks of pitches by means of numbers, have had a decisive and generally lasting influence on Western European music culture as we know it, and it is reasonable to claim that the diatonic scale and its pitch material is a system concept that "fully is based on the numbers and a mathematical-logical way of thinking—apparently far away from any musical practice and aesthetic concern" (Hansen, 1999, p. 152 [author trans.]).

As such, the reading out or the uncovering of a pitch system based on the sovereignty of numbers—as scaffolding—dominates Western culture throughout history since the Hellenes. On the one side, it is noteworthy that the Western culture never succeeded in constructing a satisfying pitch system that "comes right" in the perspective of numbers; on the other side, it is perhaps even more noteworthy that precisely the world of numbers has delivered the compromise, the equal temperament, within which only the octave is "pure" or "just" and all other pitch intervals are out of tune constructed as they are by dividing the octave (1:2) into 12 equal steps number ($\sqrt[12]{2}$) – thus it comes right by being wrong.

The pitch system along with the gradual development of a notational system with reference hereto further has paved the way for the emergence of a particular complex harmony and counterpoint that are distinctive to Western music and which are common to both the classical tradition as well as to styles and genres within popular music. Since the early 19th century, these systems have taken almost all Western instruments hostage and in late capitalism and the age of globalization, the systems have realized its imperialistic potential as well by forcing adjustments upon foreign nonoccidental pitch systems, recently in narrow interaction with global mass-media and digital music.

In this sense, we can talk of a fatal reading whose cogency and dominance instead of declining seems stronger and stronger the closer we get to present times, maybe most prominently in the digital age's dependency on fixed protocols. In spite of the many suggested alternatives that have been put forward and in spite of the many impulses from music cultures outside Western Europe, the system still penetrates the reading of pitch, even in the digital world where the number—as we know it—has ceased to exist long ago.

TIMING

When it comes to the question of musical time (the movement and gesture of music, its rhythm), the numbers constitute—in the form of time measuring series of numbers—the reference alongside which we orientate and synchronize musical events. It sounds convincing when it is claimed, "that the Greek word for number—aritmos—is related to the word 'rhytmos'" (Øhrstrøm, 1999, p. 11 [author trans.]) as rhythm, understood as constituted by a perceived regularity, normally stands out as something that is or can be counted. However there is no such thing as a complete regularity. It exists neither in music nor outside (see Knakkergaard, 2007).

The ordering or systematization of music's movement in periods, measures, and beats within the horizontal plane of the modern music notation system resembles in many ways a very coarse-cut lattice—one could claim that the same is true concerning the disposition of the vertical plane. Again the numbers and their arithmetic hide behind the notation apparatus' registration and systematization of rhythm through counting, addition, and division, and it is precisely the order the numbers and the counting make possible that stands out as the lattice.[9]

The determination of events upon the horizontal axis, the time line of the system, requires the measuring of homogeneous quanta or units: pitch values or durations. These quanta are further developed into hierarchies through subdivision in mainly two or three smaller quanta, but even when this procedure is carried out in so called odd divisions—5, 7, 11, etc.—the unit is profoundly undisturbed. It is as if the unit is given before the music. However, as Kvifte shows, there is a considerable difference between the actual performances of a piece of music and its notation (Kvifte, 2007), indicating that the theoretical understanding is an edifice constructed upon sand, just as the modern tone system is inadequate regarding tonal implications of traditional Norwegian folk music that is inherited by the ear, as documented by Sinding-Larsen (Sinding-Larsen, 1988, p. 105).

The concrete actualization of these quanta is taking place with reference to a time count, a time count that in the latter part of the history of the notation apparatus specifically is tied to a chronometric constant. By this operation, the tempo—as the breathing and pulse of music—is deprived of its possible reference to the rhythm of the human body, instead the body has to submit to the clock's mechanical rhythm. Music is in this way conceptually and theoretically tied up in a narrow arithmetically defined framework, which is, however, miles away from most forms of musical performances shaped as they are by dynamic practices of the human body. Human speech is as an example not unfolded in rigid and stereotyped rhythmic patterns, and although practices within rap music do come close to speech, it is brought into a recitative performance that is fundamentally rhythmitized as "instrumental" or "vocal" music.

As a further regulation of the unfolding of movement, the timeline is divided into measures, thus introducing the meter. By this operation at least two things happen: (a) the cyclic series of a limited amount of—discreet—numbers is established as a musical forming element, and (b) the idea of precise synchronicity between and coordination of individual streams in parallel is introduced. Whereas the cyclic series of numbers leads to the dividing of the timeline into segments of generally equal length—periods—eventually introducing the notion of the bar, harmonic thinking—and chords—emerges from the coordination of parallel streams each of which refers to a common stock of notes. It is important to hold on to that the development of the equal tempered tone system implies a reduction of the tone material to 12 unique and equally important steps that is depended upon the notion of identity of the octave. This equality—that is achieved through numbers and arithmetic—implies that it is possible to work inside the stock of tone material as a given matrix inside which transformable vectors can be defined and identified.

The number thus indirectly pervades all levels of the notational system's handling of gesture, rhythm, time—as it does toward pitch—and it is in this way, by means of the number and through the number, that the specific kind of complexity that signifies Western European music can arise (see also Weber, 1958).

THE SYSTEM

One could say that the number is an insufficient premise setter for understanding, as it is fundamentally not related to the matter it is applied toward. It acts as a metaphor, stressing its descriptive and explanatory element, but it is not really part of the matter. This very fact, however, in turn liberates the number to produce the conditions, the adapted system, for how we do understand the matter. This way the number shifts from the descriptive domain of the metaphor to the operational domain of the analogy.

Numbers do constitute a system on their own, and apparently we generally feel confident when we understand phenomena as systems, or believe that we understand the system behind. Traditionally we seem to find it very difficult to distinguish between what is part of the system and what is shaped by the system. Therefore we resort to focusing on the system. This has been the case for musicology up until very recently, a practice, as noted previously, that flows from the ancient Greeks, and which was considerably strengthened in the "golden centuries" of Western classical music by theorists such as Zarlino, Rameau, Riemann, Schenker et al. The result, as Wittgenstein states, is that the system is pulled forward as what is understood, while the sensation and the mental event that is caused by the understanding is neglected (Wittgenstein, 1999, p. 93). Even when turning toward the performative aspects striving to consider the sensation and denote music's determination as intentional sound brought about from human practices and actions, this is generally done with references to either an explicit (written) source —a score—as is the case for the theorists previously mentioned, or, especially regarding the music that falls within the popular traditions, with reference to an implicit—invisible—note-based score, as the music is created within the framework of traditionally note-based understanding and matrix.

As long as the number is merely used as an abstract symbol, an analytic indicator of distinguished incidents, a metaphor, no real harm is done, but with the application of norms and rules that relate to the number, and thus are numerically based, it is another thing entirely. The music is captured by the numerical system where it can stand out as pure number magic. The unification of the two systems—both, as all numerical systems, characterized by the discreet step as opposed to the continuous—thus gives rise to considerations regarding the basically numerical constitution of not only the music notation apparatus, but of man's concept of and approach to music in general. Music is organized, composed, and even understood and evaluated within the framework of a cell- or field-based system that allows for numerical operation. This obviously has led to the hegemony of the note. Musical instruments are designed and manufactured to perform notes in reference to the pitch system, and aside from the violin-family (and of course the human voice) it is almost impossible to go beyond the system's ordering proportions and limits. Efforts to do so lead to the development of new instruments and hence construction of an alternative to go along with them or vice versa. Whereas many composers in the 20th century such as Federico Busoni and Harry Partch envisioned—and in Partch's case also constructed —new pitch systems and instruments, others, primarily the dodecaphonists and serialists, sought to expand the possibilities within the existing tone system and the traditional acoustic instruments by applying new techniques for organizing the material of the matrix, leading to a situation where it is fair to say, that

> In the final throes of Schoenberg's twelve-note serialism in the 1960s, composers such as Pierre Boulez insisted on a mathematical rigidity that almost sucks their music dry of expression and makes onerous demands of the listener's ability to perceive ordered forms. (Ball, 2008, p. 160)

Even though focusing on the numerical implications of the musical tone system can lead to a music, which to the majority is close to incomprehensible, it still might be so that it is exactly the discreet constitution of the series of numbers, of entities that makes the system attractive, just like the "finite, definite—matter" is what is required when making music and art, as stated by Stravinsky (Stravinsky, 1960, p. 67). This may well be true regarding exactly the poetic "side," where the music is conceived and prescribed, but in trying to capture a "real" and sounding musical event in its every detail, the system is however lost in endless decimals, and it becomes obvious that the system is manifest and relevant only as a reference and its proportions are not at all absolute. And maybe this is where the promise of the music has its place; there, the cleft or scratch, that Heidegger idealizes, opens, the cleft that is the product of the conflict between the closed earth, which is given ahead, and the lived open world, that it encloses (Heidegger, 1994, p. 72 [author trans.]). And modern digital technology may in a way have brought this cleft within reach by making it possible to work with what is already closed—or even dead—within a system that is so small meshed in entities that we cannot spot the steps anymore.

This complicates the well-known embarrassment the musicologist may find herself in with respect to precise descriptions of rhythm, and it stresses the descriptive system's insufficiency and its limitation to act only as a gross reference. This, however, does not abolish the system as a necessary prerequisite—a basis—for the articulation to stand out no matter if the music is literally written or not; the system is given a priori and the articulation (still) has to acknowledge the system in order to identify and legitimize itself as music. What in one respect is considered an unsatisfying descriptive system is in fact the lattice—the scaffolding—within which we are able to refer to music and to the expression of our concept or understanding of musical matters with or without a score. The immanent system does not stand out as more than just a coherent framework of reference that allows us to communicate inside a specific understanding of music, a discourse, which as a construct is older than the actual notation. Notation is on the contrary a product of a specific understanding, a concept, and does, as such, give witness to the existence of systemic principles of musical structuring that has been developed through musical practice, a practice that might be derived from perceived "structures of the environment" (Clarke, 2005, p. 17).

The tension between the immanent rigidity of the system and the sounding musical articulation—between the structure and its expression—is maybe the strongest impetus to the emergence of a "musical sense" in as far as the system allows for the construction of specific stable "languages of elements" giving rise to formation of specific genres or "paroles." Thus one could say that the articulation of musical sense is based on the existence of a system, but at the same time on the continuous challenging of the same system.

If it is only the product, the notated musical work of art, the score, as a bearer of the abstract meaningful idea[10] one is concerned about, the number is secretly active and is only the object of discussion in relation to attempts to change notational practice. However, as soon as music as performed, "organized sound" is drawn into the framework of comprehension, numbers stand out in what Heidegger designates "the unhiddenness." It is in the crossing between the text —the idea or intention—and the sound, no matter if notation is involved or not, that there is a lack of true correspondence. The general notion of temporal implications in music does however imply that our understanding of the musical gesture is striving for this correspondence. Trying to put performance implications into numbers easily turns into an attempt to digitize the performance, no matter it is through the digitization the Heideggerian cleft may become within reach.

THE DIGITAL AGE

In the digital age, numbers have acquired an absolutely central position in the making and distribution of music. They are everywhere from the level of the idea to the storage and distribution of the recording. It is all nothing but arrays of numbers, be it the control data that gives us the image of a note on the computer screen, the sound from a digital instrument (played by hand or computer), or the recording of a singing voice as well as the processing of a virtual space. The digital domain allows for extreme manipulation by means of numerical operations freeing every sound and performance from the limits of the real world as they are transformed into these enormous arrays and tables.

Recalling the Jackson example, one could argue that in the encounter between the two fundamentally numerical but axiomatically different registration systems a kind of liberation process is initiated. Part of the formatting and understanding of music, which derives from concepts of the traditional system, is losing ground.[11] But still, in the way digital music applications generally are designed, they are actually recycling traditional concepts and axioms, at least as metaphors.

This, however, does not exclude that digital music technology holds the power—and is used—to weaken if not yet eliminate the rigidity of the numbers and also to liberate the shaping of musical expression from the rationale of the numbers returning to a practice that is based on what is actually heard, not unlike the notion of second orality, as suggested by Walter Ong (Ong, 2002, p. 10f). This may also weaken the implicit numbers of the music system as constructive elements.

The digital domain provides a basis for distribution of sound and events—incidents—that is freed from standard notation's underlying divisive principle and also, partly as a result thereof, from common idealized and stereotyped performance practices. Any kind of musical event can emerge at any possible position inside any given time span. This is truly independent of rhythmical level, micro through macro. Digital editors provided by the common application for music production include formats that allow for meticulous distribution and control of onsets of any kind of data unconstrained by the limits governing musical notation, and at the same time they provide object-oriented interfaces that allow for arbitrary placement of graphical objects representing simple or complex sonorous gestalts with reference to a timeline.

Implicitly this opens for a musical practice that is not only liberated from the rationale of Western notation—and tone systems—but also from performance practices that are closely related to standardized body movements and various forms of communal social activities. Within the digital domain, musical expression can take any form and direction imaginable. The narrow ties to arithmetic thinking and understanding that dominate traditional musical practice are suspended leaving the premises for music making seemingly completely open. As a sign of this it is evident, that the use of notes is somewhat reduced in much music of today partly in favor of an increased focus of the shaping of sound by itself and also the application of real world sounds.[12]

However, once the distribution of musical events is left open, a complex problem stands out: how are we supposed to recognize musical compositions as such when they are organized with no or limited reference to known system-based practices and norms? The absence of an a priori order, an implicit system, may easily evoke a sense of loss or horror vacuum.

This might well be the main reason why, underneath the hood of modern music applications, everything is internally organized according to—though not actually restricted to—principles and standards inherited from traditional music technologies and systems. MIDI (musical instrument digital interface) is for instance fully codified in accordance with the well-established principles of the Western tone system. And even when it comes to time implications, which strictly speaking take just a little of the code space in MIDI, the implicit organizing principle clearly is built upon the notion of musical time where events are organized according to references to tics per quarter note instead of according to pure time code.

In this respect, the attempts to liberate music from the established technologies that were carried out by leading avant-garde composers in the 1950s greatly surpass what immediately appears to be technically within the reach of modern technologies, as these technologies are caught up in metaphors and analogies to traditional music making, ranging from the notational system to the concept of musical instruments.

In other words, at a time in history where it should be easy to introduce and explore new forms of musical expression, many are held back by factors that are deliberately build in to modern technologies. But is this really interesting? New music and new musical thinking do not seem to make up a particular, concerted discourse anymore. And when they do it is not as part of current popular culture; instead they belong to a particular cultural field that refers to a modernist paradigm, the avant-garde, and even to elitism.

In the Jackson example, it is intriguing to reflect upon the way and the degree in which modern technology is utilized. The special subdivision takes place inside a stereotyped format, a typical 4/4 rock-beat feel with the shuffle in question reinforced by a hoppling lift in the snare drum at the end of the bar just before one. Thus it all takes place on solid ground. The challenge—if indeed considered as one—is introduced inside well-known territories and, as stated, does not really present itself as such. This suggests that in order to be acknowledged as a possible reformulation or break, as a function of new technologies, a move has to take place inside an already established discourse. If it does not, it is very likely ignored.

Another reason why modern technology does not seem to evoke and support new musical forms to any substantial degree could be the fact that the development of modern technologies is increasingly tied to economic interests. Just like the development of both the tonal and the notational system was carried out through many centuries by scientists, philosophers, and musicians—to a certain degree controlled by official instances like the church, though—the introduction and development of digital techniques in the 20th century came about inside research institutions on the one side and through the work of individuals who were motivated by personal interest on the other. Much of the development today is, however, carried out by large corporations whose main motivation is financial. This naturally implies addressing as large a market as possible, and one way of doing this is by stressing references to the well-known and ordinary with the obvious consequence that, instead of emphasizing how new technology fundamentally differs from the old musical technologies, it is the principles and characteristics of the old technology that are stressed (even though they are only present as metaphors and analogies), leaving the end user with a sense of the familiar.

New technology is presented as a continuation of an established practice, a remediation (Bolter & Grusin, 1998) of the whole and well-known musical apparatus providing new possibilities within this practice, not initially encouraging the emergence of new forms or radical rethinking in any way. The manufacturer's interest in selling as many items as possible seems as such a major factor in the extension of an aesthetical practice that is closely related to technologies whose limited potential was surpassed long ago.

The prevailing concept of music is thus still closely tied to systems that are in turn closely dependent upon numbers. The system acts as condition provider, and the numbers or at least numbering are needed in order to navigate inside the system. Abstract numbering or counting provides the framework inside which it is possible to establish patterns and vectors that are open to transformation and variation. In the dominant musical discourse, repetition and recognition are crucial elements for establishing what is considered meaningful musical structures evidently independent of specific culture. The lattice, which stands out as the product of the combination of the notation system and the tone system, forms the stable grammar inside which musical expression can take place by means of combination and variation procedures. Whether the discussion is centered on music's composition, performance, perception, or reception, it is highly dependent upon grammatical foundation. Inside modern culture, a musical semiotic still is only possible inside a system that allows for loss of symmetry. That is a system inside which the intervals—melodic or rhythmic—are not equal. Where there are specific scales comprising intervals of different proportions, hierarchically ordered in such a way that the fundamental of the scale, the first step, the one, has the highest priority and greatest weight, and where the beats in the bar and the length of the notes are not of equal value.[13]

However, it is well-known that the far-reaching possibilities given by modern digital technology have not entirely been left unused. Besides the continuous experimenting within the avant-garde, electronica and to a certain degree also music associated with the somewhat vague appellation New Age, seem to have pursued aesthetic ideals that aim to avoid traditional musical "shaping" in favor of sonorous atmospheric states, typically discarding the use of clear meters and specific tonalities. But even here the reference is still clear. It points unmistakably toward the system that it is fundamentally dependent upon. Ever since the stringent rationalization of the musical means of expression in the Middle Ages, primarily instigated by the Roman Catholic Church, the role and the power of the system, which holds the numbers in its midst, has formed the spine of the notion of music.

Contrary to what ideally could be expected, there are no real indications that the importance and status of 1—or numbers as a whole—in music is in retreat. Digital music applications do hold the power to ignore numbers entirely, but in practice they still make extensive use of the number as a means for communication thus implicitly maintaining an understanding of music that is axiomatically dependent upon numbers and counting. With their design we are actually just entering another domain of numerically ordered and weighted restrictions and rules. We are simply applying another scaffolding, whose imprint on the music—however subtle—is even more fundamental as nothing in the digital world is what it seems to be not even the digits.

NOTES

1. The mathematical or ideal swing-ratio, 2:1, is hardly ever heard in real life. Generally swing-feeling covers a large span ranging from hardly no differ-

ence—the length of two successive beats are almost the same—to perfor-mances where the length of the first beat is more than three times the second. Furthermore the ratio varies with respect to tempo ranging from 3.5:1 at slow tempi to 1:1 at high. (Friberg & Sundström, 2002)

2. The closest approximation to the golden mean inside a total of 480 tics is not 300:180 but 297:183. However, the difference between the two is not audible with the tempo in question, e = 86–88, so the rounded numbers are used throughout the article.

3. See also Danielsen, 2010.

4. According to the linguist Peter Gordon in more known cultures the highest number is 4. The Pirahã culture hasn't even developed higher numbers than 2 (Gordon, 2004). It is however necessary to consider that recently new stud-ies suggest that the ability to count probably is innate—and does not rely on numbers (Butterworth, 1999).

5. The list Danish of kings is a brilliant example of this clearly revealing a ten-dency to seek order by means of numbers regardless of the fact that such an order actually does not express anything at all except in this case telling us who came first.

6. Early electronic works by Stockhausen like Studie 1 and Studie 2 in the mid 1950s and are examples of such efforts as are most of the works—and instru-ments—of for instance Harry Partch.

7. The oldest known description is found in Euclid 3. Century B.C. (Hansen, 2003, p.1642).

8. For a discussion of this see Klempe, 1991, p.23ff.

9. The English composer Trevor Wishart claims that "the priorities of notation do not merely reflect musical priorities—they actually create them" (Wishart, 1996, p. 11).

10. An idea which "sich weder im akustischen Substrat noch in der subjektiven Reaktion des einzelnen Hörers erschöpft" Dahlhaus i Carl Dahlhaus og Hel-ga de la Motte-Haber *Systematische Musikwissenschaft* (Neues Handbuch der Musikwissenschaft, bd. 10), Laaber 1982 (cit. Sørensen, 2004, p. 82).

11. The extensive use of musique concrete-techniques in modern music is also a factor that supports this observation, which is also evident in the experimen-tal works of many artists. See for instance Okkels, 2008, p. 103 ff.

12. Today some conservatories do not require their students to be able to read notes when they begin their studies.

13. See also Kjeldsen (2004) and Ball (2008).

REFERENCES

Ball, P. (2008, May 8). Facing the music. *Nature, 453,* 160–162.

Bolter, J., & Grusin, R. (1998). *Remediation: Understanding new media.* Cambridge, MA: MIT Press.

Butterworth, B. (1999). *What counts? How every brain is hardwired for math.* New York, NY: Free Press.

Clarke, E. (2005). Ways of listening. An ecological approach to the perception of musical meaning. New York, NY: Oxford University Press.

Danielsen, A. (Ed.). (2010). *Musical rhythm in the age of digital reproduction*. Burlington VT: Ashgate.

Friberg, A., & Sundström, A. (2002, Spring). Swing ratios and ensemble timing in jazz performance: Evidence for a common rhythmic pattern. *Music Perception, 19*(3), 333–349.

Gordon, P. (2004, October 15). Numerical cognition without words: Evidence from Amazonia. *Science, 306*, 496–499.

Hansen, F.E. (1993). Æblets navn Om 1200-tallets motet. In F. Gravesen *Musikken har ordet* (pp. 19–32). København, Denmark: G.E.C. Gad.

Hansen, F. E. (1999). Musik – logisk konstruktion eller æstetisk udtryk? In J. Holmgaard *Æstetik og logik* (pp. 151–167). Viborg, Denmark: Medusa.

Hansen, F. E. (2003). Tonesystem. In F. Gravesen & M. Knakkergaard, *Gads musikleksikon* (pp. 1641–1646). Århus, Denmark: Gads Forlag.

Heidegger, M, (1994) *Kunstværkets oprindelse*, (original title, *Der Ursprung des Kunstwerks*, 1950). Haslev, Denmark: Samleren.

Kjeldsen, J. (2004). Tonale gruppesymmetrier versus tonale gennembrud–semiotikken mellem struktur og tilbliven. In T. Thellefsen and A. M. Dinesen (Eds.), *Semiotiske undersøgelser: Semiotiske undersøgelser*. København, Denmark: Hans Reitzel.

Klempe, H. (1991). *Musikkvitenskapelige retninger: En innføring*. Oslo, Norge: Spartacus.

Knakkergaard, M. (1998). Den obligate tambourin og den gyldne shuffle. In F. Egeland Hansen *Col Legno* (Vol. 1: pp. 1–11). Aalborg, Denmark: Aalborg Universitet.

Knakkergaard, M. (2007). Klingende tidsrum. Om vilkår for opnåelse af indsigt i forhold mellem musik og tid. In *Psyke & Logos, Tema Musik og psykologi*, Årg. 28, nr. 1 (red.) Lars Ole Bonde. pp. 138-159.

Kvifte, T. (2007). Categories and timing: On the perception of meter. *Ethnomusicology, 51*(1), 64–84.

Øhrstrøm, P. (1999). *Tidens gang i tidens løb*. Århus, Denmark: Steno Museets Venner.

Okkels, I. (2008). *Teknologi og musikopfattelse. En undersøgelse af den digitale musikteknologis rolle i den collage-baserede elektroniske musik*. København, Denmark: Københavns Universitet.

Ong, W. (2002). *Orality and literacy. The technologizing of the word*. London, England: Routledge.

Sinding-Larsen, H. (1988). The history of a tool of description and its domain to be described. In H. Sinding-Larsen *Artificial intelligence and language*. Oslo, Norway: Tano.

Sørensen, S. M. (2004) Studiet af det performative. Begreb og projekt. *Musik & Forskning, 29*, 81–106.

Stravinsky, I. (1960), *The poetics of music*. New York, NY, Random House.

Weber, M. (1958). *The rational and social foundations of music*. Carbondale, IL: Southern Illinois University Press.

Wishart, T. (1996). *On sonic art*. Amsterdam, The Netherlands: Harwood Academic.

Wittgenstein, L. (1999). *Filosofiske undersøgelser*. Kobenhavn, Denmark: Munksgaard
    Rosinante.
Zahavi, D. (1999). *Indledning in Martin Heidegger. Spørgsmålet om teknikken – og andre
    skrifter*. København, Denmark: Samleren.

CHAPTER 16

THE LANGUAGE FALLACY IN PSYCHOLOGY

Sven Hroar Klempe[1]

Language is probably the most important communication system for human beings. Yet verbal communication is not just one thing, but may appear on many different levels. There are, for example, great differences between scientific language and informal chatting. The same scale of differences can be traced by comparing a cake recipe with romantic poetry, or an instruction for an electrical device with a Jane Austen novel. In these examples language is used so differently that we probably can say the different authors are "not speaking the same language." This expression is supposed to depict the situation when two people of the same mother tongue have a talk without understanding each other at all.

On the one hand, this is what some parts of psychology is about, namely to clearing up conversational misunderstandings in everyday life. Yet there is one crucial question that has to be asked: To what extent do we know all the ways language is used? Even within poetry there are a lot of differences. There are for example immense differences between Alfred Lord Tennyson's and Dylan Thomas's poetry. Whereas the former is clear and easy to understand, the latter is rather diffuse in this respect. The same must be said about the relationship between Jane Austen and James Joyce,

Cultural Psychology of Musical Experience, pages 319–338
Copyright © 2016 by Information Age Publishing

for example. What is interesting with these examples, however, is that both Dylan Thomas and James Joyce attempt at making their language more into music. This musicalization (Wolf, 1999; Kristeva, 1982) of the language however is not just a literary construct. It is a phenomenon that also may appear in natural and everyday use of language. This is probably a term that can be applied on the situation Wilhelm Wundt described in *Outlines of Psychology* (Wundt, 1902). The small child starts its development of talk with expressive sounds as reflex phenomena accompanied by pleasurable feelings and emotions. "They are produced on all possible occasions and without any intention of communicating anything, so that they are by no means to be classed as elements of speech" (Wundt, 1902, p. 291). These sounds are often a result of the child's imitation of what the parents and others are saying around him or her. However there is not only the child that imitates. Also the parents imitate the child, but this imitation may represent another understanding of the use of the sounds. "In fact, as a rule, it is the adults who begin the imitating; they repeat the involuntary articulations of the child and attach a particular meaning to them, as, for example, 'pa-pa' for father, 'ma-ma' for mother, etc." (Wundt, 1902, p. 291). In other words, Wundt declares that the parents take the child's utterances as if they were language, whereas they are not. This mistaken of utterances is what here is called "the language fallacy," i.e., if an expression is understood as if it is language while it is primarily something quite different.

This is what communication is about, namely that it is unfolded on many different levels and in many different systems. In addition to language, we may communicate through the body, through drawings, through music, dancing, and whatever means of expression we may have at disposal. If it is so that we communicate on many different levels and in many different systems, why should not also thinking be governed by the same different spectre of systems? Albert Einstein says for example: "The words or the language, as they are written or spoken, do not seem to play any role in my mechanism of thought" (Ghiselin, 1952, p. 43). He talks instead about "visual signs," in which he thinks. For others it might be different. Like Mozart, for example, he talked about hearing the *tout ensemble* when he composed music (Ghiselin, 1952, p. 45). One aspect of this is of course that he did not go via language when he wrote down his music, like no composers do. Another and even more interesting aspect of this quotation of Mozart is that the mind does not necessarily follow a sequential order, which is a linguistic requirement. By regarding the mind as if language is the only system that governs these situations and thinking in general are probably the most éclat *ant* examples of the language fallacy. Thus some scholars have tried to avoid this fallacy by nuance the differences in thinking. One way is to talk about different intelligences (Gardner, 1983). Another is to refer to different layers of the consciousness (Freud, 1933). A third strategy is to use metaphors that refer to other systems, like the musical, for example. This can be traced in the use of metaphors like cognitive dissonance (Festinger, 1957) or polyphony (Bakhtin, 1984), but also in a metaphor like the dialogical self (Hermans & Kempen, 1993; Valsiner & Connoly, 2003). These contributions are important in pointing out the need for more variety in the understanding of the mind. However there is a need to go further into this and look at scholars who have managed to follow up Wundt's interesting observation of the child's preverbal form of communication. One of these is the almost forgotten developmental psychologist Heinz Werner (1890–1964), who in the first part of 20th century defined some alternative premises for how the development of mind can be understood.

BACKGROUND

In one of his late articles Werner *just en passant* follows up the Wundtian considerations about the child's stage of babbling (Werner, 1957b). What Werner is focusing on here is a stage between that of babbling and naming. "It seems plausible to interpret this period as one during which the awareness of soundpatterns as verbal symbols emerges" (Werner, 1957b, p. 137). Two aspects of this quotation became important for Werner during his lifelong research. One is the concept of development as a prerequisite for understanding perception, and the other is that language is related to and depending on other forms of communication. In line with this, his psychological research may in many ways reflect some aspects of the biographical components. He started playing violin at the age of 7; he studied composition and music history at the University of Vienna for a while before he ended up studying philosophy and psychology at the same place (Witkin, 1965). His PhD thesis from 1914 was entitled "The Psychology of Esthetic Enjoyment," and in 1917 he published a monograph about the invention of melodies in early childhood (Werner, 1917) as a result of his stay at the Psychological Institute of the University of Munich (Wapner & Kaplan, 1964).

Despite the fact that Werner later on did not focus so much on music directly, some musical perspectives became still present indirectly. Hence, his approaches in psychology is of special interest from a musical point of view; in his authorship he refers very often to music-related phenomena to illustrate an alternative perspective on some general aspects of the human mind that apparently do not have much to do with music. Three principles seem to be important in this respect: movement, form, and complexity, united in an organismic perspective. Movement is not only related to time, but also to changes and development. Some has regarded these as the most salient traits of music (Lévi-Strauss, 1981). The term form may refer to many different aspects. What are to be highlighted here however are the formalistic aspects, which refer to abstract meanings (Kivy, 1993). In music, complexity is first of all present through the harmonic texture. This is probably the most basic trait of music, even when we talk about melodic singing. As long as singing is tonal, harmony forms the framework in which the melodic progression is unfolded (Schenker, 1979). The three terms movement, form, and complexity are not only core terms in musicology, but also in Werner's psychology. The first study to reveal this is his analysis of the origin of the metaphor (Werner, 1919). Yet it is traced in other publications like "The Origins of the Lyric" (1924) and not least in the accomplishing *Comparative Psychology of Mental Development* (Werner, 1957a), which was originally in German and published for the first time in 1926. Later on it was translated into English (1940), revised and enlarged with the last edition so far from 1957. The last important contribution was written together with Bernard Kaplan about symbol formation in a developmental perspective, in which some of his musical perspectives can be traced, too (Werner & Kaplan, 1963/84).

THE STUDY OF MELODY SINGING (1917)

When Werner in his first independent study focused on melodic singing in early childhood, he followed up a rich tradition in German experimental psychology. Wertheimer, Koffka, and Köhler did focus on music in their early psychological experiments (Ash, 1995), but also Wundt and many more did so as well (Klempe, 2011). Werner is also regarded as representing Gestalt psychology, but he sympathized rather with the Leipzig than the Berlin group (Witkin, 1965). The reason was that the Leipzig group with Krueger, Sander, and Volkelt focused more on development than what Wertheimer, Koffka, and Köhler did. This perspective is crucial in Werner's analyzing of the development of singing in early childhood. The investigation he implemented involved children at the age of 2 to 5 years. The children should both spontaneously create their own melodies and reproduce melodies they had heard from others. What he found in this study was that there were clear patterns that governed both spontaneous and copied singing: "It is likely that the genuine melodic germ is a diffuse descending glissando, out of which the so-called 'ur-motif' (primary motif) may have developed as a descending two-toned pattern with the interval of a minor third" (Werner, 1957a, p. 125).

The main point in this investigation is not to have found the primary motif of a descending minor third, which is the most obvious aspect of spontaneous child singing. It is rather that this motif is not present as a clear structure at the early stage. Spontaneous singing in the early stage is characterized by an undifferentiated form of singing, which is recognized through several aspects. One is the direction of the melodic movement, which at the early stage is solely descending, whereas children have to be more than 39 months to apply form-building contrasts like ascending/ descending movements. The most important aspect, however, is that the youngest child never repeats parts, just the whole formula. It is after 42 months the child sorts out parts and construes a musical form by repeating parts. This illustrates the main conclusion of the investigation, namely that the child's singing appears as undifferentiated at the early stages, yet after some months becomes more and more differentiated. This is also true for other musical aspects. The ending tone is for example always the lowest tone, and the ambitus is limited to the beginning. The number of different tones in a motif is also delineated to two for the youngest children.

This investigation demonstrates first of all how development by Werner is understood in terms of how the child perceives forms. Yet it demonstrates also in an eloquent way how such a study can be done with referring to music. In his analysis of the children's actual singing, Werner makes exact analyses of the music. Every single song is transcribed into notes and placed in the tonal system. Even the individual variants in pitches are included in the transcriptions. This implies that this study is not only good psychology, but also excellent musicology. This fact demonstrates that a musicological approach can form a basis when the aim is to deal with the formal aspects of a child's development.

THE METAPHOR

The study on musical development in children from 1917 is the last investigation Werner did on music. The next study on metaphor (Werner, 1919) does not mention music at all. Nevertheless it has a certain perspective on metaphor which is quite interesting, not only from a musical point of view, but also when it comes to achieve an understanding of how Werner regards language. There are many ways to understand language, but also many ways to define it properly. A scientific perspective on language will emphasize its preciseness. This is an aspect that is embedded in grammatical rules as well. Thus some linguists regard unequivocal sentences as the ideals in grammatical analysis. This is even a prerequisite in transformational grammar and the reason for why it operates with deep structures (Chomsky, 1957/1975). In this respect the metaphor appears as a problem, and according to transformational grammar the metaphor has to be regarded as a deviation (Chomsky, 1964). On the other hand, linguists also acknowledge metaphor as an enrichment of the human language and "not a mere stylistic option to literal language" (Benveniste, 1966, p. 122).

By focusing on the metaphor in his next thesis, Werner is moving toward the verge of language. The metaphor represents a complex event, and it is exactly the complexity Werner is interested in. He is focusing on the role of metaphor as the creator of complexity in language. However, there is a big discussion what a metaphor is or is not. A normal, but analytic definition of a metaphor can be "A is B" (Danesi, 1993, p. 123). This is sufficient to underline that the metaphor includes complexity, yet it is not sufficient in an attempt at understanding all the forms of complexities that govern human use of language. Werner's thesis is first of all about the latter aspect, namely how to understand the different forms of complexity metaphors may represent. His perspective is that this complexity is first of all a result of a dynamic use of language. In a discussion about the origin of metaphors, his answer is quite simple: "There is no origin, just an endless unfolding of forms" (Werner, 1919, p. 2). Thus there are two aspects that characterize the metaphor: an unstopping dynamic process, which creates variety on the one hand, and on the other hand some uniting forms, which also are governed by development and changes.

In this understanding of the metaphor, three important aspects of Werner's psychology are already touched. One is the role of dynamic changes. This is fundamental in Werner's psychology, namely that development is not restricted to a certain part of psychology, but something that forms the basis for our cognition, personality, biology, and social interactions. Metaphors must be regarded as the best example of how language is changing. We have worn out metaphors because they have been applied too much. This reveals that metaphors are invented, used, adopted, and familiarized; in other words they are living their lives, which are embedded with changes. This use of language is driven by a need to grasp something that is superior to the lexical meaning of each of the words applied. This is the form, which is another fundamental term in Werner's psychology. However, forms are highly related to feelings, which Werner understood as something quite different from the James/Lange theory. Feelings are not primarily located in the body, but must be regarded as an "abstract form of consciousness" (Werner, 1919, p. 12), yet consciousness is not the same as cognition, but rather about awareness. This implies that feelings are the unity of the complexity embedded in a sense impression. However, this is a unity that goes beyond what language can convey, and this explains the third important factor in this context, namely feelings. Werner's understanding of complexity, form, and feelings points in directions that go beyond language, and therefore these aspects of language almost subvert language as well.

THE CONCEPT OF 'DEVELOPMENT'

The term "development" is probably one of the most challenging terms in psychology. It is strongly related to "change," which still is problematic to describe adequately. The reason is quite simply that development is embedded with a paradox, namely that something is both one thing and its opposition. If we look away from the time factor, learning can be defined in terms of the fact that the same person is both with and without knowledge about the same thing. This may apparently violate the Aristotelian principle of contradiction, and we have to bring in time to justify that this is not a contradiction, but a consequence of the fact that changes really have happened. Time is of course an aspect of our understanding we cannot omit. Yet it is emphasized differently in different cultures. For example, in Hebrew culture the time factor is much more salient than in the Greek. When Moses heard saying from God: "I am that I am" (King James, Exodus 3:14), it can be understood from two very different perspectives. The Greek perspective would be that God is the being, the logos, the universal static order; whereas the Hebrew understanding would be that God is the creator—the one who defines a beginning and an end of the history (Boman, 1960). Thus changes are included in the Hebrew thinking, whereas when Plato shall explain learning in the dialogue *Menon*, he demonstrates first of all that knowledge has always been there and the learning process is just a question of recollection. Thus the classic Greek perspective on learning does not involve any radical changes, and the principle of contradiction therefore is not violated. The modern Western culture represents a combination of the Hebrew and the Greek (Boman, 1960), but the problem with changes and development is still there.

Werner is dealing with the problem of development by referring to Goethe, who formulated the thesis of "organic development" (Werner, 1957a). Werner includes one quotation from Goethe, which summarizes very well both Goethe's thesis of organic development and the explanatory model for development Werner is applying.

> The more perfect the creature becomes, the less similar become the (morphological) parts to one another. On the one genetic pole, the whole is more or less similar to the parts, and on the other the whole is dissimilar to its parts. The more nearly equal parts, the less are they subordinated one to another. Subordination of the parts indicates a perfect creature. (Werner, 1957a, p. 40)

Through this quotation, Werner signalizes that development includes an aspect of stability, but it is combined with a dynamic process. The whole is the stable aspect that unites the individual, but also the species and the organic as such. The whole is the paramount category that is very different from its parts. The whole is also different from the sum of its parts, but it is still the unifying aspect that exists on a formal level. The parts, on the other hand, are the dynamic forces that provide growth and development.

The aspect of complexity is crucial in the understanding of dynamic forces, but complexity appears in two different versions, which represent two extremes on a continuous line. The primitive organism is complex in the sense that the parts are undifferentiated and quite similar to the whole, whereas the more "perfect creature" is complex because parts are differentiated and stand in opposition to one another. Development, therefore, is regarded as a movement from the undifferentiated to the differentiated. This can be seen both in a phylogenetic and an ontogenetic perspective, and these perspectives share some similarities. Yet the relationship between the phylogenetic and the ontogenetic is more subordinated. The crucial aspects, however, are the ontogenetic relationships that are established between the parts, especially when it comes to the mental aspects of human beings. To illustrate this we can see the babbling stage as one type of relationship between the sound element and a meaningful discourse as another. The differentiation process implies also centralization and hierarchic integration. Thinking as a centralized activity compares and relates data and information produced by activities that are more subordinated, like sensation, perception, and imaginations. The complexity, therefore, is provided by the order of the parts and how they interact in many different ways and on many different levels. Even an adult might include some babbling aspects in an apparently rational discourse.

These terms, therefore, form the basis in Werner's understanding of development. The undifferentiated represents the point of departure for an organic growth. It stands for potentiality and possibilities. Thus development is a progress from potentiality to reality in terms of a movement from the undifferentiated to the differentiated. Yet this movement is following a certain order, which form the relationship between the parts, and this order is a hierarchic order. Some parts are superior and others are subordinated. Since all the parts form a unity, they have to be coordinated, which implies a form of centralization. The higher organism, the more parts, and the more the organism are characterized by centralization. This implies, of course, that the human being is portrayed by a high degree of centralization, differentiation, and hierarchic order. Yet this perspective represents just one aspect of development. The organismic perspective implies that all elements reflect the totality, which means that even in a higher organism, which consists of many parts, each part includes some aspects of undifferentiated functions. This is also true for the mental parts. This implies that mental activities represents both higher, but also lower, mental functions at the same time.

Werner applies some selected terms to depict the ambiguity of the mental functions, like "(a) syncretic—discrete, (b) diffuse—articulated, (c) indefinite—definite, (d) rigid—flexible, [and] (e) labile—stable" (Werner 1957a, p. 53). All these pairs can be summarized in the antinomy "precise versus imprecise" or "univocal versus ambiguous." The point is that both aspects are embedded with almost same force in mental activity. Despite the fact that an adult is more precise in use of terms than a child, it is striking how imprecise the most meticulous person also can be. We go in and out and in between the two extremes all the time and the question is not how to avoid this split, but how to integrate them. This is exactly what is referred to when we talk about an integrated personality in our daily speech. It is normal that a person may have many different sides, but the crucial question is how integrated all these sides are. In this respect there is a process of unification on many different levels. One level is the cognitive functions, but unification is also a feature of sensation. This is true when it comes to the phenomenon of synesthesia. The literature tells us that synesthesia is much more widespread among children compared to adults (Werner, 1957a). But what about those of us who still in mature age perceive colors in connection with characters and chords? Are we dysfunctional or underdeveloped in a sense? According to some psychologists, probably yes, but not according to Werner. He would rather say that this is exactly how the mental functions are enriched, specifically by combining the undifferentiated with the differentiated functions.

Development therefore is not following a well-defined line, in which every stage appear gradually and in a certain order. The relationship is far more dynamic and the developing process is much more precisely described in terms of a spiral: "This formal parallelism—the initial return to more primitive means in the attempt to attain more complex ends— is another instance of the operation of the genetic principle of spirality" (Werner & Kaplan, 1963/1984, p. 170). Development represents, on the one hand, a movement in a certain direction toward higher differentiation, but it is not linear. It represents a movement that goes back and forth because the major challenge in the movement from undifferentiation to differentiation is to compensate for isolation of the parts in the process of compartmentalization. This compensational strategy is integration. The point here is that stages are not something a person just goes through and then leaves behind, but rather the opposite. All the stages form parts of a personality, and in this respect a personality is characterized by a multitude of components, which have to be taken into account if one aims at understanding the whole personality.

LANGUAGE IN A DEVELOPMENTAL PERSPECTIVE

Language is probably one of the most important aspects of an individual's development. It is through language human beings become a part of their own species. Yet it is through language one can express oneself as an individual. Thus language is both something that unites the group, but at the same time provides differentiation by creating individuals. In this respect language is not just a practical tool in the exchange of information, but rather the most intimate part of the environment in which the individual lives are unfolded. This encompassing role of language must be reflected in the understanding of it, and a psychological understanding of language does not necessarily coincide with a linguistic understanding of the same. Werner took these challenges seriously and his theory about language—and not least his understanding of the development of language in an individual's lifespan—represents a complexity that makes his theory different from what linguists would focus on.

Werner's analysis of language, therefore, is focusing on "symbolic forms" (Werner & Kaplan, 1963/1984). Together with his good colleague Bernard Kaplan, he developed a theory on an "organismic-developmental approach to the psychology of language" as his latest work, and it was published just a year before he died. The development of symbol formation in language is following the same pattern as the organismic perspective admits in all sorts of development. This implies a movement from undifferentiation to differentiation, which implies a certain understanding in language. Differentiation is exactly what linguists would highlight as a core aspect of language. If the words do not stand in opposition to each other, then they would not have any meaning. When Werner and Kaplan focus on the undifferentiated aspects of language, the semantic dimension of language gets a more subordinated role. What comes in focus instead is the phonetic dimension. Yet to talk about phonetics represents also a too narrow perspective on this. Linguists normally understand phonetics as a system of units (phonemes) that are without meaning themselves, but are rather defined in terms of differentiating meaning. When being compounded they constitute or alter the meaning of the word. Thus phonetics is highly related to semantics, which forms the perspective in which phonetics is understood. Consequently, Werner and Kaplan are focusing on paralinguistic cues in the articulation of language, which are intonation, rhythm, and the sound of the words, among others.

This brings a link back to the introductory quotation from Wilhelm Wundt, who stated that the child at the stage of babbling does not use language as expected from a linguistic point of view, but rather as if it was a kind of music. In line with this, the language fallacy was defined in terms of the fact that the parents understood the child as if the articulated sounds could form meaningful words like "mama" and "daddy," whereas they in fact were just meaningless syllables, like "ma-ma-ma-ma," "da-da-da-da," or "pa-pa-pa-pa." These sounds are not meaningless for the child, though. They express exactly what the child really want to express, namely that he or she wants to express his or her position as a part of the "sounding" family, and with the same dignity as all the other family members. Thus in an undifferentiated use of language as babbling, meaning is not absent from the articulation, but it is provided by some other factors than the lexical meanings of the words. This is the symbol formation, which includes language the way linguists define it, but it includes also a lot of paralinguistic cues, which may be musical, but also bodily expressional. This lack of limits in symbol formation underlines the undifferentiated aspects of communication, but it underlines also that the movement toward more differentiated stages does not exclude the undifferentiated aspects. We never stop using paralinguistic cues in our conversation, but we learn how to separate and differentiate between the different devices in our communication. Werner and Kaplan address four different components that determine the symbol situation: "addressor, addressee, vehicle, and referent" (Werner and Kaplan, 1963/1984, p. 252). Out of these, the vehicle, or the signifier, gets a certain attention, but it is the relationship between these components that determine the degree of differentiation and the level of development.

Werner and Kaplan are focusing on a phenomenon, which is normally regarded as a kind of deviation and abnormal use of language, namely "lapse of meaning" (Werner & Kaplan, 1963/1984, p. 30). This

> refers to the fact that linguistically meaningful sound-pattern or written pattern, a 'word' when uttered or seen in continuous repetition, suddenly begin to sound or look strange, to lose its status as a meaningful word, and in extreme cases to become a mere configuration of sounds or lines. (Werner & Kaplan, 1963/1984, p. 30)

In other words, language can in some situations lose its most essential characteristics, namely to contain lexical meanings, and by this become something else, namely pure sound or, if it is written, mere text lines. The exercise they are depicting here demonstrates very well how language might be applied in different ways, and not least that the user can switch between the different ways of using it. This demonstrates how an abnormal use of language does not necessarily imply abnormality by its user. This subversion of the meaning in language makes connections to the stage of babbling, but on the other hand, we will find this "lapse of meaning" in contemporary poetry and vocal music. Since highly normal and well-educated individuals may enjoy these expressions in art, they demonstrate very well that this is a normal use of language and it is quite normal to go in and out of such a use of language in daily speech. This is normal, and it "is one of the most fallacious notions one may hold about language, says Humboldt, to attribute the origin of speech to pragmatic need or mutual help" (Werner & Kaplan, 1963/1984, p. 160). Thus language is much more than what linguists define it to be, and its different qualities like its "musical" aspects are of high importance to make it to that kind of environment a human being in whatever age enjoys to be embraced with.

LANGUAGE AND MUSIC AS TWO DIFFERENT SYSTEMS

To capture the different systems with descriptive adequacy is an important scholarly task. We have seen that metaphor is an element in language that goes beyond what is adequately described by linguists. When Werner focused so much on linguistic borderlines, such as metaphors and paralinguistic aspects, he goes beyond what can be captured by the grammatical rule system with descriptive adequacy. Yet this does not necessarily imply that the grammatical rule system is useless, only that its applicability is limited and restricted to a small part of language. What is suggested by this reading of Werner, however, is that language is infiltrated by music in some sense. If so, this suggestion presupposes that language and music can be defined as two separate and different systems. There are different pathways to follow in an attempt at doing this, but a Saussurian approach is probably one of the most efficient because he presents clear criteria for the linguistic system, yet at the same time compares it with music.

According to Saussure, the linguistic system represents an abstraction, which is expressed in the French term *langue* that stands in opposition to *parole*—the actual speech. The linguistic system is first of all characterized by a limited number of smallest units that can be used in an endless way and by this generate the whole use of languages. These smallest units are the phonemes, which are the syllables the whole language is based upon. They are the elements that differentiate meaning, but they are meaningless without being placed in a larger context: the word and the sentences. These phonemes are nevertheless interesting because they constitute the linguistic system, and because of this they are supposed to be studied *in abstracto*, not as a part of the actual speech, but as the elements that constitute the linguistic system. In this respect Saussure is drawing a parallel to music: "a musical series, do, re, mi, can be treated only as a concrete series in time, but if I select one of its irreducible elements, I can study it in abstract" (Saussure, 1974, p. 40). Music, in other words is supposed to have the same sort of basic elements as language, which implies that it has a limited number of pitches that can generate the whole tonal system. By presupposing a tempered system, which implies that and e̱ in C major is the same as e̱ in A major, and octave equivalence, which implies that one stroked e̱ is the same as two stroked and three stroked e̱ etc., the musical pitch system can be reduced to consist of 12 single units that generate the whole tonal system with descriptive adequacy. It is not only language and music that are characterized by being a system in these terms, also the mathematical system shares the same characteristics in the sense that the decimal system contains 10 discrete units that generate the whole mathematical system. Thus to be a system there must be a final number of discrete units that generate the whole and endless system.

Another aspect that characterizes both the linguistic and the mathematical system is what the linguist Louis Hjemslev called the "paradigmatic dimension of language." This is what Saussure called the "associative relationship in language," which consists of the nonarticulated potentiality of units that are contained in the grammatical classes. If a certain unit is chosen then all the other units in the same class have to be put aside. This is what another French linguist, André Martinet, called a mutual exclusion between the smallest units in language. If certain units are chosen in the syntagmatic chain, all the other units are excluded to exist *in praesentia*, but they are there still *in absentia* (Saussure, 1974, p. 123). This criterion of mutual exclusion in language is not so dominating in music. A melody consists of a chain of pitches, which are articulated one at the time and in this respect a melody may follow this principle of mutual exclusion. Yet music does not only consist of melodies, but even more of harmonies, which means that the pitches are not chosen one by one, but rather appear in combination. There are of course certain restrictions in how they can be combined. In a Bach fugue, for example, it might be easy to recognize a failure, so the options for combining pitches are rather restricted in that type of music. The restrictions that may exist are, on the other hand, a question of style. Thus the history of music tells us about a continuous line of development, along which more and more combinations of pitches have been legitimized and accepted.

Music can in many respects be compared with language, and according to the Saussurian criteria presented here it can also easily be understood as if it is a language. Yet the same criteria underline very well that there is one important difference, and this is given by the harmony, which does not have a clear pendant in language. Musical harmony is characterized by multiplicity in the sense that several elements can be articulated at the same time without violating the system. The verticality in music, therefore, is not just an abstract phenomenon that merely exists in absentia, as is the case in language. Music articulates verticality *in praesentia*, which is exactly what the score is supposed to mirror, namely to be a visual representation of all the articulations that take place at the same time in a piece of music. This verticality in music is normally regarded as its dimension of space, but music is even more a form of art that is unfolded in time. In this regard, the term polyphony is the term that covers both the fact that mutual exclusion is not a valid criteria in the vertical dimension of the musical system, but also that music unfolds in time. Polyphony can rather be defined as the criteria of mutual inclusion in the sense that it designates the fact that each melodic line in a polyphonic texture stands in opposition to the other. This is the content of counterpoint, which implies that every voice in the musical texture shall move in different directions and by this signalizes individuality, albeit they have to follow the harmonic rules for the applied musical style. An anecdote from Mahler's life may illustrate how far this term can be stretched in a musical perspective. It says he once was visiting a marketplace in which there were several sorts of sounds articulated at the same time: a brass band sounded from one corner, a street organ from another, and several vendors were shouting out about their commodities. Mahler should allegedly have commented: "This is the real polyphony" (Mitchell, 2002). Actually some of his movements, for example the two in the middle of his ninth symphony, reflect very much this conceptualization of polyphony.

INTEGRATING DIFFERENT SYSTEMS

There is apparently an immense difference in Saussure and Werner's understanding of language. The arbitrary sign is a key term in the Saussurian conception of language, and it is a *sine qua non* for explaining why there are different languages that almost express the same and why languages continuously are in change (Saussure, 1974). Yet Werner and Kaplan, on the other hand, state that their view is "that symbols are not arbitrary signs but dynamic representational forms" (1963/1984, p. 38). However, there are reasons for suggesting that they are referring to very different perspectives. If we bring in a musicological perspective on the musical sign, it is rather difficult to talk about the sign as arbitrary. In music we will not find the same distinction between the sign and the signification, because the musical meaning is embedded in the sign itself. This is especially clear in German and Nordic languages where the term for the signifier (*ausdruck*) is applied when it is referred to the musical content. In English a similar point would be clear by making a distinction between the expression and the expressed. In music, therefore, the expression is at the same time the expressed.

What Werner and Kaplan do in their understanding of language is to define language so broad that the term includes, not only the indefinable paralinguistic elements, but also the more definable system of music. Werner did some discoveries in his studies on music and musical development, which he included in his psychological understanding of language. This is how synesthesia is embedded in Werner's conceptualization of language, in the sense that one may use the language as a musical instrument, like the child does at the stage of babbling. This use of music triggers at the same time its parents' linguistic capacity. The parents and the child can even interact very well despite this fundamental misunderstanding in their "conversation" or "choir singing," depending on which perspective one would like to take. It is important to emphasize that this synesthetical interaction goes in both directions; the parents talk triggers also the child's musical capacity.

This does not mean, however, that uses of language as a musical device just belongs to a preverbal stage of development. As was referred to in the introduction of this paper, language can be used so differently among adults that similar misunderstandings or even lacks of understanding appear between adults as between children and grown-ups. The mentioned examples demonstrate also some aspects of the genetic principle of spirality. There is an aspect of synesthesia in different ways of using language. As mentioned, James Joyce and Dylan Thomas are probably the most obvious examples of how a combination of the musical and the linguistic systems enriches literature. We may not be aware of the fact that we read their writings even as much music as literature, but we are very much aware of the fact that they have to be read very differently from instructions for a device, for example.

COMPLEXITY IN THINKING

It is not only Martinet that talks about mutual exclusion as a characteristic of language. It is central in transformational grammar that univocality represents the ideal, and ambiguity necessitates an analysis on a deeper level. Ambiguity is normally that two terms are condensed into one, and this has to be disclosed by an analysis on a deeper level. In language, therefore, one dimensionality and unambiguity are the ideals we expect language to contrive. Complexity stands in opposition to univocality and linearity, but complexity is first of all a result of these characteristics. Thus the musical system is in itself not more complex than language, rather the opposite probably. The reason why Saussure is referring to the musical system is because it is easier to understand as a system. Complexity, therefore, occurs not necessarily within one and the same system, but rather when different systems are integrated to a whole and then cause confusion and obscurity. In this sense, a combination of the musical and the linguistic system will cause complexity, and this combination of different systems is what Werner calls integration.

It is normal to define thinking in terms of the different systems. In this respect the linguistic and mathematical systems have been used as models for thinking. The musical system has almost never been used, but here is one important exception in psychological theory. This is represented by Johann Friedrich Herbart, who referred to the musical system of harmony in his attempt at explaining the process of apperception, i.e., the phenomenon that our consciousness is able to assimilate new impressions and at the same time appears as a unity. This requires a concept of multidimensionality language has severe problems with providing because of the principle of mutual exclusion. The harmony in the musical system, however, is characterized by inclusiveness in multiplicity. As long as the human being can enjoy the polyphonic texture in music, it is also capable to combine multidimensionality with rationality. Thus it is not a coincidence that it was Mozart who allegedly said he heard the music *tout ensemble* when he composed.

Wholeness implies that many levels are present at the same time, and this is exactly what musical polyphony is about. However, real complexity appears when this musical capacity is applied on systems that do not include multidimensionality.

Multidimensionality of the mind is what have been tried to grasp when metaphors like, cognitive dissonance, polyphony, and the dialogical self have been applied. It is the same motivation that lies behind Werner's conceptualization of mental development. One thing is that the undifferentiated represents a form of complexity, but quite another thing is to talk about spirality, which means that an individual is moving back and forth between undifferentiation and differentiation. This requires a differentiated understanding of the different systems that are involved. Werner does not define the musical system in his books, and after 1917 he is not paying music so much attention any more. His psychological understanding seems to presuppose that well-defined systems are lying under his term of complexity. But there are probably many of them, and this attempt at defining music as different from language is just a start in disclosing the complexity of the mind, which Werner is highlighting.

THE UNITING ASPECT: FORM

There is, however, one systematic aspect that Werner refers to during his whole authorship and that is the concept of form. This is what he concludes with in his first study on small children's spontaneous song formula, and it is this concept that unites his and Kaplan's immense work on language and communication as his last academic contribution. On the one hand, Werner is highly influenced by Goethe, but he was also very much influenced by the neo-Kantian Ernst Cassirer, whom he worked with in Hamburg and who published a three volume work on the philosophy of symbolic forms in the 1920s. Cassirer states quite clearly that his concept of form is an extension of Kant's critical philosophy:

> The object does not exist prior to synthetic unity but is constituted only by this synthetic unity; it is no fixed form that imprints itself on consciousness but is the product of formative operation effected by the basic instrumentality of consciousness, by intuition and pure thought. (Cassirer, 1972, p. 29)

This quotation from Cassirer summarizes very much what Werner also stood for. The role of the term form is in itself slightly ambiguous as well. On the one hand it stands for something definite and well defined, but here it is also presented as an aspect of unpredictability. This is, however, the most fascinating with this term, specifically that it intrigues our intellectual curiosity to investigate and define what it is about on the one hand, but on the other hand has the character of slipping out of our hands when we try to grasp it. It is at least obvious that we often miss the target when our framework for understanding is too narrow. The language fallacy is an example of this, namely that we try to understand a phenomenon as if it is language, whereas it is in many cases something quite different, and in some of these cases we should rather talk about or even understand the phenomenon as if it is music.

MUSIC AND DIFFERENTIATION

On this background we have to say that Heinz Werner represents a radical understanding of development. By denying that development has a certain origin, he is at the same time denying that it has a certain goal. Development must be regarded as an eternal change of forms in which differentiation is the key word. Yet this does not imply that all changes have to go solely in the direction of differentiations. Change may imply that differentiation is achieved in a certain area, albeit undifferentiation might be a factor in other. When different areas and different levels of differentiations are integrated, complexity is the result.

In line with this music seems to play a certain role. Music is, on the one hand, a system that may appear as highly differentiated in the sense that it forms an independent system in terms of harmony and rhythm. Yet it may also appear as undifferentiated shapes of sound with no clear forms. This was exactly what Werner found in his early study on young children's spontaneous singing. We have also seen that when singing is performed on the stage of babbling, it is hard to differentiate between music and language. In other words, even the systems are not clearly differentiated on an early stage in children's development, and consequently it is hard to tell what forms the basis: music or language. According to Werner it is none of them, and they are in the beginning of child's life hard to discern because they are present in an undifferentiated manner. This implies also that they are equalled important in a young child's world. The other point Werner made in line with this was that some undifferentiated aspects still remain during the whole life. Applied on the relationship between music and language, we may trace musical aspects in an adult's use of language and vice versa. The first is exemplified by focusing on sound elements in language, like we do by means of rhymes, alliterations, and certain types of repetitions, but also by focusing on the rhythm in language. Those elements may appear as irrational from a logical perspective, but not from a musical and aesthetical perspective. Not admitting that other forms of expressions can govern language is to commit the language fallacy.

SOME PERSPECTIVES ON MUSIC IN CULTURAL
PSYCHOLOGY IN THE FUTURE

There is no doubt that psychology has been very much focusing on language during the 20th century. Freud's concentration on word representations in the psychoanalytic process forms just a start of it. Although psychoanalysis, behaviourism, and cognitive psychology can be regarded as the main competing directions in the 20th century's psychology, the three have nevertheless in common a language oriented understanding of psychology. In this respect one may accuse the 20th century's psychology for having committed a sort of language fallacy.

However, this seems to slightly change now at the beginning of the 21st century. As mentioned in an earlier chapter in this book, there has been a tendency to look at music as a model for understanding social gatherings and human communication already in the late 20th century (Rodriguez in this book). Julia Kristeva is just one example that has contributed on this. Werner Wolf's publication of "The Musicalization of Fiction: A Study in the Theory and History of Intermediality" (Wolf, 1999) must be regarded as following up on this tendency. The same must Stephen Malloch and Colwyn Trevarthen's anthology with several contributions that highlight music as an alternative way to understand human communicative interaction (Malloch & Trevarthen, 2009). Here it is alleged that the use of discrete pitches in combination with rhythm is exactly what makes music different "from other forms of human communication" (Eckerdal & Merker, 2009, p. 247).

All contributions here are steps on the right way. Yet in this anthology we have tried to go even a step further by bringing in some factors in cultural psychology that actually touch some musicological issues, and some factors in musicology that may shed some new light on psychological issues. In the future therefore we have to

- Revitalize the close connection between aesthetics and psychology
- Focus on sound in everyday life as a semiosphere
- Find the meeting point between mythical thinking and music of today
- Trace local identities through music activities
- Search for musicalizations of the reality
- Dive into the aspect of ambiguity from a musical perspective
- Investigate creative processes in emotion regulations
- Define cultural borders and identities in terms of musical genres
- Catch the cultural meaning of time in terms differences in timescales
- Rethink the use of music in psychiatry
- Interrogate imaginations based on music

- Intervene due to the local based culture in therapy
- Mobilize a learning awareness to non-Western cultures
- Examine the play between sound and silence
- Question our assumption about how to understand music

Although the chapters in this book are contributions to all these points, they represent just a beginning, and there are a lot of challenges in progressing along these lines. And one of them is to avoid to be trapped in the language fallacy.

NOTE

1. This chapter is worked out in collaboration with and is dedicated to the Werner-expert Professor Emeritus Roger Bibace at Clark University, Worcester, MA.

REFERENCES

Ash, M. G. (1995). *Gestalt psychology in German culture, 1890–1967: Holism and the quest for objectivity.* New York, NY: Cambridge University Press.

Bakhtin, M. M. (1984) *Problems of Dostoevsky's poetics* (C. Emerson, Trans. & Ed.). Minneapolis, MN: University of Minnesota Press.

Benveniste, É. (1966). *Problémes de linguistique génerale* (Vol. 1). Paris, France: TEL Gallimard.

Boman, T. (1960). *Hebrew thought compared with Greek* (J. L. Moreau, Trans.). London, England: SCM Press.

Cassirer, E. (1972). *The philosophy of symbolic forms* (Vol. 2): *Mythical thought.* London, England: Yale University Press.

Chomsky, N. (1957/1975). *Syntactic structures.* Paris, France: Mouton.

Chomsky, N. (1964). Degrees of grammaticalness. In J. A. Fodor & J. A. Katz (Eds.), *The structure of language: Readings in the philosophy of language* (pp. 384–389). Englewood Cliffs, NJ: Prentice-Hall.

Danesi, M. (1993). *Vico, metaphor and the origin of language.* Indianapolis, IN: Indiana University Press.

Eckerdal, P., & Merker, B. (2009). 'Music' and the 'action song' in infant development: An interpretation. In S. Malloch & C. Trevarthen (Eds.), *Communicative musicality: Exploring the basis of human companionship* (pp. 241–262). Oxford, England: Oxford University Press.

Festinger, L. (1957). *A theory of cognitive dissonance.* Evanston, IL: Row, Peterson.

Freud, S. (1933). *New introductory lectures on psycho-analysis.* New York, NY: W.W. Norton.

Gardner H. (1983). *Frames of mind: The theory of multiple intelligences.* New York, NY: Basic Books.

Ghiselin, B. (Ed.). (1952). *The creative process.* New York, NY: Mentor.

Hermans, H. J. M., & Kempen, H. J. G. (1993). *The dialogical self: Meaning as movement.* San Diego, CA: Academic Press.

Kivy, P. (1993). *The fine art of repetition: Essays in the philosophy of music.* New York, NY: Cambridge University Press.

Klempe, S. H. (2011, Spring). The role of tone sensation and musical stimuli in early experimental psychology. *Journal of the History of the Behavioral Sciences, 47*(2), 187–199.

Kristeva, J. (1982). *Powers of horror: An essay on abjection.* New York, NY: Columbia University Press.

Lévi-Strauss, C. (1981). *The naked man.* New York, NY: Harper & Row.

Malloch, S., & Trevarthen, C. (Eds.). (2009). *Communicative musicality: Exploring the basis of human companionship.* Oxford, England: Oxford University Press.

Mitchell, D. (2002). *Gustav Mahler: Songs and symphonies of life and death: Interpretations and annotations.* London, England: Faber & Faber.

Saussure, F. D. (1974). *Course in general linguistics.* London, England: Owen.

Schenker, H. (1979). *Free composition.* New York, NY: Longman.

Valsiner, J., & Connolly, K. J. (Eds.). (2003). *Handbook of developmental psychology.* Thousand Oaks, CA: Sage.

Wapner, S., & Kaplan, B. (1964, September). Heinz Werner: 1890–1964. *The American Journal of Psychology, 77,* 513–517.

Werner, H. (1917). *Die melodische erfindung im frühen kindesalter. Eine entwicklungspsychologische untersuchung.* Wien, Austria: In Kommission bei Alfred Hölder.

Werner, H. (1919). *Die ursprünge der metapher.* Leipzig, Germany: Verlag von Wilhelm Engelmann.

Werner, H. (1957a). *Comparative psychology of mental development* (Revised ed.). New York, NY: International Universities Press.

Werner, H. (1957b). The concept of development from a comparative and organismic point of view. In D. B. Harris (Ed.), *The concept of development: An issue in the study of human behavior.* Minneapolis, MN: University of Minnesota Press.

Werner, H., & Kaplan, B. (1963/1984). *Symbol formation.* London, England: Lawrence Erlbaum.

Witkin, H. A. (1965, June). Heinz Werner: 1890–1964. *Child development, 30*(2), 307–328.

Wolf, W. (1999). *The musicalization of fiction: A study in the theory and history of intermediality.* Atlanta, GA: Rodopi.

Wundt, W. (1902). *Outlines of psychology* (4th ed.; C. H. Judd, Trans.). Leipzig, Germany: Wilhelm Engelmann.

ABOUT THE CONTRIBUTORS

Christian G. Allesch is an associated professor at the Department of Psychology, Paris-Lodron University, Salzburg, Austria. His research interests include psychological aesthetics, cultural psychology, and history of psychology.

Jacob A. Belzen holds doctorates in social sciences, history, philosophy, and sciences of religion. He specialized in cultural psychology, in particularly in its application to the study of religion. Widely published, he is a chair professor of psychology at the University of Amsterdam.

Arild Bergh completed his PhD on the topic of music and conflict transformation at the SocArts group at the University of Exeter, with fieldwork in Norway and Sudan. He is currently working as a senior researcher at the Norwegian Defense Research Establishment.

Katarina Mårtenson Blom, PhD, is a licensed psychologist, licensed psychotherapist, supervisor, and associate trainer in psychotherapy, and also an associate trainer in the Bonny Method of Guided Imagery and Music. She has a private practice in Stockholm, Sweden.

Lars Ole Bonde is a professor in music therapy at Aalborg University, Denmark, and professor at the Center for Music and Health, the Norwegian Academy of Music, Norway. He is a clinical supervisor and primary trainer in the Bonny Method of Guided Imagery and Music.

Cultural Psychology of Musical Experience, pages 339–341
Copyright © 2016 by Information Age Publishing
All rights of reproduction in any form reserved.

Anne Danielsen is a professor of popular music studies at the Department of Musicology, University of Oslo. She has published widely on rhythm, groove, and music production in postwar African American popular music.

Petter Dyndahl is a professor of musicology, music education and general education at Hedmark University of Applied Sciences, Norway, where he is head of the PhD program in teaching and teacher education. He has published in music education, cultural studies, popular music studies, music technology, and the media.

Rolf Inge Godøy is a professor of music theory at the Department of Musicology, University of Oslo. His main interest is in phenomenological approaches to music theory as the point of departure for music theory, and also exploring the relationships between sound and body motion in our experience of music.

Lise Jaastad is a research fellow at the University of Nordland, Center for Practical Knowledge. Her current research explores impacts of rhythm in everyday life and in health promotion, but her background is in music performance and teaching (Grieg Academy, University of Bergen (UIB) and ethnomusicology (Norwegian University of Science and Technology, NTNU) including field work in Kenya on traditional (Giriama and Kamba) musical health strategies.

Sven Hroar Klempe is an associate professor in psychology at the Department of Psychology, Norwegian University of Science and Technology (NTNU), Trondheim. He is a former full professor in musicology and an associate professor in media studies. His research interests are in the history of psychology, culture and psychology, theory of science, communication, and music psychology.

Martin Knakkergaard is associate professor in musicology and former long-time head of the music programme at the University of Aalborg, Denmark. His research interests are primarily within the field of music technology, but also directed toward fundamental questions in musicology, like music and time, music and numbers, etc.

Andrea Korenjak is an Austrian musicologist, psychologist, educationalist, and flutist. Currently she is conducting the project "Music, Medicine, and Psychiatry in Vienna (c. 1780–1850)" at the Institute for the History of Art and Musicology in the Austrian Academy of Sciences.

Viggo Krüger holds a position as researcher and music therapist at Aleris Omsorg Norge. He is also an associate professor at GAMUT, Grieg Academy Music Therapy Research Centre, University of Bergen.

Olga V. Lehmann is currently affiliated with the Norwegian University of Science and Technology (NTNU), Trondheim, Norway, as a PhD candidate in psychology. She has graduated in psychology from La Sabana University, Colombia, and in clinical psychology from Università Cattolica del Sacro Cuore, Italy. Her research interests include death beliefs, humanistic and existential psychology, silence in ordinary life, poetic instants, cultural psychology, and idiographic science.

Karen Rodríguez holds a PhD in Cultural Studies. Her research interests include small cities, the arts as a non-violent way to confront the Other, language and psychoanalysis. She is currently writing a book about artist-psychoanalyst Bracha Ettinger and serving as Dean of Studies at Bard Early College–Cleveland.

Brynjulf Stige is a professor of music therapy at the University of Bergen, Norway, and head of research at GAMUT, The Grieg Academy Music Therapy Research Centre (University of Bergen and Uni Research Health). Stige's research evolves around a particular interest in culture-centered music therapy and community music therapy.

Tania Zittoun is a professor of psychology and education at the University of Neuchâtel, Switzerland. As a sociocultural psychologist, her work has addressed life course development, the nature of semiotic processes, and the methodological challenges raised by such phenomena. She has a long-standing interest in the role of art and fiction in our understanding of reality.

Lightning Source UK Ltd.
Milton Keynes UK
UKHW021319300320
361075UK00007B/2148